Deserted Villages:
Perspectives from the
Eastern Mediterranean

Unless otherwise indicated,
all material in this book appears under a

Creative Commons
By Attribution
4.0 International License.

2021 The Digital Press @ The University of North Dakota

Book Design: William Caraher and Rebecca M. Seifried
Cover Design: Rebecca M. Seifried

Library of Congress Control Number: 2021932585
The Digital Press at the University of North Dakota, Grand Forks, North Dakota

ISBN-13 (paperback): 978-1-7364986-8-2
ISBN-13 (PDF): 978-1-7364986-1-3

Cover photo is the interior wall of a ruined building in Keria, a village in the Mani Peninsula. Photo by Rebecca M. Seifried.

DESERTED VILLAGES

Perspectives from the Eastern Mediterranean

edited by
Rebecca M. Seifried
Deborah E. Brown Stewart

The Digital Press at the University of North Dakota
Grand Forks, ND

The contributions to this volume have been reviewed through a double-blind peer review process.

Table of Contents

Acknowledgments i

Introduction..1

Part I: Abandonment in the Archaeological Record

Chapter One
Positive Abandonment: The Case from Çadır Höyük
Marica Cassis and Anthony Lauricella 27

Chapter Two
The Deserted Village of Anavatos on the Island of Chios, Greece
Olga Vassi 67

Chapter Three
Ayios Dimitrios (Paliochora) and Georgadika in Kythera:
Abandoned Settlements in a Historically Abandoned Environment
Lita Tzortzopoulou-Gregory and Timothy E. Gregory 101

Chapter Four
The Stone-Built *Palaiomaniatika* of the Mani Peninsula, Greece
Rebecca M. Seifried 153

Part II: Abandonment in the Recent Past

Chapter Five
Landscapes of Home and Thereafter: The Condition, Educational Potential, and Natural Environment of Penteskouphi Hamlet
Isabel Sanders, Miyon Yoo, and Guy D. R. Sanders..................................209

Chapter Six
Life in Abandonment: The Village of Lakka Skoutara, Corinthia
David K. Pettegrew and William R. Caraher..269

Chapter Seven
Roads, Routes, and Abandoned Villages in the Western Argolid
William R. Caraher, Dimitri Nakassis, and Ioanna Antoniadou..............319

Chapter Eight
Drones and Stones: Mapping Deserted Villages in Lidoriki, Greece
Todd Brenningmeyer, Kostis Kourelis, and Miltiadis Katsaros 347

Chapter Nine
Wheelock, North Dakota: "Ghost-Towns," Man Camps, and Hyperabundance in an Oil Boom
Richard Rothaus, William R. Caraher, Bret Weber, and Kostis Kourelis 389

The Authors..421

Acknowledgments

While this volume is a showcase for the current research being carried out by medieval and post-medieval archaeologists in the Mediterranean, it is also a model of collaboration and collegiality. It began with a network of villagers and archaeologists offering hospitality and conversations to Kostis Kourelis on his research travels during the summer 2014, a rich experience which inspired Kostis and Deb Brown Stewart to organize a double session on the topic of "Deserted Villages" at the 2016 Annual Meeting of the Archaeological Institute of America. The publication was made possible thanks to the persistence of its editors, the intellectual contributions and hard work of its authors who agreed to join our unorthodox endeavor to publish the volume digitally and open-access, the effort of two anonymous reviewers who offered their critical feedback on individual chapters and the collection as a whole, and the immeasurable support from Bill Caraher and The Digital Press at the University of North Dakota in every stage of the publication process. Additionally, the projects highlighted here join an ever-expanding body of research on historical archaeology of the eastern Mediterranean, which itself owes gratitude to the countless individuals who have contributed to the study of the recent past through their time, their hard work, and their writing—whether typed in academic publications, scrawled on the margins of field notebooks, or shared over a meal.

Map on the following page was designed by Rebecca M. Seifried. Country boundaries and bathymetry from Natural Earth. Elevation data from GMTED2010. Compass from the "Map of Saint Paul," by the H.M. Smyth Printing Co. (1921) and digitized by Stanford University Libraries (https://searchworks.stanford.edu/view/mj221qh8338).

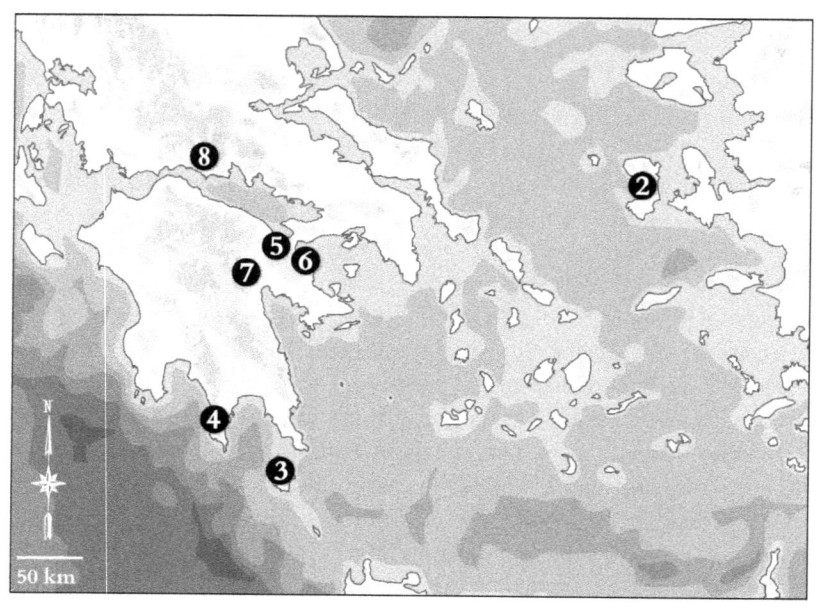
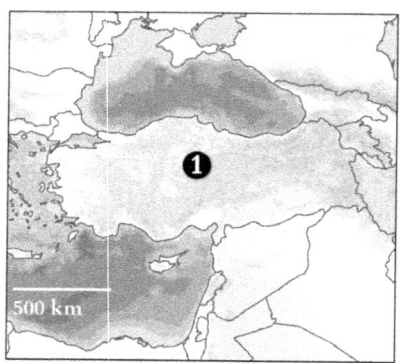
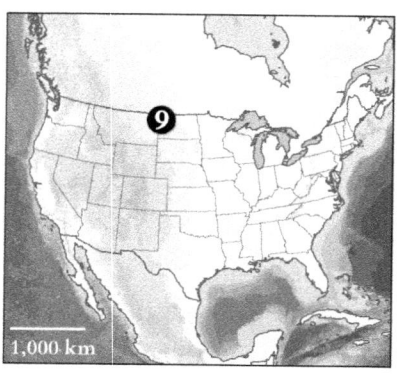

Turkey
1 – Çadır Höyük, Yozgat

Greece
2 – Anavatos, Chios
3 – Ayios Dimitrios, Kythera
    Georgadika, Kythera
4 – Koulouvades, Mani
5 – Penteskouphi, Corinthia
6 – Lakka Skoutara, Corinthia
7 – Chelmis, Argolid
    Koutsopoulou, Argolid
8 – Aigition, Phocis

United States
9 – Wheelock, North Dakota

Introduction

Deborah E. Brown Stewart and Rebecca M. Seifried

The deserted rural village has often been presented as a foil to the grand narratives of modernity. Indeed, early modernity is usually defined by the sweeping political, technological, economic, and cultural changes that disrupted the agrarian societies of the European Middle Ages. Over the last few decades, the rapid climate change, globalism, and consumerism of so-called supermodernity have threatened what remains of the rural countryside and the lifeways of agropastoralism, in part because it privileges urban and suburban modes of living. In 2007, the relocation of human populations reached a pivotal point, when the inhabitants of the world's cities finally outnumbered rural populations. As people have sought the opportunities and amenities of modern urban life, the depopulated village and the aging shepherd/farmer have become tropes for an allegedly simpler past and—in some places—for cultural identity itself (Gerstel 2020:viii). In short, the abandonment of the countryside has become a powerful motif that influences both popular culture and academic scholarship alike (Kourelis 2010:209).

By elucidating what is missing or misrepresented in these narratives, archaeologists are uniquely equipped to trace the continuities, discontinuities, and transformations that are an integral part of the abandonment process. The papers in this volume are a collection of archaeological case studies that explore this theme in different ways. The collection stems from a two-part colloquium on "Deserted Villages" held at the 117th Annual Meeting of the Archaeological Institute of America (AIA) on January 8, 2016, in San Francisco, California, and organized by Deborah Brown Stewart and Kostis Kourelis. The colloquium is one of several sponsored by the Medieval and Post-Medieval Archaeology interest group that have resulted in publications. The first was a volume on *The Archaeology of Xenitia: Greek Immigration and Material Culture* edited by Kostis Kourelis (2008). The next was a special issue of *International Journal of Historical Archaeology* on the topic of "The Abandoned Countryside: (Re)Settlement in the Archaeological Narrative of Post-Classical Greece," edited by Kostis Kourelis and William R. Caraher (Kourelis 2010). The most recent, a section in *Journal of Greek Archaeology* on "The Medieval Countryside in the Aegean and Anatolia: An Archaeological Perspective," edited by Effie Athanassopoulos (2020). While all of the collections invariably deal with abandonment, this volume makes the focus explicit, challenging the authors to elucidate how archaeologists of the medieval and post-medieval eras (broadly understood to mean the sixth century AD and later) understand the process of abandonment as it plays out in the eastern Mediterranean.

The authors who first presented their work in the 2016 colloquium have revised their content to incorporate new insights from fieldwork and expanded research, and additional contributions are included here from colleagues who were unable to participate in the colloquium but offered papers or their services for peer review. The dialogue that was launched by both the colloquium and the creation of this volume has succeeded in connecting researchers who share methodological and theoretical approaches to studying an endangered category of material culture, regardless of the place or primary time period of their research. The variety of ways in which deserted villages can be studied is, indeed, the overarching theme that connects the papers, which otherwise deal with case studies that are separated not only temporally—with regional chronologies often reflecting the unique historical trajectories of each area—but also geographically. For example, while most of the contributions focus on medieval and post-medieval villages in the eastern Mediterranean, one team applies the insights they gained from conducting intensive survey in the Mediterranean to their own backyard: the oil fields of North Dakota.

Research on Deserted Villages in Historical and Geographical Perspective

Research on the medieval and post-medieval villages in the eastern Mediterranean has emerged from the timely convergence of several important trends. Archaeology in the region has a fairly well-deserved reputation for privileging the monumental and spectacular over the mundane, as well as for being preoccupied with large tells and famous ancient sites where archaeologists hope to uncover monumental architecture, valuable artifacts, and even traces of major historical events and historical figures. Until recently, medieval and post-medieval archaeology struggled to advance beyond cultural-historical approaches that gave primacy to cultural descriptions and historical events recorded in textual evidence. Because of the subdiscipline's alignment with history, geography, art history, and folklore, the value of material culture to research—as well as to cultural heritage—was tied closely to its perception as a record of history or a direct link to a valued ancestral past. Therefore, monuments of art historical or historical value, such as churches or fortifications, have dominated the literature. Furthermore, to many minds, archaeological research on the more recent past seemed entirely unnecessary. Fortunately, the archaeology of quotidian pasts has always had its advocates, who argue that too many perspectives are omitted from texts and documentary records, and who have sought to advance research through the best technologies, methods, and theoretical approaches.

One area where archaeological research on deserted villages has benefited from this kind of advocacy is the United Kingdom. Medieval archaeology in this region owes a great debt to the multidisciplinary and multiscalar research agendas of the Deserted Medieval Villages Research Group, which was founded in 1952 and later renamed the Medieval Settlements Research Group (MSRG; for history, see Bentz 2008; Dyer 2017). As described by a founding member, the participants sought to bring different disciplinary expertise to myriad research questions, including the materials and methods of construction of individual buildings, the physical and social structures of villages, diverse strategies for land utilization and communications, and "the growth and decay of the village, and the possible connections of this with broad climatic changes" and other crises (Hurst 1956:267). For decades, the MSRG focused on two projects: the large-scale excavation at Wharram Percy, which continued until 1990, and the sampling and documentation of sites across the landscape. The results of these projects appear in *Wharram Percy: Deserted Medieval Village* (Beresford and Hurst 1990) and *Deserted Medieval Villages: Studies* (Beresford and Hurst 1971). Although the excavations at Wharram Percy have ended, similar questions about the origins, development, and abandonment of medieval villages and their hinterlands continue to drive other excavation projects in the U.K., which benefit from new technologies, scientific analyses, improved archaeological methods, and, in many cases, financial support from the MSRG. Since the advent of processualism and ongoing debates influencing landscape studies, archaeology in the U.K. remains in close conversation with prehistoric and historical archaeology in the Americas (Egan and Michael 1999; Gerrard 2003), as well as with developments in landscape archaeology in Italy and the eastern Mediterranean (Harkel and Bewley 2018; Smith 2018).

The scale, resources, output, and coordinated agenda of the British research group are admittedly unmatched in the rest of Europe, where "preventive archaeology," also known as salvage or rescue archaeology, is responsible for most of the excavation, survey, and documentation of abandoned or at-risk medieval and post-medieval villages. In recent decades, anxieties about heritage at risk from conflict or development, increasing interest in the archaeology of households, and ongoing questions about the origins, expansion, contraction, and abandonment of villages has prompted academics and professional archaeologists in several European countries to re-engage with the archaeology of villages (Carré et al. 2009; Dyer and Jones 2010; Fernández Fernández and Fernández Mier 2019).

Research on medieval and post-medieval villages has progressed along a somewhat different trajectory in the eastern Mediterranean. For most of the twentieth century, occupied and deserted villages in the region were the purview of anthropologists, folklorists, and architectural historians who documented either current/disappearing rural lifeways or vernacular architecture (see discussion in Brenningmayer et al., this volume). However, beginning about 50 years ago, and under the influence of Anglo-American archaeological discourse, archaeological landscape surveys began documenting detailed settlement histories, rural landscapes, and the material signatures of peoples' everyday activities, including evidence from the medieval and early modern eras (Athanassopoulos 2010:256; Diacopoulos 2004:185). As John Cherry (2003:141) explains, what made these projects "so distinctively new and different was their intensity, diachronic focus, interdisciplinarity, and use of the region as the conceptual basis for addressing historical or anthropological questions." Ethnographers and ethnoarchaeologists also joined the archaeologists in the form of interdisciplinary survey teams—both to help with the investigation of the modern communities and to seek analogies for premodern behaviors related to pastoralism, agriculture, craftsmanship, and village social dynamics. Ultimately, these teams produced research findings that challenged "long-standing assumptions of stability, longevity, and essential uniformity among Greek villages" (Sutton 1994:314), revealing instead the "fluidity and flexibility of the nature of settlement over time" (Jameson 2000:xi) and "an understanding of the material condition of rural Greek life as mutable and negotiated" (Sutton 2000:2). In addition to the stimulus that landscape survey provided to the field of medieval and post-medieval archaeology in the eastern Mediterranean, several excavation directors have dedicated time and resources to studying medieval and post-medieval levels at complex, multiperiod sites where earlier levels traditionally had been the priority. The increasing amount of finds and data recovered from excavations and surveys in the last few decades have galvanized efforts to develop typologies and chronologies for common archaeological artifacts such as ceramics and glass.

In tandem with these new research avenues, archaeologists began partnering with historians to explore archival lines of evidence—especially Venetian and Ottoman administrative records—and gain additional insights into the villages they were documenting materially (e.g. Bennet 2007; Davies 2004; Doorn 2009; Given 2007; Kiel 1999; Price et al. 2008; Zarinebaf et al. 2005). On this point, it is worth highlighting that the field of history is currently undergoing a parallel shift toward centering the material cultural heritage and people who live within the rural landscapes they study (e.g. Kolovos 2015). However, as Thomas Gallant (2018:178) points out, archaeologists and modern Greek historians would benefit from working more closely together (and citing one another) in order to fruitfully combine two different avenues for exploring abandoned rural villages.

As a consequence of these comparatively late developments to the archaeology of the medieval and post-medieval Mediterranean, reflective and reflexive practitioners, such as our authors, have engaged with critical discourses and methods developed within the approaches of processualism, social archaeology, environmental humanities, and historiography. As surveys continue in the eastern Mediterranean, albeit with modified research agendas and new technologies, they continue to evaluate changes to rural settlement patterns and land use through time, comparing their findings to what was known about the dramatic historical events and socioeconomic changes that impacted important centers, and identifying rural sites for further inquiry. It is no coincidence that many of the contributors to this volume have returned to medieval and post-medieval villages they first encountered while participating in large-scale surveys, now equipped with a variety of new archaeological methods, technologies, and research questions. Thus, this volume not only records medieval and post-medieval villages for the sake of expanding the corpora of known sites of archaeological and cultural interest, but also demonstrates the ways in which critical and multidisciplinary approaches have been internalized and emerge as research questions for this generation of medieval and post-medieval archaeologists.

Archaeology and Abandonment

The overarching theme of this collection is the exploration of the complex processes that are at work during the abandonment of rural settlements and the formation of archaeological sites, with conscious attention to their medieval, early modern, and modern contexts. Rather than supply a narrative that end with a site's abrupt and final abandonment (as viewed from a much later point in time), each paper thoughtfully considers histories of occupation, abandonment, and postabandonment that can be traced through documentation, oral histories, and the investigation of abandoned or partially abandoned material culture. Abandonment is considered both as a site-formation process and as a human phenomenon that intertwines the seemingly conflicting threads of memory and amnesia, opportunity and loss. This approach offers a more nuanced understanding of the reasons why people abandon rural homes and villages, the behaviors associated with abandonment of these places, and the significance of deserted villages in cultural landscapes. Most importantly, the case studies presented here reframe abandonment and postabandonment as dynamic, sometimes cyclical, and sometimes protracted processes, and they explore a vast range of environmental, political, social, and economic factors that are believed to contribute to abandonment and formative processes. Through all these papers weaves a challenge to archaeologists to reconsider how they interpret abandoned landscapes and the cultural assemblages that are deposited both upon and within them.

Abandonment—as both a sociocultural process and a process through which material culture enters the purview of archaeologists—is of fundamental concern to the discipline. Following Robert Ascher's (1961) pioneering work on formation processes, archaeologists utilized experimentation, observation, and ethnoarchaeological studies, primarily in the Americas, to investigate the ways in which artifacts, structures, and sites are transformed into archaeological record both during and after abandonment. For processual archaeologists such as Michael Schiffer (1972, 1983, 1985) and Lewis Binford (1981), a better understanding of the creation of artifact assemblages and stratigraphy was essential to establishing scientific methodologies and improving archaeological fieldwork and analysis. In particular, they sought to dispel what they termed the "Pompeii Premise," which suggested that what is uncovered in excavation necessarily correlates with the mundane activities before abandonment. Of enduring value to the discipline is the understanding that "whether one sees abandonment processes as transforming the material record ... or as integral components of site formation ... all archaeologically recovered remains have been conditioned by abandonment processes" (Tomka and Stevenson 1993:191). More recently, archaeological studies of abandonment have expanded beyond a focus on site formation processes to include strategies involved in abandonment, mobility, and place-making (e.g. Beaudry and Parno 2013; Lamoureux-St-Hilaire and Macrae 2020; Preucel and Meskell 2004).

A critical engagement with abandonment is central to the fervent discourse surrounding the archaeology of the contemporary era or recent past, which is rapidly being established as a specialization within the broader discipline. After all, as Alfredo González-Ruibal (2019:18) argues, "[c]ontemporary archaeology also deals with what is in the process of being dematerialised and dissassembled—things that in some cases become rematerialised and reincorporated into extant assemblages through recycling, lateral cycling, curation, collection and so forth." In part, this echoes a point that Ascher (1961:324) raised decades earlier in an article that greatly influenced the development of ethnoarchaeology and abandonment studies: "In a certain sense a part of every community is becoming, but is not yet, archaeological data ... The observational fields of ethnology and archaeology overlap on that proportion of a living community which is in the process of transformation."

Proponents of an archaeology of the contemporary era maintain that archaeology should resist the artificial temporal boundaries that prevent an archaeological study of material culture in the present and recent past (Buchli and Lucas 2001; Gould and Schiffer 1981; Harrison 2011:150; Harrison and Schofield 2010; Lucas 2005:118; Olsen and Pétursdóttir 2014:21; Rathje 1979; Thomas 2004). By challenging the discipline's identity as the study of abandoned things *only* from the remote past, they argue that archaeology will confront its complicit role in the political and cultural production of "heritage." Such reflexivity does not aim to abdicate responsibility, but rather to embrace activism and develop its potential to include subaltern voices that are often omitted from the documentary record (González-Ruibal 2019:20-21; Hamilakis and Anagnostopoulos 2009:66; Harrison and Schofield 2010:9-15; Witmore 2013:138).

Without question, the rapid pace of environmental, technological, and cultural change over the last century is unprecedented, and researchers in many disciplines are documenting the abandonment of houses, settlements, and the broader countryside, as well as the disappearance of rural lifeways. Current archaeological thinking about the collapse of earlier complex societies favors a "cyclical model in which societies oscillate from periods of urbanism and sociopolitical centralization to intervals of ruralism and local autonomy" (Schwartz 2006:4 citing Yoffee 1979) and posits that rural resilience after collapse at urban centers has been fundamental for the regeneration of new entities following collapse (Schwartz

2006:9 citing Adams 1978, Graffam 1992, and Van Buren 2000). Therefore, it is not surprising that recent abandonment of rural communities produces anxieties not only for at-risk archaeological sites, but also for the fate of humanity.

Yet, archaeology moves between illuminating grand narratives and producing "highly specific, localized narratives" (González-Ruibal 2019:17). Depending on the focus and research methods, it operates between Braudelian short-, medium-, and long-term timescales (Braudel 1972). In order for archaeologists to evaluate what is being perceived as rural collapse in our contemporary modernity, there still remains considerable work to be done recording, analyzing, and interpreting what has happened both at individual rural sites and within regions through time. Twenty years ago, archaeologist Oliver Creighton and ethnographer Joan Segui warned that "cultural processes underlying abandonment and structuring the material remains of [agropastoral] sites as they enter the archaeological record await controlled academic scrutiny in the Mediterranean context" (Creighton and Segui 1998:31). This volume adds to a small but growing body of archaeological work on the abandonment of rural settlements during the last millennium and a half.

Each of the papers in this volume presents a somewhat different—and, as we see it, complementary—approach to its particular case study, but they all cohere in representing abandoned rural settlements as highly contingent. On the one hand, prior to abandonment, villages and other rural sites are dynamic spaces that are configured by (and, in turn, configure) social experiences that still need to be explored archaeologically. As ethnographers and ethnoarchaeologists have documented over the last few decades, modern agriculturalists, pastoralists, and tradespeople in rural Mediterranean landscapes adapt their behaviors to local, regional, and global market forces, as well as to social and political changes. Furthermore, abandonment and reuse can be deliberate strategies for facilitating these adaptations (Costello and Svensson 2018; Creighton and Segui 1998; Forbes 2007; Gould and Schiffer 1981; Harrison 2011; Lucas 2001; Mientjes 2004, 2010; Sutton 2000). Although anthropology as a whole engages with issues of urbanization, mobility, migration, and displacement (Herzfeld 2015), there has been a renewal of interest in contemporary, not-yet-deserted villages as dynamic sites that are "never inert but always becoming," "localized sites for the negotiation of meanings" (Sorge and Padwe 2015:241), "continuously contested" (Schut and Mulder 2019:10), "translocally connected spaces" (Stasch 2017:441), and important "zones of entanglement" especially within globalization (Cochrane 2019:88). Even in what appear to be postabandonment phases, deserted villages continue to undergo transformations from natural and human causes. Yet, they also bear meaning to individuals and communities as places significant to a family or community's history; as ruins with the potential to either add to or detract from the tourism of aesthetic or cultural experiences; as structures and materials that have the potential for reuse; and, indeed, as objects of study for archaeologists, historic preservationists, and other researchers.

Part I: Abandonment in the Archaeological Record

The papers in Part I deal with case studies of long-abandoned sites that are being investigated via excavations, archaeological survey, and/or historical and archival research. While these methodological approaches are not new to the broader field of historical archaeology, their application to medieval and post-medieval domestic cultural heritage in the eastern Mediterranean is a recent—and growing—trend (e.g. Diacopoulos 2004; Gallant 2018; Murray and Kardulias 1986). Through their own fieldwork and analyses, the authors illustrate what the surviving evidence can reveal and what remains obscured about the sites' abandonment as they evaluate long-term change, rural resilience, adaptation, and memory based on fragmentary archaeological and documentary evidence.

Focusing on an excavated farmstead at the site of Çadır Höyük, Turkey, Marica Cassis and Anthony Lauricella employ resilience theory to explore episodes of change that are documented through the seventh to twelfth centuries. They find evidence for both slow and sudden abandonments, as well as reorganization among the site's identifiable phases. They argue that changes to structures and activities reflect adaptive behaviors to a variety of internal and external stimuli that occurred at varying magnitudes, but also often concurrently. Through this thoughtful study of adaptive cycles, they identify the impact of large historical events, such as the nearby Battle of Manzikert in 1071, but also argue for cycles of growth and release that reflect upon locally specific conditions and the capabilities of residents to adapt.

At Anavatos on Chios, the Greek Ministry of Culture has made considerable effort to excavate, restore, and commemorate a village lost to war and natural disaster. In this volume, Olga Vassi provides the first English description of the site, its surviving structures, and its portable finds. Based on her team's findings, she argues that the village was founded in the fifteenth century, when defense against piracy was foremost among the concerns of the residents. During the eighteenth century, the settlement expanded beyond the fortification walls, but a massacre in 1822 desolated the population. Anavatos continued to be occupied until a violent earthquake wreaked destruction in 1881. Thereafter, the village was abandoned, yet never forgotten, its ruins standing as a monument even before the 1998–2001 archaeological project.

In their contribution to the volume, Lita Tzortzopoulou-Gregory and Timothy Gregory explore collective memory and long-term processes associated with the abandoned villages of Ayios Dimitrios (Palaiochora) and Georgadika on the island of Kythera, Greece. In addition to their ongoing field survey and historical research, the team has traced stories of population displacement, resettlement, and revival through interesting toponyms, local legends, cults of saints, and archival records related to once-distinguished families. They frame the abandonment experienced on this island as part of an ongoing process of change—whether intentional or unintentional—rather than as the result of sudden and catastrophic events.

Rebecca Seifried makes a case for future excavations at the household level in the rural settlements known as the *palaiomaniatika* in the Mani, Greece. Her chapter offers a thorough review of the published art historical and architectural studies of the villages and summarizes the limited evidence about the settlements' chronology, which spans the eighth through late seventeenth centuries. Through field survey and in-depth archival research, with the village of Koulouvades as a case study, she demonstrates how archaeological sampling can provide deeper insight into the abandonment of the villages at the generational scale. Ultimately, she argues that survey is limited in the ways it can elucidate the lived experiences in the *palaiomaniatika* and assist in interpreting settlement strategies in remote and rural landscapes.

Part II: Abandonment in the Recent Past

Part II focuses on houses and villages that have been abandoned within living memory, contributing to a small but important set of case studies from elsewhere in the region that harness scientific methods and ethnoarchaeological approaches to understand the process of abandonment in real time (e.g. Andreasen et al. 2017; Chang 1994; Erny and Caraher 2020; Murray and Chang 1981; Papadopoulos 2013). As the authors observe, former residents, their descendants, and other unidentified individuals return occasionally to the villages, standing structures, discarded artifacts, and open spaces. As a result, many of the villages are still undergoing what archaeologists recognize as the abandonment process. Documenting the transformative stages of abandonment provides important lessons about archaeological interpretations of patterns in material culture. These papers shed light on the kinds of intermediary events that can take place between the initial transition from domestic space to its final abandonment and, furthermore, offer insights into the complex social dimensions of abandonment and reuse.

Integrating knowledge and methods from archaeology and ecology, **Isabel Sanders, Miyon Yoo, and Guy Sanders** demonstrate the value of interdisciplinary research to understanding the life cycle of the mostly abandoned village of Penteskouphi, which lies only a short distance from the American School of Classical Studies at Athens' excavations at Ancient Corinth, Greece. They combine years of observation, local knowledge, and their disciplinary expertise to elucidate stages in the abandonment of structures and fields in the village. In addition, their study of the area's flora and geomorphology provides clues to the village's subsistence base that would have been missed by most archaeologists. They demonstrate that aspiring archaeologists and public audiences can learn a great deal about site formation processes and interdisciplinary fieldwork by studying the availability and exploitation of natural resources at a given site.

The contribution by **David Pettegrew and William Caraher** is the culmination of 17 years of close observation and documentation of site formation processes at Lakka Skoutara in the Corinthia, Greece. Although no longer home to year-round residents, the village continues to undergo changes, interventions, and short-term habitation, in large part because of its proximity to a modern road. The work of the team (part of the Eastern Korinthia Archaeological Survey) was informed by observing the maintenance, repurposing, and deterioration of abandoned structures and the curation or discard of artifacts in what remains of the modern village. Using interviews with local informants and the results of the intensive pedestrian survey, together with the lessons learned at Lakka Skoutara, the authors extrapolate complex material signatures and historical contingencies that shape the rural landscape.

The paper by **William Caraher, Dimitri Nakassis, and Ioanna Antoniadou** further advances the argument that landscapes are dynamic and contingent spaces. Seeking to understand movement, connectivity, and agropastoralist strategies in marginally productive "intermediate zones" during the nineteenth and twentieth centuries, the Western Argolid Regional Project in Greece studied the two seasonal settlements of Chelmis and Koutsopoulou, the hilltop fortification known as Daouli, now-abandoned routes, and local memories. In addition to shifting subsistence strategies, they argue that state investment in paved roads elsewhere and the absence of strong social and economic ties between intermediate-zone settlements contributed to the abandonment of these sites.

Todd Brenningmeyer, Kostis Kourelis, and Miltiades Katsaros examine the impact of more extreme historical and economic changes on the village as a social unit, using Aigition in the region of Lidoriki, Greece, as their case study. Founded by the middle of the nineteenth century, the village endured a number of economic, ecological, and humanitarian crises during the twentieth century and was abandoned fully by 2001, except for occasional short-term use by pastoralists. Their research at Aigition not only documents what remains of the village's infrastructure, but also analyzes the mechanisms of resilience in a village that coped with emigration, war, internal displacement, episodic resettlement, modernization, abandonment, and postabandonment attempts at preservation.

At first glance, a paper on Wheelock, North Dakota, might seem somewhat out of place in a volume dominated by Byzantine, Ottoman, and early modern Greek villages whose existence relied primarily on agropastoralist activities. Yet the authors **Richard Rothaus, William Caraher, Bret Weber,** and **Kostis Kourelis** apply their combined experiences on archaeological field surveys in the eastern Mediterranean to the University of North Dakota Man Camp Project, identifying critical parallels that inform a broader archaeological interpretation of abandonment. As a settlement more ephemeral than others within the scope of their project, Wheelock became a case study for how humans behave and adapt in circumstances marked by scarcity of resources and instability without deep historical or social ties to a particular place. Situating this paper at the end of the volume invites readers to consider how the process of abandonment is experienced in different geographical, temporal, and economic contexts. Furthermore, it leaves us with a prophetic glimpse into what the archaeological assemblages of abandonment will look like in the future, particularly as more and more of the materials we leave behind are the products of modern manufacturing.

Conclusion

As so many of the papers within this volume illustrate, the study of deserted villages does not belong to the field of archaeology alone. Villages are inherently social spaces that are built up over generations through new construction, renovations, demolitions, repeated behaviors, and innovative reuses, and naturally they invite approaches from anthropology, architecture, ecology, and political science. One of the main takeaways from this collection is the need for further cross-pollination between these fields as we strive to understand more about how these places come to exist, how they are affected by processes of abandonment and postabandonment, and how they are transformed eventually into archaeological assemblages. A second takeaway is the poignant reminder that rural depopulation is not a phenomenon of the past, but rather a very modern and ever-present problem. The reasons why people ultimately choose to leave their homes are as numerous as the people themselves, ranging from the allure of economic opportunity in urban centers to the horror of violence and warfare and the fallout from environmental disaster. It remains to be seen whether recent economic crises, higher costs of living in urban areas, and the pandemic of 2020 will reverse these trends, and, if so, what strategies will emerge for such essentials as subsistence and employment. This volume emphasizes that studying abandonment in the past is deeply relevant to the abandonment that is taking place today. Through it all, we remember that the deserted village is not only a painful or romantic icon of the past, but also a product of economic, political, and social forces at differing scales that alter rural communities and their connections to the landscape. It is our hope that the lessons offered here will be carried forward to inform a critical examination of the modern forces that are at work in the abandonment and postabandonment of rural landscapes all across the globe.

References Cited

Adams, Robert McC.
   1978   Strategies of Maximization, Stability, and Resilience in Mesopotamian Society, Settlement, and Agriculture. *Proceedings of the American Philosophical Society* 122(5):329–335. https://www.jstor.org/stable/986687

Andreasen, Niels H., Panagiota Pantzou, Dimitris Papadopoulos, and Andreas Darlas (editors)
   2017   *Unfolding a Mountain: An Historical Archaeology of Modern and Contemporary Cave Use on Mount Pelion.* Monographs of the Danish Institute at Athens 19. Aarhus University Press, Aarhus.

Ascher, Robert
   1961   Analogy in Archaeological Interpretation. *Southwestern Journal of Anthropology* 17(4):317–325. https://doi.org/10.1086/soutjanth.17.4.3628943

Athanassopoulos, Effie F.
   2010   Landscape Archaeology and the Medieval Countryside: Settlement and Abandonment in the Nemea Region. *International Journal of Historical Archaeology* 14(2):255–270. https://doi.org/10.1007/s10761-010-0106-x
   2020   Introduction. Colloquium: The Medieval Countryside in the Aegean and Anatolia: An Archaeological Perspective. *Journal of Greek Archaeology* 5:367–376.

Beaudry, Mary Carolyn, and Travis G. Parno (editors)
   2013   *Archaeologies of Mobility and Movement.* Springer, New York.

Bennet, John
   2007   Fragmentary "Geo-metry": Early Modern Landscapes of the Morea and Cerigo in Text, Image, and Archaeology. In *Between Venice and Istanbul: Colonial Landscapes in Early Modern Greece*, edited by Siriol Davies and Jack L. Davis, pp. 199–217. American School of Classical Studies at Athens, Princeton, New Jersey.

Bentz, Emma
   2008   'More than a Village': On the Medieval Countryside as an Archaeological Field of Study. In *Archives, Ancestors, Practices: Archaeology in Light of its History*, edited by Nathan Schlanger and Jarl Nordbladh, pp. 97–108. Berghahn Books, London.

Beresford, Maurice, and John Hurst
   1990   *Wharram Percy: Deserted Medieval Village*. B. T. Batsford, London.

Beresford, Maurice, and John G. Hurst (editors)
   1971   *Deserted Medieval Villages: Studies*. Lutterworth Press, London.

Binford, Lewis R.
   1981   Behavioral Archaeology and the "Pompeii Premise." *Journal of Anthropological Research* 37(3):195–208. https://doi.org/10.1086/jar.37.3.3629723

Braudel, Fernand
   1972   *The Mediterranean and the Mediterranean World in the Age of Philip II*. Translated by Siân Reynolds. 2 vols. Collins, London.

Buchli, Victor, and Gavin Lucas
   2001   *Archaeologies of the Contemporary Past*. Routledge, London.

Carré, Florence, Vincent Hincker, Nadine Mahé, Édith Peytremann, Sébastien Poignant, and Élisabeth Zadora-Rio
   2009   Histoire(s) de(s) village(s): L'archéologie en contexte villageois, un enjeu pour la compréhension de la dynamique des habitats médiévaux [Histor(ies) of Village(s): Archeology in Rural Contexts, a Tool for Comparing the Dynamics of Medieval Habitats]. *Les Nouvelles de l'archéologie* 116:51–59. https://doi.org/10.4000/nda.727

Chang, Claudia
   1994   Sheep for the Ancestors: Ethnoarchaeology and the Study of Ancient Pastoralism. In *Beyond the Site: Regional Studies in the Aegean Area*, edited by P. Nick Kardulias, pp. 353–371. University Press of America, Lanham, Maryland.

Cherry, John
    2003   Archaeology Beyond the Site: Regional Survey and its Future. In *Theory and Practice in Mediterranean Archeology: Old World and New World Perspectives*, edited by John K. Papadopoulos and Richard M. Leventhal, pp. 137–141. Cotsen Institute of Archaeology, Los Angeles.

Cochrane, Thandeka
    2019   'The Village' as Entangled: An Exploration of Rural Libraries in Northern Malawi. *Etnofoor* 31(2):87–102. https://www.jstor.org/stable/26856487

Costello, Eugene, and Eva Svensson (editors)
    2018   *Historical Archaeologies of Transhumance across Europe*. Themes in Contemporary Archaeology 6. Routledge, New York.

Creighton, Oliver H., and Joan R. Segui
    1998   The Ethnoarchaeology of Abandonment and Post-Abandonment Behaviour in Pastoral Sites: Evidence From Famorca, Alacant Province, Spain. *Journal of Mediterranean Archaeology* 11(1):31–52. https://doi.org/10.1558/jmea.v11i1.31

Davies, Siriol
    2004   Pylos Regional Archaeological Project Part VI: Administration and Settlement in Venetian Navarino. *Hesperia* 73(1):59–120. https://www.jstor.org/stable/3182019

Diacopoulos, Lita
    2004   The Archaeology of Modern Greece. In *Mediterranean Archaeological Landscapes*, edited by Effie F. Athanassopoulos and Luann Wandsnider, pp. 183–198. University of Pennsylvania Press, Philadelphia.

Doorn, Peter
    2009   Population and Settlement in Post-Medieval Doris, Central Greece. In *Medieval and Post-Medieval Greece: The Corfu Papers*, edited by John Bintliff and Hanna Stöger, pp. 199–213. BAR International Series 2023. Archaeopress, Oxford.

Dyer, Christopher
   2017   The Origin and Early Development of the Medieval Settlements Research Group. *Medieval Settlement Research* 32:1–6.

Dyer, Christopher, and Richard Jones
   2010   *Deserted Villages Revisited.* University of Hertfordshire Press, Chicago.

Egan, Geoff, and R.L. Michael (editors)
   1999   *Old and New Worlds: Historical/Post-Medieval Archaeology Papers from the Societies' Joint Conferences at Williamsburg and London 1997 to Mark Thirty Years of Work and Achievement.* Oxbow Books, Oxford.

Erny, Grace, and William R. Caraher
   2020   The Kingdom of Chelmis: Architecture, Material Culture, and the Modern Landscape of the Western Argolid. *Journal of Field Archaeology* 45(3):209–221. https://doi.org/10.1080/00934690.2019.1704990

Fernández, Jesús Fernández, and Margarita Fernández Mier (editors)
   2019   *The Archaeology of Medieval Villages Currently Inhabited in Europe.* Archaeopress, Oxford.

Forbes, Hamish Alexander
   2007   *Meaning and Identity in a Greek Landscape: An Archaeological Ethnography.* Cambridge University Press, Cambridge.

Gallant, Thomas W.
   2018   Social History and Historical Archaeology in Greece. The Kefalonia and Andros Project, 2010–2014. In *An Age of Experiment: Classical Archaeology Transformed (1976–2014)*, edited by Lisa Nevett and James Whitley, pp. 177–193. McDonald Institute for Archaeological Research, Cambridge.

Gerrard, Christopher M.
   2003   *Medieval Archaeology: Understanding Traditions and Contemporary Approaches.* Routledge, London.

Gerstel, Sharon E. J.
   2020   Perspectives on the Greek Village. *Journal of Modern Greek Studies* 38(1):vii–x. https://doi.org/10.1353/mgs.2020.0000

Given, Michael
   2007   Mountain Landscapes on Early Modern Cyprus. In *Between Venice and Istanbul: Colonial Landscapes in Early Modern Greece*, edited by Siriol Davies and Jack L. Davis, pp. 137–148. American School of Classical Studies at Athens, Princeton, New Jersey.

González-Ruibal, Alfredo
   2019   *An Archaeology of the Contemporary Era*. Routledge, New York.

Gould, Richard A., and Michael B. Schiffer (editors)
   1981   *Modern Material Culture: The Archaeology of Us*. Studies in Archaeology. Academic Press, New York.

Graffam, Gray
   1992   Beyond State Collapse: Rural History, Raised Fields, and Pastoralism in the South Andes. *American Anthropologist* 94(4):882–904. https://doi.org/10.1525/aa.1992.94.4.02a00060

Hamilakis, Yannis, and Aris Anagnostopoulos
   2009   What is Archaeological Ethnography? *Public Archaeology* 8(2–3):65–87. https://doi.org/10.1179/175355309X457150

Harkel, Letty Ten, and Robert Bewley
   2018   An Incredible Journey? Understanding Ancient Landscapes from England to the Middle East and North Africa. *Medieval Settlement Research* 33:40–59. https://doi.org/10.5284/1059016

Harrison, Rodney
   2011   Surface Assemblages. Towards an Archaeology *in* and *of* the Present. *Archaeological Dialogues* 18(2):141–161. https://doi.org/10.1017/S1380203811000195

Harrison, Rodney, and John Schofield
   2010   *After Modernity: Archaeological Approaches to the Contemporary Past*. Oxford University Press, Oxford.

Herzfeld, Michael
    2015   The Village in the World and the World in the Village: Reflections on Ethnographic Epistemology. *Critique of Anthropology* 35(3):338–343. https://doi.org/10.1177/0308275X15589977

Hurst, John
    1956   Deserted Medieval Villages and the Excavations at Wharram Percy, Yorkshire. In *Recent Archaeological Excavations in Britain: Selected Excavations 1939–1955*, edited by Rupert Leo Scott Bruce-Mitford, pp. 251–273. Routledge & Paul, London.

Jameson, Michael H.
    2000   Foreword. In *Contingent Countryside: Settlement, Economy, and Land Use in the Southern Argolis since 1700*, edited by Susan Buck Sutton, pp. xi–xii. Stanford University Press, Stanford.

Kiel, Machiel
    1999   The Ottoman Imperial Registers: Central Greece and Northern Bulgaria in the 15th–19th Century; The Demographic Development of Two Areas Compared. In *Reconstructing Past Population Trends in Mediterranean Europe (3000 B.C.–A.D. 1800)*, edited by John Bintliff and Kostas Sbonias, pp. 195–218. Oxbow Books, Oxford.

Kolovos, Elias (editor)
    2015   *Ottoman Rural Societies and Economies. Halcyon Days in Crete VIII: A Symposium Held in Rethymno, 13–15 January 2012.* Crete University Press, Rethymno.

Kourelis, Kostis
    2010   Introduction: In the Comfort of Perpetual Abandonment. *International Journal of Historical Archaeology* 14(2):209–214. https://doi.org/10.1007/s10761-010-0102-1

Kourelis, Kostis (editor)
    2008   *The Archaeology of Xenitia: Greek Immigration and Material Culture.* New Griffon 10. American School of Classical Studies at Athens. Princeton, New Jersey.

Lamoureux-St-Hilaire, Maxime, and Scott Macrae (editors)
   2020   *Detachment from Place: Beyond an Archaeology of Settlement Abandonment.* University Press of Colorado, Louisville.

Lucas, Gavin
   2001   *Critical Approaches to Fieldwork: Contemporary and Historical Archaeological Practice.* Routledge, London.
   2005   *The Archaeology of Time.* Routledge, London.
   2014   Conduits of Dispersal: De-Materializing an Early Twentieth-Century Village in Iceland. In *Ruin Memories: Materialities, Aesthetics and the Archaeology of the Recent Past*, edited by Bjørnar Olsen and Þóra Pétursdóttir. Routledge, London. https://doi.org/10.4324/9781315778211.ch17

Mientjes, Antoon C.
   2004   Modern Pastoral Landscapes on the Island of Sardinia (Italy). Recent Pastoral Practices in Local Versus Macro-Economic and Macro-Political Contexts. *Archaeological Dialogues* 10(2):161–190. https://doi.org/10.1017/S1380203804001230
   2010   Pastoral Communities in the Sardinian Highlands (Italy): A View on Social Mobility. *Ethnos* 75(2):148–170. https://doi.org/10.1080/00141841003678759

Olsen, Bjørnar, and Þóra Pétursdóttir (editors)
   2014   *Ruin Memories: Materialities, Aesthetics and the Archaeology of the Recent Past.* Routledge, London. https://doi.org/10.4324/9781315778211

Murray, Priscilla, and Claudia Chang
   1981   An Ethnoarchaeological Study of a Contemporary Herder's Site. *Journal of Field Archaeology* 8(3):372–381. https://doi.org/10.2307/529576

Murray, Priscilla, and P. Nick Kardulias
   1986   A Modern-Site Survey in the Southern Argolid, Greece. *Journal of Field Archaeology* 13(1):21. https://doi.org/10.2307/529910

Papadopoulos, Constantinos
    2013   An Evaluation of Human Intervention in Abandonment and Post-Abandonment Formation Processes in a Deserted Cretan Village. *Journal of Mediterranean Archaeology* 26(1):27–50. https://doi.org/10.1558/jmea.v26i1.27

Preucel, Robert W., and Lynn Meskell
    2004   Places. In *A Companion to Social Archaeology*, edited by Lynn Meskell and Robert W. Preucel, pp. 215–229. Blackwell, Malden, Massachusetts. https://doi.org/10.1002/9780470693605.part3

Price, Simon R. F., Oliver Rackham, Machiel Kiel, and Lucia Nixon
    2008   Sphakia in Ottoman Census Records: A *Vakif* and its Agricultural Production. In *The Eastern Mediterranean Under Ottoman Rule: Crete, 1645–1840*, edited by Antonis Anastasopoulos, pp. 69–99. Crete University Press, Rethymno.

Rathje, William L.
    1979   Modern Material Culture Studies. *Advances in Archaeological Method and Theory* 2:1–37. https://www.jstor.org/stable/20170141

Schiffer, Michael B.
    1972   Archaeological Context and Systemic Context. *American Antiquity* 37(2):156–165. https://doi.org/10.2307/278203
    1983   Toward the Identification of Formation Processes. *American Antiquity* 48(4):675–706. https://doi.org/10.2307/279771
    1985   Is There a "Pompeii Premise" in Archaeology? *Journal of Anthropological Research* 41(1):18–41. https://www.jstor.org/stable/3630269

Schut, Thijs, and Nikki Mulder
    2019   Introduction: The Vibrant Village. *Etnofoor* 31(2):7–12. https://www.jstor.org/stable/26856482

Schwartz, Glenn M.
    2006   From Collapse to Regeneration. In *After Collapse: The Regeneration of Complex Societies*, edited by Glenn M. Schwartz and John J. Nichols, pp. 3–17. University of Arizona Press, Tucson.

Smith, Christopher
    2018   J.B. Ward-Perkins, the BSR and the Landscape Tradition in Post-War Italian Archaeology. *Papers of the British School at Rome* 86:271–292. https://doi.org/10.1017/S006824621700037X

Sorge, Antonio, and Jonathan Padwe
    2015   The Abandoned Village? Introduction to the Special Issue. *Critique of Anthropology* 35(3):235–247. https://doi.org/10.1177/0308275X15588618

Stasch, Rupert
    2017   Afterword: Village Space and the Experience of Difference and Hierarchy Between Normative Orders. *Critique of Anthropology* 37(4):440–456. https://doi.org/10.1177/0308275X17735369

Sutton, Susan Buck
    1994   Settlement Patterns, Settlement Perceptions: Rethinking the Greek Village. In *Beyond the Site: Regional Studies in the Aegean Area,* edited by Nick P. Kardulias, pp. 313–335. University Press of America, Lanham, Maryland.
    2000   Introduction: Past and Present in Rural Greece. In *Contingent Countryside: Settlement, Economy, and Land Use in the Southern Argolid since 1700,* edited by Susan Buck Sutton, pp. 1–24. Stanford University Press, Stanford, California.

Thomas, Julian
    2004   *Archaeology and Modernity.* Routledge, London.

Tomka, Steve A., and Marc G. Stevenson
    1993   Understanding Abandonment Processes: Summary and Remaining Concerns. In *The Abandonment of Settlements and Regions: Ethnoarchaeological and Archaeological Approaches,* edited by Catherine M. Cameron and Steve A. Tomka, pp. 191–195. Cambridge University Press, Cambridge.

Van Buren, Mary
  2000   Political Fragmentation and Ideological Continuity in the Andean Highlands. In *Order, Legitimacy, and Wealth in Ancient States*, edited by Janet Richards and Mary Van Buren, pp. 77–87. Cambridge University Press, Cambridge.

Witmore, Christopher
  2013   Which Archaeology? A Question of Chronopolitics. In *Reclaiming Archaeology: Beyond the Tropes of Modernity*, edited by Alfredo González-Ruibal. Routledge Handbooks Online, London.

Yoffee, Norman
  1979   The Decline and Rise of Mesopotamian Civilization: An Ethnoarchaeological Perspective on the Evolution of Social Complexity. *American Antiquity*. 44:5-35. https://doi.org/10.2307/279187

Zarinebaf, Fariba, John Bennet, and Jack L. Davis (editors)
  2005   *A Historical and Economic Geography of Ottoman Greece: The Southwestern Morea in the 18th Century*. Hesperia Supplement 34. The American School of Classical Studies at Athens, Athens. https://www.jstor.org/stable/i388452

PART I

Abandonment in the Archaeological Record

Chapter One
Positive Abandonment: The Case from Çadır Höyük

Marica Cassis and Anthony Lauricella

Houses are deceptive artifacts. Their permanence privileges them in the archeological record, and as archaeologists we often use them as proxies for the societies we study. In defining them, however, houses often come to represent binary categories: public vs. private, domestic vs. military or religious, elite vs. poor. Yet, houses do not represent *all* culture and society. Rather, they reflect choices made by particular communities in specific circumstances, and they can be misinterpreted through assumptions about the past (Bowes 2010:82–83). Further, houses change with societies. Both architectural choices and the internal artifacts within them are constantly changing, representing the decisions of the populations who own, utilize, or control the building. These changes are made in response to a variety of stimuli ranging from the global to the mundane. But the fact remains that changes in domestic structures reflect specific reactions to specific stimuli.

The concept of abandonment is at the center of archaeological discussions of houses because abandonment is the process that bridges the gap between a house's use and its appearance in the archaeological record. Archaeologists have most frequently thought of abandonment in terms of the processes that produce the archaeological record—that is, the passage from the systemic context to the archaeological (Schiffer 1972). This line of thought, which conceptualizes abandonment in terms of process, produces readily testable hypotheses and frameworks for interpreting the specifics of the material past. These approaches tend to ignore the cultural context and ramifications of abandonments (Smith 2008), and, increasingly, scholars have started to focus on the enduring material presence of abandoned places, landscapes, and structures that exist as part of the modern landscape in the form of ruins (e.g. Andreassen et al. 2010; Gordillo 2014; Olsen and Pétursdóttir 2014). All formulations of abandonment must contend with explaining the break between use and occupation and what is encountered in the archaeological record.

In considering the material past, we too often think of forced and sudden abandonment as corresponding to macrohistorical events, such as war or invasions. But abandonment as a process happens across a variety of spatial and temporal scales (Cameron 1991). Abandonment also represents choice and continuity as populations reject past styles or unnecessary objects. It is also a process as walls are moved and floors refurbished in response to changing populations or resources. Both minor changes (e.g. architectural adjustments) and major ones (e.g. the desertion of a room full of artifacts) mark forms of abandonment (Baker 1975; Cameron 1991; Schiffer 1985). Identifying forced and unforced abandonment (whether sudden or gradual) is a way of understanding how a society changes and adapts to internal or external stimuli. Among the most useful theoretical approaches to abandonment can be found in the field of household archaeology, which focuses on the use and reuse of artifact assemblages as well as the continued use of space by communities in constant flux (Allison 1999, 2008; Beaudry 2015; Gilchrist 2007; Hendon 2007; Souvatzi 2010).

While abandonment provides the background to this chapter, episodes of change and reaction are, in turn, a major component of resilience theory (Holling and Gunderson 2002; Redman and Kinzig 2003; Redman 2005). This model, grounded in an ecological perspective, recognizes that archaeological sites go through an "adaptive cycle" of exploitation (r), conservation (K), release (Ω), and reorganization (α; Figure 1; Redman 2005:Figures 1 and 2), while functioning within a large hierarchy. The entire system is known as *panarchy*. As Redman (2005:72) defines it, "[r]esilience theory seeks to understand the source and role of change—particularly the kind of changes that are transforming—in systems that are adaptive." The model posits that multiple cycles of varying magnitude can affect communities at the same time, feeding into and influencing and/or constraining each other in both time and space. Further, the size and complexity of the society affected has a direct impact on the nature and speed of the reaction to the affecting cycles. When stressed societies are forced into reorganization, this often includes abandonment in one form or another. Resilience theory allows archaeologists to analyze multiple systems at multiple interrelated scales. Seemingly small and short-lived cycles may connect to longer-lasting processes. If we consider abandonment—whether major or minor—as a component of the release portion of this cycle, we begin to have a way to theorize the change in

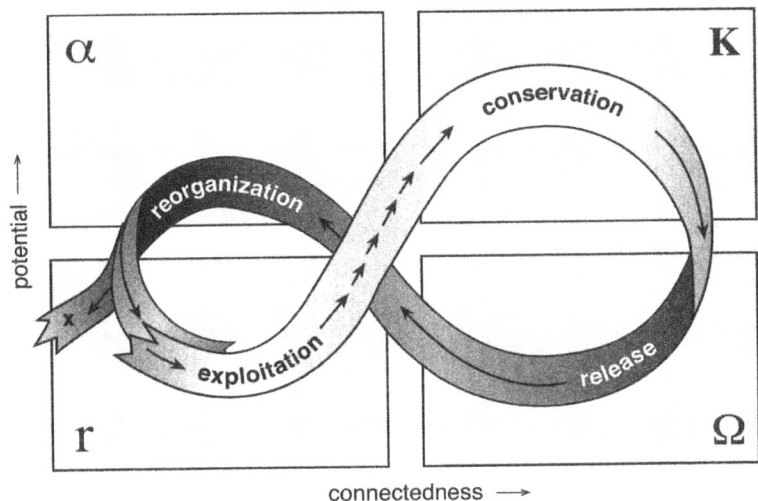

Figure 1. Resilience theory: "a stylized representation of the four ecosystem functions (r, K, Ω, α) and the flow of events among them" (Holling and Gunderson 2002:Figure 2-1). Image copyright © 2002 Island Press. Reproduced by permission.

archaeological sites. The cyclical model of resilience theory, when applied to the analysis of abandonment, represents a more nuanced picture of change over time.

Older classic models of abandonment focus on artifacts and assemblages and posit more-or-less linear movements from use to reuse (Ascher 1968; Schiffer 1972), while resilience theory allows for analysis at different (and multiple) scales. This approach can be of particular significance in relation to rural medieval sites, where there has been a tendency to consider them in relation to the larger empires and kingdoms known from written sources. The resultant assumptions about rural sites have little connection to the lived realities of the people inhabiting them. The application of resilience theory in these archaeological contexts offers an enhanced view of the complex changes that have affected regions and specific sites. Several recent studies have successfully utilized the model in relation to both the eastern and western medieval worlds (Haldon et al. 2014; McCormick et al. 2012; Roberts et al. 2018).

The model also works on a microscale, however, and this chapter approaches the concept of abandonment through the lens of resilience theory and seeks to explain the *longue durée* trajectory of a domestic structure punctuated by multiple instances of abandonment (Cassis et al.

2018). Useful application of this analysis to medieval European sites illustrates subtle changes as opposed to abrupt abandonments (Jervis 2017; Schreg 2011; see also Brenningmeyer et al. and Tzortzopoulou-Gregory and Gregory, this volume). Here, we follow Redman and Kinzig's (2003) assertion that resilience theory provides "a better understanding ... of human ecosystems" by illustrating that change in communities—large and small—is episodic, far from uniform, and frequently the result of destabilization, and that communities naturally lose resilience over time (Redman 2005). Considering small rural communities as independent ecosystems linked to, but not defined by, larger hierarchies allows for much more nuanced views of these populations.

Çadır Höyük—Defining Abandonment

The Byzantine site of Çadır Höyük is located in Yozgat province, Turkey (Figure 2), an area which was part of the Byzantine theme of Charsianon. The *höyük* (mound) has been occupied since the mid sixth millennium BC. During the periods discussed in this chapter, occupation occurred in two areas: the mound itself and the terrace to its north (Figure 3 and Figure 4). For the purposes of this chapter, however, we are interested in the period that ranges from approximately the first century AD to the twelfth century AD, an occupation sequence that occurs in both locations. Over this approximate millennium, shifts in material culture delineate four identifiable phases: Early Roman (first to fourth centuries), Late Roman (fourth to seventh centuries), Early Byzantine (seventh to ninth centuries), and Middle Byzantine (ninth to twelfth centuries). A fifth discernible phase in the medieval period (twelfth to thirteenth centuries) can be identified with the arrival of the Turkic nomads among the Greek population. While chronologically Seljuk, it remains unclear how much the courts of the Seljuks influenced their population in the countryside.

Although the site contains two major areas of use throughout these periods, this chapter will focus on the domestic architecture on the north terrace, where the four phases of discernible occupation provide a good example of a house utilized in repeated cycles and, thus, offers the opportunity to apply these models of abandonment and resilience to explain change. In each phase, we see a house manipulated by its inhabitants to adapt to changes arising from a series of abandonments. Each abandonment reflects the release and reorganization phases of the adaptive cycle, and within each shift it is possible to identify the flexibility of the household to adapt to changes in both the microenvironment and the

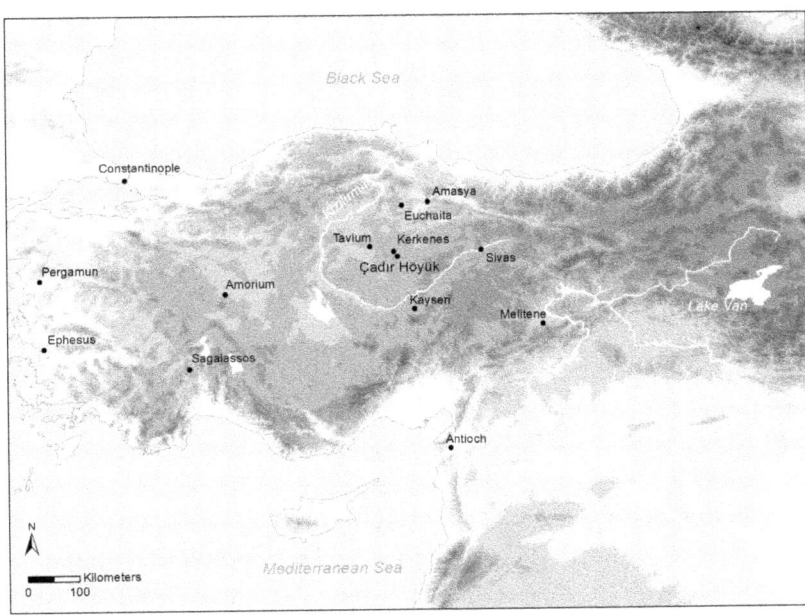

Figure 2. Map of Central Anatolia. Map courtesy of Anthony Lauricella.

Figure 3. View of Çadır Höyük, looking north. Photo courtesy of Marica Cassis.

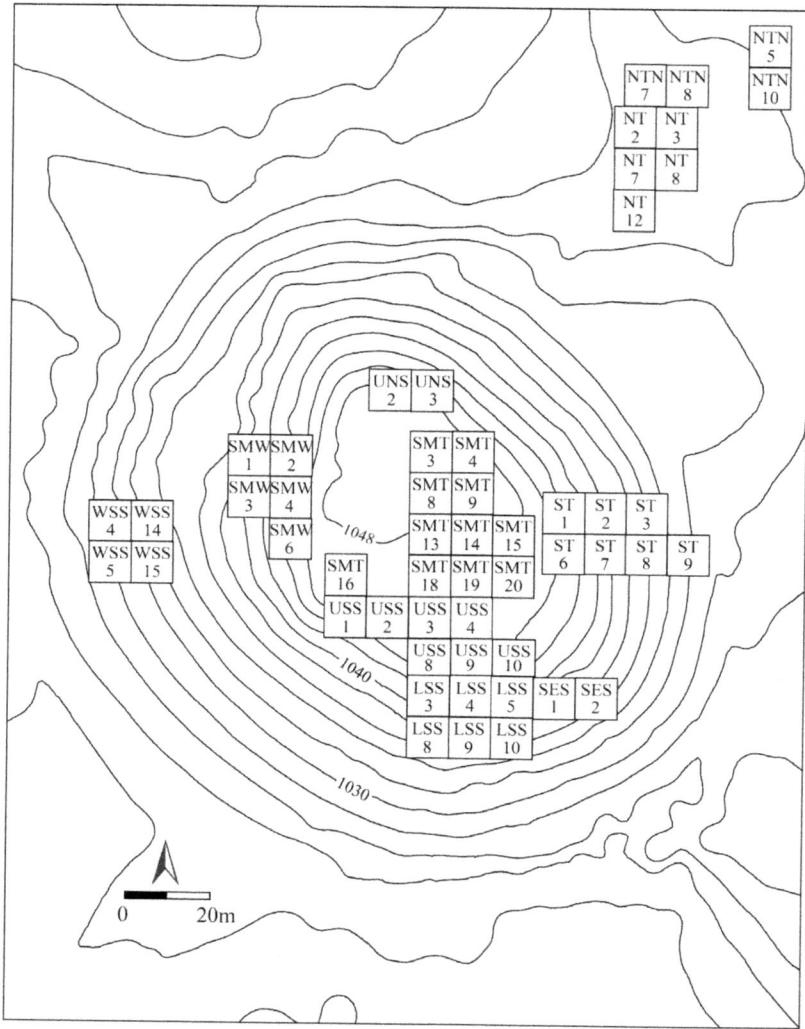

Figure 4. Topographic map of Çadır Höyük. Map copyright Çadır Höyük Excavations.

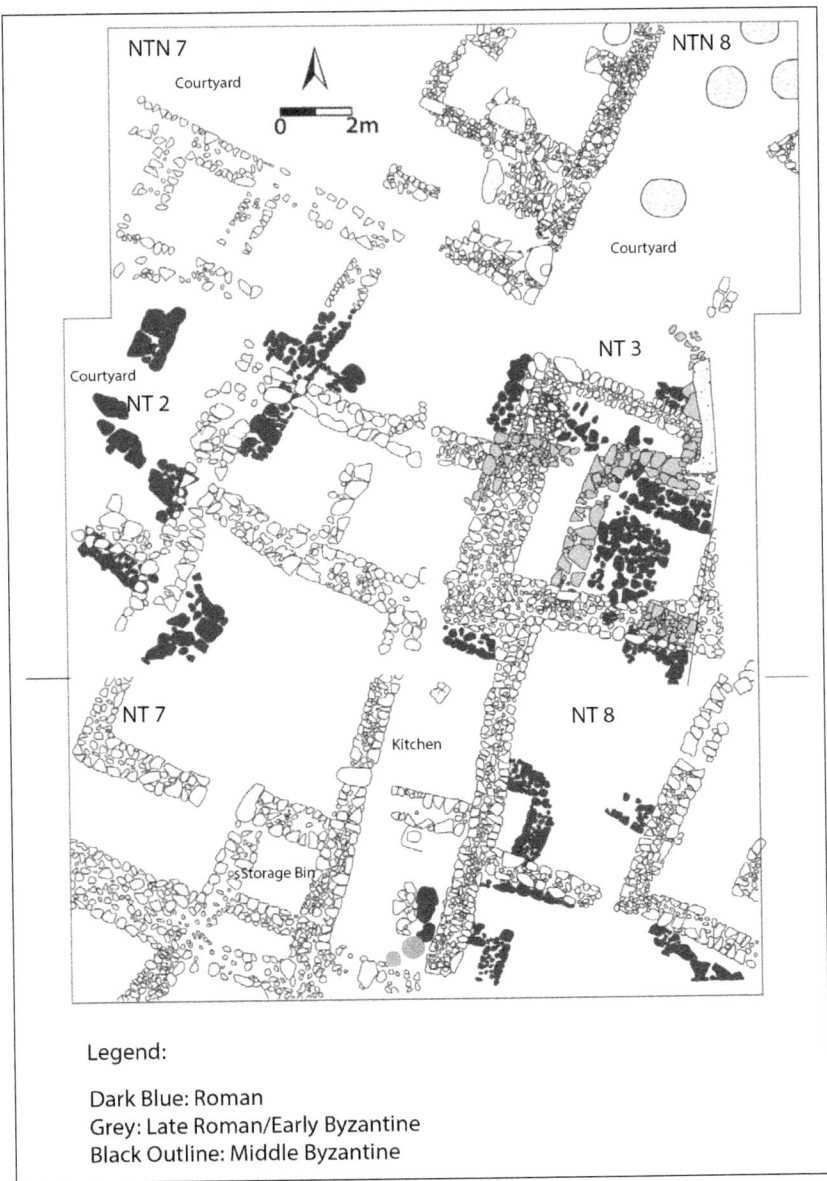

Legend:

Dark Blue: Roman
Grey: Late Roman/Early Byzantine
Black Outline: Middle Byzantine

Figure 5. Plan of the terrace at Çadır Höyük. Map copyright Çadır Höyük Excavations.

macroenvironment of the Byzantine Empire. This, in turn, provides a more nuanced view of an area little understood in Byzantine history, particularly leading up to the Seljuk period of occupation.

Traditional approaches to Byzantine history and archaeology have paid little attention to the Anatolian hinterland, instead focusing on urban environments and their subsequent decline in the sixth and seventh centuries. Older studies have presented the Byzantine era as a stark, violent period of repeated occupations and destructions, largely based on our knowledge of the historical events that only loosely affected the region (Foss 1977; Vryonis 1971). However, excavation and survey at a number of sites in Anatolia, such as Amorium (Lightfoot 2017) and Ephesus (Ladstätter 2017), have illustrated that this was not, in fact, the reality for most of the population in these regions. The stratigraphy at Çadır Höyük suggests continuous, if varied, occupation, which needs to be seen as part of a cycle of growth and release. Further, the activities of the population of the site should be seen as reactions to both internal and external stimuli, often happening simultaneously.

Abandonment 1: The Late Roman Period—Abandonment as Resilience

The most extensive occupation of the northern terrace at Çadır Höyük began in the Late Roman period. Based on ^{14}C dates and the remnants of large, mostly robbed-out walls on the terrace (particularly in trenches NT 2, NT 3, and NTN 7; see **Figure 4**), we know that there was some habitation of the site in the Early Roman period (Steadman et al. 2015:90). Not enough is visible yet to clarify whether this was a precursor to the large house that marks the Late Roman habitation, nor to understand what the transition between these periods looked like. However, by the late fourth century—based on ^{14}C dates, ceramics, and coins—we know that a large domestic structure was inhabited on the terrace (Steadman et al. 2015:90). It was a large house, possessed of at least one large courtyard and possibly two, which contained some characteristics of a Late Roman elite household (**Figure 5**), including plastered walls and imported wares. By the seventh century, however, some of these elements were deliberately abandoned in a rebuilding episode that reflects a substantial adaptation of this population to the changing Late Roman world.

The original structure is difficult to define, but some attempt is necessary in order to understand the resilience of the structure in the subsequent period. To date, the majority of Late Roman Anatolian structures that have been published are either located in an urban context or represent the identifiable elite classes (Bowes 2010; Ellis 1988, 2004; Eyice 1996). Simon Ellis divides housing into two categories for this period: the true peristyle house of the Roman upper classes and a more complex Early Byzantine house that draws on both Roman and local elements. Ellis admits that:

> This "middle ground" of housing ... continues to be the most difficult stratum of housing to tackle ... Housing at this social level is less constrained by aristocratic convention, although it may pay lip service to peristyle traditions by using an odd mosaic or column. Equally these houses are beyond the realm of the villager peasant—they may have good décor, and were often owned by relatively wealthy tradesmen. [Ellis 2004:43]

While this definition still describes an urban context, it provides a key to understanding space from a different perspective than through the eyes of the elite. Perhaps the key to the resilience of the house at Çadır Höyük lies precisely in the fact that it represents a liminal and largely unknown class of domestic structure in Anatolia, one that borrowed from both elite Roman and local norms.

As the plan of the terrace shows, understanding the original layout is quite difficult since the structure was reused and rebuilt throughout the Roman, Late Roman, and Byzantine periods (see **Figure 5**). In earlier publications, we assumed this to be a variation of the peristyle structure (Cassis 2009; Cassis and Steadman 2014), but after increased excavation, it seems more likely that this falls into the category of a provincial Late Roman or Early Byzantine house as defined by Ellis. The entrance seems to have been from an external courtyard (NT 2, NTN 7), from which a passageway ran along two rooms (**Figure 6**), ultimately arriving in a large internal courtyard which had at least two more rooms lining it (NTN 8, NT 3; **Figure 7**). The earliest levels of this Late Roman structure offer evidence for more elaborate workmanship than in later periods. For example, the walls in this structure are decorated with painted plaster, a decorative element with parallels throughout the Late Roman world. Most notable is a large plaster basin set into a painted wall in NTN 7/8 (**Figure 8**). Taken in conjunction with the plastered and painted walls, this basin suggests a household of some means, with the ability to commission decent workmanship. Within the stratigraphic levels associated with this house, we have found coins dating to the late fourth and fifth

Figure 6. View of NTN 7 and 8, looking east: the courtyard and passageway between rooms. Photo copyright Çadır Höyük Excavations.

Figure 7. View of the large internal courtyard, NTN 8. Photo copyright Çadır Höyük Excavations.

Figure 8. Late Roman room with a basin, NTN 8. Photo copyright Çadır Höyük Excavations.

Figure 9. Late Roman imported African Red Slip ware. Photo copyright Çadır Höyük Excavations.

Figure 10. Late Roman entrance, USS 1, looking south. Photo copyright Çadır Höyük Excavations.

Figure 11. Late Roman room, USS 3, looking west. Photo copyright Çadır Höyük Excavations.

centuries as well as examples of a local variety of African Red Slip ware (ARS) and a few imports (Figure 9). The house represents owners with some standing in society, if not an extravagant lifestyle, but the difference in layout from the standardized Roman peristyle makes it difficult to categorize and, thus, may suggest a local population of moderate wealth, a constituency in Late Roman society that Ellis (2004) has hypothesized.

What is particularly striking about the evidence at Çadır Höyük is that it stands in stark contrast to some of the other elements of Late Roman culture in the region. For example, an unexcavated structure at nearby Kerkenes suggests precisely the type of Late Roman elite culture that Ellis defines in his work, since it contains an apsidal hall (Summers 2001). A recently discovered mosaic near Kerkenes (Turkish Daily News 2015) and the spectacular Roman remains of the bath complex at Sarakaya speak to the type of material that was available to an elite population in the region (Chantre 1898; Şenyurt 2016). Thus, the variation among Roman houses suggests social differentiation within the context of Late Roman society in the area. At present, then, our assessment of this structure suggests that it was the house of a member of a local family of some standing living in proximity to the mound. The mound, largely used in the Middle Byzantine period for defense and storage, had some Late Roman structures, the nature of which remains somewhat uncertain. Nevertheless, after the 2017 season, we now know it had a more established usage in the Late

Roman period than we had previously understood, as USS 1 and USS 2 provide evidence of an entrance to the Late Roman site, and USS 3 is a small isolated room that dates to this period (**Figure 10** and **Figure 11**). The house on the terrace thus represents a localized architectural form that was part of a regional network of domestic sites ranging from the aristocratic Roman to the vernacular local.

The end of this Late Roman phase is marked by the first of the site's abandonments, and it was a slow one. The seventh century was a period of extensive change in the Late Roman world. Plague, political turmoil, and environmental degradation—noted in the sixth-century writings of Procopius and others—were significant forces (Telelis 2008). By the start of the seventh century the region suffered invasion by the Sasanian Persians, which, while short-lived, devastated Antioch and lands across northern Syria and southern Anatolia. Weakened by these events, the Late Roman world was no match for the arrival of the Muslims in the Levant in the seventh century. The Muslims pushed the Byzantine army back into Anatolia and, although they were not able to pursue them further, created havoc in the Late Roman heartland through seasonal raids that destroyed crops and livestock and weakened the communities in southern Anatolia. It has been argued, most successfully by Mark Whittow (2009) and John Haldon (1990), that it was the culmination of crises that led to a substantial reorganization of society in the seventh century. Urban life changed considerably with a move away from the grandiose symbols of patronage and empire visible in the old Roman cities. Reduced public infrastructure was the result of less money and less patronage, and older buildings were divided, subdivided, and repurposed. While the older historical narrative suggested that many centers were abandoned, archaeology has now proven that there was an adjustment and a shrinking of cities.

While the change is readily apparent in the urban centers, excavation at rural settlements has been limited, and there is a particular dearth of information about houses in this period as a result. The commonly held belief is that the aristocratic elite withdrew from the countryside and smaller regional centers, leaving behind populations whose domestic organization was neither visible nor particularly interesting. However, if we consider that the more well-known peristyle houses were not, in fact, indicative of all levels of local society, we can hypothesize a more vernacular housing style alongside those houses that were representative of elite Roman norms. Further, if these houses reflect a local population, it seems even more likely that these people did not flee or disappear but

Figure 12. Local Early Byzantine Imitation Red ware (NTN 8). Photo copyright Çadır Höyük Excavations.

rather adapted to changes in ways that their Roman elite counterparts either did not or could not. Indeed, perhaps we have been looking for the wrong thing.

The stratigraphy of Çadır Höyük bears this out. While there is no evidence either for or against a change in population, the stratigraphy of the house indicates that it continued with a change in material culture. Within the Early Byzantine period, walls were repaired, small subdivisions occurred, and new floors were laid down (Cassis 2009). There was not, however, any major new building in this period. Indeed, the transformation at Çadır Höyük largely reflected an abandonment of the past and an adaptation to the needs of the present. While the original population had adopted at least some of the norms of the elite Roman worldview, in the seventh century residents were unable or unwilling to continue using the earlier structures as they existed. This change reflects a deliberate rejection of past norms or an adjustment to changes in the economic and social structures present in the early Byzantine period. This is most evident in the material culture. While coinage was never extensive, these seventh- to ninth-century phases are marked by the dearth of coinage that characterizes the period in Anatolia generally. This is a notable change as well, because the earlier levels—while not particularly rich in coinage—do provide examples of coins from the fourth through sixth centuries. On these later floors we find the evidence for changing material culture as local and imported ARS gave way to locally made ceramics that were meant to stand in for the earlier objects (Figure 12; Cassis 2009).

So, what happened? By the seventh century many of the cities of the empire had contracted substantially. The narrative of ruralization, long accepted as indicative of this period, reflects the ability of the people in the rural landscape to adapt more easily than those in urban areas. Although there is written evidence to suggest more of a peasant economy—notable, for example, in saints' lives such as the *Vita* of Theodore of Sykeon (Haldon 1990)—this does not fully explain the period. Nor, frankly, does the readily accepted belief that all of the wealthy inhabitants fled as society collapsed. Instead, if we return to resilience theory, we can see the Early Byzantine period as one of first conservation (K) and then of release (Ω), a release that would eventually give way to the reorganization of the ninth and tenth centuries, a period which resulted in a society based around a local economy with an agricultural focus.

The evidence for this lies in the reuse and restructuring of the house in order to adapt to the changes that were affecting rural communities throughout Anatolia. This continuity is evident at Çadır Höyük, where the population attempted to hold on and adapt to these changes. We see this in several places on the terrace where the original house was rebuilt and reused as the community adapted to the lack of contact with the wider world (Cassis 2009). New floors, for example, were laid down in NT 2, NTN 7, and NTN 8. While the house changed even more in later periods, the material culture changes were substantial. The evidence does not suggest that the population itself changed but rather that access to certain types of material culture changed, which in turn affected the way that the surviving society expressed itself. The adaptations visible in the ceramics, while not as fine as in the Late Roman period, nevertheless provide evidence for attempted consistency with the vanishing world of the elite Late Roman household. In places like Çadır Höyük it may be possible to ask whether this was a local class that, because it was more adaptable to the specific environment, survived the changes of this period better than the elites of the fine peristyle manor houses or the urban centers. Regardless, the adaptation of this population—visible in the site's continuity— marks a slow abandonment of the past to create a new type of settlement. In short, it reflects the release and reorganization phases of resilience theory.

Abandonment 2: The Eleventh Century—Forced Abandonment

By the ninth century, things were beginning to change in central Anatolia. A brief lull in the continuous raids along the southern border during the Umayyad–Abbasid transition meant that the Byzantine Empire had time to reclaim territory and reestablish control over areas in central and southern Anatolia. By the tenth century, the empire had a more stable government, a reorganized thematic system, and a series of emperors who understood the significance of the rural world and the agricultural population. This led to a new world order which allowed for an empire consolidated symbolically on the Emperor in Constantinople but more practically focused on individual leaders in provincial centers. Overall, it was a period of prosperity, which historians have largely understood in economic and political terms. However, archaeologically speaking, this can also be seen in terms of resilience theory, as this period represents one of new exploitation (r) and conservation (K) following reorganization (α).

While historians understand that the increasing political fragmentation of the empire meant that power resided more consistently in the hands of local families in the themes, we have given little thought to how communities adjusted to the change and how this resulted in a new architectural and material culture legacy. On a microscale, this plays out with developments in housing. Once again, we are stymied by a lack of understanding of what houses looked like in the Middle Byzantine period in the rural parts of the empire. The majority of work has been done on elite housing in urban centers (Rheidt 1990), and there has been little interest in attempting to trace the material lives of the urban or rural poor. Indeed, Oikonomides (1990) once remarked that the houses of peasants were not studied because they contained little of interest. Nevertheless, since the last century, increased excavation of the Middle Byzantine period at places like Ephesus and Amorium, as well as in Greece, has suggested that Middle Byzantine houses—at least the elite ones—can be characterized as inward-looking, multifunctional spaces built on reused Late Roman structures (Sigalos 2004).

Çadır Höyük displays precisely this type of restructuring. It is in roughly the tenth century that the Late Roman house was refurbished with beautiful stone paving and plastered courtyards, directly over the location of the earlier house (NT 7 and NTN 7; Figure 13). The rebuilt part of the house indicates a return to wealth. The format of the house was different, however, and reflects an inward, vernacular style of the local population. The house did not need to be completely redesigned but rather was rebuilt and extended. Earlier structures were demolished entirely in the southern

Figure 13. Middle Byzantine house, NTN 7. Photo copyright Çadır Höyük Excavations.

part of the house, although extant wall stubs and floors suggest that the original house had been at least as large as the later structure. To the south of the richly refurbished rooms, a large kitchen area was added (Cassis 2009). This was a long room containing two ovens, a hearth area, and at least two benches, one against the northern wall and one in the center of the room (NT 7 and NT 8; Figure 14). There are several parallels to this type of house in excavations in Greece, and Sigalos (2004:60–61) suggests that Middle Byzantine houses were characterized by long kitchens used for a variety of household activities.

That being said, the dates for this structure at Çadır Höyük remain difficult to pin down, as there is remarkably little coinage or fine ware. Parallel construction on the mound suggests a tenth-century date, based primarily on some very small pieces of diagnostic fine ware, including one piece of White ware. Circumstantial historical evidence, largely from works like those of the eleventh-century historian John Skylitzes, suggests that this was a period of relative security in central Anatolia and that this house represents a return to wealth of a local family or village. Settlement on the mound was reestablished in this period, and a large fortification was constructed (Cassis and Steadman 2014; Steadman et al. 2015). The combination of the two building programs points to local societal organization and defense. While there is little here to suggest a major thematic family, we do know that in Charsianon, the province

Figure 14. Middle Byzantine kitchen, NT 7 and NT 8, looking north. Photo copyright Çadır Höyük Excavations.

that included Çadır Höyük, there were notable imperial figures. These included Samuel Alusianos, a Bulgarian general who had married into one of the thematic families and whose eleventh-century seal was excavated on the mound (Cassis 2009; Skylitzes 2010). Defining these families remains difficult, however, since we remain uncertain about the precise location of the thematic capital as well as the connection between it and minor sites like Çadır Höyük and Kerkenes. But as the region as a whole regrouped, local families also began to reestablish themselves.

The release (Ω) or abandonment of the site, however, marks a very different end to the population than what took place at the end of the Late Roman period. This abandonment can be seen through two separate events: a slow decrease in the prosperity of the site, probably starting in the early or mid eleventh century, followed by a forced abandonment around the time of the Battle of Manzikert in 1071. There are no guidelines to understand precisely what happened in the eleventh century in Anatolia. The archaeology indicates that the prosperity of the tenth and early eleventh centuries was relatively short-lived and that the population associated with this domestic complex—and the fortification on the mound—became increasingly fearful. Most of the evidence for this comes from the mound itself, which exhibits substantial rebuilding in the eleventh century. However, the majority of this is poorly constructed, ephemeral architecture, built in stages over earlier structures. New stone walls were constructed against the earlier fortification wall, creating new rooms, and then mud brick was added on top of these walls in a second rebuilding (SMW 1 and 2; **Figure 15** and **Figure 16**). At present, we believe that the population, fearing attacks, decreased substantially and moved to the mound for protection. This occupation phase is characterized by an increased number of tools, including agricultural implements like grinding stones (**Figure 17**), as well as religious artifacts (**Figure 18**). By the mid eleventh century, these populations were at risk of raids from early Seljuk groups and renegade mercenaries (Haldon 2008).

The cause of the final abandonment remains uncertain, but in the past few years we have been able to reconstruct events with more security. Two particular elements suggest that the majority of the population left under its own steam with a clear intention of returning. First, as noted in other scholarship on Çadır Höyük, the inhabitants left a large collection of animals penned up on the mound. New analysis by Ben Arbuckle and his team has identified the animals as cattle, many of which were old and diseased (Steadman et al. 2017). Recent excavations on the mound have now found the remains of at least six people. The partial remnants of two

Figure 15. Secondary eleventh-century mud-brick construction, SMW 1 and 2, looking north. Photo copyright Çadır Höyük Excavations.

Figure 16. Eleventh-century rooms appended to ninth or tenth-century fortifications, SMW 1 and 2, looking north. Photo copyright Çadır Höyük Excavations.

Figure 17. Agricultural implement (SMW 2). Photo copyright Çadır Höyük Excavations.

Figure 18. Reliquary cross (SMW 2). Photo copyright Çadır Höyük Excavations.

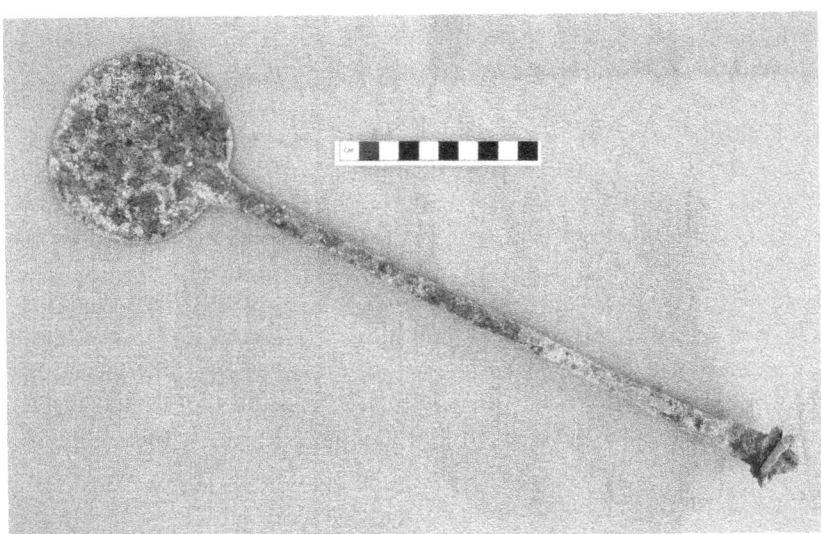

Figure 19. Metal kitchen implement (NTN 8). Photo copyright Çadır Höyük Excavations.

people were found in guard rooms on the mound: one on the west side and one on the south side. Both were found in proximity to weapons, and the room against the fortification wall in SMW 2 also provided a piece of a Byzantine helmet and some chain mail. Other remains, including those from adolescents, were found near SMW 2 and in the stable with the remains of animals. All of these people seem to have died in violent circumstances, suggesting that a small group was left to defend the mound, ultimately unsuccessfully.

The circumstantial evidence of the mound is confirmed by the material found in the excavations of the Middle Byzantine house on the terrace. While there are no human remains on the terrace and little to suggest violence in this part of the settlement, the objects that were left behind suggest that the inhabitants intended to return to the site shortly after they had left. This is most clear in the kitchen area, where a collection of tools was identified, including bone saws, horse paraphernalia, and a variety of other good-quality metal artifacts (**Figure 19**). Although the deposit was itself quite disturbed, this almost certainly reflects a secondary treatment of the artifacts, as we will discuss below. While not found in their original context, the presence of these tools suggests that they were both replaceable and awkward to carry, and that the population felt it unnecessary to remove them during their temporary displacement.

This abandonment marks the end of a cycle of rebuilding that had begun probably in the tenth century. By the mid eleventh century, central Anatolia was changing. Increased trouble in the capital led to political instability in the provinces, although how much that would have affected these populations is uncertain (Beihammer 2017). More problematic was the increased number of mercenaries and Turkic nomads in proximity to these small rural sites, especially in light of a weak centrally controlled response. The local families, so prominent in the tenth century, were increasingly vying for power in the capital and abandoning their themes to external attacks. The eleventh century also exhibited signs of increased environmental change (Haldon et al. 2014), which certainly contributed to the arrival of the Turkic nomads. Thus, after a period of relative comfort and prosperity throughout the tenth century, the population was forced into a position of forced release (Ω) as the political and environmental landscapes changed.

Abandonment 3: The Twelfth Century—Adaptive Seasonal Abandonment

As noted in previous publications, it had been our assumption for many years that the site fell into complete disuse after the middle of the eleventh century (Cassis 2009). However, we have had to substantially revise this view with further exploration of the mound (Cassis 2017).

Exploration of the east side of the fortification of the mound between 2016 and 2017 (SMT 9 and SMT 4) has revealed that this area was, in fact, reoccupied. A new population—probably Turkic—rebuilt and reoccupied some of the Middle Byzantine structures sometime in the late eleventh or early twelfth century. It is impossible to say with any real certainty who this population was, as the Turkic groups who had arrived in the region were largely nomadic with little adherence to an organized central authority. Nevertheless, rebuilding—coupled with some distinctive material culture—suggests that part of the mound was reutilized for at least brief periods of time.

Much of this new construction was ephemeral, suggesting that the reoccupying population was transient. Along the east wall of the mound, some of the Byzantine rooms were reused. The original stone fortifications, as well as two small rooms along this wall, were rebuilt with mud brick, a reconstruction that included a built mud-brick bench in one of the rooms (SMT 9; Figure 20). Immediately to the south of this, at least one small windbreak was established, probably to protect livestock (SMT 15; Figure 21). In SMT 9, an excavated pile of shells in proximity to a hearth, as well as some Seljuk metalwork (Figure 22) and medieval

Figure 20. Twelfth or thirteenth-century mud-brick reconstruction, SMT 9, looking east. Photo copyright Çadır Höyük Excavations.

Figure 21. Twelfth or thirteenth-century windbreak, SMT 15, looking west. Photo copyright Çadır Höyük Excavations.

Figure 22. Seljuk-period metalwork (SMT 9). Photo copyright Çadır Höyük Excavations.

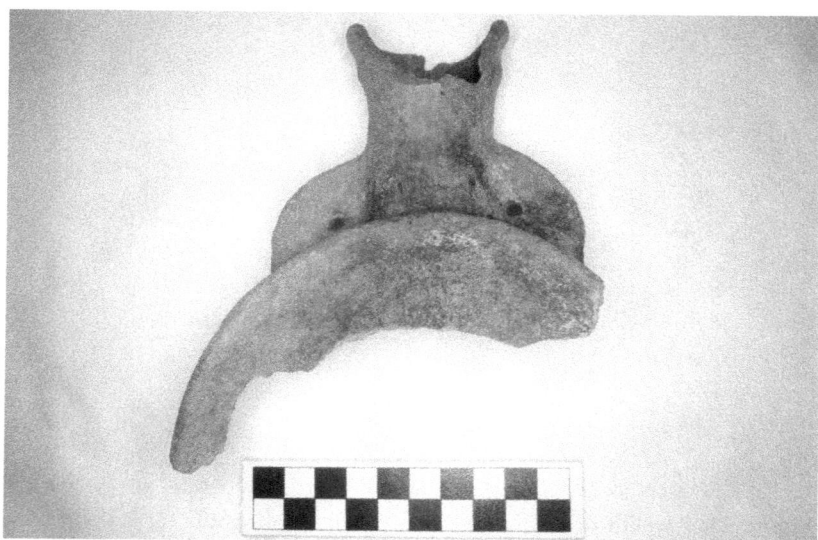

Figure 23. Medieval traveler's flask (SMT 9). Photo copyright Çadır Höyük Excavations.

ceramics (**Figure 23**), were also found in this occupation level. While the ceramics at the site are primarily course ware, the wares evolve throughout the Byzantine period into this occupation level, and Joanita Vroom (personal communication 2015) has tentatively placed these ceramics in the late twelfth or early thirteenth century. They are handmade course wares with a micaceous slip which represent a long-standing pottery tradition in the area. However, these ceramics are less finely made than those of the previous centuries, even though the rough shapes remain consistent with those of the previous century (Cassis 2017).

While these changes are relatively small, they stand in marked contrast to the architecture and stratigraphical contexts on other parts of the mound that were not disturbed after the eleventh-century abandonment. The stable full of animals, for example, was simply covered over and a windbreak placed over it. On the south and west sides of the mound, guard chambers remained untouched after they were abandoned, complete with religious artifacts and remnants of armor. The reoccupation of the site—even if temporary or seasonal in nature—thus marks part of the cycle of resilience theory. As noted above, the mid eleventh century provides evidence of the release (Ω) phase of the cycle, while the return to the site in the late eleventh or early twelfth century marks a different type of reorganizational phase (α) in Anatolia. That is, as the new Turkic population arrived and added to the chaos in Anatolia, the old societal organization gave way to a new one that was temporary or seasonal in nature. Although the nature of the settlement changed—reflecting the arrival of the Turkic people—the similarities in ceramics suggests that there was also a return of some of the Byzantine population, with a resulting mixed population (Redford 2015). While this is admittedly speculative, given the lack of corresponding archaeological or literary evidence for the region and the period, it is clear that the reorganization (α) took into account the environmental and social changes of the eleventh century and allowed for the creation of a new society.

The reuse on the mound, some of which covers the eleventh-century abandonment, provides a terminus post quem for resettlement and reuse on the mound. The abandoned Middle Byzantine house on the terrace provides more evidence for continued use by a transient population. First, there is ample evidence that the house underwent some architectural renovation. This is most obvious in the kitchen, where the doorway was blocked. Outside, the courtyard was subdivided and small storage bins were created out of standing walls (**Figure 24**). The dates for these changes again remain somewhat nebulous, but this would have resulted in a major reorganization and reorientation of the walls of this area, suggesting that there was a different set of intentions behind this use. The small amount of research on Turkic housing in Anatolia—which comes primarily from an ethnographical perspective—suggests that built houses often incorporated a work area that mimicked the space and function of a tent (Bammer 1996). The kitchen area, which had two hearths, would have served that function well but may have needed to be reoriented for the reorganization phase of reuse, resulting in the blocked doorway. Further, within this space, a number of utilitarian artifacts were found which have parallels at other Middle Byzantine sites in Anatolia (e.g. Berti 2012; Ferrazzoli 2012), but they were reused and consequently redistributed in the later period. Reuse was also confirmed by the excavation of NT 7 in 2001, which uncovered a wealth of intact ceramics and metal objects, again tentatively dated to the early twelfth century (Figure 25 and Figure 26). A surface find of a possible Danishmendid coin in the vicinity adds to the circumstantial evidence for dating this occupational level. The presence of a grave at the bottom of the east side of the mound is also significant (ST 3; Figure 27). There, a woman was carefully interred in the shallow grave (Steadman et al. 2015). She was positioned facing Mecca rather than toward the east, and a rock was placed deliberately at her neck, possibly in keeping with the animistic fears of the Turkic tribesmen who were new to Islam (Peacock 2010:123–124). Buried at her hip was a small pot of the same type found in NT 7, suggesting a twelfth- or thirteenth-century date. Who she was remains a mystery, but her burial points to a transient population—either Turkic or mixed—in the area after the abandonment of the site.

The next abandonment phase, when the transient population that reoccupied the east part of the mound finally left, is part of both release and reorganization as Anatolia—and the Turkic groups—adapted to the new world order. What differentiates this phase from the earlier ones is that the transitory nature of the settlement in the late eleventh and early twelfth centuries suggests continuous cycles of abandonment and reuse, which, taken together, form a new type of reorganization (α) that probably lasted until the Ottoman period provided more permanent settlement in the region. This original Turkic population that arrived in the region was nomadic in the main part, and it seems likely that their arrival at places like Çadır Höyük reflected a slow adaptation to a new land and to the remnants of old populations. We cannot yet trace whether this population change was singular or happened repeatedly as Anatolia changed, but, given what we know of the early Turkic populations, it seems likely that we are looking at the cycles of release and reorganization that would eventually result in the mixed resettlement of Anatolia.

Figure 24. Blocked doorway and storage bins, NT 7, looking southwest. Photo copyright Çadır Höyük Excavations.

Figure 25. Ceramic vessel (NT 7). Photo copyright Çadır Höyük Excavations.

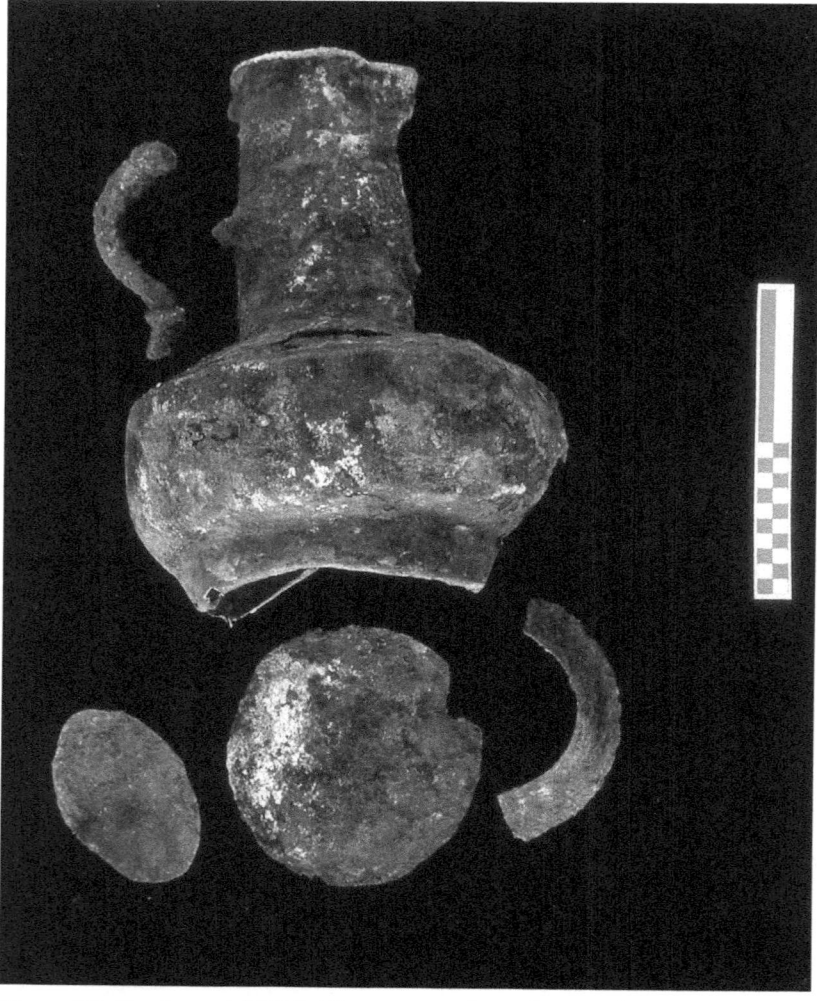

Figure 26. Metal vessel (NT 7). Photo copyright Çadır Höyük Excavations.

Figure 27. Medieval burial (ST 3). Photo copyright Çadır Höyük Excavations.

Conclusions

From the Late Roman period until the end of Byzantine control in Anatolia, a single complex at the foot of Çadır Höyük housed generations of residents. The history of this building was punctuated by three abandonments. The first of these was the seventh-century abandonment of the Late Roman world as the population was faced with the challenges of the Early Byzantine period in Anatolia, which was marked by the loss of many of the trappings of the Roman Empire. This abandonment can be seen as a slow change, an adaptation to a changing world. The second abandonment, that of the mid eleventh century, marked the sudden demise of the population as environmental change and the resultant social upheaval led to a complete reorientation of society. Finally, the third abandonment occurred not once, but repeatedly in the eleventh and twelfth centuries, as a nomadic Turkic population adapted to a new environment and the remnants of the Byzantine population. These, we propose, are best considered as adaptive reorganizations and not necessarily as final events. Thus, for example, the regional economic and military insecurity of the seventh century impacted rural Çadır Höyük, although the result was not the devastation that traditional top-down models would suggest. Instead, the changes we observe were active choices to adapt to new realities. Successive moments of abandonment as new populations moved onto the plateau were intentional decisions by individuals and communities to minimize loss and instability.

Local changes at Çadır Höyük reflect larger historical trends, but they also were shaped by locally specific conditions. Rather than interpreting change through a macrohistorical or political lens, we must see processes of abandonment as rational localized responses to historically contingent phenomena. Abandonment in its broadest definition can, indeed, mean the cessation of settlement at a site, but it can also refer to abandonment of past practices as a society reorganizes. Viewed this way, abandonment is not inherently negative but rather potentially adaptive—a normal part of the cycle of change in an archaeological site. Resilience-centered models allow us to highlight continuity and reorganization over the simplistic models of conquest, catastrophe, and abandonment. In short, these models provide a more realistic and human interpretation of archaeological settlement.

Acknowledgments. Research at Çadır Höyük was supported by the Social Sciences and Humanities Research Council of Canada (SSHRC Insight Grant 435-2014-0944).

References Cited

Allison, Penelope
   1999   *The Archaeology of Household Activities*. Routledge, London.
   2008   Household Archaeology. In *Encyclopedia of Archaeology*, edited by Deborah Pearsall, pp. 1449–1458. Academic Press, Oxford.

Andreassen, Elin, Hein Bjartmann Bjerck, and Bjørnar Olsen
   2010   *Persistent Memories: Pyramiden—A Soviet Mining Town in the High Arctic*. Tapir Academic Press, Trondheim.

Ascher, Robert
   1968   Time's Arrow and the Archaeology of a Contemporary Community. In *Settlement Archaeology*, edited by Kwang-Chih Chang, pp. 43–52. National Press Books, Palo Alto.

Baker, Charles M.
   1975   Site Abandonment and the Archaeological Record: An Empirical Case for Anticipated Return. *Journal of the Arkansas Academy of Science* 29(5):10–11. https://scholarworks.uark.edu/jaas/vol29/iss1/5

Bammer, Anton
   1996   Çadır ile Anadolu Evi İlişkileri [The Relationship Between the Tent and the Anatolian House]. In *Tarihten günümüze Anadolu'da konut ve yerleşme [Housing and Settlement in Anatolia: A Historical Perspective]*, edited by Yıldız Sey, pp. 234–247. Tepe Architectural Culture Center, Istanbul.

Beaudry, Mary C.
   2015   Households Beyond the House: On the Archaeology and Materiality of Historical Households. In *Beyond the Walls: New Perspectives on the Archaeology of Historical Households*, edited by Kevin R. Fogle, James A. Nyman, and Mary C. Beaudry, pp. 1–22. University Press of Florida, Gainesville.

Beihammer, Alexander Daniel
   2017   *Byzantium and the Emergence of Muslim-Turkish Anatolia, ca. 1040–1130*. Routledge, New York.

Berti, Fede
    2012   Grave Goods from the Necropolis in the Agora of Iasos. In *Byzantine Small Finds in Archaeological Contexts*, edited by Beate Böhlendorf-Arslan and Alessandra Ricci, pp. 187–211. Byzas 15. Yayınları, Istanbul.

Bowes, Kim
    2010   *Houses and Society in the Later Roman Empire.* Bristol Classical Press, London.

Cameron, Catherine M.
    1991   Structure Abandonment in Villages. *Archaeological Method and Theory* 3:155–194.

Cassis, Marica
    2009   Çadır Höyük: A Rural Settlement in Byzantine Anatolia. In *Archaeology of the Countryside in Medieval Anatolia*, edited by Tasha Vorderstrasse and Jacob Roodenberg, pp. 1–24. Nederlands Instituut voor het Nabije Oosten, Leiden.
    2017   Çadır Höyük. In *The Archaeology of Byzantine Anatolia: From the End of Late Antiquity Until the Coming of the Turks*, edited by Philipp Niewöhner, pp. 368–374. Oxford University Press, Oxford.

Cassis, Marica, Owen Doonan, Hugh Elton, and James Newhard
    2018   Evaluating Archaeological Evidence for Demographics, Abandonment, and Recovery in Late Antique and Byzantine Anatolia. *Human Ecology* 46(3):381–398. https://doi.org/10.1007/s10745-018-0003-1

Cassis, Marica, and Sharon R. Steadman
    2014   Çadır Höyük: Continuity and Change on the Anatolian Plateau. In *From West to East: Current Approaches to Medieval Archaeology*, edited by Scott D. Stull, pp. 140–154. Cambridge Scholars Publishing, Newcastle.

Chantre, Ernest
    1898   *Recherches archéologiques dans l'Asie occidentale. Mission en Cappadoce: 1893–1894 [Archaeological Research in Western Asia. Mission to Cappadocia: 1893–1894].* Ernest Leroux, Paris.

Ellis, Simon P.
 1988 The End of the Roman House. *American Journal of Archaeology* 92(4):565–576. https://doi.org/10.2307/505251
 2004 Early Byzantine Housing. In *Secular Buildings and the Archaeology of Everyday Life in the Byzantine Empire*, edited by Ken Dark, pp. 37–52. Oxbow Books, Oxford.

Eyice, Semavi
 1996 Türkiye'de Bizans Yerleşimi Hakkında Notlar [Observations on Byzantine-Period Dwellings in Turkey]. In *Tarihten günümüze Anadolu'da konut ve yerleşme [Housing and Settlement in Anatolia: A Historical Perspective]*, edited by Yıldız Sey, pp. 206–220. Tepe Architectural Culture Center, Istanbul.

Ferrazzoli, Adele Federica
 2012 Byzantine Small Finds from Elaiussa Sebaste. In *Byzantine Small Finds in Archaeological Contexts*, edited by Beate Böhlendorf-Arslan and Alessandra Ricci, pp. 289–307. Byzas 15. Yayınları, Istanbul.

Foss, Clive
 1977 Archaeology and the "Twenty Cities" of Byzantine Asia. *American Journal of Archaeology* 81(4):469–486. https://doi.org/10.2307/503279

Gilchrist, Roberta
 2007 Archaeology and the Life Course: A Time and Age for Gender. In *A Companion to Social Archaeology*, edited by Lynn Meskell and Robert W. Preucel, pp. 142–160. Blackwell, Malden. https://doi.org/10.1002/9780470693605.ch6

Gordillo, Gaston
 2014 *Rubble: The Afterlife of Destruction.* Duke University Press, Durham, North Carolina.

Haldon, John F.
 1990 *Byzantium in the Seventh Century: The Transformation of a Culture.* Cambridge University Press, Cambridge.
 2008 *The Byzantine Wars.* The History Press, Stroud.

Haldon, John, Neil Roberts, Adam Izdebski, Dominik Fleitmann, Michael McCormick, Marica Cassis, Owen Doonan, Warren Eastwood, Hugh Elton, Sabine Ladstätter, Sturt Manning, James Newhard, Kathleen Nicoll, Ioannes Telelis, and Elena Xoplaki
    2014   The Climate and Environment of Byzantine Anatolia: Integrating Science, History, and Archaeology. *Journal of Interdisciplinary History* 45(2):113–161. https://doi.org/10.1162/JINH_a_00682

Hendon, Julia
    2007   Living and Working at Home: The Social Archaeology of Household Production and Social Relations. In *A Companion to Social Archaeology*, edited by Lynn Meskell and Robert W. Preucel, pp. 272–286. Blackwell, Malden. https://doi.org/10.1002/9780470693605.ch12

Holling, C. S., and Lance H. Gunderson
    2002   Resilience and Adaptive Cycles. In *Panarchy: Understanding Transformations in Human and Natural Systems*, edited by Lance H. Gunderson and C. S. Holling, pp. 25–62. Island Press, Washington, DC.

Jervis, Ben
    2017   Assessing Urban Fortunes in Six Late Medieval Ports: An Archaeological Application of Assemblage Theory. *Urban History* 44:2–26. https://doi.org/10.1017/S0963926815000930

Ladstätter, Sabine
    2017   Ephesus. In *The Archaeology of Byzantine Anatolia: From the End of Late Antiquity Until the Coming of the Turks*, edited by Philipp Niewöhner, pp. 238–248. Oxford University Press, Oxford.

Lightfoot, Christopher S.
    2017   Amorium. In *The Archaeology of Byzantine Anatolia: From the End of Late Antiquity Until the Coming of the Turks*, edited by Philipp Niewöhner, pp. 333–341. Oxford University Press, Oxford.

McCormick, Michael, Ulf Büntgen, Mark A. Cane, Edward R. Cook, Kyle Harper, Peter Huybers, Thomas Litt, Sturt W. Manning, Paul Andrew Mayewski, Alexander F. M. More, Kurt Nicolussi, and Willy Tegel
    2012   Climate Change During and After the Roman Empire: Reconstructing the Past from Scientific and Historical Evidence. *The Journal of Interdisciplinary History* 43(2):169–220. https://doi.org/10.1162/JINH_a_00379

Oikonomides, Nicolas
    1990   The Contents of the Byzantine House from the Eleventh to the Fifteenth Century. *Dumbarton Oaks Papers* 44:205–214. https://doi.org/10.2307/1291629

Olsen, Bjørnar, and Þóra Pétursdóttir (editors)
    2014   *Ruin Memories: Materialities, Aesthetics and the Archaeology of the Recent Past*. Routledge, New York. https://doi.org/10.4324/9781315778211

Peacock, A. C. S.
    2010   *Early Seljūq History: A New Interpretation*. Routledge, London.

Redford, Scott
    2015   The Rape of Anatolia. In *Islam and Christianity in Medieval Anatolia*, edited by A.C.S. Peacock, Bruno De Nicola, and Sara Nur Yıldız, pp. 107–116. Ashgate, Farnham.

Redman, Charles L.
    2005   Resilience Theory in Archaeology. *American Anthropologist* 107(1):70–77. https://doi.org/10.1525/aa.2005.107.1.070

Redman, Charles L., and Ann P. Kinzig
    2003   Resilience of Past Landscapes: Resilience Theory, Society, and the *Longue Durée*. *Conservation Ecology* 7(1):14. https://www.jstor.org/stable/26271922

Rheidt, Klaus
    1990   Byzantinische Wohnhäuser des 11. bis 14. Jahrhunderts in Pergamon [Byzantine Houses from the 11th to 14th Centuries in Pergamon]. *Dumbarton Oaks Papers* 44:195–204. https://doi.org/10.2307/1291628

Roberts, Neil, Marica Cassis, Owen Doonan, Warren Eastwood, Hugh Elton, John Haldon, Adam Izdebski, and James Newhard
    2018   Not the End of the World? Post-Classical Decline and Recovery in Rural Anatolia. *Human Ecology* 46:305–322. https://doi.org/10.1007/s10745-018-9973-2

Schiffer, Michael B.
    1972   Archaeological Context and Systemic Context. *American Antiquity* 37(2):156–165. https://doi.org/10.2307/278203
    1985   Is There a "Pompeii Premise" in Archaeology? *Journal of Anthropological Research* 41(1):18–41. https://doi.org/10.1086/jar.41.1.3630269

Schreg, Rainer
    2011   Feeding the Village—Reflections on the Ecology and Resilience of the Medieval Rural Economy. In *Food in the Medieval Rural Environment: Processing, Storage, Distribution of Food*, edited by Jan Klápště, and Petr Sommer, pp. 301–320. Brepols, Turnhout. https://doi.org/10.1484/M.RURALIA-EB.1.100175

Şenyurt, Hasan K.
    2016   Sarıkaya Roma Hamamı Tarihçesi ve 2010–2015 Yılı Kazı Çalışmaları Sonuçları [The History of the Sarıkaya Roman Bath and Results of the 2010–2015 Excavations]. In *Bozok Üniversitesi. I. Uluslararası Bozok Sempozyumu 05–07 Mayıs 2016 Bildiri Kitabı*, I. Cilt [*Bozok University. I. Proceedings of the International Bozok Symposium 05–07 May 2016*, Vol. I], edited by Kadir Özköse, pp. 110–121. Bozok University Publications, Yozgat.

Sigalos, Lefteris
    2004   Middle and Late Byzantine Houses in Greece (Tenth to Fifteenth Centuries). In *Secular Buildings and the Archaeology of Everyday Life in the Byzantine Empire*, edited by Ken Dark, pp. 53–81. Oxbow Books, Oxford.

Skylitzes, John
   2010   *John Skylitzes: A Synopsis of Byzantine History, 811–1057. Translation and Notes*. Translated by John Wortley. Cambridge University Press, Cambridge. https://doi.org/10.1017/CBO9780511779657

Smith, Angèle
   2008   Landscapes of Clearance: Archaeological and Anthropological Perspectives. In *Landscapes of Clearance: Archaeological and Anthropological Perspectives*, edited by Angèle Smith and Amy Gazin-Schwartz, pp. 13–24. Left Coast, Walnut Creek, California.

Souvatzi, Stella
   2012   Between the Individual and the Collective: Household as a Social Process in Neolithic Greece. In *New Perspectives on Household Archaeology*, edited by Bradley J. Parker and Catherine P. Foster, pp. 15–44. Eisenbrauns, Winona Lake, Indiana.

Steadman, Sharon R., Gregory McMahon, Jennifer C. Ross, Marica Cassis, T. Emre Şerifoğlu, Benjamin S. Arbuckle, Sarah E. Adcock, Songül Alpaslan Roodenberg, Madelynn von Baeyer, and Anthony J. Lauricella
   2015   The 2013 and 2014 Excavation Seasons at Çadır Höyük on the Anatolian North Central Plateau. *Anatolica* 41:87–123.

Steadman, Sharon R., T. Emre Şerifoğlu, Gregory McMahon, Stephanie Selover, Laurel D. Hackley, Burcu Yıldırım, Anthony J. Lauricella, Benjamin S. Arbuckle, Sarah E. Adcock, Katie Tardio, Emrah Dinç, and Marica Cassis
   2017   Recent Discoveries (2015–2016) at Çadır Höyük on the North Central Plateau. *Anatolica* 43:203–250.

Summers, Geoffrey D.
   2001   Keykavus Kale and Associated Remains on the Kerkenes Dağ in Cappadocia, Central Turkey. *Anatolia Antiqua* 9:39–60.

Telelis, Ioannis G.
   2008   Climatic Fluctuations in the Eastern Mediterranean and the Middle East AD 300–1500 from Byzantine Documentary and Proxy Physical Paleoclimatic Evidence—A Comparison. *Jahrbuch der Österreichischen Byzantinistik* 58:167–207. https://doi.org/10.1553/joeb58s167

Turkish Daily News
   2015   Treasure Hunters Find Late Roman Mosaics. 8 February. http://www.hurriyetdailynews.com/treasure-hunters-find-late-roman-mosaics--78059, accessed November 8, 2020.

Vryonis, Speros
   1971   *The Decline of Medieval Hellenism in Asia Minor and the Process of Islamization from the Eleventh through the Fifteenth Century.* Publications of the Center for Medieval and Renaissance Studies, UCLA, 4. University of California Press, Berkeley.

Whittow, Mark
   2009   Early Medieval Byzantium and the End of the Ancient World. *Journal of Agrarian Change* 9(1):134–153. https://doi.org/10.1111/j.1471-0366.2009.00199.x

Chapter Two
The Deserted Village of Anavatos on the Island of Chios, Greece

Olga Vassi

During the fifteenth century, when the island of Chios was under Genoese rule, the settlement of Anavatos was founded in the mountains. It was invisible from the sea and nearly inaccessible.[1] The houses, streets, public spaces, churches, and small level areas (plateaus) were necessarily adapted to the steep natural contours. A defensive wall followed the brow of the cliff, and the gate to the fortified space guarded its single passable point. The domestic architecture was almost primitive: the houses were small, two storied, and with flat roofs. A large church dedicated to the Archangel Michael was built at the top of the hill, and another, dedicated to the Virgin, was erected above the village's only water cistern.

During the eighteenth century the village began to expand outside the wall, a development that was cut short violently in 1822 by a massacre of the local population by Ottoman troops and, a few decades later in 1881, by a great earthquake. The medieval village now stands abandoned and in ruins.

The Location

The island of Chios is located in the northern Aegean Sea, opposite the western shore of Asia Minor. Within its central mountainous terrain is nestled the settlement of Anavatos. About 23 km to the east is the coastal city of Chios (Chora), and to the west the settlement is connected to the coast by a pathway approximately 3.5 km long. Anavatos is situated at the top of a steep and rocky hill (Figure 1), within pastures and small fields of almond, olive, pistachio, and fig trees, all interspersed with vineyards. It is not discernible from the sea, as it is surrounded by high mountains to the west, north, and south. Its name, Anavatos (< ἀνάβασις = ascent), is testimony to the inaccessibility of its high and rugged terrain (Zolotas 1921:579).

---

[1] All photos were generated by the author unless otherwise noted.

Figure 1. View of Anavatos from the southeast.

The Written Sources about Palio Chorio

Beyond its impressive natural surroundings, the settlement is of particular interest because its medieval presence remains unchanged. Today, it comprises three distinct areas: (1) Palio Chorio (old village) or the *kastro* (fortification) at the peak, now destroyed and enclosed within a fortified wall; (2) the village outside the enclosure with its two-story houses on the slope of the hill (Philippa-Apostolou 2004); and (3) the new village at the foot of the hill with its tiled roofs, which was built after 1881 when much of the older village was destroyed by an earthquake and abandoned (Figure 2).

Anavatos was first mentioned in written sources in the sixteenth century: Hieronimus Giustiniani, who had lived on the island and was the presumed son of the last Genoese *podestà* (chief magistrate) of Chios, published a history of Chios in 1586 and briefly mentioned that a settlement called Anavato existed in the central part of the island (Giustiniani 1943:87). Some years later in 1638, Francesco Lupazzolo of Piedmont included the fortification of Anavatos in a map of Chios and mentioned the village in his text, although he probably never visited the place himself. After that, Anavatos was known to travelers who also wrote about the village but most probably never visited. These include the English priest John Covel in 1677 and the French botanist Joseph Pitton de Tournefort

Figure 2. View of Anavatos from the northeast.

in 1791 (Argenti and Kyriakidis 1946:319, 613). In the mid seventeenth century, the Italian jurist and diplomat Francesco Piacenza wrote that it had only 150 inhabitants.

In 1822, during the days-long massacre of Chios by Ottoman troops, the population was either annihilated or enslaved (Axiotakis 1994 [1976]:38–42). A few decades later, in 1881, an earthquake greatly impeded the development of the island and marked a milestone in the history and monuments of Chios, destroying whatever had survived destruction by the Ottoman forces (Bouras 1982a:40, 43, 53; Delopoulos 1983).

The Plan of Palio Chorio

The oldest section of Anavatos is at the top of the hill, and it is surrounded by a defensive wall that was entered via a single gate at the end of a steep pathway that leads up from its base (Figure 3 and Figure 4). In the past, the village within the walls—the *kastro*—was called Palio Chorio, and according to oral tradition it was divided into four neighborhoods: Taxiarchis (a reference to the Archangel Michael), Panayia (the Virgin), Kakouin (rough place), and Stenes Portes (narrow doors). There exists one more place name, Stis Portes (at the doors), which refers to the lowest southern end of the ruins (Axiotakis 1994 [1976]:156; Zolotas 1921:579).

Figure 3. Satellite view of Anavatos. Image courtesy of Google Earth.

The desertion of the upper section of the settlement began with the massacre of 1822. The finishing blow to its abandonment was the earthquake of 1881 that left Palio Chorio in ruins, collapsing the roofs of all the buildings, the surrounding walls, the churches, and the entrance gate, and burying the roads of the village under the debris. In the years between 1998 and 2001 the Greek Archaeological Service undertook large-scale excavations at Palio Chorio, which revealed many houses under the piles of fallen stones, as well as the existence of paved roads that were hitherto indiscernible under the debris. After the completion of widespread cleaning and consolidation of the ruins, this endeavor—the "Restoration and Enhancement of Anavatos at Chios"—in essence brought to light an entire village in ruins, but with all its features sufficiently visible and distinct for it to be reconstructed.

Figure 4. Topographic plan of the fortified village of Anavatos after the excavation works in 1998–2001: (a) pathway, (b) entrance gate, (c) church of the Panayia, (d) church of the Taxiarchis. Illustration courtesy of the Ephorate of Antiquities of Chios and used with permission.

Thanks to these enhancement works, the ground plan of the medieval village is now apparent. The axis of approach was the path that rose from the foot of the hill and followed a natural course wherever the rocky terrain was smooth enough to allow passage (Figure 4a). Today the path is 2 m wide at all points and paved with flagstones in order to facilitate visitors' approach. The pathway led to the gate, which opened on the east side of the fortification (Figure 4b). Inside the fortified village, the path was hewn from the rock and continued under an arched passageway until it reached a small plateau in front of the church dedicated to the Panayia (Figure 4c). From this point it branched out into many passages leading to all the neighborhoods of the village: the church of the Taxiarchis (Figure 4d) and the top of the hill, the east and west slopes, and the lowest and most rugged part of the hill on the south slope. Aside from the narrow lanes and the small level space in front of the church, communal areas do not exist. It seems that the central role of this plateau, which one encounters shortly after the entrance to the fortified settlement, served as the main *plateia* (village square) and probably also for assemblies and commercial exchange. It also provided access to a large public cistern now enclosed beneath the south aisle of the church. Apparently, the confined space of the fortification and the resulting cramped conditions did not allow for the creation of other public spaces. A similar configuration and use of the area relative to the town's entrance were found at Geraki in the Peloponnese during the Late Byzantine period (Simatou and Christodoulopoulou 1989/1990:69).

The lanes are narrow and constantly change in direction and orientation; they never intersect at a right angle and often have sharp inclines. The central lanes are about 1.3 m in width, while the secondary lanes are narrower, serving as passages—sometimes ending in cul-de-sacs—between houses, rather than as routes of circulation throughout the village. We know that the factor that determined the width of many roads in medieval villages was the smallest breadth of a fully laden pack animal (i.e. 2.0–2.5 m; Bouras 1982b:35). At Anavatos, the paths are often so narrow (0.8 m) as to preclude the passage of beasts of burden. Another clue is the lack of beveled corners in the houses themselves, a feature that is found in many other medieval towns, such as Mystras (Orlandos 1999 [1937]:89, Figures 77 and 81). These beveled corners facilitated the passage of mules and donkeys, and their absence from the architecture in Anavatos may indicate that many of these animals were sheltered somewhere outside the village. This is in contrast to the villages of southern Chios and other Byzantine-period settlements, where people cohabited with their animals.

Figure 5. Vaulted passageway in Palio Chorio, Anavatos.

In only two locations do we find vault-covered passages. Most probably there were more originally, but the collapse of almost all the multi-storied buildings did not allow for the preservation of additional examples. One is close to the entrance (Figure 5), and the other is east of the church of the Taxiarchis in the upper neighborhood. We know that these passages were constructed in medieval times for many reasons and that they served many purposes: they buttressed the vaults of the adjoining houses, thus creating a powerful anti-seismic system (Lampakis and Bouras 1960:10, 35); they created new living quarters when there was an increase of population and conditions were necessarily crowded; and last but not least, they provided pedestrians with protection from adverse weather conditions.

The division of the village into neighborhoods was imposed by the terrain itself (see Figure 3 and Figure 4). At the top of the hill, where the tract of land surrounding the church of the Taxiarchis is small in area (Figure 4d), the slope is abrupt and there are fewer than 30 buildings, including dwellings and storehouses. In contrast, in the area around the church of the Panayia (Figure 4c), where the terrain is smoother and creates a natural plateau, we find the greatest concentration of buildings and the densest population among all the neighborhoods (excavations revealed approximately 80 buildings). And finally, the very steep south slope also has fewer buildings. In all the neighborhoods of the settlement, the houses are joined to one another in additive succession, creating a pattern that is notable for its disorder and lack of planning.

Certainly not all the buildings within the fortified enclosure were destined for housing alone. Based on Anavatos' similarity to other Late Byzantine settlements with multi-functional buildings (such as Geraki or Mystras in the Peloponnese or Pergamon in Asia Minor; Rheidt 1990:195–204), it is likely that many of the buildings were used as storehouses or served other activities of the inhabitants (e.g. workshops). However, the buildings' present dilapidated state does not allow for further speculation regarding their other possible uses. Two churches were used to hold services before the village was abandoned, and each was built on one of the level areas on the hill: the church of the Taxiarchis, which sits upon a ridge of the terrain and has a commanding position over the ruins (Figure 4d), and the church of the Panayia, which is located lower down on the plateau near the entrance to the *kastro* (Figure 4c).

The above observations lead us to the conclusion that there was no town planning before the village was established, which is corroborated by comparison with other towns and villages of the Late Byzantine period (Bouras 1998:90, 92). Urban planning presumes a central authority, and its immediate result is apparent in a geometric network of streets or in a system of central roads that connect nuclei, even when the natural contours of the landscape constrain or complicate such plans. This leads to the arrangement of space into sections and, in particular, to the designation of free spaces with specific functions for society as a whole, rather than for private needs alone. These features are entirely absent from the plan of Anavatos; at the same time, their absence provides clues with which to date the *kastro*. The suffocating town plan might be evaluated as sufficient for the defense of the village, but in no way did it provide adequate amenities for the inhabitants or ensure healthy living conditions. In short, Anavatos appears to be a characteristic example of a village of this period, founded when the overarching concern was the safety of the inhabitants and the organization of space for any other type of human interaction was considered secondary.

The *Kastro*: The Wall and Gate

The wall surrounding the *kastro* is not extant in its entirety; however, its course along the brow of the hill, which is by itself a natural fortification, is abundantly clear. The natural formation of the hill was taken into account and incorporated into the wall that was raised upon it. Places where there were depressions or cavities in the bedrock were built up with stones in order to support the wall. It is notable that the same method was employed in the settlement of Kato Kastro in Andros, which is dated to the thirteenth to fourteenth centuries (and definitely before 1385; Deliyanni-Dori 2006:473, 479).

The wall is approximately 400 m long and encircles an area of 6,000–6,500 m². In many places the wall is not an independent construction, but rather is formed by the walls of the houses at the edge of the village; thus, the fortification is not a continuous, separate construction (see **Figure 3** and **Figure 4**).

On its north side, which allowed access to the village, the wall reaches a height of 8 m and is in good condition on both sides of the gate. On its east side, the wall forms a projection due to its partial demolition and the later construction of a three-story complex that protrudes from the delineated wall (**Figure 2**, **Figure 3**, and **Figure 4**). This complex, with an imposing height of 12.2 m that dominates the landscape, incorporates the church of the Panayia on its third level, the old schoolhouse on its second level, and an oil press on its ground level. On the west side of the *kastro*, which sits above an unapproachable gorge, the wall is weak, with a narrow width (0.6–1.0 m) and low height (0.5–1.0 m). The northwest part of the wall atop the hill is also weak and low, while the south wall is completely destroyed, with only traces of its outline remaining. All of the fortification walls were built of common small and medium-sized local stones without bricks, while the lime mortar was thin and has been almost entirely washed away.

The entrance gate to the village has not been preserved, but evidence of its existence—found on both sides of its opening—permits us to reconstruct it with certainty (Figure 4b). At its opening the gate was quite thick (1.68 m in width), and here we also find bricks that were incorporated into the masonry. The opening was wedge-like in plan as it expanded inward. Its height was approximately 3.35 m, and 2.13 m at its greatest width. It was topped with a broad arch that was built with porous-stone voussoirs—one is extant—with an alternating series of bricks in between (Figure 6). The lintel or spandrel that sealed the arch was most probably monolithic, as were the parts of the two doorjambs. The gate was secured in the back with a wooden bar (the *romanesion*, according to Byzantine terminology; Orlandos 1999 [1937]:71), which would have been nestled into holes 0.32 m tall and 0.22 m wide in the masonry walls on either side. The articulation of the gate was similar to that found at other settlements on Chios, such as the Mastichochoria (Mastic Villages) of Mesta (Figure 7) and Olympoi in the south of the island, which are dated to the fourteenth to fifteenth centuries (Bouras 1982b:32–44; Lampakis and Bouras 1960:1–40, Figures 3 and 4; Smith 1962:59–68, 111–120, Figures 117 and 163).

The Water Supply

The inhabitants of Anavatos, which was built directly upon the top of a rocky hill, could not have accessed naturally flowing water from the nearby spring found northeast of the village (at Ayios Yannis). It is certain that water was in short supply and that the inhabitants were frequently faced with the threat of drought. The solution was either to carry water up from the foot of the hill, where the water from the spring still flows today, or to collect rainwater in cisterns in the basements of some of the homes. At the same time the village was established, a large public cistern was built on the plateau near the entrance, and it was later covered over by the south aisle of the church of the Panayia (Figure 4c). The cistern is rectangular and barrel-vaulted, with its long axis parallel to the contour of the hill. Its internal dimensions measure 7.0 × 3.5 × 3.5 m, and it could have held about 45 m^3 of water (Paschalidis 2012:444–445, Figure 2), which would have been sufficient to meet the basic needs of the community. Its interior walls were plastered with waterproof mortar in accordance with Byzantine building tradition (Orlandos 1958:115–119; Vassi and Faïtaki 2015:3–12), while its floor was covered with earthenware tiles.

Figure 6. Remnants of the arch above the gate of Palio Chorio, Anavatos.

Figure 7. The gate of the village of Mesta in the Mastichochoria (after Lampakis and Bouras 1960:Figure 3). Drawing courtesy of Maria Christeli.

The Churches

There were two churches within the fortified settlement, protected by its walls: the Taxiarchis (dedicated to the Archangel Michael) and the Panayia (dedicated to the Presentation of the Virgin in the Temple). They were parish churches that ministered to the daily needs of each neighborhood, as well as to the village as a whole. They commemorated two major religious holidays of the Orthodox Church: the feast-day of Archangel Michael on November 8, and the Presentation of the Virgin on November 21.

Figure 8. The church of the Taxiarchis in Palio Chorio, Anavatos.

The church of the Taxiarchis (**Figure 4d** and **Figure 8**) is double-aisled and measures 12.25 × 10.8 × 8.0 m. The south aisle is covered with a flat roof, while the north has a tiled hip roof. Above the north aisle is a series of three lowered saucer domes, while a domical vault covers the south aisle.

The church underwent several building phases. Its original form, which should be dated to the same period as the establishment of the *kastro*, was as a single-aisled church with a semicircular apse built into a recess of the rocky hill. The next stage saw the construction of a new, somewhat larger, church that extended to the south, but still not very large in size. The second church was again single-aisled with a tiled saddle roof and (most probably) an internal barrel vault. In the final phase, the church was extended once more to the south, but this time the extension rested on barrel-vaulted passageways that ran parallel to the rocky slope. This is when it acquired its current monumental style as a double-aisled church, with a large and high south aisle added to the pre-existing north part of the building and divided from it by a series of arch-bearing columns (Delinikola et al. 2008:40–41). This final phase should be dated in accordance with its morphological characteristics (e.g. doorframes, vault form and construction, relief decoration; Smith 1962:87, Figures 169.1–5 and 171.1–2) to the beginning of the nineteenth century, a few years before the catastrophe of 1822.

Throughout the centuries of its existence, the church of the Panayia (Figure 4c and Figure 9) experienced a similar evolution to that of the Taxiarchis with regard to the additions and remodeling it underwent. Today it occupies the top section of a three-story complex that protrudes beyond the outline of the east defensive wall (see Figure 2) and faces toward the natural plateau on the hill, a short distance from the entry to the *kastro*. It is a double-aisled, barrel-vaulted church (measuring 14.0 x 10.0 x 5.6 m) with tiled saddle roofs and an apse that is etched into the width of the east wall (Paschalidis 2012:447-454, Figures 1 and 4). The two aisles are separated by arches set upon a column and a pillar. The history of the church and the monument as a whole is outlined as follows: initially, there was a plateau that allowed access to the public cistern from which the inhabitants could draw their water. Its north side carried a small single-roomed edifice, which leaned against the east wall and may have been a simple house rather than a church. This phase should be assigned to the period when the village was established and its population moved into the walled area. Later, the building was almost completely demolished in order to erect the church; all that remains today is a section of the wall that bears a pillar supporting the arcade. The church was then expanded to the east and south by an aisle that blocked access to the cistern. This indicates a late date, when it was safe to dismantle a section of the wall and destroy access to the only common cistern in the *kastro*. In accordance with the stylistic elements of the wall-painting of the Pantokrator in the apse of the Panayia, which dates to the beginning of the nineteenth century, we should date the final form of the church to this era (Figure 10). Churches that incorporate the wall of a fortress also have been noted at Mystras: specifically, the Metropolis and the church of the Odigitria (Marinou 2009:55, 64, 79).

The Buildings and Houses

The general characteristics of the buildings and houses in the ruined part of Anavatos may be summarized as follows: in their entity, all were stone-built two-story edifices with narrow fronts, and most of them had barrel vaults that were perpendicular to the contours of the natural landscape. This standard form was repeated in all cases—with minor, unimportant differences between the buildings—and the area they covered was about the same, with only small variations. Their fortress-like character and mentality were abundantly obvious, since they employed closed shapes and flat roofs, had no balconies or outside stairs, and had few openings in the outer walls of the houses. The aggregate of unplastered stone façades

Figure 9. The church of the Panayia in Palio Chorio, Anavatos.

Figure 10. Wall painting of the Pantokrator in the apse of the church of the Panayia in Palio Chorio, Anavatos. Photograph courtesy of the Ephorate of Antiquities of Chios and used with permission.

was adjusted so as to be confused with the rocky terrain and, thus, not easily discerned from afar. This was an effective camouflage for reasons of security. Architecturally, the articulation of a medieval fortified village is pronounced.

The excavations in 1998–2001 revealed about 110 buildings, most of which were houses. The inhabitants created small housing clusters by attaching one house to another at random, in this way managing the available space. The same solution has been noted in other medieval settlements in both Greece and Asia Minor, such as Mystras and Pergamon (Bouras 1998:90).

The buildings consisted of a ground floor and an upper floor with a wooden mezzanine. The only type of roofing found in the houses of Anavatos was the barrel vault; there are no other vaults (e.g. groin vaults, domical or cloister vaults, or blind domes) to be found. In contrast, all types of vaults were employed in the southern Mastichochoria settlements, which were influenced by Western practices (Lampakis and Bouras 1960:35; Smith 1962:34, Figure 21).

With few exceptions, the ground floor and upper floor contained only one room. On the ground floor (the Byzantine *katoyion*), only the entrance door led into the building, and no other openings pierced the wall. The external dimensions of the buildings, which were square or rectangular, were on the average 7.5 x 4.5 m.

Access to the upper floor (the Byzantine *anoyion*) was gained only from the inside, since no exterior staircases were found in any of the houses. The interior staircase was made of wood or, if space allowed, stone. When the interior space was tall enough, mezzanines were created with wooden beams, as concluded from the presence of small mortises (0.22 x 0.25 m) preserved on the side walls. The second story had only one room, was square or trapezoidal in shape, and averaged between 14 and 24 m^2 in area (e.g. Building no. 42 measured 4.0 x 3.8 m; Building no. 50, 4.9 x 2.5 m; and Building no 51, 6.5 x 3.8 m). The Byzantines called this room the *triklinos,* and this was where people spent the day, slept, and conducted daily activities. This room usually contained a fireplace.

The construction of recessed niches or closets in the interior walls of the upper floor for storage (of food, household utensils, etc.) indicate that this area hosted everyday activities. In contrast, the area of the ground floors in many instances was restricted by rocks and boulders, and people were forced to use the space for storing food, other agricultural products, supplies, and tools, and for the other secondary needs of the household.

Some houses, mostly in the neighborhoods of the Taxiarchis and the Panayia, had a barrel-vaulted basement that was accessed through a trapdoor and could be used in various ways, perhaps even as a cistern.

An important element of the *triklinos* in other medieval settlements, such as at Mystras or even Pyrgi in southern Chios, was the small private family shrine. At Anavatos, such evidence of piety, devoutness, and private worship was not found in any of the collapsed buildings; however, this does not preclude the possibility that niches may have been used as iconostases.

Built-in hearths or fireplaces used for cooking and to provide heat are not extant in most of the homes because they were built in the upper-floor living space, which in most cases has collapsed. In the two preserved examples, the fireplace is located in the corner of the upper floor. Its protruding section has a parabolic shape that rests on stone corbels, and the stone-built chimney is square in plan. The houses that did not have fireplaces were likely heated by means of portable braziers.

Doors were always situated on the narrow side of a building, and they were similar in architectural design to the windows in that they were arched and closed with a single flap of wood. Lean-out windows not only allowed light into the rooms, but also were the only obvious sign of extroversion in the otherwise solid bulk of the buildings. The tympanum of the arch above the lintel was always blind, obstructed by either masonry or a monolithic slab, and the opening was rectangular (Mamaloukos 2012:1–38). In some of the house windows in the *kastro*, we note the exclusive use of bricks or a combination of hewn-stone voussoirs and bricks in the articulation of the crowning arch. This is in keeping with the centuries-old Byzantine practice employed in Chios.

The roof was always flat, following the building practice that has characterized the Aegean islands since antiquity. A thin layer of waterproof plaster (called *astrakia* in the local dialect) was then applied to the roof, which was slightly rounded down its length due to the extrados of its barrel vault. A low stone ledge was laid around the circumference of the roof. The roof of one house was used as the courtyard of a neighboring house that rose above it, a practice also found in other island villages (Philippidis 1984:50).

The outer appearance of the façades of the buildings was very simple: they were built with rough stones and remained unplastered. In certain houses—which may be the oldest, since this is typical of Byzantine practice—bricks were inserted between the stones. Arches were usually, if not exclusively, built with stone. When the masonry of a wall contained pieces of brick (of which there are only a few examples), then brick was again included in the construction of the arches over the doors and windows of the house. Brickwork patterns or other decorations that are found in other settlements, such as Mystras, are not evident in the façades of Anavatos (Orlandos 1999 [1937]:84–90).

As far as size and form are concerned, none of the buildings or houses in Palio Chorio are more or less prominent than any others; therefore, one might discuss a possible lack of social stratification at Anavatos. In contrast, in the upper town of Mystras, mansions and homes that belonged to members of the social class of the Despot were built as symbols of grace, prestige, and acknowledgment, and they differed enormously from the small single-roomed units found elsewhere in the city (Marinou 2009:56).

The Portable Finds from the Excavations

Most of the 110 buildings revealed during the excavations were filled with rubble from the upper floor. The clearing and digging brought to light a large number of sherds, metal finds, shells, and animal bones (i.e. remains of meals), as well as a number of coins.

The metal finds were mostly building accessories and equipment. They included nails of various types and sizes—such as a broad-headed nail from a wooden chest—locks; keys; knockers; hinges from doors and windows; household items made of copper and brass, such as tableware (forks, knives, spoons); and ammunition and weaponry made of iron, such as a small cannonball or a large knife blade. Finally, there were many small finds from everyday life, such as bronze thimbles, scissors, incense censors, oil lamps, and buttons, as well as finds like inexpensive jewelry and amulets. An amber bead attests to the usage of *komboloi* (worry beads) for relaxation or amusement, a habit that was popular among males in the Ottoman era.

A large number of ceramic vessels was recovered from the surfaces of the house floors, resting among the other debris. Most belong to everyday vessel forms, including large- or medium-sized storage vases and water-carrying containers. Glazed bases of open table wares (i.e. bowls and plates) comprise only a minority of the samples recorded.

Most of the storage vessels are pithoi, and they bear decorations of various types, including inscribed, additional, or impressed decorations (i.e. bands of incised wavy lines, round relief coils with potters' fingerprints, marks from strings, small crosses framed by parallel right angles, herring-bone patterns, or rhombuses). They all belong to a well-known pithos type that was widely distributed throughout the Aegean during the eighteenth and (mainly) nineteenth centuries and was manufactured in the town of Ainos (present-day Enez, near Edirne) in Thrace. Very few samples from pithoi of different provenance occur: there are a few ridged sherds, possibly identified with pithoi from Messenia in the Peloponnese ("Koroneika"; Giannopoulou 2009, 2010), and others that may come from Siphnos or Naxos in the Cyclades (Korre-Zografou 1995:254, Figure 467, 2003:59, Figure 62). Among the sherds of storage containers are a few pieces that might be attributed to Chian eighteenth-century production; they bear round seals with six- or seven-pointed asterisks stamped either on the flat rim or below the neck (Giannopoulou and Demesticha 2008; Liaros 2016:62–63; Yangaki 2008:133–138). These seals are reminiscent of similar stamps on Middle Byzantine amphorae (Hayes 1992:77–78, Plate 14.19) and have parallels in unglazed domestic wares from other parts of Greece during the Ottoman period (Vroom 2003:179–180, Figure 6.14, W38.2-5).

Many handles of locally produced plain water jars were also collected. The jars were made in the pottery workshops of Harmolia in southern Chios, which were active from the eighteenth century until the first half of the twentieth century. However, the majority of these finds from Anavatos should be dated to the nineteenth century—and mostly to the latter half (Korre-Zografou 2003:144–145). Among the exceptions are two peculiar fragments of green-glazed raki jugs (i.e. ewers) dating to the eighteenth to early nineteenth centuries. They bear a perforated clay addition between the neck and the spout, known as "the cock's wattle" (*to leiri tou kokkora*), and they originated in either Macedonia or Epirus and were distributed widely across the southern Balkans (Korre-Zografou 1995:89, 133–134, 137, Figures 151, 227, 230, 238–239; Vlahos 2018).

An important factor in determining the date of the establishment of the village is the collection of numerous sherds from Late Byzantine to early post-Byzantine glazed tableware vessels, most of which were deep bowls with a monochrome, shiny-brown, or pale-yellow glaze that were typical of the second half of the fourteenth to fifteenth centuries (François 1995:110, Figure 18d; Makropoulou 1995:No. 29, 15, 34, Figure 15). They have a relatively high base ring, and their exterior surface was left unglazed. On many of them, traces of tripod marks are distinct. There are also examples of fourteenth-century Spatter ware, Derivative Zeuxippus ware (or Late Sgraffito ware; François 1995:95; Yangaki 2012:58–60, Figure 51), and others from early post-Byzantine times (i.e. the fifteenth to sixteenth centuries) with a green-painted decoration on the rim. Not one sherd from previous historical periods—either Greek antiquity or the Roman through Middle Byzantine periods—was found.

Chios' close ties with Italy and its centers of ceramic production continued until the end of the sixteenth century, as testified to by a berettino plate that was found in the *kastro*. The plate's design—abstract blue-cobalt motifs formed on an azure background—is representative of the pottery workshops of Liguria (i.e. of Savona, Albisola, and Genova; Skartsis 2009:189, 197; Vassiliou 2017:342, Figure 15).

Later on in the nineteenth century, post-Byzantine ceramics coexisted with imports from Italy, England, the Netherlands, and Asia Minor and were used alongside these imports by the inhabitants. Examples found together include vessels from Didymoteicho in Thrace (Skartsis 2009:38); plates imported from the southern Italian region of Puglia (Papadopoulou 2018:15) or from Cerreto in Campania near Naples, with floral patterns of the period circa 1850 (Korre-Zografou 2003:107, Figure 123); and dishes typical of the English Staffordshire porcelain produced after 1840 (i.e. the transfer technique). It is well known that in the Aegean islands such vessels were not only used as tableware, but also often arranged on walls and mantelshelves in a purely decorative manner (Skartsis 2009:213–215). A sample of a red Dutch decorative plate was also found with them (Korre-Zografou 2003:179, Figure 233).

The Turkish Çanakkale shallow dishes, with either stylized vegetal motifs in dark brown or abstract linear motifs (such as a sort of whirl), also make an appearance among the finds from Anavatos. This is to be expected, since this kind of pottery was extremely widespread in the Aegean from the mid eighteenth century until the beginning of the twentieth century (Borboudaki 2007:170–171, 173). The very few sherds of Ottoman Kütahya ware—found throughout Greece (Skartsis 2009:219)—and a clay pipe discovered among the archaeological remains corroborate the textual evidence that smoking and drinking coffee were very popular habits in the Ottoman Empire during the eighteenth and nineteenth centuries (Vroom 2003:353–357).

A total of 306 coins were collected from approximately half (52) of the buildings. There were two impressive cases in which a considerable concentration of coins was found, leading us to believe that the use of these buildings was not restricted to housing, but also that they were places where financial transactions took place. In the first example (Building 32), located close to the entrance gate just beyond the settlement's vaulted passage, a collection of 35 coins from all eras was found. In the other example

(Building 57), located in the neighborhood on the south slope, excavation yielded 25 coins of the Ottoman Empire, 21 of them minted in the year 1808 during the reign of Mahmud II.

The majority of the coins are bronze, but they also include 2 gold coins from the period of Ottoman rule (i.e. the nineteenth century) and 21 silver coins, the majority of which also date to the Ottoman period. The large number of coins dated to the late fifteenth and sixteenth centuries (44) and to the nineteenth century (152) reflect the two main periods when economic activity in the settlement was on the rise. Of the sixteenth-century coins, the majority (38) were minted in Chios during the years of Genoese rule and are classified according to familiar numismatic types to the first half of the sixteenth century (Valakou 2010). From the output of the Chian mint, 3 silver coins stand out: a counтермarked *grosso* of the late fifteenth century, another *grosso*, and a *mezzo grosso* of the year 1520 that bears the initials F and I of the *podestà* Francesco di Lorenzo Giustiniani Banca (Lunardi 1980:218, 227, 229; Mazarakis 2003:195, 201, 202; Schlumberger 1882:430, Figures 15.8 and 15.10). Also notable is the presence of 2 bronze coins of the late fifteenth century from the city of Genoa itself. The majority of the nineteenth-century coins were minted by the Ottoman Empire, the Greek and French states, and Germany—the latter of which were mainly accounting coins or tokens.

With regard to the older coins that were found (6 from Roman Chios and Samos, 3 from the Early Byzantine Empire [fourth to sixth centuries], and 6 from the Middle Byzantine period [tenth to twelfth centuries]), we do not believe—as has been posited elsewhere (Kavvadia 2012:241–248)—that they indicate that Anavatos was inhabited either in antiquity or during the Early and Middle Byzantine periods. Rather, we believe the coins are singular objects that belonged to a collection or a hoard. This seems to be the case for a *follis* of Justinian I (524–565 AD) and a Middle Byzantine *follis* of the eleventh century (Kavvadia 2012:no 824, no 813, 242, Figures 4 and 7), which were found in the same building (No. 32) together with 33 coins from different historical periods, including Venetian (sixteenth century), Ottoman (possibly seventeenth and certainly eighteenth and nineteenth centuries), and later Greek coins (i.e. from the newly-formed Greek state of the nineteenth century). The assertion that Anavatos existed during the Early and Middle Byzantine periods does not, for that matter, accord with direct evidence of the typology, morphological characteristics, and architectural physiognomy of the settlement, nor with the ceramic assemblage, which contains no examples from the Early or Middle Byzantine periods. On the other hand, the evidence from some of the coins is extremely crucial for determining the latest dating of the settlement's establishment. These are coins that were found either within the walls of buildings (C1034, C920) or accidentally embedded in the construction of the extrados of the vaults in the late fifteenth century (C1093, C936, C938). Another coin that was found on the north protective wall of the settlement dates to the year 1520 (C843).

Chronology—Conclusions

Previously, it had been proposed that Anavatos was a possible guard post, fortified and equipped to house sentries to watch for possible piratical excursions from the western shores of Chios (Smith 1962:120). At that time, no date was proposed for its establishment. Later, Anavatos was considered to have been formed during the period of Ottoman rule in Chios—that is, after the year 1566, when Admiral Piyale Pasha conquered the island on behalf of the Ottoman Sultan Suleiman the Magnificent (Bouras 1982b:45). Recently, a new suggestion was put forth, on the basis of numismatic evidence, for an early Byzantine dating (Kavvadia 2012:241–248). However, the type and form of the buildings, the town plan, and the ceramic and numismatic evidence all indicate that the village was a typical medieval settlement, which should be dated to the fifteenth century. This is the period when the island came under the rule of the Mahona of Chios and Phocaea (1346–1566; **Argenti** 1979:1–35). In the year 1346, Admiral Simone Vignoso conquered Chios in the name of the Republic of Genoa. During the period of Genoese rule, the island was administrated by a Genoese commercial company, the Mahona; after 1362, the members of this company belonged to the *albergo* (family/clan) of the Giustiniani of Genoa and thereafter bore this surname. When Chios came into the possession of the Genoese, the production and trade of mastic, the exclusive product of the island, took on new dimensions. The Mahona organized both of these activities in a systematic manner (Argenti 1958; Balard 1978).

While it appears that Anavatos was established during the years of Genoese rule, its characteristics are clearly those of a Byzantine settlement; even though Westerners were responsible its establishment, it lacks any apparent influence from Western elements In short, the fortified village of Anavatos presents the appearance of a typical fortified town of the Byzantine era. The building practices and architectural forms were those that had been handed down through the years to the fifteenth century. The Mahona permitted the local population to organize the settlement in order to protect themselves from piracy or other threats, but it did not intervene in the organization of its space. What took place here was the opposite of what happened in the towns of southern Chios, where mastic, the "gold" of Chios, was produced and where the Mahona was particularly interventionist in its policies (Eden 1950:16–20).

There is nothing innovative in the organization and management of space in Anavatos. The rule of safety prevailed for its inhabitants, and this led to a strictness in the economy of space. Its synthesis is characterized by introversion, but one that is in complete harmony with the surrounding environment into which the mass of buildings gradually proceeds down the hill. Defense was the primary concern, and the fortified enclosure that protected the residents was formed by the exterior walls of the outermost houses, in accordance with the ancient Aegean practice (Philippa-Apostolou 2000:22–23, 35–55). The houses were reiterating units of a basic, minimally organized home, and they were served by an elementary network of roads that began at the gate of the fortress. An extremely abstemious way of life emerges from the architectural physiognomy of the village: two small churches covered the religious needs of the population, and a small plateau, the social and economic.

About 110 buildings were erected within the village's walls; not all of them served as houses. The population can be estimated at around 500 people at a minimum if we follow Angeliki Laiou's calculations for post-Byzantine Macedonia of two parents and three children per house (Laiou 1977:372–392). The inhabitants were indigenous and Orthodox in religious affiliation, and they lived in a small remote village in the countryside, far from the political, social, and economic center that was then the *kastro* in the main city of Chios. The inhabitants of Anavatos depended primarily on agricultural production and the rearing of domesticated animals and livestock. The few remains of seashells and animal bones also show that their consumption of meat and fish was limited.

The area outside the walls belongs to a second historical phase at the end of the seventeenth century, when the threat of piracy ceased to exist and the population increased (Krantonelli 1991:9–14, 266, 375), resulting in the settlement's expansion. The various particular characteristics of the buildings remained the same, the only difference being that space was no longer limited by the defensive walls (Philippa-Apostolou 2004). The year 1822 was a catalyst for the function of the settlement as a whole: the massacre that took place in Chios by Ottoman troops, well known from many sources, caused its partial desolation. However, the fact that has been made clear by the excavations is that the settlement was not totally deserted after the slaughter—as has been believed and repeatedly published until now—but rather that life in the fortified village at the top of the hill went on. According to the evidence provided by the ceramics and coins,

Palio Chorio was not abandoned at once; obviously, its population decreased drastically, but its inhabitants continued to live in the same space. On top of that, it appears that the settlement was, in fact, an extroverted one: it imported products from other cities of Ottoman-ruled Greece and Asia Minor, as well as from Italy and even England and the Netherlands. Financial transactions and imports continued even after the earthquake of 1881 (Altınok et al. 2005:719–722) and up until the beginning of the twentieth century. It seems that the destruction and abandonment of the village that can be seen today took place gradually over the span of a (relatively) few years, from the end of the nineteenth century to the early decades of the twentieth century. Nevertheless, if any inhabitants were living in the upper village in the early twentieth century, they would have been rather few in number; life had moved outside the walled village to the slope and foot of the hill. Palio Chorio was irrevocably deserted only after the earthquake of 1881, when its residents moved to the foot of the hill. There, the sole surviving permanent inhabitant of Anavatos still lives.

The determining factors in the complete desertion of the settlement as a whole were internal and external migration—phenomena that also have been observed in other rugged areas in both island and mainland Greece (see Seifried, this volume). Today, there is only a single resident left in the lower part of the village, living across from the church of Kato Taxiarchis (Lower Taxiarchis). Ottoman tax and population records, as well as other kinds of administrative documents (e.g. decrees by the central authority, court rulings, land registries) that are written in Ottoman Turkish and kept either in Greece or in Istanbul, should be extremely useful for tracking the process and mechanism of Anavatos' abandonment (Balta 1989). Unfortunately, the provincial historical archive of Chios has little information about the subject (Topping 1952:254, 255). Such research, however, being of a different nature and belonging to another major area of inquiry, is beyond the scope and intentions of the present study. Nonetheless, this work paves the way for additional research in related specialties that can benefit from the archaeological conclusions presented here.

Acknowledgments. I would like to express my warmest thanks to the editors Deborah Brown Stewart and Rebecca Seifried for their most appreciated help and their boundless support throughout the whole process of publishing this paper. I also wish to thank the two reviewers for their fruitful suggestions, with which they contributed to the improvement of the final text.

References Cited

Altınok, Yıldız, Bedri Alpar, Naşide Özer, and Cem Gazioğlu
   2005   1881 and 1949 Earthquakes at the Chios-Cesme Strait (Aegean Sea) and Their Relation to Tsunamis. *Natural Hazards and Earth System Sciences* 5:717–725. https://hal.archives-ouvertes.fr/hal-00299270

Argenti, Philip P.
   1958   *The Occupation of Chios by the Genoese and their Administration of the Island, 1346–1566. Described in Contemporary Documents and Official Dispatches.* 3 vols. Cambridge University Press, Cambridge.
   1979   The Mahona of the Giustiniani: Genoese Colonialism and the Genoese Relationship with Chios. *Byzantinische Forschungen* 6:1–35.

Argenti, Philip P., and Stilpon Kyriakidis
   1946   Η Χίος παρά τοις γεωγράφοις και περιηγηταίς: από του ογδόου μέχρι του εικοστού αιώνος [*Chios According to Geographers and Travelers: From the Eighth to the Twentieth Centuries*]. Estia Editions, Athens.

Axiotakis, Andreas
   1994 [1976]   Ο Ανάβατος της Χίου. Ιστορία-τέχνη-λαογραφία [*Anavatos of Chios: History–Art–Folklore*]. 3rd ed. Translated by A. Dallas-Damis. Veltiomeni Editions, Chios.

Balard, Michel
   1978   *La Romanie génoise (XIIe–début du XVe siècle)* [*Genoese Romania (12th to Early 15th Centuries*]. 2 vols. Società Ligure di Storia Patria, Genova.

Balta, Evangelia
   1989   Οθωμανικά αρχεία στην Ελλάδα. Προοπτικές της έρευνας [*Ottoman Archives in Greece: Research Perspectives*]. *Mnimon* 12:241–252. https://doi.org/10.12681/mnimon.440

Borboudaki, Maria (editor)
2007   Πηλός και χρώμα. Νεώτερη κεραμική του ελλαδικού χώρου (15ος–19ος αι) [Clay and Color: Modern Ceramics of Greece (15th–19th c.)]. Exhibition Catalogue, Hellenic Ministry of Culture, Byzantine and Christian Museum, Athens.

Bouras, Charalambos
1982a   Nea Moni on Chios, History and Architecture. Commercial Bank of Greece, Athens.
1982b   Χίος [Chios]. In Ελληνική παραδοσιακή αρχιτεκτονική [Greek Traditional Architecture], Vol. 1, edited by Dimitris Philippidis, pp. 143–182. Melissa, Athens.
1998   Πολεοδομικά των μεσοβυζαντινών και υστεροβυζαντινών πόλεων [Urban Planning in Middle and Late Byzantine Cities]. Deltion of the Christian Archaeological Society 20:89–97. https://doi.org/10.12681/dchae.1197

Deliyanni-Dori, Eleni
2006   Η έρευνα στο Επάνω Κάστρο της Άνδρου. Μερικές σκέψεις [An Archaeological Survey of the Epano Kastro of Andros: Some Considerations]. Deltion of the Christian Archaeological Society 27:471–480. https://ejournals.epublishing.ekt.gr/index.php/deltion/article/view/4296

Delinikola, Efi, Anna Kairou, and Kitsa Athanasiadou
2008   Ιερός ναός Ταξιάρχη Αναβάτου - Τεκμηρίωση και πρόταση αποκατάστασης [The Church of the Taxiarchis in Anavatos – Design Project for the Restoration]. Paper presented at Η οχυρωματική αρχιτεκτονική στο Αιγαίο και ο μεσαιωνικός οικισμός Αναβάτου Χίου. Διεθνές συνέδριο [International Conference on The Architecture of Fortifications in the Aegean and the Medieval Settlement of Anavatos of Chios], Chios.

Delopoulos, Kyriakos (editor)
1983   Λεύκωμα των ερειπίων της Χίου συνεπεία των σεισμών της 23/24 Απριλίου 1881. Φωτογραφίες αδελφών Καστάνια [Album of the Ruins of Chios after the Earthquakes of 23/24 April 1881. Photographs by the Kastania Brothers]. Gennadius Library, Athens.

Eden, W. A.
    1950   The Plan of Mesta, Chios. *Annual of the British School at Athens* 45:16–20. https://doi.org/10.1017/S0068245400006687

François, Véronique
    1995   *La céramique byzantine à Thasos [Byzantine Ceramics of Thasos]*. Études Thasiennes 16. École Française d'Athènes, Paris.

Giannopoulou, Mimika, and Stella Demesticha
    2008   Τα μεταβυζαντινά αποθηκευτικά αγγεία των Μαστιχοχωρίων της Χίου [Post-Byzantine Storage Vessels of the Mastic Villages in Chios]. In *Γη – Μήτρα ζωής και δημιουργίας. Πρακτικά επιστημονικής συνάντησης 19-21 Μαρτίου 2004 [Gaia – Uterus of Life and Creativity. Proceedings of the Scientific Meeting 19–21 March 2004]*, edited by Eugenia Daphne, pp. 187–193. Ministry of Culture, Museum of Greek Folk Art, Athens.

Giannopoulou, Mimika
    2009   Τα κρασοπίθαρα της Πελοποννήσου [The Wine Pithoi of the Peloponnese]. In *Οἶνον ἱστορῶ IX. Επιστημονικό συμπόσιο, Πολυστάφυλος Πελοπόννησος [The Story of Wine IX. Scientific Symposium, Polystafylos Peloponnese]*, edited by Yiannis A. Pikoulas, pp. 153–173. Union of Peloponnese Wine Producers. Athens.
    2010   *Pithoi: Technology and History of Storage Vessels through the Ages*. BAR International Series 2140. Archaeopress, Oxford.

Giustiniani, Hieronimo
    1943   *Hieronimo Giustiniani's History of Chios,* edited by Philip Argenti. Cambridge University Press, Cambridge.

Hayes, John W.
    1992   *Excavations at Saraçhane in Istanbul: 2. The Pottery*, Princeton University Press, Princeton, New Jersey.

Kavvadia, Aristea
2012 Ο μεσαιωνικός οικισμός του Αναβάτου υπό το φως της νεώτερης αρχαιολογικής έρευνας [The Medieval Settlement of Anavatos of Chios in Light of the Latest Archaeological Research]. In *Διεθνές συνέδριο. Η οχυρωματική αρχιτεκτονική στο Αιγαίο και ο μεσαιωνικός οικισμός Αναβάτου Χίου. Πρακτικά, Χίος, 26-28 Σεπτεμβρίου 2008 [The Architecture of Fortifications in the Aegean and the Medieval Settlement of Anavatos of Chios: Proceedings of the International Conference, Chios, 26–28 September 2008]*, edited by Aristea Kavvadia and Panayiotis Damoulos, pp. 239–248. Alpha-Pi Editions, Chios.

Korre-Zografou, Katerina
1995 Τα κεραμεικά του ελληνικού χώρου *[The Ceramics of Greece]*. Melissa, Athens.
2003 Τα κεραμεικά του Αιγαίου (1600-1950) *[Ceramics of the Aegean (1600–1950)]*. Ministry of the Aegean, Athens.

Krantonelli, Alexandra
1991 Ιστορία της πειρατείας, στους μέσους χρόνους της Τουρκοκρατίας 1538-1699 *[History of Piracy in the Middle Years of the Turkish Period, 1538–1699]*. Estia Editons, Athens.

Laiou-Thomadakis, Angeliki E.
1977 *Peasant Society in the Late Byzantine Empire: A Social and Demographic Study*. Princeton University Press, Princeton, New Jersey.

Lampakis, Antonis, and Charalambos Bouras
1960 Τα μεσαιωνικά χωριά της Χίου [The Medieval Villages of Chios]. In *Το ελληνικό λαϊκό σπίτι [The Greek Traditional House]*, edited by Panayiotis A. Michelis, pp. 5–40. National Technical University of Athens, Athens.

Liaros, Nikos
2015   Post-Medieval Large Jar (*Pithos*) Production on the Island of Chios in the East Aegean Sea. In *Jarres et grands contenants entre Moyen Âge et Époque Moderne. Actes du 1er Congrès International Thématique de l'AIECM3, Montpellier-Lattes, 19–21 Novembre 2014 [Jars and Large Containers between the Middle Ages and the Modern Era. Proceedings of the 1st International Thematic Congress of the AIECM3, Montpellier-Lattes 19–21 November 2014]*, edited by Henri Amouric, Véronique François, and Lucy Vallauri, pp. 59–70. Lucie Editions, Nîmes.

Lunardi, Giuseppe
1980   *Le monete delle colonie Genovesi [The Coins of the Genoese Colonies]*. Atti della Società Ligure di Storia Patria, Nuova Serie 20 (94). Società Ligure di Storia Patria, Genova.

Makropoulou, Despoina
1995   Κεραμεική [Pottery]. In Συλλογή Δημητρίου Οικονομοπούλου. Βυζαντινή και μεταβυζαντινή κεραμεική, μεταλλικά αντικείμενα, νομίσματα *[Collection of Dimitrios Oikonomopoulos: Byzantine and Post-Byzantine Ceramics, Metal Objects, Coins]*, edited by Evangelia Kypraiou, pp. 6–30. Ministry of Culture, Fund of Archaeological Proceeds, Athens.

Mamaloukos, Stavros
2012   Observations on the Doors and Windows in Byzantine Architecture. In *Masons at Work: Architecture and Construction in the Pre-Modern World*, edited by Robert Ousterhout, Renata Holod, and Lothar Haselberger. University of Pennsylvania, Philadelphia.

Marinou, Georgia
2009   Η πολεοδομική συγκρότηση του οικισμού [The Urban Planning of the Settlement]. In Τα Μνημεία του Μυστρά. Το Έργο της Επιτροπής Αναστήλωσης Μνημείων Μυστρά *[The Monuments of Mystras: The Work of the Committee for the Restoration of the Monuments of Mystras]*, edited by Stephanos Sinos, pp. 55–78. Finance Management Fund for Archaeological Projects, Athens.

Mazarakis, Andreas
2003 Τα νομίσματα της Χίου, 1346-1566 [The Coins of Chios, 1346–1566]. Andreas Mazarakis, Athens.

Orlandos, Anastasios
1958 Μοναστηριακή αρχιτεκτονική [The Architecture of Monasteries]. 2nd ed. Archaeological Society at Athens, Athens.
1999 [1937] Τά παλάτια καί τά σπίτια τού Μυστρά [The Palaces and Houses of Mystra]. 2nd ed. Archaeological Society at Athens, Athens.

Papadopoulou, Barbara (ed.)
2018 Νεώτερη κεραμική από την Ήπειρο. Συλλογή Φώτη Ραπακούση [Modern Ceramics from Epirus: The Fotis Rapakousis Collection]. Hellenic Ministry of Culture, Ephorate of Antiquities of Arta, Arta.

Paschalidis, George
2012 Το τριώροφο στον Ανάβατο. Ο δημόσιος πολυθεματικός χώρος στον οχυρωμένο οικισμό [The Three-Story Building: A Public Multi-Functional Place in the Fortified Settlement]. In Διεθνές Συνέδριο Η οχυρωματική αρχιτεκτονική στο Αιγαίο και ο μεσαιωνικός οικισμός Αναβάτου Χίου. Πρακτικά, Χίος, 26-28 Σεπτεμβρίου 2008 [The Architecture of Fortifications in the Aegean and the Medieval Settlement of Anavatos of Chios: Proceedings of the International Conference, Chios, 26–28 September 2008], edited by Aristea Kavvadia and Panayiotis Damoulos, pp. 441–454. Alpha-Pi Editions, Chios.

Philippa-Apostolou, Maro
2000 Μικροί οχυρωμένοι οικισμοί του Αιγαίου. Στα ίχνη της ιστορικής τους ταυτότητας [Small Fortified Settlements of the Aegean: On the Tracks of Their Historical Identity]. Erinni Editions, Athens.
2004 Ανάβατος Χίου. Αρχιτεκτονική, μορφολογική και αρχαιολογική ανάλυση και τυπολογία [Anavatos of Chios: Architectural, Morphological and Archaeological Analysis and Typology]. D.E.P.O.S.A.E., Athens.

Philippidis, Demetrios
1984   Νεοελληνική αρχιτεκτονική. Αρχιτεκτονική θεωρία και πράξη (1830-1980) σαν αντανάκλαση των ιδεολογικών επιλογών της νεοελληνικής κουλτούρας [Modern Greek Architecture: Architectural Theory and Practice (1830–1980) as a Reflection of the Ideology of the Modern Greek Culture]. Melissa, Athens.

Rheidt, Klaus
1990   Byzantinische Wohnhäuser des 11. bis 14. Jahrhunderts in Pergamon [Byzantine Houses from the 11th to 14th Centuries in Pergamon]. *Dumbarton Oaks Papers* 44:195–204. https://doi.org/10.2307/1291628

Schlumberger, Gustave
1882   *Numismatique de l'Orient latin* [Numismatics of the Latin Orient]. 2nd ed. E. Leroux, Paris.

Simatou, Anna-Maria, and Rosalia Christodoulopoulou
1989/1990   Παρατηρήσεις στον μεσαιωνικό οικισμό του Γερακίου [Observations on the Medieval Settlement of Geraki]. *Deltion of the Christian Archaeological Society* 15:67–88. https://doi.org/10.12681/dchae.1035

Skartsis, Stephania
2009   Chlemoutsi Castle (Clermont, Castel Tornese), Peloponnese: Its Pottery and Its Relations with the West (13th–Early 19th c.). PhD dissertation, Centre for Byzantine, Ottoman & Modern Greek Studies, Institute of Archaeology and Antiquity, University of Birmingham.

Smith, Arnold C.
1962   *The Architecture of Chios, Subsidiary Buildings, Implements and Crafts*, edited by Philip P. Argenti. A Tiranti, London.

Topping, Peter
1952   The Public Archives of Greece. *American Archivist* 15(3):249–257. https://www.jstor.org/stable/40289093

Valakou, Parisianthi
2010   Νομίσματα της Γενουατοκρατίας στη Χίο (1346-1566). Η συλλογή του Βυζαντινού Μουσείου Χίου [Coins of the Genoese Period in Chios (1346–1566): The Collection of the Chios Byzantine Museum]. In *Το νόμισμα στα νησιά του Αιγαίου. Νομισματοκοπεία, κυκλοφορία, εικονογραφία, ιστορία. Πρακτικά συνεδρίου της Ε' Επιστημονικής Συνάντησης, Μυτιλήνη, 16-19 Σεπτεμβρίου 2006, τομ. II: Μέσοι-Νεώτεροι χρόνοι [Coins in the Aegean Islands: Minting, Circulation, Iconography, History. Conference Proceedings of the 5th Scientific Meeting Mytilene, 16–19 September 2006, Vol. II: Middle Ages–Modern Times]*, edited by Panagiotis Tselekas, pp. 109–118. Οβολός 9. Friends of the Numismatic Museum, Athens.

Vassi, Olga, and Stella Faïtaki
2015   Η κινστέρνα της Νέας Μονής στη Χίο [The Cistern of Nea Moni in Chios]. *Deltion of the Christian Archaeological Society* 36:1–20. https://doi.org/10.12681/dchae.1770

Vassiliou, Anastasia
2017   Κεραμική ιταλικών εργαστηρίων στο βενετοκρατούμενο Ναύπλιο [Ceramics of Italian Workshops in Venetian Nafplio]. In *Ναυπλιακά Ανάλεκτα IX. Της Βενετιάς τ'Ανάπλι -300 χρόνια από το τέλος μιας εποχής, 1715-2015. Επιστημονικό Συμπόσιο, Ναύπλιο, 9-11 Οκτωβρίου 2015, Πρακτικά [Nafpliaka Analekta IX. Nafplion of Venice – 300 Years from the End of an Era, 1715–2015. Proceedings of the Scientific Symposium, Nafplio, 9–11 October 2015]*, edited by Eftychia Liata, pp. 331–348. Deme of Nafplio, Ioannis Kapodistrias Intellectual Foundation, Nafplio.

Vlahos, Vangelis
2018   Η κεραμική στη περιοχή των Πρεσπών κατά την ύστερη Οθωμανική περίοδο. Οι περιπτώσεις των αγγειοπλαστικών κέντρων της Φλώρινας και της Ρέσνα [Ritual Pots from the Towns of Florina and Resen in the Late Ottoman Period]. Paper presented at the 12th Congress on Medieval and Modern Period Mediterranean Ceramics, Athens, Greece.

Vroom, Joanita
2003 *After Antiquity: Ceramics and Society in the Aegean from the 7th to the 20th century A.C. A Case Study from Boeotia, Central Greece.* Faculty of Archaeology, Leiden University, Leiden.

Yangaki, Anastasia
2008 Χιώτικα αγγεία από την Συλλογή του Κέντρου Μελέτης Νεώτερης Κεραμικής [Chian Vessels in the Collection of the Centre for the Study of Modern Ceramics]. In *Γη - Μήτρα ζωής και δημιουργίας. Πρακτικά επιστημονικης συνάντησης 19-21 Μαρτίου 2004 [Gaia – Womb of Life and Creativity. Proceedings of the Scientific Meeting 19–21 March 2004]*, edited by Eugenia Daphne, pp. 133–149. Ministry of Culture, Museum of Greek Folk Art, Athens.
2012 *Εφυαλωμένη κεραμική από τη θέση «Άγιοι Θεόδωροι» στην Ακροναυπλία (11ος-17ος αι.) [Glazed Ware from Ayioi Theodoroi in Akronafplia (11th–17th c.)]*. National Research Institute, Institute of Historical Studies, Department of Byzantine Research, Athens.

Zolotas, George
1921 *Ιστορία της Χίου. Ιστορική τοπογραφία και γενεαλογία, ιστορική τοπογραφία [History of Chios: Historical Topography and Genealogy, Historical Topography]*. Vol. 1Α^Α. P. D. Sakellariou, Athens.

Chapter Three
Ayios Dimitrios (Paliochora) and Georgadika in Kythera: Abandoned Settlements in a Historically Abandoned Environment

Lita Tzortzopoulou-Gregory and Timothy E. Gregory

The phenomenon of deserted settlements and its causes and effects have been of interest to scholars throughout the world and across time. Our paper, like most of the others presented here, bases its approach on the theoretical considerations of scholars from the 1970s through the 2000s who worked primarily in the eastern Mediterranean (Cherry et al. 1991; Jameson et al. 1994; Renfrew 1972). One of the most important conclusions of the study of abandonment in the past is that it was not normally a single event but rather something that was part of a normal process of settlement use (Cameron and Tomka 1993; McLeman 2011). Indeed, in certain circumstances, abandonment was closely connected with intentional patterns of life, such as migration, the utilization of non-renewable resources, and preferences for certain kinds of agriculture. To be sure, abandonment can sometimes be connected with catastrophic change, caused by both human and natural or environmental agents (such as invasions or climate change and natural disasters), but it seems more commonly connected with intentional and/or unintentional change than with disaster.

Our own particular approach will certainly correspond to what has been presented in this volume, with a broad view of abandonment (as well as survival) primarily in the Mediterranean area in the historical past. We hope that our contribution will emphasize the concept that, in an archaeological context at least, "abandonment" does not simply mean an "end" to things. Rather, it is a part of an ongoing process that involves both beginnings and endings, but also change and resilience—where settlements can, of course, be completely abandoned but, more commonly, are likely to transform and develop different functions over time. In our paper, we have decided to focus on a specific case study of abandonment and settlement transformation on the island of Kythera that may or may not be characteristic of other parts of the Mediterranean world. In this particular case, we view the abandonment of the rural settlement pattern of the island of Kythera as a result of a complex web of environmental, sociocultural, economic, and political responses, or what Butzer and Endfield (2012) refer to as "cascading feedbacks" connected to broader temporal and spatial phenomena and societal collapse. They argue that: "Societal collapse represents transformation at a large social or spatial scale, with long-term impact on combinations of interdependent variables: (i) environmental change and resilience; (ii) demography or settlement; (iii) socio-economic patterns; (iv) political or societal structures; and (v) ideology or cultural memory" (Butzer and Endfield 2012:3628).

In a recent publication, Knapp and Meyer (2020) argue for the application of such an approach to examining collapse, demise, and regeneration in academically controversial large-scale phenomena such as the transition from the Bronze Age to the Iron Age in Cyprus. Our own case study on Kythera certainly does not compare in terms of temporal scale to such large phenomena; nevertheless, we argue that there is enough evidence (archaeological, historical, and archival) that can warrant a similar investigation into the transition from the late medieval to early modern periods (thirteenth to sixteenth centuries AD) and into the present day. As such, we argue for a number of interrelated factors or cascading feedbacks connected with the phenomenon of a broader collapse of Kythera's centuries-long peculiar feudal organization as the leading force behind the oscillating changes in the local settlement system and its demographics. Especially significant in this regard is a major shift in the social structure of the northern part of Kythera from at least the sixteenth century, and especially in the eighteenth century. This shift was marked by various incidents of population dispersal within the island, depopulation and repopulation of settlements, and immigration as well as outward migration from the island. Some of these events could not have taken place in earlier times due to the various and complex historical and political realities associated with a controlling land-based aristocracy alongside Venetian imperial rule throughout the late Middle Ages. As we have discussed these historical developments in more detail elsewhere (Tzortzopoulou-Gregory and Gregory 2017), our present paper will focus briefly on the shifting attitudes from aristocratic and hereditary-based land ownership to private freehold ownership and the associated socioeconomic implications, including demographic fluctuations and the increasing importance of women in the running of households and local economies.

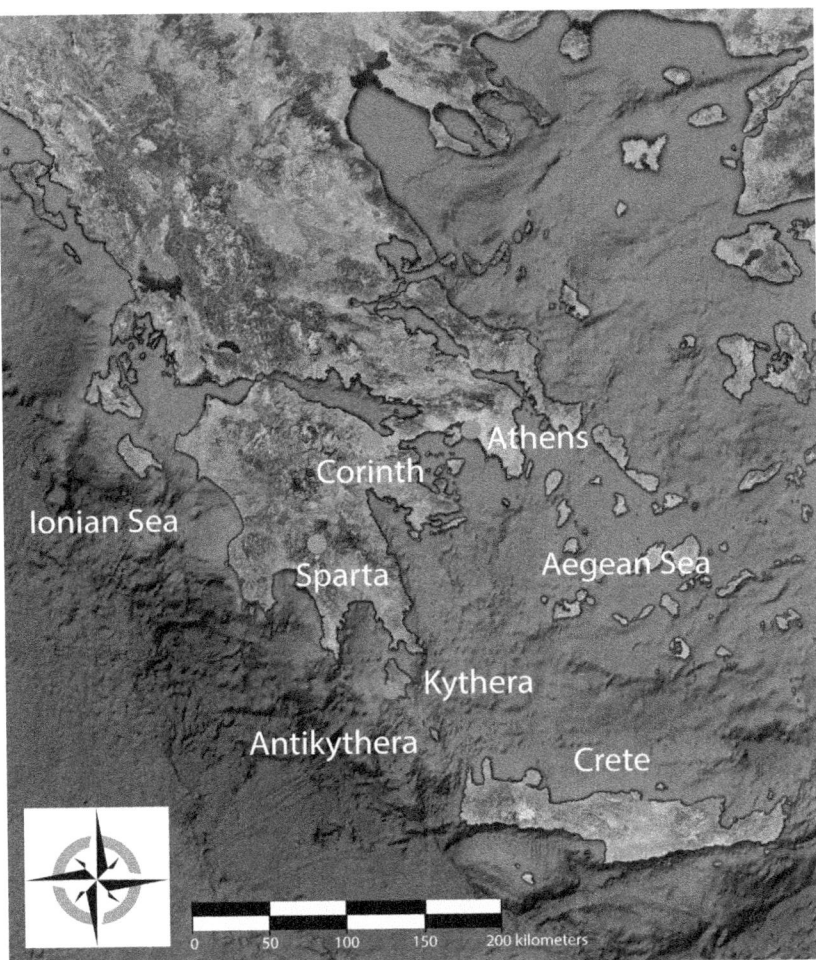

Figure 1. Map of Greece showing the location of Kythera.

Focus on Kythera

The island of Kythera is located just off the southeast corner of the Peloponnese, midway between the mainland of Greece and Crete and astride the main shipping routes of the eastern Mediterranean (**Figure 1**).

Indeed, its location and the relatively small human population have historically led to a phenomenon of apparent abandonment of peoples on Kythera over long periods (from prehistory to the present), something studied over time by foreign observers and the inhabitants themselves. One of the more common views of this is the (generally accepted) claim that, up to the present, Kythera has suffered from either "partial" or "total" abandonment possibly as many as six times, each followed by repopulation and new periods of prosperity and general well-being. In this view (among other things), it is frequently believed that "long-range" abandonment or, in some cases, what can be called the "seventh period" of abandonment, will signal either "the end of the world!" or at least a phenomenon that leads to "catastrophic disaster" (Gregory 2009:113–117; Sathas 1885).

Such very large vacillations in population or other monumental change, of course, are known throughout the world and throughout time, sometimes perhaps the result of worldwide or regional causes but also sometimes apparently the result of very local events.[1] In the case of Kythera, for example, it is easy to see what seem to be peaks of population throughout the past, most notably in (1) the Early Helladic and (2) the Protopalatial periods of prehistory, (3) the Classical and (4) later Roman periods, perhaps (5) the later Middle Ages, and (6) the nineteenth century—all of these presumably followed by significant population collapses in the areas considered. Many of these "disasters" seem to be accompanied by the abandonment of significant settlements: for example, the Minoan city in the vicinity of Kastri (Paliopoli), the Classical city of Kythera (Paliokastro), the Hellenistic–Roman city of Kythera (Skandeia), and the medieval city of Ayios Dimitrios (Paliochora; Figure 2; Gregory 2006, 2009). It is notable that none of these early cities exist today except as abandoned or archaeological sites, and the precise location of some of them is still debated.[2]

The "story" or "impact" that such "abandonments" are supposed to have on various phenomena frequently have been thought to be tied closely to the revival of life in an area as a whole, so that the abandoned settlements, perhaps ironically, have been connected with stories concerning the revival of the island and its ultimate resettlement, presumably because local culture has more interest in explaining the revival than in considering the abandonment. Thus, the martyrdom of Ayia Elesa (a local saint whose martyrdom on Kythera has granted her a position as one of the three patrons of the island), supposedly in 395 AD, and the miracles attributed to

---

[1] Kalligeros (2011:26–30) provides a number of reasons for the abandonment of settlements on Kythera, including plague, pirate raids, and relocation due to migration and environmental phenomena.

[2] According to Kalligeros (2011:42–53), many of the settlements listed in medieval documents are yet to be located and/or identified on the landscape.

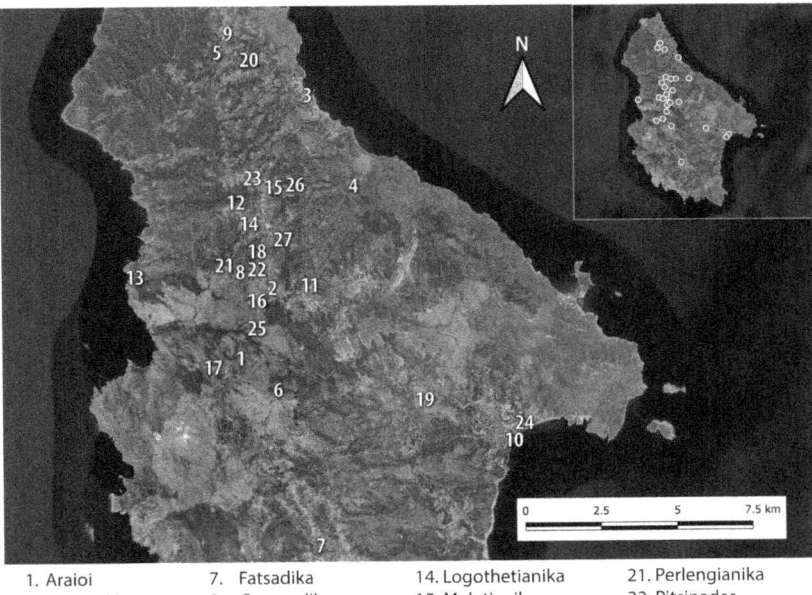

Figure 2. Map of Kythera showing the location of major settlements mentioned in the article, including Ayios Dimitrios (Paliochora) and Georgadika in the central part of the island. Map courtesy of Matthew Crum.

1. Araioi
2. Aroniadika
3. Ayia Pelayia
4. Ayios Dimitrios (Paliochora)
5. Diakopoulianika
6. Dokana
7. Fatsadika
8. Georgadika
9. Karavas
10. Kastri (Paliopoli)
11. Kastrisianika
12. Katsoulianika
13. Koufoyialos
14. Logothetianika
15. Meletianika
16. Mount Skliri
17. Mylopotamos
18. Osios Theodoros
19. Paliokastro
20. Panayia Despina
21. Perlengianika
22. Pitsinades
23. Potamos
24. Skandeia
25. Spastiras
26. Triphylianika
27. Zaglanikianika

her have been thought to be responsible for the repopulation of Kythera after a period of "collapse" in late antiquity, even though the chronology of her miracles may also be historically questionable (Metallinos 2003).

Perhaps the best example of "renewal stories" or "founding myths" of this type may be the arrival and death of Osios Theodoros on Kythera supposedly in 921 AD, a time when, according to the saint's hagiography, the island was deserted, presumably as a result of the attacks of the Arab pirates from Crete along the coasts of Greece (Gregory 2006:491–496). Thus, the stories of the two saints (Ayia Elesa and Osios Theodoros) who "tamed the abandoned wilderness" of the island and allowed its repopulation through postmortem interventions are remarkably similar to each other, and it is likely that there was some literary borrowing from one to the other.[3] Furthermore, it is notable that the concept of Kythera as a "desert" or "deserted place" (*erimos topos*) seems to be common among both of these saints' biographies, and, indeed, it is a topic worthy of more detailed discussion.

Ayios Dimitrios (Paliochora)

One of the more recent historical abandonments on Kythera was the destruction of Ayios Dimitrios in August of 1537 as a result of the attack of Khizr Hayreddin, more generally known as "Barabarossa" (Bradford 1968). There are no clearly eyewitness accounts of this event, but the basic results are known largely from the accounts of the Venetian officials who reported to the Serene Republic in the decades after the catastrophe, seeking (generally unsuccessfully, as it turned out) to secure funds to restore the defenses of the old city. Local traditions on the island—depending now primarily on oral reports that were written down presumably generations after the event—maintain that the devastation and depopulation of the settlement was complete and total, except that a few residents of the city fled to the church of the Panayia (or Virgin) near the outer walls, where through a miracle the Panayia prevented the pirates from gaining entrance and saved the residents. It is significant that the present-day residents of the nearby settlements of Triphylianika, Meletianika, Logothetianika, and Zaglanikianika frequently claim that they are the direct descendants of these few survivors of Barbarossa's massacre. Such stories culminated in an annual celebration of the miracle of the Panayia toward the end of August each year, which, ironically, also marks the anniversary of the massacre itself and at the same time draws attention back to this phenomenon of the "desolation and repopulation nexus."

Interestingly, a scholarly debate has arisen in recent years about the chronology of the abandonment of Ayios Dimitrios and the degree to which it was, on the one hand, sudden and total or, on the other, a gradual process. This may seem like a minor historical issue, since the results were, in any case, eventually complete as far as the city itself was concerned. The place was relegated to a ruin that was haunted and cursed by the spirits of those who were killed in the massacre but who continued to "reside" in the vicinity and drive away any who came to disturb their peace. As time went on, Ayios Dimitrios became known as Paliochora (the "Old City").

---

[3] See Caraher 2008 for a very interesting article on the life and miracles of Osios Theodoros; his evaluation is certainly appropriate in the context of abandonment that we are investigating here.

In the absence of any systematic excavation within the medieval site, and while the findings of an archaeological survey carried out by a Greek–British team in the 1980s is yet to be fully published, it is difficult at this stage to ascertain the degree to which the city of Ayios Dimitrios developed from the time of its founding to its eventual demise and relegation to a "ghost town" and a *paliochora* (Ince et al. 1987, 1989). Guy Sanders (1996:158) is one of the few scholars to suggest that the city continued to be occupied as late as the seventeenth century. Based on a list of inhabited settlements drawn up by Petros Kastrofylakas in 1583, in which S. Dimitri (as Ayios Dimitrios was known to the Venetians) is also listed—as well as anecdotal, but persuasive, evidence in the form of pottery from the sixteenth and seventeenth centuries at the site—we agree with Sanders that the city of Ayios Dimitrios continued to function past its destruction, albeit in a significantly different way. The evidence suggests that the city may not have been completely destroyed at a single moment and that some inhabitants might have survived or returned, with activity continuing for some time after its destruction (Gregory and Tzortzopoulou-Gregory 2015:259). How one defines this activity—whether permanent or seasonal habitation, partial habitation of specific areas within the city, or no habitation at all but simply a transfer of function of some of the buildings to housing sheep and goats (as indeed was the case until a few years ago)—is yet to be determined.

Ince and Ballantyne's (2007:24) counterargument to the gradual abandonment of the site is that the destruction of Ayios Dimitrios led to its immediate abandonment. Their argument is based on the hypothesis that Ayios Dimitrios was essentially a "feudal" settlement, in which the nobility dominated the luxurious urban spaces while the peasants who tilled the land huddled within the poorly defended areas of the urban center. They argue that the breaching of the walls of the castle in 1537 made it impossible for the peasants to live there, and so they scattered to the surrounding countryside (which had not been of any value to the upper-class families) and thus founded numerous settlements, many of which exist to this date.

This issue may seem to be merely a scholarly squabble, but in fact it has real significance in terms of our broader understanding of the phenomenon of the abandonment of Ayios Dimitrios. The findings of the Australian Paliochora-Kythera Archaeological Survey (APKAS), in contrast to the argument made by Ince and Ballantyne, demonstrate that even before 1537 there were significant settlements already established in the wider vicinity of the Ayios Dimitrios town (Coroneos et al. 2002).[4] Thus, in this view, some of the small settlements that are scattered broadly from Potamos in the north to Aroniadika in the center were presumably where the vast majority of free peasants lived well before the destruction of Ayios Dimitrios in 1537, as well as later (Gregory 2008:260).[5]

The destruction of Ayios Dimitrios and the subsequent depopulation that followed forced the Venetian Republic to intervene. Reluctantly, the nobles agreed to emancipate all serfs, keeping the population from fleeing and encouraging settlers who had fled to return, presumably back to the settlements surrounding the medieval center (Leontsinis 1987:68–71). This argument is further supported by later historical accounts, especially notarial records of contracts of land transactions in the form of land sales and leases between nobles and free farmers, which were an attempt to encourage new settlers on the island and to increase productivity (Leontsinis 1987:72). Records from this period also indicate the growing gap between the nobles and those who worked the land as either serfs (*paroikoi*) or free farmers, with the latter often having to borrow from the nobles in order to pay unreasonably high taxes and thus entering them into a perpetual cycle of debt. In the event that they could not pay their debts, they would either have their lands confiscated or be forced to provide free service by working the lands of the nobles, a fate as equally bad as being a serf.

If the reconstruction presented by APKAS is correct, at least to any degree (i.e. that the settlements around Ayios Dimitrios existed already before its destruction and grew exponentially postdestruction), then our understanding of an abandonment/revival phenomenon may need to be reevaluated as a much more complex series of events.

Something that may be of help in the investigation of this question is the analysis of the disappearance of many other settlements, most of which are neither necessarily monumental nor part of a "grand vision" that is often viewed as the focus of medieval and/or modern historians.

---

[4] APKAS was initiated in 1999, and its focus was an examination of the Ayios Dimitrios–Paliochora hinterland and the diachronic development of settlements within that area.

[5] Many of these free farmers may have ended up on Kythera as refugees, especially after the falls of Constantinople in 1453 and the Despotate of Mystras in 1458. Many family names on the island may be derived from the titles of Byzantine officials who found refuge on Kythera from the fifteenth century onward: families such as those of Komenos, Megalokonomos, and Strategos, which are found in the aforementioned settlements.

Such settlements are, of course, documented in tax records, chronicles, and other sources, but little is normally said about the process of their founding and abandonment and its possible causes.

Georgadika[6]

In the interest of space, we will focus here only on one very different example of what we might characterize as an "abandoned" place: a settlement located in the central part of the island and known from the eighteenth-century Venetian census records as Georgadika. The discussion will include its church, dedicated to Ayia Triada (the Holy Spirit), constructed apparently in the tenth–twelfth centuries, and now significantly damaged.

The settlement of Georgadika is today completely deserted, and the land is used only for occasional agricultural purposes.[7] We were alerted to the existence of the settlement during the early phases of APKAS in 1999–2003 and our investigations into the network of churches that could be identified in the broader survey area. Thus, on the basis of the eighteenth-century censuses carried out by the Venetians, we know that a church of Ayia Triada existed in Georgadika and that its inhabitants were recorded by name through all the censuses carried out in the eighteenth century, but the exact location of the church and the buildings of the settlement were unknown (Patramani et al. 1997). With the help of local informants, the APKAS team was able to identify the location of the settlement, partway between the small (but active) villages of Pitsinades (in the east) and Perlengianika (to the west), just south of the monastery of Osios Theodoros (mentioned briefly above), and north of Aroniadika and the two main roads that run south and north in that part of the island (see **Figure 2**).

During the Venetian period, Georgadika belonged administratively to the *distretto* of Kastrisianika, and, as we might have imagined, it was historically connected with the nearby villages mentioned above and the northern settlements near Logothetianika, as well with as the tenth-century monastery of Osios Theodoros. The following provides a basic

---

[6] The transliteration used for the name of the settlement is based on its modern Greek pronunciation, which differs from its Venetian version in the seventeenth-century censuses.

[7] Georgadika is not a unique "abandoned" medieval/post-medieval settlement by any means; the countryside of Kythera abounds in deserted settlements like this. For an archaeological investigation of such a settlement, see **Bennet and Harlan 2015**.

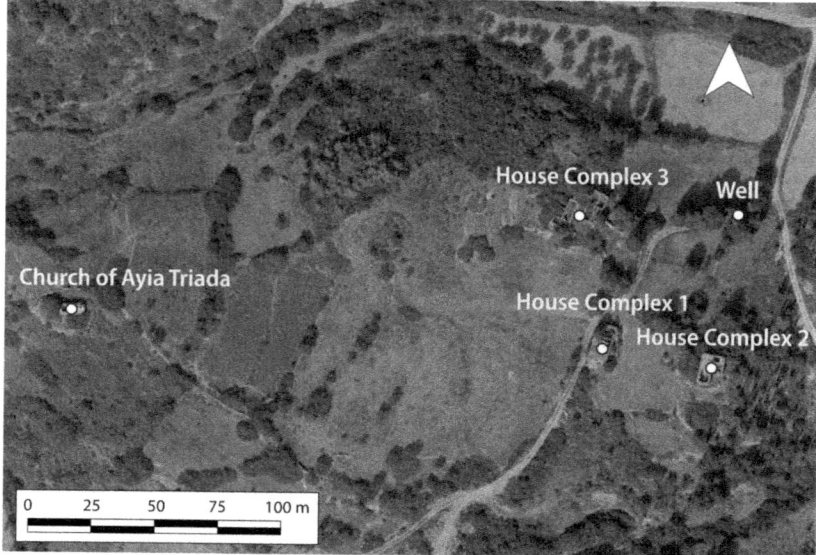

Figure 3. Aerial photo of the area showing the small settlement of Georgadika (right) and the church of Ayia Triada (left). Photo courtesy of John Fardoulis.

overview of the location and surviving remains concerning the settlement. It should be noted here that the investigations in this settlement are not yet complete, and thus there is currently no detailed architectural study of the buildings described below.

In earlier times, the road system in Kythera was significantly different from what it is now, and the oral information we collected suggests that Georgadika was once on an important route that was part of the early modern local road network. Thus, before the British-period construction of the modern north–south road system in the nineteenth century, Georgadika lay astride an earlier main road that ran north and south, west of the modern system on the island. This evidence tells us that the earlier road ran south from Pitsinades to Georgadika, then across the heights of Mount Skliri, probably through Spastiras and Araioi, and on to the south. This would have made Georgadika a major hub on the premodern road network of the period.

The aerial photograph in **Figure 3** shows that the main part of the abandoned settlement would have been in the area that is shown as relatively empty of agricultural growth. The main approach to the area is a fairly narrow road coming primarily from the east, while a relatively long line and a series of field walls (running roughly east–west) mark a water

Figure 4. Ayia Triada church, exterior. Photo courtesy of John Fardoulis.

Figure 5. Ayia Triada church from above. Photo courtesy of John Fardoulis.

line that moves towards the sea. Within the area shown in the aerial photograph are three house complexes, one *aloni* (threshing floor) associated with House Complex 3, a smaller *aloni* southwest of the same complex (in the center of the photograph), the ruined church of Ayia Triada to the west of the settlement, and a stone-constructed well alongside the road to the northeast of the settlement.

The Church of Ayia Triada

The church of Ayia Triada is located on the west edge of the settlement, just at the top of a north–south series of drops down the wide east–west watercourse mentioned above (**Figure 4** and **Figure 5**).

The church is in very poor condition, and its roof has disappeared completely. Some of the paintings on each of the original four sides of the church survive, and some are in a condition that allows us to determine their original representations (**Figure 6**). Thus, the image of Ayia Triada (the Holy Trinity) is relatively well preserved above the apse on the east wall of the church (**Figure 7** and **Figure 8**).

Slightly to the west of the image of the Ayia Triada, near the bottom of the south wall, are the frescoes dedicated to Ayia Sophia and her three female children—Pistis, Elpis, and Agapi (Faith, Hope, and Charity)—and there are many damaged frescoes of other saints on the north wall of the church (**Figure 9** and **Figure 10**). Inscriptions with the names of three different donors appear in some of the frescoes: Panayiotis and Theodoros (first names only of presumably father and son), and Grizotis (family name). One of the relatively poorly preserved images is all but certainly that of Osios Theodoros, one of the most important saints in the tenth century AD and a figure that is associated with the survival of Kythera against the threat from Arab raids at that time.

Despite this information, it is somewhat perplexing that even though Osios Theodoros is one of the two major patrons of the island, very few churches seem to have displayed representations of his image. An icon with an image of Osios Theodoros is in the saint's monastery church, just north of Georgadika and not far from Pitsinades. Following the premodern road (now overgrown and mostly inaccessible) south of Georgadika, one passes by the small (and nearly abandoned) church of Osios Theodoros Spastiras, which contains another image of Osios Theodoros, this time in the form of a fresco. In addition, this north–south roadway continues toward Mylopotamos, from which a branch strikes out (much improved in recent years) leading along the coast to the cave-church of Ayia Sophia. Not surprisingly, the church's surviving paintings include

Figure 6. Panorama of the interior of Ayia Triada church from the west. Photo courtesy of Jon Frey.

Figure 7. Interior of the apse of Ayia Triada church. Photo courtesy of Timothy E. Gregory.

Figure 8. Detail of the fresco of the Ayia Triada above the apse. Photo courtesy of Timothy E. Gregory.

Figure 9. 3D view of the interior south wall of Ayia Triada church, with frescos. Ayia Sophia and her daughters are in the center. Photo courtesy of Jon Frey.

Figure 10. 3D view of the interior north wall of Ayia Triada church, with frescos. Osios Theodoros appears at the bottom right. Photo courtesy of Jon Frey.

an image of Osios Theodoros and another representation of Ayia Sophia and her three daughters, who, it will be remembered, dominated nearly the whole of the south side of the interior of the church of Ayia Triada in Georgadika. While these connections between roadways and locations of veneration may simply be fortuitous, in view of the small number of places where evidence of the veneration of Osios Theodoros is clearly preserved, it seems reasonable to interpret them as outlining a geographic "trail" of places where the spiritual symbols and protectors (Osios Theodoros and the saints Sophia, Faith, Hope, and Charity) were remembered.

If this idea has value, it certainly suggests the importance of Georgadika as a point on this "trail," at least in an early period. Oral information also attests that Georgadika, during at least the last hundred years or so, was one of the stops along the "pilgrim" trail of the icon of the Myrtidiotissa (Virgin of the Myrtles), locally known as the *gyra* (procession), which takes place during a period of 50 days during Lent, after Easter, and possibly at other times each year.[8] The inclusion of Georgadika and the church of Ayia Triada as a stopping point in the *gyra* of the icon would

---

[8] The Panayia Myrtidiotissa is the main patron of Kythera, venerated by both the Venetians and the local population over the centuries. Her "found" icon is one of the most prized religious items in Kythera, and it is housed in the monastery of the same name in the central-west of the island. Its "tour" to the main villages of Kythera during the *gyra* is an opportunity for everyone on the island to share the Virgin's blessings. For more information on the Myrtidiotissa see Charou-Koronaiou 2018; Paspalas 2008.

Figure 11. Route of the *gyra* of the Myrtidiotissa icon between the settlement at Georgadika and the town of Mylopotamos. Map courtesy of Matthew Crum.

certainly have indicated that the settlement—even during this period of decline in its population and near abandonment (the last resident lived here in the 1950s)—was considered a major focus of traditional continuity in the religious activity of the period (**Figure 11**).

The House Complexes in Georgadika

The small settlement of Georgadika itself is located above a small, flat depression on the south side of the wide stream that runs east–west from the slopes of Mount Skliri to its outlet into the sea at Koufoyialos. Here, we refrain from labeling the settlement as a village or hamlet, as it lacks the main characteristics of either; there is no village center, and the church itself seems to be located at a distance from the houses. The settlement, comprised of three large composite house complexes, compares to other such settlements nearby and scattered across the island; they share the characteristics of rural estates or manor houses, with no obvious civic center or defense structures (see **Figure 3**).

Systematic ground-level archaeological investigation of the three house complexes primarily involved the removal of very dense and impenetrable vegetation, revealing the main features of the structures, including foundations, internal divisions, walls, and other structural characteristics. Several anomalies in the layout of the settlement were identified; most

Figure 12. Aerial photo of the settlement of Georgadika. The church of Ayia Triada is in the upper left corner (west of the settlement). Photo courtesy of John Fardoulis.

striking in this respect was the arrangement of the structures with a minimum of approximately 30 m distance between them. More remarkably, the church is located at a considerable distance from the house complexes and not in a central location within the settlement (Figure 12).

House Complex 3 is clearly the largest and most elaborate of the three (Figure 13). It is located along a relatively long east–west ridge, near the only access into the large interior area of the site. The complex has a basic center made up of two or three large, rectangular spaces, presumably built at different times and connected with each other by joining walls and doorways (**Figure 14, Figure 15,** and **Figure 16**). To the east of the main complex is a relatively large area that includes walls and small enclosures, presumably for animals, supplies, equipment, and possibly protection of access to the broader complex from enemies. Toward the central exterior of the main complex are the remains of a large *fournos* (stone-built oven), presumably for cooking. Interestingly, several of the stones built into and close to the oven/doorway area display modern graffiti scratched into the stones. Most of these are impossible or difficult to read, but some seem to contain letters that suggest parts of a name. A few also seem to contain dates, one or two of which may suggest 1947.

Figure 13. House Complex 3 from above, with a large threshing floor in the upper left corner (west of the complex). Photo courtesy of John Fardoulis.

Figure 14. House Complex 3, interior.

Figure 15. House Complex 3, west end.

Figure 16. House Complex 3, *fournos* and partly preserved chimney.

Further to the west of the main (long) rooms are a very large *aloni* (threshing floor) and several other unidentifiable structures. Another small *aloni* is located along the northeast walls of the complex and above a relatively high wall that stands above a large flat area, which has been used for agriculture until recently.

House Complex 1, also known as the Koumouli House (Koumouli being the family name of the last resident of the house in the 1950s), is a rectangular structure on a significant height, constructed on hard bedrock not far from House Complex 3 to the northwest. In fairly recent times, the complex would presumably have been entered from one of two doorways that survive on the exterior north–south wall (Figure 17, Figure 18, Figure 19, and Figure 20).

The complex is made up of two separate, but obviously (at least at some period in time) interconnected, components (Figure 21). A large roofed, vaulted room runs east–west with an entrance doorway on the south wall and two windows on either side of the vault. An internal door on the north wall connects to another east–west vaulted room with a largely collapsed roof. An impressively large fireplace is at the east end of the vaulted room, above which the roof is preserved along with an intact chimney (Figure 22 and Figure 23). On either side of the fireplace is a pot base embedded within the construction of the wall (Figure 24). A small window is in the west wall of the vaulted room. Adjacent to this vaulted room is a separate north–south rectangular structure, built at a different (and possibly later) time, with a main entrance on the west wall and a blocked entrance on the east wall. A large arch separates a small rectangular space running east–west from the remainder of the structure (Figure 25). There is no roof remaining on this building. A courtyard enclosure wall runs north–south along the east side of the complex.

Figure 17. Aerial view of House Complex 1 from the east. Photo courtesy of John Fardoulis.

Figure 18. House Complex 1, west side.

Figure 19. House Complex 1, south side.

Figure 20. House Complex 1, east side.

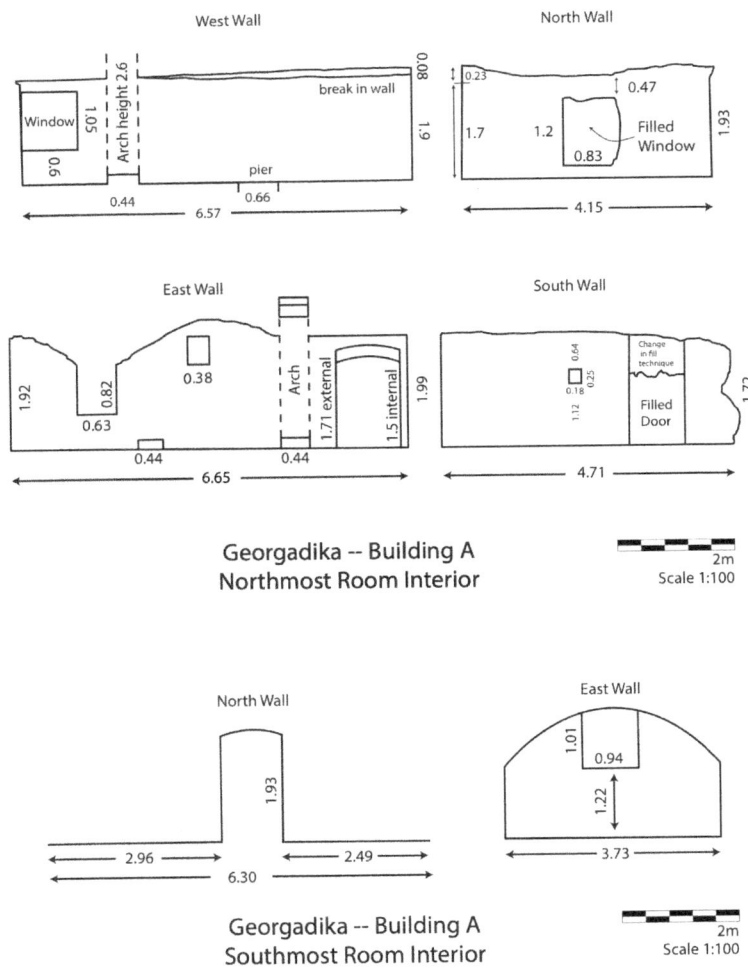

Figure 21. Sketch elevations of House Complex 1.

Figure 22. House Complex 1, fireplace.

Figure 23. House Complex 1, chimney.

Figure 24. House Complex 1, one of the pot bases embedded on either side of the fireplace.

Figure 25. House Complex 1, arch.

House Complex 2 is located almost directly east of House Complex 1 and on higher land surrounded by cliffs on all sides (Figure 26, Figure 27, and Figure 28). The L-shaped building complex is in fact comprised of two separate houses, which despite sharing a common wall have no internal connection between them. Each house has its own separate main entrance, but they both share the same courtyard, which is surrounded by a semicircular drystone wall. Each relatively low and unusually wide-arched doorway entrance (ca. 2.0 m wide x 1.5 m tall) is framed by blocks of *poria* (the local porous limestone). The rectangular house that runs north–south is a two-story building with its entrance on the south end of its west wall, two windows blocked with stones on the east wall, and its roof now missing. At the south end of the building is a vaulted room with a small window, which has been largely blocked up with stones. There is a doorway entrance on the east wall of the vaulted room. The roof of the vault shows repairs using concrete. Perpendicular to this two-story house is the entrance to a large one-story rectangular house divided by two impressive arches. A fireplace is in the northeast corner of the room immediately next to the main entrance, and a window is in the south wall (Figure 29). This building is also missing its roof, except for some olive tree trunks that are still in place. Both buildings are constructed of stones, with extensive use of pottery sherds in the mortar.

The chronology of the construction and additional phases of the buildings mentioned above are difficult to determine. The use of both vaulted and rectilinear construction is most interesting, and although each technique may reflect different phases of construction and habitation, the adaptation, modifications, and simultaneous coexistence of these spaces are worthy of more detailed architectural study. Pottery found around the buildings (including *sgraffito*) and some of the pottery that can be identified inside the construction of House Complex 2 dates to the fourteenth century. The reasonably well-preserved frescoes of the church of Ayia Triada suggest that both they and the construction of these houses may originally date to sometime around the sixteenth century. While the earliest phases of the houses may well date to that same period, the scratched graffiti in them (especially in House Complex 3) suggests that they may have been abandoned closer to the beginning or the middle of the twentieth century. Interestingly, except for the account of an elderly

Figure 26. Aerial view of House Complex 2 from the east. House Complex 1 is in the background. Photo courtesy of John Fardoulis.

woman of the Koumouli family who inhabited House Complex 1 in the 1950s, local informants generally have no recollection of the settlement being inhabited.[9]

Another peculiarity of the houses is their significant size, although (as already mentioned) one needs to keep in mind the fact that additions were clearly made to nearly all of them; families living in them were likely to have been large. Even in the proposed earlier phases of each of the structures, however, one can see that each would have been of a significant size, characteristically of rectangles ca. 10 x 20 m on a side. No cisterns were identified in any of the house complexes or near the church of Ayia Triada. However, the presence of a large stone-constructed well by the roadside to the northeast of the settlement may be evidence of an adequate communal water supply, as there is quite a large volume of water in it even today (**Figure 30** and **Figure 31**). A burial ground has not been identified in the vicinity of the settlement, although it is presumed that burial may have taken place around (or inside) the church of Ayia Triada. Alternatively, the cemetery ground at the monastery of Osios Theodoros, which also serves as the burial place for the inhabitants of nearby Pitsinades, may have been used.

---

[9] According to the same information, this woman had no children. At the time of our investigations, we were informed that the cows grazing in the immediate vicinity of House Complex 1 belonged to her nephew, who also claims title to the property.

Figure 27. House Complex 2, southeast end.

Figure 28. House Complex 2, east side.

Figure 29. House Complex 2, interior of the entrance doorway and fireplace.

Figure 30. Well by the roadside at Georgadika.

Figure 31. Mouth of the well at Georgadika.

The Eighteenth-Century Venetian Censuses and the Nineteenth-Century British Censuses

The records of eight surviving Venetian-period censuses, spread unevenly from 1721 to 1788, present the names and ages of a total of 139 individuals who were registered in the parish of Ayia Triada Georgadika[10]—an average of 17.4 persons per census (Patramani et al. 1997:A725, B724, D960). Some of these individuals are present in more than one census, which is not surprising given that many of the censuses were taken only a few years apart. Considering that three houses survive today in Georgadika, one could calculate on the basis of the census figures an average of 5.8 persons for each household. However, we do know from the census records exactly how many households are recorded, given that each household represents a separate (nuclear) family unit. It should be made clear here that even though the censuses list the individuals as belonging to a separate *famiglie* (family), the term *famiglie* conforms more to the definition of household rather than family, since it includes not only conjugal units but also servants and relatives residing within the same household (Hionidou 2015:50). At the same time, a household as such does not necessarily mean that it resides in a separate house. A house structure or house complex as that encountered in Gerorgadika may be shared by more than just one *famiglie* household. Table 1 lists the number of households and individuals per family name group for each of the surviving Venetian-period censuses, while the chart in **Figure 32** presents the total number of individuals recorded for each individual census between 1721 and 1788. Figure 33 shows the number of individuals per family group for each census year.

So, for example, in 1721 there were seven households listed: three with the surname Giorgà (the most populous family name in this census with 15 individuals), two Griscoti (with seven individuals), one Prinea (with five individuals), and one Facea (the parish priest who lived on his own). However, there are only three house complexes in the settlement of Georgadika, and we can only presume that each house complex was used to accommodate more than one household at a time. In fact, a careful study of the complex architecture of the houses described earlier may help in defining the different phases of construction, which in turn may be associated with different phases of occupancy and number of households. Of course, it is impossible for us to determine which families lived in

---

[10] In these censuses, which are recorded in Venetian, the parish of Georgadika is recorded as Santa Trinità Agiorgadicha (1721, 1724, 1753, 1760, 1784), Parochia di S(anta) Trinità a Giorgadica (1770), Parochia di S(antisssima) Trinità a Giorgadica (1772), and Santa Trinita à Giorgadica (1788).

132

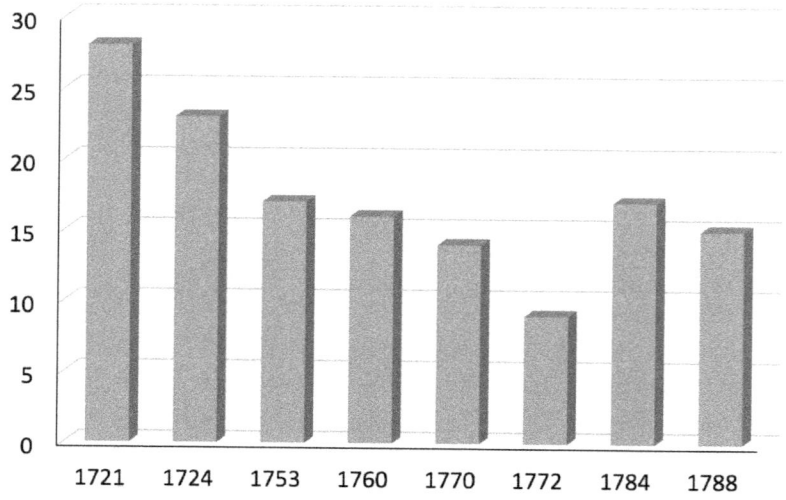

Figure 32. Chart showing the total number of individuals per census year.

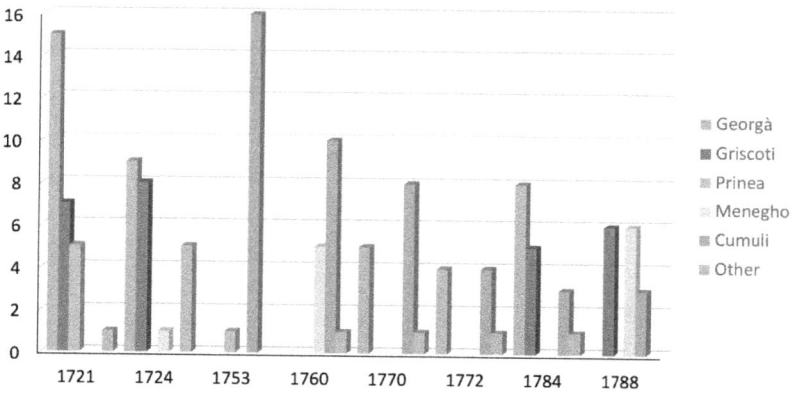

Figure 33. Chart showing the number of individuals in each family per census year.

Table 1. Number of Individuals Per Family Name and Total Number of Households Per Census—Georgadika (Giorgadica/Agiorgadicha).

	Individuals Per Family Name										Total Individuals	Households
	Gorgà	Griscoti / Grisoti	Prinea	Menegho / Menego / Menengo	Cumuli / Cumulli	Facea	Lianò	Mavromati	Logotheti	Unknown		
1721	15	7	5	–	–	1 (+)	–	–	–	–	28	7
1724	9	8	–	1	–	1 (+)	4	–	–	–	23	9
1753	–	–	1 (+)	–	16	–	–	–	–	–	17	5
1760	–	–	–	5	10	–	–	1 (+)	–	–	16	5
1770	5	–	–	–	8	–	–	–	1 (+)	–	14	4
1772	4	–	–	–	4	–	–	–	–	1 (+), no name or age	9	3
1784	8 (+)	5	–	–	3	–	–	–	–	1, female with no name	17	5
1788	–	6	–	6	3	–	–	–	–	–	15	3
Total	41	26	6	12	44	2	4	1	1	2	139	

Note: Each (+) represents a priest, included as part of the total count.

which of the three houses, let alone which part of the houses. What is certain, however, is that the families seem to appear and disappear in the different censuses, and the reasons for this may be many and complex, ranging from errors in record-keeping to real sociological phenomena such as mobility due to in-marriage, out-marriage, and seasonal and permanent migration.

Based on the information graphically presented in the charts, by far the most dominant family name groups are the Giorgà and the Cumuli/Cumulli, representing 61.2% of the individuals in the censuses across time (Table 1, Figure 33). Furthermore, when we add one other family name group (the Griscoti/Grisoti), the three family groups together represent 79.9% of the of the individuals in the censuses across time. Interestingly, while the Giorgà family dominated in the 1721 census, they dramatically declined in numbers in the 1724 census and disappeared totally from the subsequent 1753 and 1760 censuses; the family reappeared again in 1770, with a slight increase in the 1784 census. There are no Giorgà family members recorded in the last census of 1788. By contrast, the Prinea family appeared only in the 1721 and 1753 censuses (they were missing from the 1724 census), while the Cumuli/Cumulli family name appeared for the first time in the 1753 census (with an impressive size of 16 members) and in every other census until 1788, with a gradual decline in the number of members. It is worth noting that of the seven priests mentioned in the censuses, one was from the Prinea family (1753) and one was from the Giorgà family (1784), while the other five were "outsiders," bearing common family names from other parts of the island: Facea (a common name in the village of Fatsadika)[11], Mavromati (a common name from nearby Pitsinades), and Logotheti (a common name from Logothetianika). A parish priest is recorded in the 1772 census, but his name and age are missing.

As the size of the families vacillated significantly over the period reresented by the censuses, the records also clearly reflect the frequent movements of individuals who appeared, disappeared, and reappeared again in different years. It should be noted that the total numbers of individuals in each census was quite small (the highest being in 1721 with 28 individuals, and the lowest in 1772 with 9 individuals), but it is still quite remarkable to notice such high mobility in the population (see Figure 32).

It is important to stress here that the nature of the family unit or household in eighteenth-century Kythera seems to be predominantly

---

[11] The same priest was listed in both the 1721 and 1724 censuses, although his age was obviously erroneously recorded (48 years old in 1721 and 46 years old in 1724).

nuclear, accounting for 70% of all households in the 1724, 1784, and 1788 censuses for the whole island (Hionidou 2011:221). Likewise, in Georgadika, the number of households listed in each census ranged between three and six, each normally consisting of a couple and their children and occasionally an elderly (widowed) parent, usually of the male head of the household. The 1724 census recorded the largest number of households (nine in total) but not necessarily the largest number of individuals, while the 1772 census recorded the smallest number of households (three) and the smallest number of individuals (nine, one of whom was a parish priest whose name was not recorded). The seven households in 1721 included one with the parish priest (Facea) who was listed on his own with no other family members. The same priest appeared in the 1724 census, while a different parish priest was listed as the occupier of a single household in 1753 (Prinea), and yet another one in 1760 (Mavromati). In 1772, there was one parish priest but his name and age are not provided. Teodossio Giorgà di Panagioti was listed as the parish priest in the 1784 census, and he too, was listed as the only member of his household.[12] There was no parish priest listed in the final Venetian census of 1788.

Of course, it is significant that the name of the settlement we are discussing appeared in various different forms of Giorgadica or Agiorgadicha in the census records, but it is certainly possible that it was known by other names at different times. In modern times the settlement is also referred to as "Koumoulianika," as the last inhabitant, who resided in House Complex 1 until the mid 1950s, was from the Koumouli family (the Greek version of the family name Cumuli/Cumulli which appeared in the Venetian censuses). It is also referred to as "Meneyianika," referencing the Menegas family (the Greek version of the Menegho/Menego/Menengo family, whose members were mentioned only in the 1724, 1760, and 1788 censuses; see Table 1, Figure 33). It is also suggested that the settlement may be the same—or at least within the same area—as the one referred to as "Grizoti" (Γριζωτή) in a sixteenth-century census, the oldest surviving census on Kythera but one that is problematic in terms of historical topography (Kalligeros 2011:99–100). Interestingly, inscriptions in the church of Ayia Triada show that some of the surviving frescoes bear the names of two individual donors, Theodoros and Panayiotis, presumably father and son. These Christian names are common among the men of the Giorgà family both in the censuses and as they exist today (in

---

[12] It is surprising that all the parish priests in Georgadika seem not to have had any family. Most parish priests in other parts of the island are listed as heads of households along with their wives and children.

modern Greek, the family name is transliterated as Georgas).[13] Another inscription inside the church of Ayia Triada mentions a certain Grizotis as one of the church's donors. The family name Griscoti (possibly a corruption of Grizoti or Grisoti) appeared in the 1721, 1724, 1784, and 1788 censuses, and this may support Kalligeros' argument that Georgadika may be a later name for the sixteenth-century settlement of Grizoti.

Here it is interesting to note that the Griscoti/Grisoti family name is probably of Italian (and possibly Venetian) origin, and that a certain Pavlos Griziotis-Lembidis was mentioned in a sixteenth-century official register as being the head of the armor guard of Kythera (Kalligeros 2006:202). In the eighteenth-century censuses, the name appeared in the settlements of Milopotamo (Mylopotamos in Greek), Picinades (Pitsinades in Greek), and Giorgadica/Agiogiardicha (mentioned above) and disappeared from all records by the nineteenth century. There are no known present-day descendants of the Griscoti family. The origins of the Koumouli (i.e. Cumuli/Cumulli) family are unknown, but like Griscoti it, too, may be of Italian origin. As far as we know, the name did not appear anywhere else on the island and it is no longer in existence since the passing of the last resident who bore that name in Georgadika in the 1950s. Apparently, she and her sister lived together in House 1, and neither of them were married. A living, distant nephew of the Koumouli sisters (with a different family name) is allegedly their only relation and the current owner of their property and fields in Georgadika.

The present-day Georgas family name (i.e. Giorgà) is of Greek origin and can be traced to as early as the sixteenth century in a land-purchase contract from Kythera that mentions a Dimitris Giorgà. The same person is mentioned in a list of moneylenders to the governor of Kythera, Pietro Suriano (1571–1573), indicating that he was certainly a person of affluence and, perhaps, influence (Kalligeros 2006:192). The present-day family name Menegas (the Greek version of Menegho or Menego), which appeared for the first time in the 1724 census, seems to be connected to the Giorgà family name; according to Kalligeros, it is a nickname that apparently became the official family name of one of the branches of the Giorgà family—a common practice with many family names on the island that originated as nicknames. Today, descendants of the Menegas family exist only outside of Kythera, mainly in Athens (Kalligeros 2006:486).

Beyond the Venetian censuses mentioned above, the census records of the British period (1809–1864) contain information about Georgadika

---

[13] Following the customary practice of first-born male and female children being given the name of their paternal grandparents.

and the Georgas family, although these survive only sporadically.[14] The last entry for Georgadika seems to be the census of 1825, which recorded only two families: the Georgas and the Koumouli, the former with ten individuals and the latter with six, each led, respectively, by a widower (92 years old) and a widow (aged 38). There were four adults listed in this census, meaning that the other 12 individuals were all children.

The existing notarial records, in fact, nicely complement the information from the 1825 census. For example, in 1855 Pashalia Georga, the wife of Minas Georgas (son of the deceased Antonios Georgas), registered the birth of their son, Antonios. The registration of newborn children was normally the father's undertaking, but, in this case, the father is referred to as being absent from Georgadika, and almost certainly from the birth of his child. Similar to this are references to the two godparents of the infant Antonios: both were women whose husbands were also referred to as being absent from Kythera at the time of the child's baptism (**Figure 34**). This was apparently not an uncommon situation on Kythera during the early modern period when many of the men left the island to undertake seasonal work as farmers, laborers, or sea merchants on the mainland, on other Greek islands, or even as far away as Egypt, Asia Minor, or the Black Sea (**Aslani 2018**). What is interesting about this particular entry is that the baptism of the infant took place at the Ayia Triada church at Georgadika—presumably the home parish of the infant—but his mother is referred to as being originally from the village of Dokana, and each of the godmothers reside in their respective birth villages of Katsoulianika and Perlengianika. The second godmother is married to a Georgas (as mentioned previously, he was absent from the island at the time), and it is interesting that she is not residing in Georgadika (presumably the birthplace of her husband). This information is quite suggestive of the various movements and kinship interactions between Georgadika and the nearby villages, further supporting our argument for the fluidity of settlement amongst local residents. Furthermore, the phenomenon of predominantly male absence from Kythera raises interesting questions about the role of women and their obvious responsibilities and power in managing and maintaining households during this period. Relating to the phenomenon of male mobility is the information provided in an earlier entry in the parish records (from 1846), which refers to a certain Antonios Georgas (presumably the grandfather of the infant Antonios) as having died in the Peloponnese, where he was also buried (**Figure 35**).

---

[14] It is important to note here that the British-period censuses were recorded in Greek and not in Venetian, thus the Greek transliteration is applied for the name of the settlement and the family names.

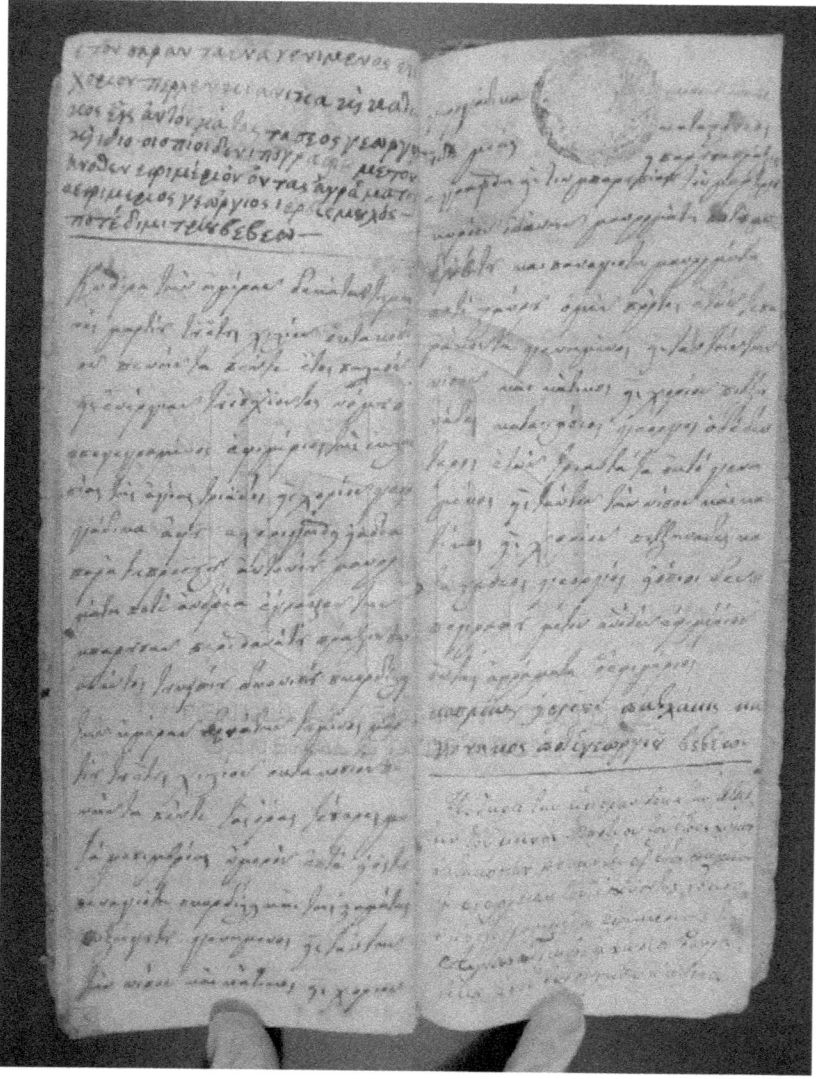

Figure 34. 1855 entry of the baptism of Antonios Georgas (the infant) in the Ayia Triada parish records. Digital image courtesy of the Local Archives of Kythera: http://gak-kyth.att.sch.gr. The translation provided for this entry is as follows: "Pashalia Georga, 25 years of age, wife of Minas Georgas who is absent, and daughter of Georgios Karydis of the village of Dokana, presented her infant son who was born on 26 October 1855 at 6:00 am, and was named Antonios. The godparents of the child were Mrs. Gianoulla Kominou, the wife of Panagioti Kominou who is absent, from the village of Perlegianika, and Mrs. Maria Georga, wife of Ioannis Georgas who is absent, born in Katsoulianika and residing in the same."

Figure 35. 1846 entry of the death of Antonios Georgas (the elder) in the Ayia Triada parish records. Digital image courtesy of the Local Archives of Kythera: http://gak-kyth.att.sch.gr. The translation of this entry reads as follows: "Antonios Georgas, son of Panayiotis, died and was buried in the Peloponnese."

The subsequent census taken by the British in 1833 shows no records for Georgadika. One would assume from this that the settlement was abandoned by then, with no inhabitants to record. The notarial records, however, continue to mention people residing in Georgadika, with the resident priest at the church of Ayia Triada maintaining the parish records. In fact, the last existing entry in the notarial records is dated to 1864. It is a mystery as to why there are no census records available for Georgadika after 1825, when we know from the above parish records that the settlement was still inhabited and its church still functioning in 1864. It is also a mystery as to why the British censuses of 1825–1844 do not mention members of any of the Georgadika families anywhere else on the island. If one were to consider these records alone, ignoring the above-mentioned parish records, it would seem as if the families had all disappeared. However, in the 1844 census, a Georgas family is found registered in the village of Karavas in the northernmost part of the island. In this census, the Georgas family was represented by seven individuals: the 62-year-old widow of the priest Ioannis Georgas and their son, Panayiotis, then also a priest, with his wife and their four children. Descendants of this family still exist in the village of Karavas, while in more recent years, some have relocated to the nearby seaside village of Ayia Pelayia.

The relocation of the Georgas family to the northernmost settlement on Kythera certainly poses a number of questions: what forced this particular family to leave Georgadika at a time when we know that Ayia Triada was still operating as a parish (at least until 1864 based on the Ayia Triada parish records mentioned above)? What happened to the other inhabitants/families (the Georgas, Koumouli, and Menegas families of Georgadika) between 1825 and 1864, and why are there no census records for the Georgadika parish available for that period?[15] Were they simply left out of the censuses, or have the records for Georgadika for the period in question simply gone missing? The latter is very likely, as the records from some other parishes in Kythera also seem to be missing; for example, Panayia Despina (Vouno) is missing from all Venetian and British censuses, even though it had existed as a thriving parish. Or could it be that the settlement was abandoned and that the inhabitants, along

---

[15] It is worth noting that, other than the Georgas family name, none of the other names exist anymore on Kythera. The Prineas family name is still quite common, especially in the nearby villages of Perlengianika and Logothetianika, and since their presence in Georgadika was for only a short period of time, one can assume that they arrived from one of these other villages, perhaps through marriage, and moved back again soon after.

with their parish of Ayia Triada, were simply integrated within the two larger nearby villages, Perlengianika and Pitsinades? If so, then why are the families not listed in the censuses for those or other villages nearby?

A centenarian descendant of the only surviving Georgas family from the village of Karavas (in the neighborhood of Diakopoulianika) relayed to us the following lore concerning the family's fate: the family originated from a place called Georgadika (the location of which is unknown to them), and they were quite prosperous. At a certain time, the people from Georgadika were accused of stealing large amounts of olive oil that belonged to the nearby monastery of Osios Theodoros. In response, the bishop invited the culprit(s) to come forward and return the stolen oil with no reprimand. As no one came forward, the bishop excommunicated the entire village. This eventually resulted in the inhabitants being cursed with a plague; some of them died, and the rest fled to avoid the same fate, thus abandoning the village. According to the legend, only one of the branches of the Georgas family survived and ended up in the Karavas area.[16]

Obviously, we cannot validate the Georgas family legend in any reasonable way, but its attempt to offer an explanation for the family's appearance in a new and different location is quite suggestive of a "radical" population movement and relocation from one part of the island to another. This correlates closely with the evidence we have for the "absence" encountered in the documentary sources, even though the causes for this are as of yet unknown (unless one believes the excommunication and plague story). Furthermore, the archaeological evidence (in the form of the surviving buildings described earlier along with the scattered artifacts found within and around them) and the census records suggest a complex series of phenomena that we cannot simply view as abandonment. The evidence for a change of function(s), at least from settlement to seasonal habitation and agricultural exploitation, is certainly worth considering. In fact, the complexity of population movements as encountered in the census records (at least for Georgadika), combined with important

---

[16] In considering the above legend, it is quite ironic that according to the 1844 census the family in question (in Karavas) included a priest and his wife! Even more fascinating is that the priest, Panayiotis Georgas (35 years old), was the son of another priest, the deceased Ioannis Georgas. The family appeared for the first time in the census records for Karavas in 1844, but it was not listed in the last surviving census for Georgadika in 1825. At that time, Panayiotis would have been 19 years old, but neither he nor his parents (Ioannis and Kerana) were listed in the Georgadika parish or in any other of the parishes. Is it possible that the family was away from Kythera and not residing on the island at that time?

information from the notarial and parish records, as well as the rapidly fading oral traditions of the area, make it an exciting and most fascinating topic for further archaeological and other investigations. One of the future goals of the APKAS project is to carry out a systematic archaeological survey of the Georgadika settlement and its immediate vicinity, including the church of Ayia Triada, as well as a detailed architectural survey of the buildings, which will provide a better understanding of the settlement and its relationship to the region at large.

Conclusion

Our paper focused on two different, yet closely connected, examples of abandoned settlements on the island of Kythera. While Ayios Dimitrios represents a historically documented, catastrophic destruction of an urban establishment from a calculated and targeted external invasion, the small and insignificant rural settlement at Georgadika presents us with a challenging set of local responses to broader island-wide (and perhaps regional and beyond) socioeconomic phenomena for examining the complexities of abandonment as a process of adaptation, transformation, and resilience. Thus, these two separate case studies should be analyzed together in terms of their connection to a broader system of cascading feedbacks that reflect the collapse of the centuries-long feudal organization of Kythera's economy and the decline in its "imperial" (Venetian) administration.

The destruction of Ayios Dimitrios in 1537 did not mark an end, but rather the beginning of a "new order of things"—not just for the northern part of Kythera, but for the whole island. The defensive characteristics of the city were obviously adequate in the early years after its founding (presumably in the twelfth century), but its walls were not equipped to withstand the Ottomans' cannons and gunpowder. From a military viewpoint, Ayios Dimitrios was no longer viable. The fact that the city's defenses had not been reconfigured in the event of an imminent attack with the latest in military siege warfare shows a lack of interest (or resources) on the part of the island's administration to invest in its northern defenses. The failure to defend Ayios Dimitrios can only be symptomatic of the weakness of the Venetian Republic to respond to the military threats to its possessions in the eastern Mediterranean and the beginning of the decline of its influence in the region.

After the city's destruction, and as the focus of the island's defenses and military presence shifted to the west and south, the Venetians made no attempts to refurbish Ayios Dimitrios' fortifications, nor to provide adequate defenses in the north and east. However, instead of abandoning the region, a reorganization of the countryside in terms of land ownership opened up tremendous new opportunities for private freeholders who were brave enough to risk investing in a part of the island that was largely defenseless against pirate and other raids. As the now-weakened aristocrats residing in the south found themselves unable to hold onto their northern possessions after many of the peasants working the land were either taken into slavery or fled the region because of insecurity, an opportunity arose for local and immigrant farmers to become landowners themselves.

In fact, it was not the first time that Kythera's nobility was confronted with issues regarding land productivity and labor. The island never boasted a large population, and its environment was not favorable to wheat cultivation, which was the main focus of production for the Venetians. The landscape, although intensively transformed for wheat cultivation from the fourteenth century onwards (i.e. with the arrival of the Venetians), it was never easy to manage, and labor intensity always outnumbered productivity. This is a classic example of the Venetian administration imposing an economic system based on its imperial ideology onto a landscape ill-suited to provide the revenue it needed to support its naval capacity. Furthermore, the peculiar political system that developed on the island saw the influential Venetian family of the Venier (which had close ties to Crete) take control of the island's agricultural economy, while the Venetian Republic was in charge of all military and mercantile activity (Leontsinis 1987:68–71). The peasants who worked both the state-owned and Venier lands were largely serfs (*paroikoi*), and only a few were independent small farmers. As time went on, a growing gap between the nobility of the island and the peasants led to tension, which the Venetian administrators were forced to mediate and contain. The destruction of Ayios Dimitrios in 1537 along with the continuous threat of pirate raids that afflicted the countryside finally forced the Venetian state and the reluctant Venier feudal lords to emancipate the serfs (Leontsinis 1987:72).

Between the sixteenth and nineteenth centuries, various attempts were made by the Venetian state and the Venier family to increase agricultural production, including a policy of inviting immigrant farmers from abroad (especially Greeks from the Ottoman-held provinces of the mainland and the Aegean) and demanding the return of farmers who had fled the island by threatening to confiscate the lands they left behind (Leontsinis 1987:75–84). In addition, the authorities by now recognized that the specialized production of wheat was not a viable policy; farmers were now encouraged to focus on cash crops, which led to a transformation of land use practices, including intensive terracing for olive cultivation and stone-constructed fencing of individual properties. As a result of these policies, the population of Kythera saw resurgence, and between 1545 and 1760 it rose from 1,850 to 6,000. Also, because of land reforms and redistribution, the amount of private land ownership increased, while state-owned land significantly diminished (Leontsinis 1987:92–93).

This is the backdrop against which the settlement pattern encountered in our investigations of the north part of Kythera developed. While it is uncertain as to when exactly small, rural settlements like Georgadika were established, we can hypothesize that their existence reflects the adaptation of revolutionary agrarian policies that transformed the physical landscape and its use. These polices also paved the way for a new social order that was dominated by private freeholders in charge of their own destinies, who most likely bypassed the authority of the feudal lords by meeting their tax obligations directly to the Venetian state. Thus, families like the Griscoti, Cumuli, and Georgà—obviously with adequate means to acquire their own lands—established their individual manor houses and estates in the area of Georgadika and their own parish affiliated with the Ayia Triada church, while also maintaining close kinship ties with other established settlements, such as Pitsinades, Dokana, and Logothetianika.

The transition from a predominantly feudal system of large estates to freehold ownership by the peasant population marked an important milestone in Kythera's history. While the agrarian reforms certainly impacted the northern part of the island, they must have had limited impact in the south, where the nobles still held onto large estates that were now most likely worked by free peasants whose plight was probably no better than that of serfs. Through a system of land rental, these peasants had to pay their share of taxes to both the nobles and the Venetian state, setting them up for perpetual debt and an inability to rise independently. Thus, a unique socioeconomic pattern developed, dividing the island's population between the south (characterized by large estates owned by nobles) and the north (with its small freeholder estates). The continuous influx of immigrants to the north over the next couple of centuries saw the increase of more freehold farmers, but also an emerging class of merchants and tradespeople, making Potamos a populous and thriving commercial center, as well as a hotbed of progressive and often revolutionary political ideologies (Leontsinis 1987).

After the demise of Venetian rule in the eighteenth century and several successions of control of the island by other great powers, including the French and the British, Kythera finally united with Greece in 1864. During this time, very little had changed for the Kytherian farmer, whose continuous plight to overcome poor yields led to a perpetual state of debt to pay taxes and make ends meet. The French, soon after their arrival in 1797, attempted to take away the rights of the nobles; meanwhile, the nobles still continued their oppressive treatment of the local population, and with the support of the British, they were reinstated as the main economic and political authority on the island until its unification with Greece.

The authorities' reluctance to get rid of an adapted, but now outdated, feudal system—despite the fact that feudalism was by now aborted in most parts of western Europe—was detrimental for the island. As sea travel became safer, many of the local farmers found opportunities abroad to supplement their meager income from farming. Thus, out-migration, as witnessed in the parish records at Georgadika, became the norm for many of the young and able male family members. Like many other similar settlements, Georgadika saw fluctuations in its male population, with the evidence suggesting that many of the farming responsibilities (and the household economy in general) were transferred to the hands of the women who were left behind (Hionidou 2011:223). While the added responsibilities were certainly burdensome, one can imagine the empowerment and certain level of independence of these women in terms of economic and social decision-making. Seasonal migration to nearby overseas destinations on the mainland and other islands—and as far as Egypt and Smyrna in Asia Minor—was common throughout the nineteenth century, and this mobility to and from the island was rather fluid, with people returning back to their homes once the season's labor was over. Usually the workers were involved in unskilled physical labor mainly as farm hands, but the same mobility pattern was also followed by sea and land merchants, tradespeople, fishermen, and seamen (Aslani 2018). During the early to mid twentieth century (and especially up to the period immediately after World War II), the pattern changed to that of more systematic and mass migration to destinations that offered more permanent employment opportunities, like Athens and Piraeus, and, more significantly, to distant continents such as the Americas and Australia. Although the settlement at Georgadika may have already been deserted by then, given that we lack any population data from 1825 onwards, the impact of the twentieth-century mass migrations on the immediate region and the surrounding settlements is quite well documented (Bottomley 1984; Diakopoulos 2003; Hionidou 2015).

With the advent of time, and as circumstances demanded, families either dispersed, relocated (as in the case of the Georgas family), or vanished with no descendants to carry on with farming the family lands, leading to the settlements' eventual abandonment in terms of habitation and to their transformation in terms of land use (in this case, as a grazing ground for cows). Thus, the processes leading to the establishment, development, and eventual abandonment of settlements such as Georgadika are intricately connected with broader temporal and complex socioeconomic and political phenomena, including the gradual rise and collapse of institutions and their ideologies and practices. Similar studies of other "abandoned" settlements in the APKAS survey area, as well as in other parts of the island, will hopefully allow for further inter- and intrasettlement comparisons and analyses that could illuminate the processes involved in the development and gradual abandonment of Kythera's complex settlement system during the medieval and post-medieval periods up to the present day.

Acknowledgments. The authors would like to thank Jon Frey for his contribution of photographs and drawings of the church of Ayia Triada and House Complex 1, John Fardoulis (Mobility Robotics) for providing drone-derived documentation of the site of Georgadika, and Matthew Crum for the maps used in this paper. We are also grateful to APKAS co-director Stavros Paspalas and to all the APKAS participants who helped us with collecting information, especially Richard Macneill, Anthoulla Vassiliades, and Matthew Baumann.

References Cited

Aslani, Karolina
    2018   *Τα Αγγλικά Διαβατήρια που εκδόθηκαν στα Κύθηρα 1814–1864* [*The British Passports Issued on Kythera 1814–1864*]. Kytherian World Heritage Fund, Chora, Kythera.

Bennet, John, and Deborah Harlan
    2015   Academic Bilingualism: Combining Textual and Material Data to Understand the Post-Medieval Mediterranean. In *Medieval and Post-Medieval Ceramics in the Eastern Mediterranean – Fact and Fiction. Proceedings of the First International Conference on Byzantine and Ottoman Archaeology, Amsterdam, 21–23, October 2011*, edited by Joanita Vroom, pp. 17–46. Brepols, Turnhout.

Bottomley, Gillian
    1984   The Export of People: Emigration from and Return Migration to Greece. Centre for Multicultural Studies Occasional Papers 1, University of Wollongong. Research Online. https://ro.uow.edu.au/cmsocpapers/2, accessed October 17, 2020.

Bradford, Ernle
    1968   *The Sultan's Admiral: The Life of Barbarossa*. Hodder & Stoughton, New York.

Butzer, Karl W., and Georgina H. Endfield
    2012   Critical Perspectives on Historical Collapse. *Proceedings of the National Academy of Science of the United States of America* 109(10):3628–3631. https://doi.org/10.1073/pnas.1114772109

Cameron, Catherine M., and Steve A. Tomka (editors)
    1993   *Abandonment of Settlements and Regions: Ethnoarchaeological and Archaeological Approaches*. Cambridge University Press, Cambridge.

Caraher, William R.
    2008   Constructing Memories: Hagiography, Church Architecture, and the Religious Landscape of Middle Byzantine Greece: The Case of St. Theodore of Kythera. In *Archaeology and History in Roman, Medieval and Post-Medieval Greece: Studies on Method and Meaning in Honor of Timothy E. Gregory*, edited by William R. Caraher, Linda Jones Hall, and R. Scott Moore, pp. 267–280. Ashgate, Burlington, Vermont.

Charou-Koronaiou, Eleni
2018   Το Προσκύνημα των Μυρτιδίων [The Pilgrimage of the Myrtidia]. 2nd ed. Kythera Association of Athens, Athens.

Cherry, John F., Jack L. Davis, and Eleni Mantzourani (editors)
1991   Landscape Archaeology as Long-Term History: Northern Keos in the Cycladic Islands from Earliest Settlement until Modern Times. University of California Los Angeles Institute of Archaeology, Los Angeles.

Coroneos, Cosmos, Lita Diacopoulos, Timothy E. Gregory, Ian Johnson, Jay Noller, Stavros A. Paspalas, and Andrew Wilson
2002   The Australian Paliochora-Kythera Archaeological Survey: Field Seasons 1999–2000. *Mediterranean Archaeology* 15:126–143.

Diakopoulos, Lita
2003   Επίδραση της βιομηχανοποίησης και της μετανάστευσης στον παραδοσιακό τρόπο ζωής: μια αρχαιολογική μελέτη του 20ου αιώνα στα Κύθηρα [The Impact of Industrialisation and Migration on Traditional Lifeways: An Archaeological Investigation of 20th-Century Kythera]. In Α΄ διεθνές συνέδριο Κυθηραϊκών μελετών, 20–24 Σεπτεμβρίου 2000. Κύθηρα: Μύθος και πραγματικότητα. *[First International Conference of Kytherian Studies, 20–24 September 2000. Kythera: Myth and Reality]*, Vol. 3, edited by Athanasia Glykofryde-Leontsini, Georgios Leontsinis, and Nikos Glytsos, pp. 121–136. Open University of the Municipality of Kythera, Chora.

Gregory, Timothy E.
2006   Narrative of the Byzantine Landscape. In *Byzantine Narrative: Papers in Honour of Roger Scott*, edited by John Burke, Ursula Betka, Penelope Buckley, Kathleen Hay, Roger Scott, and Andrew Stephenson, pp. 481–496. Byzantina Australiensia 16. Brill, Melbourne.
2008   Sklere: A Place of Refuge after the Ottoman Sack of Kythera in 1537. *Deltion of the Christian Archaeological Society* 29(4):259–268. https://doi.org/10.12681/dchae.625

2009 Landscape and Cultural History in Medieval and Early Modern Kythera. In *Η' διεθνές Πανιόνιο συνέδριο, Κύθηρα, 21–25 Μαΐου 2006 [Proceedings of the 8th International Panionian Conference, Kythera, 21–25 May 2006]*, Vol. 1, pp. 102–124. Society of Kytherian Studies, Athens.

Gregory, Timothy E., and Lita Tzortzopoulou-Gregory
2015 *The Archaeology of Kythera*. Meditarch, Sydney.

Hionidou, Violetta
2011 Independence and Inter-Dependence: Household Formation Patterns in Eighteenth Century Kythera, Greece. In *The History of the Family* 16(3):217–234. https://doi.org/10.1016/j.hisfam.2011.03.005
2015 From Modernity to Tradition: Households on Kythera in the Early Nineteenth Century. In *The History of Families and Households: Comparative European Dimensions*, edited by Silvia Sovič, Pat Thane, and Pier Paolo Viazzo, pp. 47–68. Brill, Leiden.

Ince, Gillian E., Theodore Koukoulis, and David Smyth
1987 Paliochora: Survey of a Byzantine City on the Island of Kythera. Preliminary Report. *The Annual of the British School at Athens* 82:95–106. https://doi.org/10.1017/S0068245400020347

Ince, Gillian E., and Andrew Ballantyne
2007 *Paliochora on Kythera: Survey and Interpretation. Studies in Medieval and Post-Medieval Settlements*. BAR International Series S1704. Archaeopress, Oxford.

Ince, Gillian E., Theodore Koukoulis, Andrew N. Ballantyne, and David Smyth
1989 Paliochora: Survey of a Byzantine City on the Island of Kythera. Second Report. *The Annual of the British School at Athens* 84:407–416. https://doi.org/10.1017/S0068245400021079

Jameson, Michael H., Curtis N. Runnels, and Tjeerd H. van Andel
1994 *A Greek Countryside: The Southern Argolid from Prehistory to the Present Day*. Stanford University Press, Stanford.

Kalligeros, Emmanuel
2006 Κυθηραϊκά Επώνυμα. Ιστορική, γεωγραφική και γλωσσική προσέγγιση [Kytherian Surnames. A Historical, Geographical and Linguistic Approach]. 2nd ed. Society of Kytherian Studies, Athens.
2011 Κυθηραϊκά Τοπωνύμια. Ιστορική γεωγραφία των Κυθήρων [Kytherian Toponyms. A Historical Geography of Kythera]. Society of Kytherian Studies, Athens.

Knapp, A. Bernard, and Nathan Meyer
2020 Cyprus: Bronze Age Demise, Iron Age Regeneration. In *Collapse and Transformation: The Late Bronze Age to Early Iron Age in the Aegean*, edited by Guy D. Middleton, pp. 237–246. Oxbow Books, Oxford.

Leontsinis, George
1987 *The Island of Kythera: A Social History (1700–1863)*. National and Kapodistrian University of Athens, Athens.

McLeman, Robert A.
2011 Settlement Abandonment in the Context of Global Environmental Change. *Global Environment Change* 21:S108–S120. https://doi.org/10.1016/j.gloenvcha.2011.08.004

Metallinos, Georgios
2003 Θεολογικές κριτικές προσβάσεις στην αγιολογική ταυτότητα των Κυθήρων [Theological Critical Approaches to the Hagiological Identity of Kythera]. In Α΄ διεθνές συνέδριο Κυθηραϊκών μελετών, 20-24 Σεπτεμβρίου 2000. Κύθηρα: Μύθος και πραγματικότητα. [*First International Conference of Kytherian Studies, 20–24 September 2000. Kythera: Myth and Reality*], Vol. 4, edited by Athanasia Glykofrydi, Georgios Leontsinis, and Eleni Leontsini, pp. 257–270. Open University of the Municipality of Kythera, Chora.

Paspalas, Stavros A.
2008 The Panagia Myrtidiotissa: The Changing Image of a Kytherian Icon. In *Archaeology and History in Roman, Medieval and Post-Medieval Greece: Studies on Method and Meaning in Honor of Timothy E. Gregory*, edited by William R. Caraher, Linda Jones Hall, and R. Scott Moore, pp. 197–225. Ashgate, Burlington, Vermont.

Patramani, Maria G., Antonia K. Marmareli, and Emmanuel G. Drakakis
 1997   Απογραφές Πληθυσμού Κυθήρων 18ος αιώνας *[18th-Century Population Censuses of Kythera]*. 3 vols. Society of Kytherian Studies, Athens.

Renfrew, Colin
 1972   *The Emergence of Civilisation: The Cyclades and the Aegean in The Third Millennium BC*. Methuen, London.

Sanders, Guy D. R.
 1996   Two *Kastra* on Melos and their Relations in the Archipelago. In *The Archaeology of Medieval Greece*, edited by Peter Lock and Guy D. R. Sanders, pp. 147–177. Oxbow Monographs 59. Oxbow Books, Oxford.

Sathas, Konstantinos N.
 1885   L'antique memorie dell'isola di Cerigo [The Ancient Memories of the Island of Kythera]. In *Documents inédits relatifs a de l'histoire de la Grèce au Moyen Âge [Unpublished Documents Relating to the History of Greece in the Middle Ages]*, Vol. 6, pp. 299–311. Maisonneuve, Paris.

Tzortzopoulou-Gregory, Lita, and Timothy E. Gregory
 2017   The Karavas Water Project: An Archaeological and Environmental Study of Interaction and Community in Northern Kythera. In *Journal of Greek Archaeology* 2:343–376.

Chapter Four
The Stone-Built *Palaiomaniatika* of the Mani Peninsula, Greece

Rebecca M. Seifried

The Mani peninsula, the southernmost projection of the Peloponnese in Greece, is the location of over 170 settlements with preserved stone-built architecture from the premodern era (**Figure 1**). These remarkable places are known locally as *palaiomaniatika* (old Maniat settlements) or *palaiochores* (old villages). The settlements are small, comprising between 10 and 50 houses, and they were built and occupied by local residents of the Mani peninsula. The vernacular architecture of the houses is relatively homogenous, constituting the typical one- or two-story rectangular layout (i.e. the "longhouse") that is common throughout rural landscapes in the Peloponnese (Sigalos 2004a, 2004b:66; Stedman 1996:185–186). Roughly half of the settlements are still inhabited today, with the same houses that were built centuries ago serving as the foundations for modern homes and newer buildings constructed in the spaces between to form the nucleated settlement layout that is typical of modern Greek villages. The others are now abandoned, the ruined houses enshrouded by wild olives and shoulder-high thorny shrubs. These deserted villages of Mani are some of the most numerous in Greece, rivaled only by those in the neighboring peninsula of Messenia (Antoniadis-Bibicou 1965:404).

Previous studies suggested that these settlements were established as early as the eighth century AD and at the latest by the thirteenth century (Moschos and Moschou 1982:263; Moschou 2004:33–34), a span of time broadly defined as the Middle Byzantine period, when the power of the Byzantine Empire was at its zenith. Despite the fact that Ottoman rule in the region began in 1463, a substantial change in settlement layout and

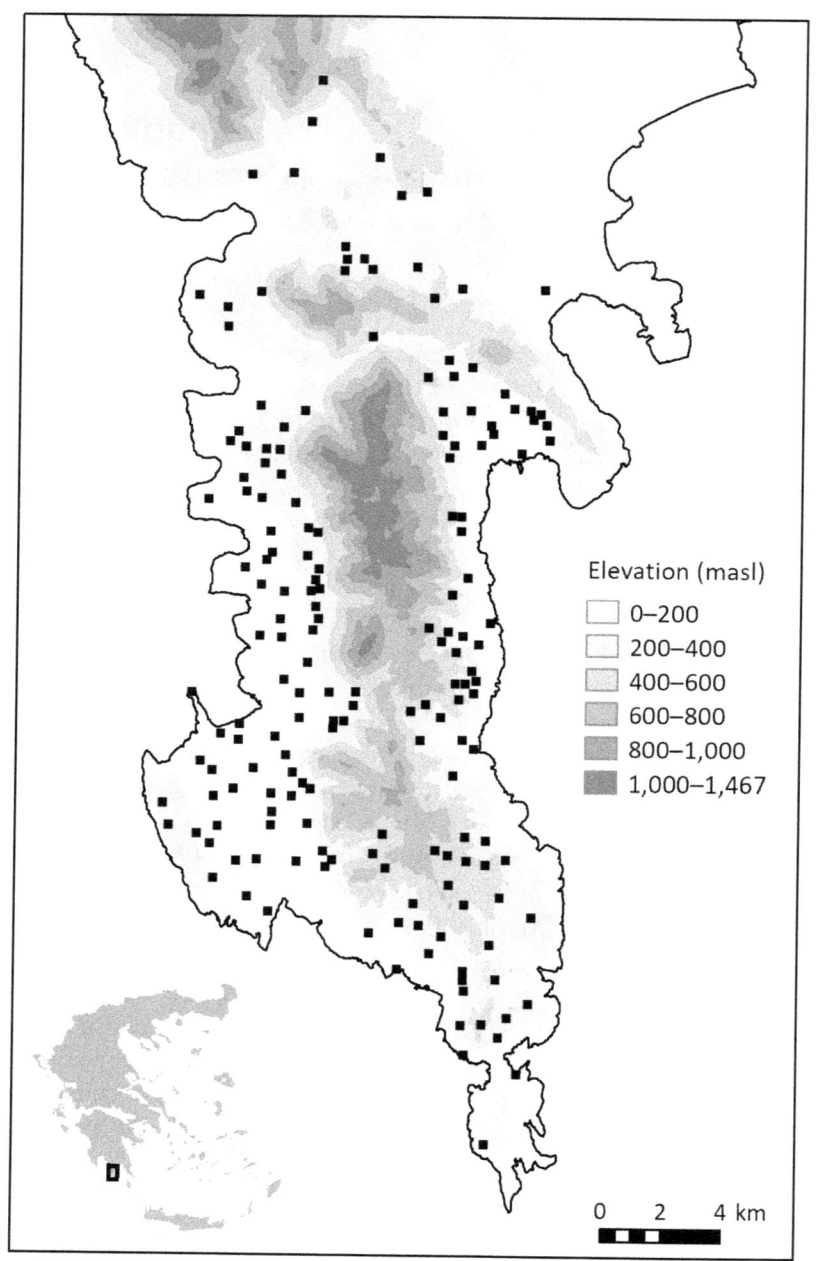

Figure 1. Map of the southern Mani peninsula, Greece, indicating the locations of the *palaiomaniatika* settlements.

architecture is believed to have occurred only after the late seventeenth century (Saïtas 2004:54).[1] New information from historical Ottoman tax registers lends weight to the claim that many of the *palaiomaniatika* continued to be occupied during the period of Ottoman rule. Of all the *palaiomaniatika* known to researchers, one-third can be matched with toponyms from historical records and roughly half are still occupied today, confirming that the vernacular architectural style of the Byzantine period continued well into what is termed, in Greece at least, the "post-medieval period."

However, there are serious limits to what we can say about the *palaiomaniatika* without further evidence from archaeological excavations. As far as I know, no systematic excavations of the *palaiomaniatika* have ever been published. With almost all of the available information coming from art historical and architectural studies, it is impossible to refine the chronology of these settlements and their architecture much further than the currently accepted range of the eighth to seventeenth centuries. This vagueness of chronology hamstrings any efforts to tease apart the process of abandonment in Mani and to understand how it may have played out in the lives of its residents. More broadly, the lack of excavations means that we cannot explore the kinds of research questions about microscale social organization that are possible through the lens of a well-theorized household archaeology (Souvatzi 2008, 2014).

The inattention to Mani's Byzantine and post-Byzantine domestic heritage is part of the broader story of archaeological research in Greece. Historically, the field of Greek Byzantine archaeology has focused exclusively on churches and the art they contain. Over the past 20 years, many scholars have called for a development of a historical archaeology of Greece that focuses on domestic material culture. Writing about the medieval houses documented by the Morea Project, Kostis Kourelis (2003:173) posited that that the Peloponnesian house type—to which the *palaiomaniatika* houses generally belong—may be part of a widespread

---

[1] The settlements were occupied exclusively by local residents of the Mani peninsula. During the Ottoman period in Mani (1463–1821), Ottoman occupation seems to have been restricted to the fortresses of Passava. Historical sources refer to Passava as a garrisoned fort up until the seventeenth century, when it was captured and destroyed by Venetian forces. According to Komis (2005:319–332), when the Ottomans reconquered the region in 1715, they rebuilt the fortress and an Ottoman village called Tourkovrisi was established nearby with about 700–800 families. Supposedly, the Maniates staged a revolt in 1780, seized the castle, and killed the people living in Tourkovrisi. To my knowledge, this is the only reference to an Ottoman village in the study region.

building tradition, but he cautioned that "conclusions must be reserved for a time when comparative material is published from a sufficient number of Greek medieval villages." In his commentary on a special issue that (like this volume) stemmed from a symposium of the Medieval and Post-Medieval Archaeology interest group of the Archaeological Institute of America, Tim Gregory (2010:303) called for more archaeological work to be carried out in Byzantine and post-Byzantine phases and for scholars of these eras to look "more closely at the methods and approaches developed by historical archaeologists elsewhere in the world." As recently as 2016, Effie Athanassopoulos (2016:38) wrote that the "archaeology of everyday life based on excavations of settlements, agricultural or industrial installations, and marketplaces is still in its infancy." Despite these calls to action, few rural settlements have been targeted by the kind of archaeological scrutiny that is necessary for producing valuable comparative data.

Southern Greece, in particular, has been the subject of many archaeological surveys since the Minnesota Messenia Expedition was launched in the 1960s (for an overview of these projects, see Kourelis 2019:167–174). However, few of the surveys have resulted in systematic excavations of rural houses from the medieval and post-medieval phases. Published examples (**Figure 2**) include a post-Byzantine house at Nichoria, Messenia (McDonald et al. 1983:427–431), a thirteenth to fifteenth-century house at Lavda, Eleia (Goester and van der Vrie 1998), two fourteenth-century houses within the fortified village at Panakton, Attica (Houses I and IV; Gerstel et al. 2003:155–165, 169–174), and a house within the fortified village at Ayios Vasileios, Corinthia, that may date to between the fourteenth and seventeenth centuries (Gregory 2013:292–301). Similar houses were recorded by the Morea Project in the provinces of Achaia and Eleia in the northern Peloponnese (Kourelis 2003, 2005). Much more common are studies of elite houses or houses in urban centers, which generally incorporate more elaborate architectural forms and designs (e.g. Bouras 1983; Cerasi 1998; Sigalos 2004b; Vionis 2009). Even the fascinating case study of Cappadocia is not readily comparable, as the rock-cut houses there "were clearly not peasant homes" and typically comprised multi-room structures frequently organized around a courtyard (Ousterhout 2005:182 and relevant critique in Kourelis 2007; Ousterhout 2017).

This paper adds another voice to the call for a household archaeology of abandoned rural villages in Greece, which have received scant scholarly attention in comparison to both their counterparts elsewhere in the eastern Mediterranean or to their older (prehistoric) and wealthier (urban) neighbors within Greece. In the first part, I lay out the typical characteristics

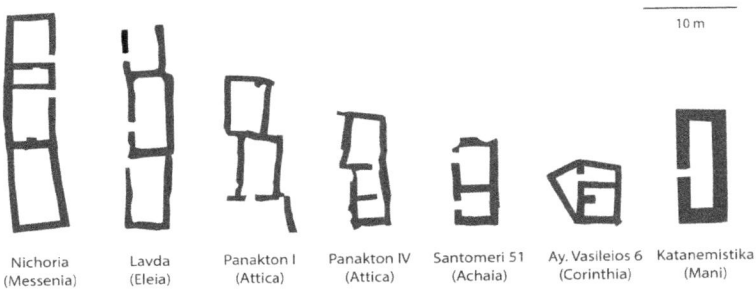

Figure 2. Plans from houses at Nichoria (after **McDonald** et al. 1983:Figure 14.1), Lavda (after Goester and van der Vrie 1998:Figure 7), Panakton (after **Gerstel** et al. 2003:Figures 6 and 20), Santomeri (after **Kourelis** 2003:Figure 284), and Ayios Vasileios (after Gregory 2013:Figure 15), compared with a typical *palaiomaniatiko* house plan from Mani (after Saïtas 1990:Figure 19).

of the houses and settlements of the *palaiomaniatika*, and in the second, I discuss different ideas about when they were established and abandoned. These sections rely on published research from the fields of art history and architecture as well as data from my own field research. The nature of this research means that the discussion is descriptive in nature and provides little real insight into the social functioning of the *palaiomaniatika* or the factors that led many of them being abandoned. Yet, the purpose of the review is to summarize the current state of knowledge and to underscore what exactly we still do not know about these places. In the third part, I present a case study of the abandoned *palaiomaniatiko* village of Koulouvades, showing how targeted archaeological sampling alongside analysis of historical sources can help refine the chronology of these settlements and open avenues for asking meaningful research questions. In the final part, I make a case for why household excavations must be carried out at sites like these—not only in Mani, but also in other rural landscapes across the eastern Mediterranean.

Typical Characteristics of the *Palaiomaniatika*

The term *palaiomaniatika* was introduced by Nikolaos Drandakis and colleagues during their research in the 1970s (e.g. Drandakis et al. 1980:158–159) and featured as the title of Takis Moschos and Leda Moschou's (1981, 1982) articles on the subject. More commonly the settlements are referred to as *palaiochores* (old villages), and the various features within them are known colloquially as *kolospites* or *kolospitakia* (houses), *kolopyrgoi* (towers), and *koloyisternes* (cisterns; Saïtas 1990:Note 39). Documentation of the architecture and layout of these stone-built settlements has been carried out by several research teams over the past few decades (Argyriades et al. 1972; Etzeoglou 1982, 1988; Moschos and Moschou 1981, 1982; Moschou 1982; Moutsopoulos and Dimitrokallis 1976/1978, 1980; Pawlowski 2020). Maps showing the general locations of the settlements have appeared in publications by Moschos and Moschou (1981:Plates 1a-d) and Yanis Saïtas (2009a:Figure 6.1; see also Saïtas 1983a, 1983b, 2009b, 2011).

Supplementing this research is original field data collected in 2014–2016 for a study on the Byzantine and post-Byzantine settlements in Mani (Seifried 2016). My project sought to document all the settlements with standing architecture in the southern half of the peninsula—an area of about 350 km²—using a combination of field visits and aerial imagery analysis to record the built structures, including houses, towers, mills, churches, cisterns, and field walls. A total of 215 permanent settlements were recorded. Based on the previous typological work done on the region's vernacular architecture, it was determined that 177 of the settlements contained evidence of occupation during the Byzantine and/or early Ottoman phases. Most of these appear on the earlier maps, but some were previously unknown to the scholarly community.

Of the *palaiomaniatika* settlements documented by my project, half (88) were still occupied. The continued use and modification of the buildings and pathways in these places made it difficult to detect the earliest phases of occupation: older buildings were frequently repointed, sometimes obscuring the stones altogether, or they were modified to create elaborate multi-room residential complexes or tower-houses (Figure 3). Many of the stone pathways that were built to expedite foot and animal traffic (*kalderimia*) have been paved over to allow for automotive travel. At times, the built features were totally destroyed to make way for a new road. But despite all this, the advantage of studying an occupied settlement is that many of the oldest buildings and paths are in excellent states of preservation due to their continued use over many centuries. Their occupants have maintained them, repairing fallen walls and preventing the kind of decay and collapse that has affect abandoned structures.

Abandoned settlements present different challenges for recording. Since the 1930s, Mani has suffered dramatic population loss as people emigrated out of the region and the economic opportunities in the Greek countryside dwindled (Allen 1976; Wagstaff 2000:Figure 2). A large Maniat community was established in Piraeus in the twentieth century as

Figure 3. A *palaiomaniatika* house in Pyrgos Dirou that has been renovated and expanded.

Figure 4. Typical state of preservation of structures in an abandoned *palaiomaniatiko*: (a) house and (b) cistern (Koulouvades).

younger generations migrated to Athens in search of work. Today, the population of a typical Maniat village may increase tenfold during the month of August, when families from all over the globe return to their ancestral village for the summer holiday, but many of the villages are almost entirely unoccupied during the majority of the year. This large-scale population movement means that agricultural activities that once kept the fields clear—including olive and grain cultivation and, especially, animal husbandry—have almost entirely ceased in most parts of Mani. As a result, the vegetation within and around the abandoned *palaiomaniatika* has been allowed to grow unchecked (**Figure 4**). Furthermore, because these buildings have been allowed to collapse and dismantle themselves naturally, the massive amounts of wall fall often obscure the structures and interior faces of the walls. In areas with several closely spaced houses, it can be very difficult to detect the underlying house plans. Still, from the perspective of an archaeologist, the benefit of abandonment is that it provides a glimpse into an older version of the settlement's layout—certainly not the original form, but one that predates the modern era of cement construction and paved roads.

House Form

Over 600 individual houses were identified in the *palaiomaniatika* during the course of my fieldwork; 406 were able to be measured in some way. Additional built structures were also recorded, most notably churches, cisterns, and defensive installations such as watch huts and towers. All of these features share in the same vernacular architectural style that characterizes the houses. The churches have been dealt with in great detail over the past century, beginning with Ramsay Traquair's (1908/1909) and Arthur H.S. Megaw's (1932/1933) early studies and continuing with Nikolaos Drandakis and a diverse group of Byzantine scholars (e.g. Drandakis 2009; Etzeoglou 1977; Gkioles 1996; Konstantinidi 1998; Menenakou 2007; Mexia 2008/2009). Recent syntheses of this work have looked at the spatial relationships between the churches and the settlements (Seifried 2021; Seifried and Kalaycı 2019). The cisterns and other aspects of the hydraulic landscape have been published separately (Seifried 2020a). The watch huts and towers comprise a small sample size (16 in total) and are discussed in the context of settlement layout below.

There is one key way in which the houses in Mani differ from their rural counterparts elsewhere in the Peloponnese. In both the scholarly literature and in popular usage, the term "megalithic" (or even "cyclopean") has been used to describe their typical dry-stone construction. Saïtas (1990:19) reported the average block sizes of the quarried limestone as ranging from 30 cm to over 140 cm on each side. Using such large blocks naturally means the walls are extremely thick—sometimes exceeding 150 cm in width. By contrast, the walls of published comparanda measure 60–65 cm at Nichoria (McDonald et al. 1983:427), 70 cm in the northern Peloponnese (Kourelis 2005:124), and 75 cm at Panakton (Gerstel et al. 2003:156). The large dimensions of the building material and thickness of the walls in Mani made the houses extremely durable and contributed to their exceptional preservation—not only from the action of natural deterioration, but also from human modification and reuse of building material in new construction (see **Figure 2**).

As with other examples of medieval houses, the houses in Mani were built of locally quarried limestone, the most common geological type in the region.[2] They typically were built as standalone structures, oriented east–west if located on a flat plain, or perpendicular to the gradient if on a hillside. At times, additional structures were added to the first in an agglomerative pattern, either along the shorter wall to form a long chain of connected houses or along the longer wall. The latter was especially common on hillsides, when building along the same terrace was more expedient. Otherwise, the houses were unconnected from one another, and walls were rarely built to delineate external courtyards.

The doors were most commonly located on the southern aspect to protect against the northern winter wind (see Kourelis 2003:179) and to allow for maximal entry of light. Few if any windows were built into the walls. The doorways were small—Saïtas (1990:19) reported an average range of 80–110 cm wide and 90–150 cm high—and were topped by a single massive limestone lintel. Measurements taken during my study shows a range in lintel size from 107 to 195 cm in width and 16 to 61 cm in height and depth. In very rare cases, engraved designs were etched into the lintels, including one in the ruined settlement of Lakkos (near Tsopaka), which bears two roughly engraved crosses, and another in the settlement of Kouvouklia (near Glezou), which bears three elaborately carved crosses and two zoomorphic figures (**Figure 5**). This same house was featured in Haris Calligas' (1974:Figure 9) architectural study of the settlements in Mani.[3]

---

[2] There are a few micro-regions in Mani, especially in the south, where schist is the predominant geological type. Houses there are built with schist and, as a result, they do not preserve as well as their limestone-built counterparts.

[3] I thank Yanis Saïtas for pointing me to this reference.

Figure 5. Lintels above doors in *palaiomaniatika* houses: (a) typical entryway with lintel (Koulouvades); (b) lintel with engraved crosses and zoomorphic figures (Kouvouklia).

Figure 6. Two-storied houses with: (a) upper and lower doorways both preserved (Soulia); (b) internal ledges built to support a floor (Palaia Tserova).

Although very few houses are preserved beyond a partial ground floor, some evidently had two stories, with a low ground floor used for storage or as a space to keep animals, and a taller second story used as the main residential area (see Saïtas 1990:18; Sigalos 2004b:71–73; Stedman 1996:185). The floors were supported with beams—either of wood (Moschos and Moschou 1982:266) or more likely of stone (Saïtas 1990:19–20)—extending across the narrower width of the structure. The beams could be secured into niches in the walls, or they could simply rest upon a protruding ledge built into the walls. My research documented 36 houses with clear evidence of a second story. Several were so well preserved that they still retained an upper doorway, staggered so that the second-story entrance was not directly above that of the ground floor. The others had niches or ledges built into the walls to support the crossbeams (Figure 6). Finally, in a few rare cases, a small enclosed area was found in the ground floor, delineated by a transverse wall and coated with plaster, possibly for water storage (see Saïtas 1990:18).

Many more houses are now filled with rubble, a perplexing artifact of the postabandonment process (Figure 7). Moschos and Moschou (1982:264) suggested that the rubble fill was the result of years of gradual accumulation as farmers collected the stones from the surrounding fields and deposited them within the walls of abandoned houses. However, it is possible that such fill may also result from wall collapse, particularly if the upper walls were built with rubble that was held together with a simple earthen mortar. Wall collapse could very well have resulted in the pattern documented at so many *palaiomaniatika* settlements.

The ground floor of the houses was probably made of packed earth, as in the examples at Panakton and Nichoria (Gerstel et al. 2003:157; McDonald et al. 1983:427). The roofs were likely formed in a similar fashion to the dividing floor in two-story houses, supported by beams resting in niches or on ledges built into the walls; however, no roofs have been preserved to confirm this hypothesis. Because of the scarcity of timber in the region and the abundance of limestone, Saïtas suggested that these beams were made of stone and that the roof would have been completed with layers of in-filling stones, pebbles, and a mixture of beaten clay earth and manure. Wooden roofs would have been rare (Saïtas 1990:20; Figure 256a).

The external dimensions of the structures averaged 10.3 m in length (SD = 2.2 m, n = 202) and 4.7 m in width (SD = 0.5 m, n = 255; for data, see house_measurements.csv in Seifried 2020b). Internal dimensions averaged 8.4 m in length (SD = 2.3 m, n = 169) and 2.7 m in width

Figure 7. House filled with rubble (Pangia).

(SD = 0.5 m, n = 169). The internal measurements were difficult to assess directly due to the prevalence of rubble fill, so in some cases they were inferred based on the external dimensions and the width of an exposed wall. The average internal area was 22.4 m^2 (SD = 7.7 m^2, n = 169), which reflects contemporary cases from elsewhere in the Peloponnese, such as two rooms in House I (19.8 m^2 and 18.9 m^2) and the three-roomed House IV (26.9 m^2) at Panakton (Gerstel et al. 2003:156, 169). Compared to longhouses of the early modern and modern periods (see Pettegrew and Caraher, this volume), the *palaiomaniatika* were significantly smaller in terms of living area. This has important implications for the availability of workspace provided by the houses, lending support to the assumption that the area immediately outside the house was used as a workspace (Kourelis 2003:175).

The wide range in internal area—by my calculations, the smallest house measured 6.8 m^2 and the largest 44.8 m^2—led Saïtas (1990:17, Figure 13) to propose a three-part classification of small, medium, and large buildings. However, this typology seems to have little interpretive value at this stage, as we do not know exactly why the houses varied in size to such a great extent. It may very well be that the smallest houses were restricted in size because of geographical considerations, as all of those with areas less than 11 m^2 are located in hillside or hilltop settlements. At the other extreme, the largest houses may reflect a very slow expansion of house size over time, as all of the houses over 40 m^2 in area were recorded in diachronic settlements with early Ottoman phases. But in terms of their overall similarity of design and layout, the houses resemble those documented by the Morea Project, about which Kostis Kourelis (2003:175–176) drew comparisons with the "unitary" or "mixed house" of northern Europe, where undifferentiated activities and co-residence of humans and animals all took place within a single rectangular longhouse.

Settlement Layout

The *palaiomaniatika* were generally made up of 10–50 houses, along with other built features such as cisterns, enclosures, churches, and less frequently, defensive installations. Data gathered during fieldwork suggests that the settlements break naturally into three size categories: small (with approx. 5–20 houses), medium (30–50 houses), and large (60–70 houses), with most falling into the small or medium categories (**Figure 8**; for data, see house_counts.csv in Seifried 2020b).

Previous scholars have suggested that, as with their modern counterparts, the *palaiomaniatika* were occupied by kin groups: Moschou (2004:36) referred to them as "small population aggregates formed on the basis of patrilineal blood relations," which laid the foundation for the later settlement pattern that arose and continued into modern times. Saïtas (1990:16) suggested that "small neighboring hamlets frequently form[ed] broader groups—units of agricultural, livestock raising communities which exploit[ed] a small productive hinterland." At present it is difficult to know exactly how the inhabitants of neighboring settlements interacted with each other in the Byzantine and early Ottoman periods, with the exception of the important insights gained from painted dedicatory panels in two Byzantine churches in Kipoula and Polemitas (Drandakis 1980, 1982). The panels name individuals from multiple surrounding settlements who helped finance the churches' construction and decoration, thereby testifying to the pooling of resources between settlements in order to build public, ritual spaces. In turn, the churches may have acted as "integrative facilities" (see **Adler and Wilshusen 1990**) that could be used to reinforce and "enact" community membership (Mac Sweeney 2011; Yaeger 2000). Therefore, in at least two documented cases, neighboring villages may have cooperated in multi-settlement clusters at least in an ideological sphere, to some degree mirroring Saïtas' hypothesis that multiple settlements may have worked together to complete communal agricultural and pastoralist activities.

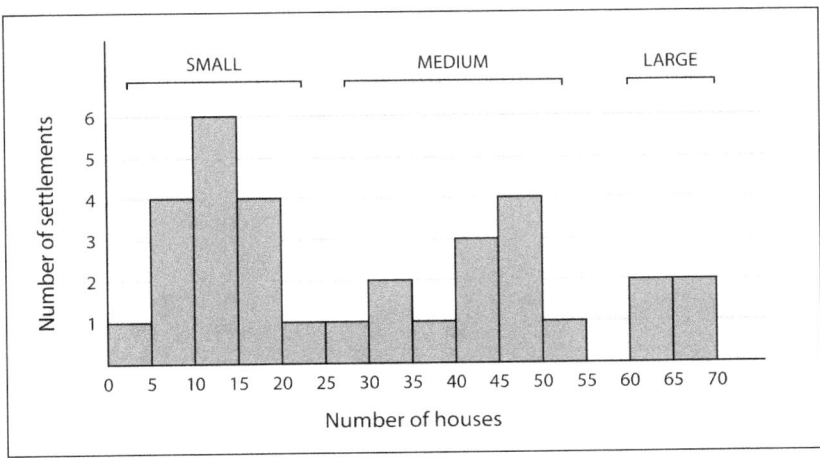

Figure 8. Number of houses recorded at the fully mapped settlements, showing possible clustering into small, medium, and large settlement size categories.

A settlement's size and layout depended to a large extent on its geographical location, with distinctions particularly noticeable between plains, hillsides, and hilltop locations. Plains settlements, which are mainly located in the flat areas along the western side of the peninsula, comprise a loose cluster of built features aligned to the same orientation and evenly dispersed throughout the site (**Figure 9**). In a few cases, the houses were built in a loose ring around a large central area, which was seemingly empty of built features and could have been used as communal garden plots or as a space for social activities. Cisterns were built throughout the site (with roughly one cistern for every two houses), but there were a few sites where the cisterns were built all together in a single part of the site. The plains settlements were generally undefended, but Saïtas (1990:16) noted that "heavy, dry stone fences" may have served basic defensive purposes around and throughout the sites. There is also at least one case—that of Kouvouklia (the same settlement in which the lintel with a zoomorphic engraving was found)—where a massive, nearly square, tower-like structure was preserved in the center of the site. The exterior of the structure measured 7.5 x 5.5 m, with its wall width ranging from 1.58 to 1.83 m. These dimensions suggest it was once taller and may have served a defensive purpose. Similar tower-like structures with "megalithic" foundations were recorded on the fringes of two other plains settlements: Charia and Ayia Varvara.

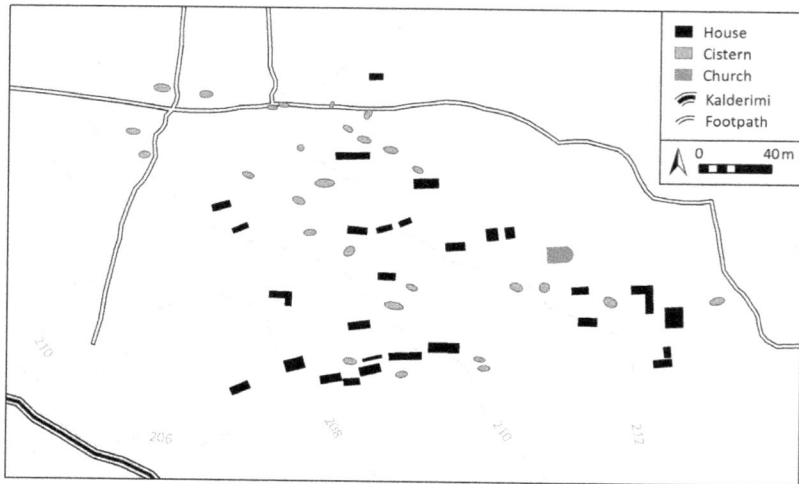

Figure 9. Plan of Koulouvades, showing a typical plains layout.

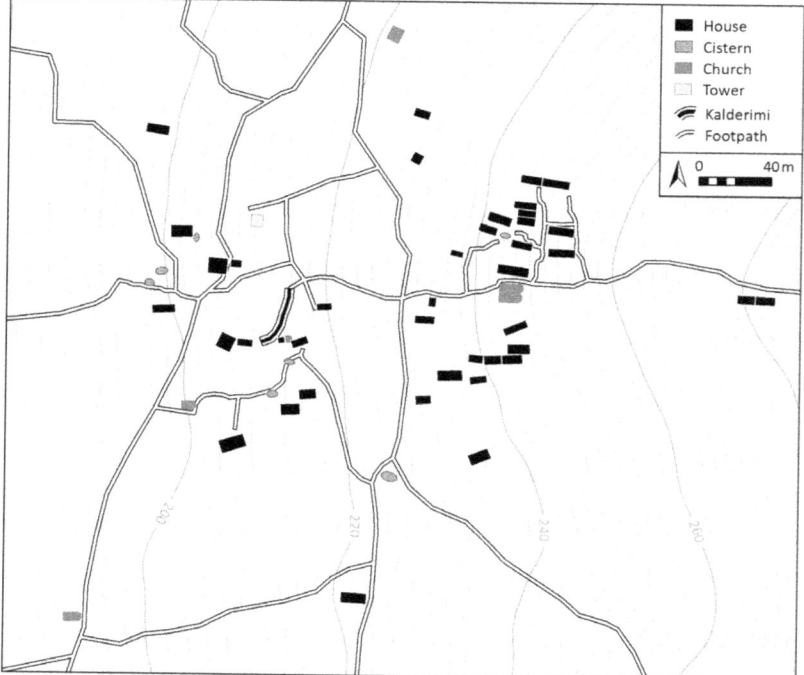

Figure 10. Plan of Briki, showing a typical hillside layout.

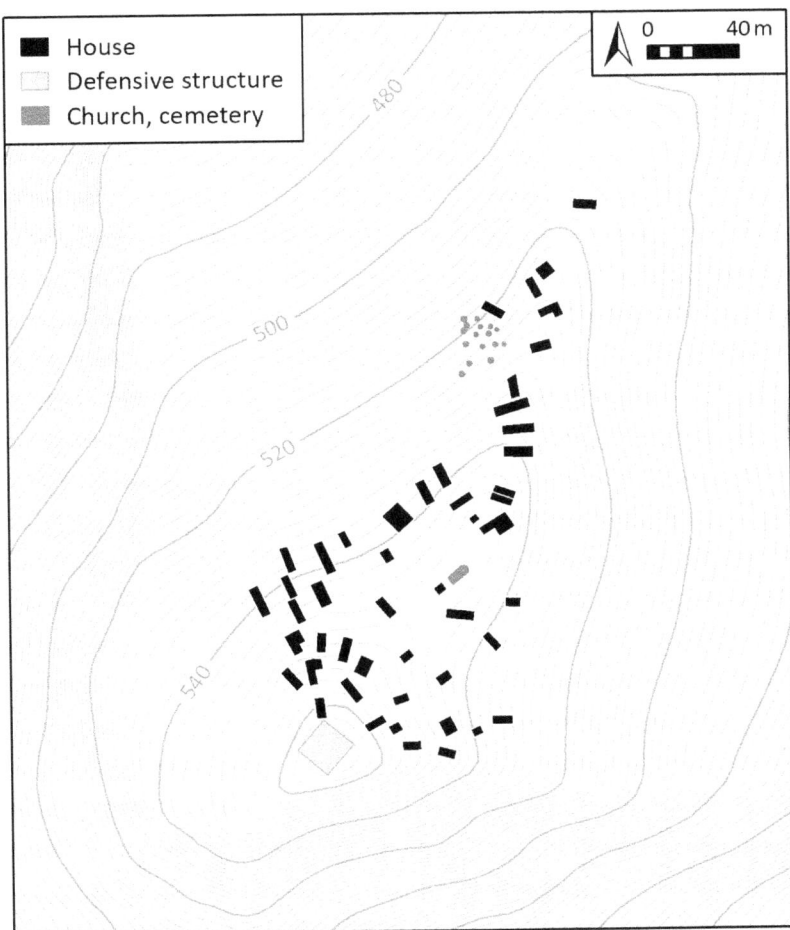

Figure 11. Plan of Palaia Tserova, showing a typical hilltop layout.

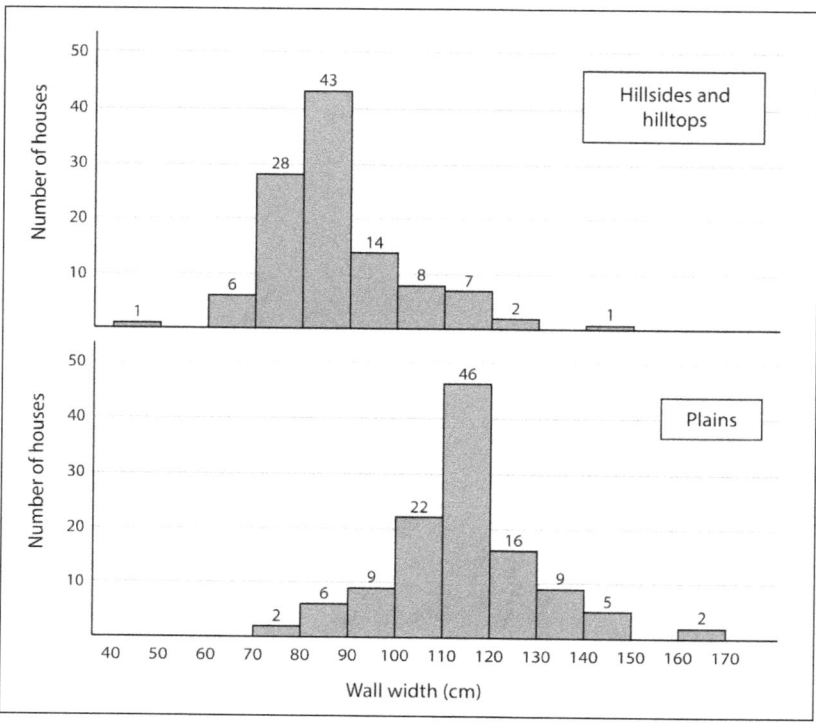

Figure 12. Histogram of house wall widths, showing distinction between hillside/hilltop settlements and plains settlements.

Hillside settlements are located along the lower slopes of the mountains that stretch down the spine of the peninsula (Figure 10). As with the plains sites, those on hillsides also comprised a loose cluster of houses, but in this case aligned perpendicular to the slope of the hill. Houses were frequently built in rows along the same elevation contour. Presumably, the primary benefits of a hillside location were the enhanced view of the surrounding landscape and the natural defensive quality of the sloping land. In some cases, defensive ability was further enhanced by building a wall to connect the downslope faces of a row of houses. It is likely that the hillside location also positioned certain settlements (i.e. those situated in the gullies and small valleys) to take advantage of the seasonal flow of rainwater from the mountains above. Today, perennial springs are known in only a few places within the study region, and water acquisition and storage for the dry summer months would have been critical needs of daily life (Seifried 2020a).[4]

---

[4] By contrast, the mountains in northern Mani are very well watered, with dozens of natural springs.

The final type of geographical setting is hilltops or ridges, which offered the most defensible positions and the best vistas but also made movement and transportation more difficult and limited access to seasonal water flows from mountain gullies (**Figure 11**). Hilltop settlements tended to be denser, with houses oriented perpendicularly to the slope and clustered around the highest elevation contours. The houses at the very highest elevation were often larger and more complex, at times with several adjacent and connected rooms (e.g. Kondyli, Skala). In two cases, the peak of the settlement was enclosed with a low encircling wall, forming a small, fortified area, or *kastro* (Palaia Tserova and Loukadika). In most cases, very few to no cisterns were discernible during fieldwork, suggesting that they were either located in unsurveyed territory or were buried or covered by vegetation.

While the *palaiomaniatika* are generally characterized by "megalithic" architecture and correspondingly thick walls, there is a discernible patterning in the thickness of house walls: some settlements tend to have houses with walls around 80–90 cm thick, while other have houses with walls around 110–120 cm thick. An independent samples t test was used to compare the mean wall widths between the two groups, and the test showed that there was a significant difference ($p = 0.00$) between wall widths in plains locations (M = 112.9 m) and hillside or hilltop locations (M = 86.8 m). The statistical test shows that wall widths reflect the choice of settlement location, with the thicker-walled houses located in plains settlements and the thinner-walled houses in hillside or hilltop settlements (**Figure 12**). In short, it seems that wall width is less a reliable chronological indicator than a reflection of the site's geography.

Chronology of the *Palaiomaniatika*

In this section, I lay out the current state of knowledge about the chronology of the *palaiomaniatika*, all of which is derived from art historical and architectural studies. Dating these remarkable settlements based on these features alone is complicated by the fact that the vernacular architectural tradition persisted for so long and changed so slowly over time. As Leda Moschou summarized:

> The construction of houses at all periods … probably belonged to a building tradition that went back to ancient times. The megalithic dry-stone masonry and the way in which the stone blocks were worked are elements to be found in many fortifications and also in some buildings of the Late Hellenistic period. They point to an age-old tradition of specialised techniques for quarrying the hard

local limestone, and also to advanced tools, tried-and-tested systems for extracting the quarried blocks, and for lifting them into position, and the experience and ability to control the statics of the courses. [Moschou 2004:35]

Thus, while the current consensus is that the *palaiomaniatika* were primarily founded and occupied as early as the eighth century and abandoned sometime after the seventeenth century, additional research is needed to narrow this chronology.

Establishment

N. K. Moutsopoulos and G. Dimitrokallis (1976/1978) were the first to attempt to date the establishment of the *palaiomaniatika*, drawing comparisons with the Neolithic "megalithic" tradition of Western Europe and hypothesizing that Mani's vernacular architecture dated to prehistoric times. This suggestion drew swift criticism from Takis Moschos and Leda Moschou (1982:263), who asserted that the settlements date to the Middle Byzantine period because they are often associated with churches that are securely dated to this time. Of course, using churches as a chronological proxy assumes that they are contemporaneous with the houses, cisterns, and other features comprising the occupied settlement. This assumption is not necessarily incorrect, but without excavations it is impossible to rule out the alternative explanations of settlement development and to determine the experience of any one settlement in particular.

To some extent, the rare examples of excavated medieval longhouses houses do support the accepted eighth to thirteenth-century dating. Two of the excavated samples from the Peloponnese date to the Middle and/or Late Byzantine periods (Lavda and Panakton), and the other two (Nichoria and Ayios Vasileios) may date to the Late Byzantine or early Ottoman periods. There is a general consensus throughout the eastern Mediterranean that a dramatic shift in house form took place between the Late Roman/Early Byzantine period and the Middle Byzantine period, when the typical complex surrounding a courtyard was replaced with a linear house form (Bouras 1983:5). This shift is said to reflect a broader societal change in how people related to each other and interacted with private/public spheres (Sigalos 2004b). Although the model of "courtyard complex to linear house" was initially developed in studies of elite houses and compounds, it may well apply to rural places like Mani.

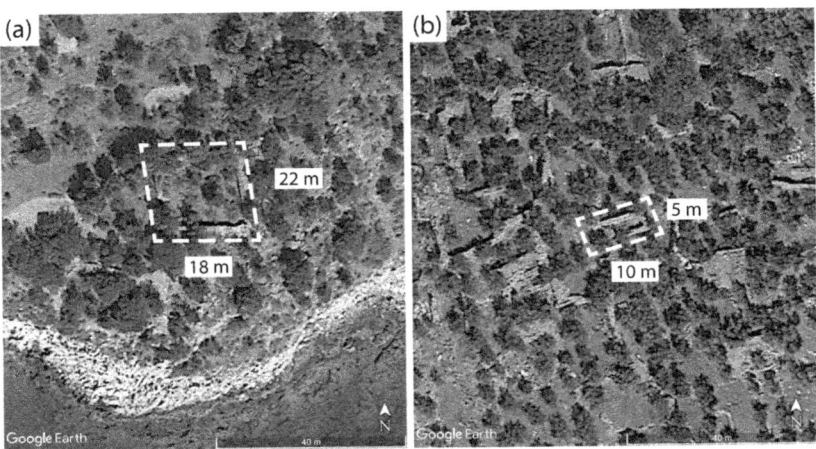

Figure 13. Aerial view comparing (a) the Late Roman compound at Mastakaria and (b) a typical *palaiomaniatiko* settlement. Image courtesy of Google Earth.

The sole intensive archaeological survey to be carried out in Mani, the Diros Project (2011–2013), sheds a glimpse of light onto the differences between Late Roman and Byzantine architecture in this rural landscape. The small survey focused on the bay north of Pyrgos Dirou, spanning an area of just under 2.5 km². The surveyors recorded a large walled enclosure on a cliff overlooking the north side of the bay in an area referred to as Mastakaria (**Figure 13**; Pullen et al. 2018). Based on the surface finds, which included a very high density of roof tiles and ceramic types indicative of domestic occupation and production (including amphorae, kitchen wares, a fragment of a beehive, and small amounts of fine ware), the surveyors dated the site to the fourth to sixth/seventh centuries AD—the Late Roman period. The dry-stone enclosure wall was built of unworked limestone and measured roughly 18 m (east–west) by 22 m (north–south). An entryway, apparently built without a lintel, was preserved in the southeast corner, where the wall stands to a height of about 1.8 m. A second entryway, only about 0.9 m high with the wall continuing above it, was located further along the eastern wall.

Mastakaria is the only example of Late Roman domestic architecture currently documented in the study region, so further examples must be studied before it will be possible to generalize about house forms at this time. However, it does provide two interesting and clear contrasts with the houses in the *palaiomaniatika*. First, large walled complexes like Mastakaria do not appear in the *palaiomaniatika*. Instead, walls used to delineate space tend to be built of loose rubble, and they are usually no more than 1 m high. Second, ceramic roof tile is extremely rare. It seems that houses in the Byzantine and early Ottoman periods were typically roofed with a less expensive material (recall that Saïtas suggested the inhabitants used packed earth or pebbles), and the roofs of older churches are sometimes covered with tiles made of slate or schist. During the course of fieldwork, ceramic roof tile was noted in only three of the *palaiomaniatiko* settlements, all of which also have later Ottoman phases. Together with the information from Mastakaria, this suggests that ceramic roof tile fell into disuse after the Late Roman period and did not come into widespread use again until around the mid seventeenth century. The insights from the Late Roman enclosure in Diros Bay seem to indicate that a shift in rural house form from the Late Roman to Middle Byzantine periods did, in fact, take place in Mani, which in turn support Moschos and Moschou's suggestion that the *palaiomaniatika* date to no earlier than the eighth century.

Abandonment

Historical records from the sixteenth to nineteenth centuries provide some insight into the abandonment of the *palaiomaniatika* and the disappearance of the supposedly "medieval" or "megalithic" vernacular architectural tradition. Recently, several *tahrir defterleri* (Ottoman tax registers) from the sixteenth century have come to light that were previously unknown to scholars of Mani's history (for further information about the defterler, see Coşgel 2002; Lowry 1992). It is now clear that Mani was the subject of full tax surveys in the years 1514 (TT80 and TT367) and 1583 (TT603 and TT677).[5] Together, these resources provide the earliest written administrative account of the settlements in Mani,[6] including settlement names and counts of households, estimates of each settlement's agricultural output, names of individual heads of households and fortress

---

[5] An earlier tahrir defteri (TT10) was compiled for the Peloponnese in the years 1460–1463, immediately following the Ottoman Empire's conquest of the region. TT10 is a phenomenal resource that has been analyzed and utilized by many historians and archaeologists alike (Alexander 1978; Beldiceanu and Beldiceanu-Steinherr 1980; Liakopoulos 2019), but unfortunately, Mani is not included in the document. The most likely explanation for this is that Mani had not been fully conquered by 1463. However, there is also a small possibility that the relevant pages dealing with Mani were lost during the document's rather exciting history and chance rediscovery (Liakopoulos 2019:35–36).

[6] While an earlier document from the year 1366 referenced the towns of Areopoli (Tsimova) and Pyrgos Dirou (Iro), territories given to the *feudarchis* (ruler or fiefowner), Nikola Acciaiuoli (Longnon and Topping 1969:253–254), it mentions no other settlements in the region.

guards, and even later scribal notes commenting on the periodic rebellions in Mani. A full publication of the Mani *defterler* is anticipated, but for now only the most relevant information on settlement names will be discussed (for preliminary information on specific settlement chronologies, see Seifried 2016:Appendix A).

Additional documents are available from the seventeenth to nineteenth centuries. The seventeenth century was a period of political upheaval in the Peloponnese, with attempted rebellions against the Ottoman Empire in the early part of the century, followed by the region's conquest by the Republic of Venice in 1685. Several relevant Italian documents from this century have been published: a settlement list from the year 1618, which was compiled surreptitiously to assess the military strength of the region (Buchon 1843:241–295; Komis 2005:41–42; Wagstaff 1977), and Venetian documents from 1692, 1695, and 1700, all conducted by Provveditor Generals of the Morea (for 1692 and 1695: Komis 2005:43–47; Moatsos 1976/1978; for 1700: Panagiotopoulos 1987; see also Seifried 2015; Topping 1976/1978). In 1715, the Ottoman Empire reconquered the Peloponnese and promptly conducted another full tax survey, resulting in another extremely detailed register. The portion of this register corresponding to Mani is TT878 and, as with the earlier *defterler*, it only recently came to light (for a similar register from the Messenian peninsula, TT880, see Zarinebaf et al. 2005). Finally, two later documents from 1813 and 1829 provide a glimpse into the settlements in Mani at the very end of Ottoman rule, which ended with the Greek Revolution of 1821–1829 (for 1813: Kremmidas 1984; for 1829: Bory de Saint-Vincent 1834:89–92; Frangakis-Syrett and Wagstaff 1992; Komis 2005:54–55).

Naturally, there are caveats to consider when dealing with historical tax registers, censuses, and other kinds of settlement lists. First and foremost is the issue of power: local residents, especially in rural or peripheral areas, did not always cooperate with tax officials or foreign military personnel. It must be assumed that some number of individuals engaged in tax evasion, whether by underreporting their household production or by fleeing altogether (such as to a seasonal camp in the mountains; Given 2007:139–144; Scott 2009). Second is the issue of access. With limited time and resources, surveyors could not possibly record every single settlement in a given region, and the smallest or least accessible usually went undocumented. Third is the issue of reliability, as not all of the documents described above were recorded by firsthand observers. While the 1514 tax register and the 1618 list appear to follow a geographical procession, suggesting that the recorder visited the region in person, the order of names in the other lists suggests that their authors did not venture into Mani themselves (Seifried 2016:137–144). All of these factors mean that the settlement lists represent only a portion of the settlements occupied in Mani. We can expect that the smallest or most remote will not have been recorded, and we must also read the names and associated content with a grain of salt, acknowledging that the people who wrote these lists were not locals and did not have expert knowledge of the region.

Still, the historical documents do provide some insight into the occupational history of many of the *palaiomaniatika* in Mani over the course of the sixteenth to nineteenth centuries. While some remained occupied, a few disappeared from the records along the way, suggesting that they may have been abandoned. These patterns allow us to categorize the settlements into three major phases of abandonment: (1) before the sixteenth century, (2) during the early Ottoman period (sixteenth to mid seventeenth centuries), and (3) during the Venetian or later Ottoman periods (mid seventeenth to eighteenth centuries).

About 50–60 of the *palaiomaniatika* may have been abandoned before or around the time the Ottoman Empire took control. This is suggested by their absence from the early Ottoman *tahrir defterleri* of 1514 and 1583 and all subsequent records, and the fact that their original names are no longer remembered by local residents. A few of the toponyms in the early *defterler* have yet to be identified, and it is possible that some of these correspond to settlements within this group; this would mean that they were abandoned a bit later, in the early Ottoman period. Interestingly, while most of these settlements remained permanently abandoned, six were reinhabited briefly in the later Ottoman period (by one or two isolated residential complexes) before those later houses, too, were abandoned.

Fourteen of the *palaiomaniatika* seem to have been abandoned during the early Ottoman period (Table 1). These settlements appear in the early Ottoman *tahrir defterleri* or the 1618 list, but in no other records after this. Within this group, 10 remained permanently abandoned, and 4 were temporarily reinhabited in the later Ottoman period—all by one or two isolated residential complexes—before being abandoned once again. Admittedly, some of the toponyms are only tenuously associated with entries in the settlement lists (due to a corruption of names in the 1618 list), but I believe them to be the most likely candidates based on geography and alignment between archaeological remains and recorded

Table 1. Settlements Abandoned During the Early Ottoman Period (1463–1685), with Corresponding Entries in the 1514 and 1618 Settlement Lists.

Modern Toponym	1514 List	1618 List
Aetopholia		Haitofoglia di Cholochitia
Kato Meri	Kato Meri	
Koulouryiani (Koulouvades and Kouvouklia together)	Kalouryiani	
Kozia		Chosea
Mesopangi		Mizopangi
Skourka		Scurca di Cholochitia
Vikolias		Voucholia de Cholochitia
Vlistiko		Viglistico
Korines[a]		Zigarismeni
Kourines[a]		Bragia di Nicliani
Lakkos[a]		Mos Sabatiani
Settlement north of Skourka[a]		Giorgicio-Poulo di Cholochitia
Settlement southeast of Vachos[a]		Panayia di Vacha

[a] Tentative identification based on the order of names in the list, the geographical location of the settlement, and alignment between archaeological remains and recorded houses.

houses. A further 13 settlements were abandoned at this time and then reinhabited in the later Ottoman period, growing to become more substantial settlements that are still occupied today.[7]

Up to 12 of the *palaiomaniatika* may have been abandoned during the Venetian or later Ottoman periods. These settlements appear in records from the seventeenth or eighteenth centuries but not in the later records from 1813 or 1829. These are the most secure examples, as in most cases there are additional historical records testifying to their abandonment and providing detailed explanations for why the residents left. Potentially

---

[7] These are (in alphabetical order): Ayia Varvara (Phtio), Charouda, Chimara, Erimos, Kaphiona, Keria, Kotraphi, Kyparissos, Ochia, Skaltsotianika, Soloteri, Vamvaka, and a small village (*xemoni*) south of Areopoli (whose name I have not yet learned) that may be a candidate for the 1618 entry for Mavroiagni.

Table 2. Settlements Abandoned During the Venetian (1685–1715) or Later Ottoman (1715–1821) Periods, with Corresponding Entries in the 1692, 1695, 1700, and 1715 Settlement Lists.

Modern Toponym	1692 List	1695 List	1700 List	1715 List
Divola	Drivola	villa Divola	Dittolla	Divala, formerly Kotrona
Kaliazi	Cagliasi	villa Caliesi	Calliasi	Kalyazi
Kondili	Candili, e Lucadia	villa Condili	Candilli	Kondili
Karyoupoli	Cariopoli	Criopoli	Cariopoli	Karyupoli
Tserova	Cottrona, e Cerova	villa Cerova	Cerova	Çerova
Porachia		Poralia		
Stavrikio	Stavri, Stavrichie, e Pangie			
Tigani[a]			Maina alta	

[a] Tentative identification proposed by Komis (2005:377–379).

eight of the *palaiomaniatika* fall into this category (Table 2), and there are an additional four that do not appear in the records but have similar abandonment profiles from an architectural standpoint (Paliochori, located on a ridge above Drymos; and ruined settlements near Skala, Vatheia, and Riganochora).

In summary, the evidence from the historical records indicates that people were still living in the majority of the *palaiomaniatika* well into the Ottoman period. Only around 30% were abandoned by the time the Ottoman Empire took over—and that is a high estimate, considering that the sixteenth-century tax officials inevitably did not record many of the settlements occupied at the time. It is plausible that even more persisted into the first phase of Ottoman rule than this analysis suggests. Over time, some of the *palaiomaniatika* were slowly abandoned, with about 15% abandoned sometime after the first phase of Ottoman rule, and another 8% after the Venetian period or later period of Ottoman rule. Over 40% of the *palaiomaniatika* have been continuously occupied from their founding roughly a millennium ago, and more than a dozen were reoccupied after a long period of abandonment.

Case Study: Koulouvades

It should be clear at this point that we know very little about the social dynamics of life in the *palaiomaniatika*. Broad strokes can be drawn about the evolution of vernacular architecture in Mani over the past millennium, but such a long-term perspective obscures the processes of daily life and abandonment in these villages. In an effort to illustrate the importance of detailed archaeological work for the study of medieval rural settlements, I turn now to the case study of an abandoned *palaiomaniatiko* settlement near the village of Pyrgos Dirou, called Koulouvades. This site has the typical plains layout, and it is a sister settlement to Kouvouklia, which lies less than 1 km to the southeast. The site is well known to locals. A resident of nearby Charia first took me to see it in the summer of 2013. He and another local resident reported that the area is known by two names: Koulouvades and Pano Chorio (Upper Village), and that together with Kouvouklia the two sites are known as Koulouryiani. It is likely that the latter toponym derives from the surname of two of the patrons of the nearby eleventh- to thirteenth-century church of the Taxiarchis in Glezou. The donors' names are inscribed on the marble beams supporting the dome arches: Eustratios Koulouras, Theodoros Koulouras, and Niketikos (Kalopissi-Verti 2003:341–342; Traquair 1908/1909:191–192; for a bibliography of the church, see Mexia 2011:77–79).[8]

The ruined structures in Koulouvades form a triangular shape, with the longest end pointing to the east (see Figure 9 above). Today the area is subdivided into olive groves that are fairly overgrown, and the walls of the abandoned houses have been incorporated into field walls in order to delineate fields or to serve as animal pens. During field research carried out in the summer of 2014, we recorded a total of 28 individual houses, some of which were connected into multi-house complexes. Most of the buildings were filled with rubble, and the walls had been reduced to only the lowest course(s). We also recorded 32 cisterns, the vast majority of which were built in the typical slab-topped style that was used until the end of the seventeenth century (Seifried 2020a). Only one cistern was of the later barrel-vaulted type. The 1-to-1 ratio of cisterns to houses is extremely high compared to other villages recorded during fieldwork, particularly considering that the cisterns are likely to be underrepresented in the final counts because of limited visibility due to vegetation growth

---

[8] I am grateful to Panagiotis Makris for calling my attention to these inscriptions.

and wall fall. A cluster of cisterns is located in the northwest part of the settlement, with several sharing a single field, while others are distributed in between the houses.

At the northeastern edge of the village is the ruined Byzantine church of Ay. Vlasis (also referred to locally as Ay. Vlasides). Angeliki Mexia (2011:179–180) reports that the church, which is otherwise unpublished, dates to the second half of the twelfth century. It is a small vaulted construction, measuring 6.6 x 4.4 m on the exterior walls. The roof and apse are in stages of collapse, and only a few traces of iconography remain on the interior walls. The church's most remarkable feature is a large marble lintel over the west entrance that is engraved with the typical Byzantine motifs of a cross and birds.

One of the unusual things about Koulouvades is the impressive size of one of the houses (T363F023) and a nearby cistern (T363F030); they are among the largest in all the *palaiomaniatika*, particularly in terms of the size of the stones used in their construction. Both are situated in the northern part of the settlement (Figure 14). The exterior walls of the house are 14.8 m long and 5.8 m wide, with an average wall width of 1.6 m (Figure 15). Because the walls are so massive, the internal living area (29.9 m²) is only slightly above average. The cistern is located about 45 m west of the house, with no intervening features (Figure 16). Its internal tank is an elongated oval measuring 8.8 m long by 1.5 m wide. Several massive limestone slabs still span the top and would have once supported a roof made of limestone rubble; however, the roof is now almost entirely collapsed. Despite the impressive length of this cistern and especially the beams spanning its roof, its internal storage capacity is only just above the average for all the cisterns measured during field research.

This cistern was one of two chosen for ^{14}C dating. A sample of the hydraulic mortar was removed from the outer layer of the mortar directly below a large limestone slab on its north wall. The sample was found to contain a charcoal inclusion that was suitable for dating via accelerator mass spectrometry (AMS), while the other sample (from a different cistern) contained no dateable material (Figure 17).[9] The uncalibrated radiocarbon date of the charcoal sample is 416 ± 16 BP (DEM-3259/MAMS-38304; charcoal; δ^{13}C = -24.6‰). When calibrated using the OxCal v.4.2.3 program (Bronk Ramsey and Lee 2013) and the IntCal13 calibration curve (Reimer et al. 2013), the age range is 1444–1463 cal

---

[9] The sample was processed by Dr. Yannis Maniatis at the National Center for Scientific Research Demokritos in Athens, Greece. AMS measurement was performed at Klaus-Tschira-Labor für Physikalische Altersbestimmung, Curt-Engelhorn-Zentrum Archaeometrie gGmbH in Mannheim, Germany.

181

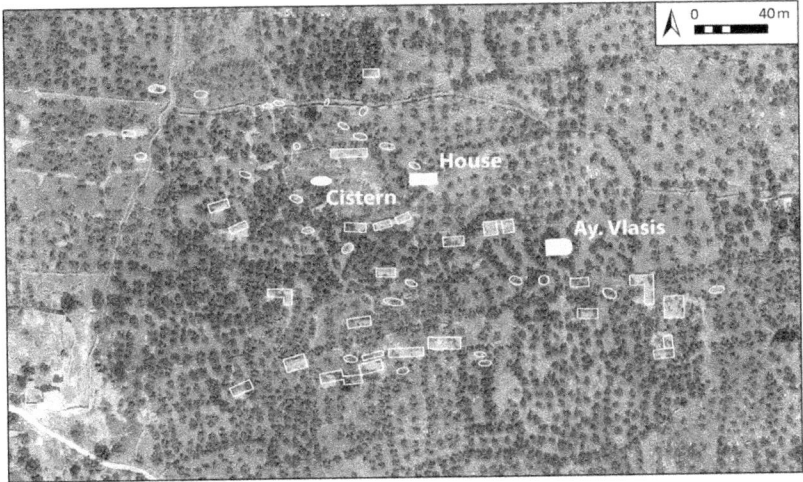

Figure 14. Aerial photo of Koulouvades showing location of the house, cistern, and church discussed in the text.

Figure 15. The large house in Koulouvades, looking southeast.

Figure 16. The large cistern in Koulouvades, looking west.

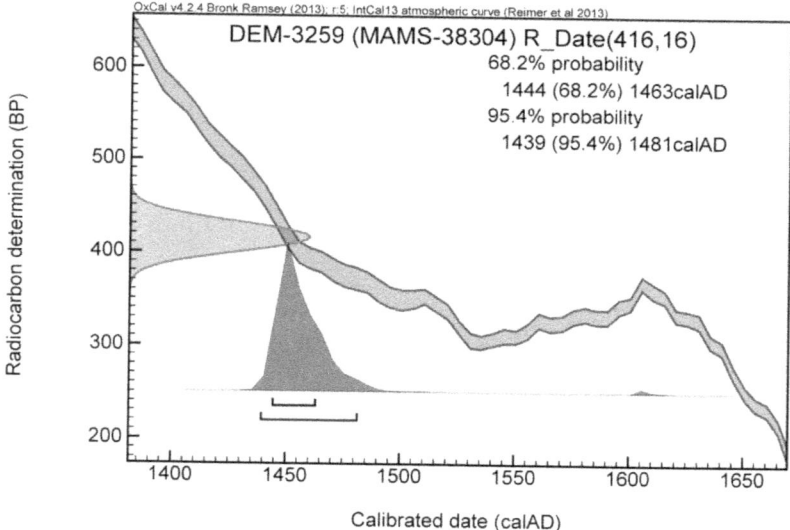

Figure 17. Calibration curve of the ^{14}C sample taken from the outer layer of hydraulic mortar in the large cistern in Koulouvades.

AD (1σ) or 1439–1481 cal AD (2σ). What this tells us is that the cistern's hydraulic mortar was last replenished in the middle of the fifteenth century, around the time that the Ottoman Empire conquered the region that is today the Peloponnese. It seems likely that the cistern went out of use within a generation or two after this event (for studies of domestic cisterns elsewhere in the Peloponnese, see Forbes forthcoming; Germanidou 2018).

The historical records confirm that Koulouvades was still occupied in the early sixteenth century. The village appears in the 1514 register (TT80) as "Kalouryiani, with Vari Matsouka, a *mezraa* in its borders." The latter name is possibly referencing another village 1 km south of Kouvouklia known as Marmatsouka. The designation of *mezraa* suggests that the area was already abandoned at the time of recording and was being used as fields by the people living in the villages of Koulouryiani. The modern village of Marmatsouka is concentrated within the more extensive layout of the original *palaiomaniatiko* and was evidently resettled after a lengthy period of abandonment. Altogether 42 heads of household, 5 bachelors, and 1 widow were recorded as living in Koulouryiani, for a total estimated number of households of around 48. The residents were assessed a tax payment of 4,145 *akçes* (the standard silver currency of the Ottoman Empire). For the sake of illustration, based on the estimated value of the currency around 1490 (Barkan and McCarthy 1975:15, Note 2), 2 akçes could buy about 1 okka (1.28 kg) of lamb. Therefore 4,145 *akçes* could buy roughly 53 lambs weighing in at 50 kg each.

Together, the ^{14}C date taken from a cistern in Koulouvades and the reference in an Ottoman tax register to the wider settlement area of Koulouryiani support a final abandonment date in the sixteenth century. In other words, the village was still functioning as a typical, vibrant rural community at the time of the Ottoman conquest. By the early sixteenth century, the settlement was already in the early stages of abandonment. Field research documented a total of 74 houses between the two settlements (28 in Koulouvades and 46 in Kouvouklia). If we suppose that most—if not all—of these houses were occupied at the settlement's height, and that each house was used by a single household (as registered in the defter), then these numbers would suggest a substantial loss of population already by 1514. The absence of Koulouryiani and its individual villages areas from the subsequent historical records (including the 1583 defter) suggests that its abandonment was probably complete by the latter half of the sixteenth century. Further fieldwork—whether that be test pits, excavation of one or more houses or cisterns, or additional radiocarbon dating—would undoubtedly open up the potential for more detailed inquiry.

Toward a Household Archaeology of Abandoned Rural Villages in Greece

Household archaeology gained traction in the 1980s with the rise of processual archaeology, particularly in Mesoamerica and the American Southwest (e.g. Blanton 1994; Flannery 1976; Netting et al. 1984; Santley and Hirth 1992; Wilk and Ashmore 1988; Wilk and Rathje 1982). Parallel studies by social theorists contributed to the field by exploring the links between built environment and households (Bourdieu 1977, 1990; Foucault 1975; Giddens 1984; Rapoport 1969, 1982). In the decades since household archaeology emerged, it has been fruitfully applied to nearly every part of human history, with particular prominence in studies of the Americas (for recent reviews, see Carballo 2011; Kahn 2016; Nash 2009; Pluckhahn 2010). What these studies show is that a focus on households and the everyday life of ordinary people provides an opportunity to explore social change from a "bottom-up" perspective, as opposed to the "top-down" view of regional approaches. It enables questions about the gendering of space, differential access to resources within a community, household-scale economic activities (including production, distribution, and consumption), the ways in which social units interact with each other, the ways in which household members bargain and negotiate in order to overcome conflicting interests, and how all these processes change over time and with respect to the wider social context.

Architecture features prominently in household archaeology, with the caveat that, just as "pots do not equal people," "houses do not equal households." The definition of households as social entities that may or may not involve cohabitation means that houses cannot be used as proxies for the people that lived within them. Similarly, household archaeologists must be careful not to apply their own conceptualizations about what a household looks like onto the architectural fabric of the settlements they left behind. But with these warnings in mind, the study of domestic architecture does allow us to ask interesting questions about the role that it played in the social processes of households over time. As with other kinds of built structures, houses can "act as sites for the construction of social memory through the repetition of practices, the construction and use of buildings over time, and the transmission of social knowledge, as well as the transmission of the buildings themselves and the objects associated with them" (Souvatzi 2012:183). While rooting people to their fellow residents and to the physical landscape, houses and other built structures are also reinterpreted and contested as new generations come and go. Thus, household archaeology allows us both literally and figuratively to dig into the idea of "architecture as process" by exploring layers of activity, deconstruction, rebuilding, and ultimately abandonment.

Stella Souvatzi (2008, 2012) has been one of the main proponents of a "social archaeology of households" in Europe, applying this approach to several of the most prominent Neolithic sites in Greece (Nea Nikomedeia, Sesklo, and Dimini). Ancient urban centers have also received a fair amount of attention at the household scale—such as the Athenian Agora, Halieis, and Olynthos, among others (e.g. Ault and Nevett 2005; Nevett et al. 2017)—but seldom with the explicitly anthropological framework that makes Souvatzi's approach so applicable to rural landscapes in the historical periods. Rural people do occasionally feature in historical texts in the form of population counts, estimates of their productive potentials, accounts of legal action, or records of birth, marriage, and death. But rarely do we have access to the kinds of insights into their daily lives that are common for wealthier people: narrative accounts, handwritten letters, biographies, or even mundane information about household contents in wills and other official records. The people who live on the socio-economic edges of the state simply do not leave behind these kinds of testimony. In this sense, studying a rural medieval village is in many ways like studying a prehistoric one. With historical documents providing (at best) limited insight into the residents' lives, the material remains they left behind become ever more important clues into the functioning of past societies at the household scale.

The fact that only two of the chapters in this volume deal with excavation data indicates how infrequently household archaeology is applied to the medieval and later phases in the eastern Mediterranean; yet the chapters also demonstrate how worthwhile this application can be. Through careful excavations of a house at Çadır Höyük (Cassis and Lauricella, this volume), the team was able to discern four phases of occupation and abandonment, which allowed them to tie the site into a broader understanding of how rural populations adapt to change at a much larger scale. The evidence they unearthed pointed to phases of the house's reuse and renovation, changes in domestic pottery assemblages, an abandonment episode that was both sudden and violent, and a collection of architectural and artifactual evidence that suggests part of the site was reoccupied by a different population. At the site of Anavatos (Vassi, this volume), a large-scale excavation program allowed archaeologists to study the layout of the post-medieval village in its entirety, including its public spaces, religious infrastructure, water supply, neighborhoods, and domestic architecture.

In turn, these data provide countless insights into day-to-day life in Anavatos. For example, the phases of construction point to a prioritization of safety and defense over other human needs, the narrow width of the roads suggests that the residents did not bring mules or donkeys into the village, and the material remains unearthed by the excavations indicate a continued (albeit much reduced) population at the site into the late nineteenth century. Both of these case studies showcase the kinds of questions that we could ask of abandoned rural villages if only we access to household-scale data.

At the same time, there are very real challenges to adopting a household archaeology of rural villages that are historically contingent and unlikely to be easily overcome, particularly for U.S.-based researchers working in Greece. I will outline four challenges that I believe most daunting to this work. Chief among them is the tradition from which Byzantine and post-Byzantine archaeology extends, which focuses specifically on religious architecture. A generation of archaeologists—many of whom are contributors to this volume—have attempted to shift their corners of the field toward a more materially informed approach that centers the quotidian experience of the rural countryside (e.g. Athanassopoulos 2016; Cloke and Athanassopoulos 2020; Erny and Caraher 2020; Kourelis 2018, 2019; Sanders 2014; Tzortzopoulou-Gregory 2010; Tzortzopoulou-Gregory and Gregory 2017; Vionis 2016, 2020). Yet, the focus of the field overall has not changed to the same degree. This is evident, for example, in the rarity of archaeological sessions at the Byzantine Studies Conference, which—when they do occur—are well attended and well received (including Kostis Kourelis' chaired sessions on "Cyprus: Archaeology, Architecture and History" in 2007 and "Archaeology of Byzantine Neighborhoods" in 2015).

Second is the discouragement of junior scholars that results from the way in which some of the foreign institutions allocate excavation and survey permits. In brief, non-Greek scholars are required to apply for archaeological permits via one of the foreign institutions; the process varies in competitiveness depending on the institution. For example, U.S.-based scholars applying through the American School of Classical Studies at Athens (ASCSA) are expected to hold a permanent position as a faculty member in their home country, and the process (if ever successful) can take many years. As the global economic situation has deteriorated over the past decade and short-term, contingent faculty positions become ever more common, the challenges facing the new generation of scholars have become increasingly difficult barriers to launching new field research programs.

Third is the reluctance of some of the more impactful institutions to welcome scholarship on medieval and post-medieval phases. A notable exception to this is *Hesperia*, the journal of the ASCSA, which frequently publishes studies on Byzantine and later topics. But others have not been so generous. The flagship journal of the Archaeological Institute of America, the *American Journal of Archaeology* (with a higher impact score and arguably more diverse readership than *Hesperia*) will not consider articles dealing with phases after Late Antiquity, even if they focus on sites within Greece whose earlier phases are published elsewhere in the journal. Policies like these serve to reinforce the low prioritization of medieval and post-medieval studies and hamper the effort to bring the field in dialogue with other archaeological and theoretical approaches throughout the world.

Last, but arguably the most important, is the impact that the global economic crisis has had on archaeology in Greece, particularly since austerity measures were first put in place in 2010 under the Papandreou government. While the recession in Greece officially ended in 2018, the effects of the austerity measures will be felt for many years to come. The coronavirus pandemic of 2020 will only add to these catastrophic economic consequences. For example, the Greek Archaeology Service has been reorganized several times, resulting in layoffs for many staff, precarity for others, and cuts in funding to support archaeological sites and continued research. In remote places like Mani, whatever resources do exist within the Greek state are unlikely to be diverted toward studying humble houses like the *palaiomaniatika*. Thus, in my view, the hope that a household archaeology of rural villages can take root in Greece will depend upon support from established institutions, particularly through access to permitting, funding, and publication venues that will push the scholarship into dialogue with the wider field.

Conclusion

In their 1982 article on the *palaiomaniatika*, Moschos and Moschou (1982:263) cautioned against "drawing premature conclusions regarding the chronological classification" of the settlements due to a paucity of archaeological excavation at the time. Unfortunately, despite the passing of more than 40 years since the earliest publication on the topic, no excavations of a *palaiomaniatika* village have been published. The current understanding is that they first appeared between the eighth and thirteenth centuries. Information from Ottoman historical records confirms that many of the settlements were still occupied into the sixteenth and seventeenth centuries. The lack of a refined chronological understanding of the *palaiomaniatika* is a major problem for broad-scale syntheses, but it also means that we have little knowledge of the day-to-day activities that took place in these settlements. Thus, the *palaiomaniatika* offer an important case study about the limits of architectural and art historical approaches in medieval and post-medieval rural landscapes, where the overarching characteristics of the vernacular architecture are its simplicity and duration through time.

The silver lining to the present state of published research on the *palaiomaniatika* is the vast potential for future study through targeted survey and excavation. With over 170 extant settlements with preserved stone-built architecture, Mani would be a valuable case study for studying rural domestic architecture in the Byzantine and Ottoman periods. Recent methodological and theoretical advances in household archaeology have had a dramatic impact on our understanding of the day-to-day cycles of activity in domestic settings, and these approaches could be used to construct a detailed picture of lived experience in the *palaiomaniatika*. Potential topics that could be explored include the relationship between built space, family composition, and the theorization of "social units," particularly in light of historical census data; patterns of household production, consumption, and exchange; movement of people and goods beyond the settlement; settlement-scale construction programs and planning; variation in building forms and functions; the gendering of space; the role of space in ritual activities and the structuring of social order; socioeconomic differentiation within and between settlements; spatial experience and its duration through time; the roles of power in influencing settlement and house form; and the visibility and the experience of seeing/being seen. These are just a few of the myriad topics that archaeologists and historians alike have been exploring in other regions over the past several decades through household-scale research.

Archaeological investigation is especially vital because of the near-total absence of other forms of documentation. There are simply no written records about the experience of living in a *palaiomaniatika*, aside from the few tantalizing inscriptions in nearby churches that attest to the pooling of resources between settlements and the wealth of certain individuals who could afford to sponsor church constructions. Historians like Angeliki Laiou (2005) have provided extremely detailed pictures of life in typical Byzantine villages, and Sharon Gerstel's (2015, 2020) recent work—with examples drawn from southern Mani—demonstrates the breadth of insight that can be gained from analyzing religious painting, written sources, and ethnographic data. At the same time, these works underscore the fact that excavations are essential to fully understanding the myriad facets of secular life in rural settings. It is imperative that targeted investigations be carried out to help refine the broad chronological framework of the *palaiomaniatika* and to gain insights into the lived experience of the residents of these enigmatic villages.

Acknowledgments. Special thanks to Deb Brown Stewart and Kostis Kourelis for organizing the "Deserted Villages" colloquium at the 2016 Annual Meeting of the Archaeological Institute of America. This paper is based on parts of my doctoral dissertation, completed in 2016 through the Department of Anthropology at the University of Illinois at Chicago. Research was funded by the National Science Foundation [BCS-1346694], ArchaeoLandscapes Europe, and the University of Illinois at Chicago. Satellite imagery was provided by the DigitalGlobe Foundation, and aerial photography and elevation data was provided by the National Cadastre and Mapping Agency, SA (Ktimatologio). Field research was conducted under the auspices of the 5th Ephorate of Byzantine Antiquities in Sparta and in collaboration with the Diros Project, an archaeological survey and excavation co-directed by Giorgos Papathanassopoulos and Anastasia Papathanasiou through the Ephorate of Palaeoanthropology & Speleology of Southern Greece. Support for final analysis, writing, and radiocarbon dating was provided by a Marie Skłodowska-Curie Individual Fellowship (750843). The libraries of the American School of Classical Studies at Athens proved immeasurably useful during the writing phase. This research would not have been possible without assistance from Billy Ridge and Chelsea Gardner (research assistants extraordinaire), Elias Kolovos, Andonis Koilakos, and the Koilakos family. An early draft of this paper benefited from comments by Tuna Kalaycı, Yanis Saïtas, Panagiotis Makris, and two anonymous reviewers. Needless to say, any remaining errors are my own.

References Cited

Adler, Michael A., and Richard H. Wilshusen
   1990   Large-Scale Integrative Facilities in Tribal Societies: Cross-Cultural and Southwestern US Examples. *World Archaeology* 22(2):133–146. https://doi.org/10.1080/00438243.1990.9980136

Alexander, John C.
   1978   Δύο Οθωμανικά κατάστιχα του Μόριά (1460–1463) [Two Ottoman Registers of the Morea 1460–1463]. In *Πρακτικά του Α συνεδρίου Μεσσηνιακών Σπουδών (2–4 Δεκ. 1977) [Proceedings of the First Conference of Messenian Studies, 2–4 December 1977]*, pp. 399–407. Peloponnisiaka Parartima 5. Society for Peloponnesian Studies, Athens.

Allen, Peter S.
   1976   Aspida: A Depopulated Maniat Community. *Annals of the New York Academy of Sciences* 268(1):168–198. https://doi.org/10.1111/j.1749-6632.1976.tb47642.x

Antoniadis-Bibicou, Hélène
   1965   Villages désertés en Grèce: Un bilan provisoire [Deserted Villages in Greece: A Provisional Assessment]. In *Villages désertés et histoire économique, XIe-XVIIIe siècle [Deserted Villages and Economic History, 11th–18th centuries]*, Centre de Recherches Historiques, École Pratique des Hautes-Études – VIe Section, pp. 343–417. S.E.V.P.E.N., Paris.

Argyriades, E., M. Kavaya, M. Korres, Y. Saïtas, S. Skamnaki, and K. Tzanaki
   1972   Οικισμοί στη Μάνη. Οικιστική ανάλυση [Settlements in Mani: Household Analysis]. Paper presented at the National Technical University of Athens.

Athanassopoulos, Effie F.
   2016   *Nemea Valley Archaeological Project: II. Landscape Archaeology and the Medieval Countryside*. The American School of Classical Studies at Athens, Princeton, New Jersey.

Ault, Bradley A., and Lisa C. Nevett (editors)
2005 *Ancient Greek Houses and Households: Chronological, Regional, and Social Diversity*. University of Pennsylvania Press, Philadelphia.

Barkan, Ömer Lutfi, and Justin McCarthy
1975 The Price Revolution of the Sixteenth Century: A Turning Point in the Economic History of the Near East. *International Journal of Middle East Studies* 6(1):3–28. https://doi.org/10.1017/S0020743800024302

Beldiceanu, Nicoară, and Irène Beldiceanu-Steinherr
1980 Recherches sur la Morée (1461–1512) [Research on the Morea (1461–1512)]. *Südost-Forschungen* 39:17–74.

Blanton, Richard E.
1994 *Houses and Households: A Comparative Study*. Plenum Press, New York.

Bory de Saint-Vincent, Jean Baptiste G. M.
1834 *Expédition scientifique de Morée. Section des science physiques: II. Géographie et géologie* [*Scientific Expedition of the Morea. Physical Sciences Section: II. Geography and Geology*]. F. G. Levrault, Paris.

Bouras, Charalambos
1983 Houses in Byzantium. *Deltion of the Christian Archaeological Society* 11:1–26. https://doi.org/10.12681/dchae.925

Bourdieu, Pierre
1977 *Outline of a Theory of Practice*. Translated by Richard Nice. Cambridge University Press, Cambridge.
1990 *The Logic of Practice*. Polity Press, Cambridge.

Bronk Ramsey, Christopher, and Sharen Lee
2013 Recent and Planned Developments of the Program OxCal. *Radiocarbon* 55(2–3):720–730. https://doi.org/10.2458/azu_js_rc.55.16215

Buchon, Jean Alexandre C.
1843   *Nouvelles recherches historiques sur la principauté française de Morée et ses hautes baronies [New Historical Research on the Frankish Principality of the Morea and its High Baronies]*, Vol. I. Imprimeurs Unis, Paris.

Calligas, Haris A.
1974   The Evolution of Settlements in Mani. In *Shelter in Greece*, edited by Orestis B. Doumanis and Paul Oliver, pp. 115–137. Architecture in Greece Press, Athens.

Carballo, David M.
2011   Advances in the Household Archaeology of Highland Mesoamerica. *Journal of Archaeological Research* 19(2):133–189. https://doi.org/10.1007/s10814-010-9045-7

Cerasi, Maurice
1998   The Formation of Ottoman House Types: A Comparative Study in Interaction with Neighboring Cultures. *Muqarnas* 15:116–156. https://doi.org/10.1163/22118993-90000412

Cloke, Christian, and Effie Athanassopoulos
2020   Late Antique and Medieval Landscapes of the Nemea Valley, Southern Greece. *Journal of Greek Archaeology* 5:406–425.

Coşgel, Metin M.
2002   Ottoman Tax Registers (Tahrir Defterleri). Electronic document, http://opencommons.uconn.edu/econ_wpapers/200247, accessed December 6, 2020.

Drandakis, Nikolaos V.
1980   Οι τοιχογραφίες του Αγίων Αναργύρων Κηπούλας (1265) [The Wall Paintings of Ayioi Anargyroi, Kipoula (1265)]. *Archaiologike Ephemeris* 119:97–118.
1982   Δύο επιγραφές ναών της Λακωνίας: του Μιχαήλ Αρχαγγέλου (1278) στον Πολεμίτα της Μάνης και της Χφυσαφίτισσας (1290) [Two Temple Inscriptions in Laconia: The Archangel Michael (1278) in Polemitas in Mani and the Chrisafitissas (1290)]. *Lakonikai Spoudai* 6:44–61.

2009   Μάνη και Λακωνία [Mani and Laconia]. 4 vols. Lakonikai Spoudai Parartima 17. Society for Laconian Studies, Athens.

Drandakis, Nikolaos V., Eleni Dori, Sophia Kalopisi, and Maria Panagiotidi
1980   Ἔρευνα στή Μάνη [Research in Mani]. *Praktika tes en Athenais Archaiologikes Hetaireias* 1978:135–182.

Erny, Grace, and William Caraher
2020   The Kingdom of Chelmis: Architecture, Material Culture, and the Modern Landscape of the Western Argolid. *Journal of Field Archaeology*:1–13.
https://doi.org/10.1080/00934690.2019.1704990

Etzeoglou, Rodoniki
1977   Ἅγιος Ἰωάννης εις θέσιν Φούρνιατα Πύργου Διροῦ [Ayios Ioannis in the Fourniata Neighborhood of Pyrgos Dirou]. *Lakonikai Spoudai* 3:459.
1982   Karyoupolis. Une ville byzantine désertée: Esquisse de géographie historique du nord-est du Magne [Karyoupolis. A Deserted Byzantine City: Sketch of the Historical Geography of North-Eastern Mani]. *Byzantion* 52:83–123.
1988   Καρυούπολις, μια ερειπωμένη βυζαντινή πόλη [Karyoupolis, a Ruined Byzantine City]. *Lakonikai Spoudai* 9:3–60.

Flannery, Kent V. (editor)
1976   *The Early Mesoamerican Village*. Academic Press, New York.

Forbes, Hamish A.
Forthcoming   Cisterns and Loutses in a Traditional Peloponnesian Village: Aspects of Function, Use, and Monumentality. In *Going Against the Flow. Wells, Cisterns and Water in Ancient Greece*, edited by Patrik Klingborg. Swedish Institute at Athens, Athens.

Foucault, Michel
1975   *Discipline and Punish: The Birth of the Prison*. Translated by Alan Sheridan. Vintage Books, New York.

Frangakis-Syrett, Elena, and J. Malcolm Wagstaff
   1992   The Height Zonation of Population in the Morea c. 1830. *The Annual of the British School at Athens* 87:439–446. https://doi.org/10.1017/S0068245400015252

Germanidou, Sophia
   2018   Mapping Agro-Pastoral Infrastructure in the Post-Medieval Landscape of Maniot Settlements: The Case-Study of Agios Nikon (ex. Poliana), Messenia. *Journal of Greek Archaeology* 3:359–404.

Gerstel, Sharon E. J.
   2015   *Rural Lives and Landscapes in Late Byzantium: Art, Archaeology, and Ethnography*. Cambridge University Press, Cambridge.
   2020   Recording Village History: The Church of Hagioi Theodoroi, Vamvaka, Mani. *Journal of Modern Greek Studies* 38(1):21–41. https://doi.org/10.1353/mgs.2020.0002

Gerstel, Sharon E. J., Mark Munn, Heather E. Grossman, Ethne Barnes, Arthur H. Rohn, and Machiel Kiel
   2003   A Late Medieval Settlement at Panakton. *Hesperia* 72(2):147–234. https://doi.org/10.2972/hesp.2003.72.2.147

Giddens, Anthony
   1984   *The Constitution of Society: Outline of the Theory of Structuration*. Polity Press, Cambridge.

Given, Michael
   2007   Mountain Landscapes on Early Modern Cyprus. In *Between Venice and Istanbul: Colonial Landscapes in Early Modern Greece*, edited by Siriol Davies and Jack L. Davis, pp. 137–148. American School of Classical Studies at Athens, Princeton, New Jersey.

Gkioles, Nikolaos
   1996   Ο ναός του Αγίου Θεοδώρου Άνω Πούλας στη Μέσα Μάνη [The Church of Ayios Theodoros in Ano Poula, Inner Mani]. *Lakonikai Spoudai* 13:277–305.

Goester, Yvonne C., and Dingenus M. van der Vrie
  1998   Lavda. The Excavation 1986–1988. *Pharos* 6:119–178.

Gregory, Timothy E.
  2010   Commentary: Medieval and Post-Medieval Archaeology of Greece. *International Journal of Historical Archaeology* 14(2):302–307. https://doi.org/10.1007/s10761-010-0108-8
  2013   People and Settlements of the Northeastern Peloponnese in the Late Middle Ages. In *Viewing the Morea: Land and People in the Late Medieval Peloponnese*, edited by Sharon E. J. Gerstel, pp. 277–306. Dumbarton Oaks Research Library and Collection, Washington, D.C.

Kahn, Jennifer G.
  2016   Household Archaeology in Polynesia: Historical Context and New Directions. *Journal of Archaeological Research* 24(4):325–372. https://doi.org/10.1007/s10814-016-9092-9

Kalopissi-Verti, Sophia
  2003   Epigraphic Evidence in Middle-Byzantine Churches of the Mani: Patronage and Art Production. In Λαμπηδών: Αφιέρωμα στη μνήμη της Ντούλας Μουρίκη *[Lampidon: Tribute to the Memory of Doula Mouriki]*, edited by Mary Aspra-Vardavaki, pp. 339–354. National Technical University of Athens Press, Athens.

Komis, Kostas
  2005   Πληθυσμός και οικισμοί της Μάνης: 15ος–19ος αιώνας *[Population and Settlements of Mani: 15th–19th Centuries]*. 2nd ed. University of Ioannina, Ioannina.

Konstantinidi, Chara
  1998   *Ο ναός της Φανερωμένης στα Φραγκουλιάνικα της Μέσα Μάνης [The Church of the Phaneromenis in Phrangoulianika, Inner Mani]*. Lakonikai Spoudai Parartima 2. Society for Laconian Studies, Athens.

Kourelis, Kostis
  2003   Monuments of Rural Archaeology: Medieval Settlements in the Northwestern Peloponnese. PhD dissertation, Department of Art and Archaeology of the Mediterranean World, University of Pennsylvania, Philadelphia. Proquest (AAI 3095902).
  2005   The Rural House in the Medieval Peloponnese: An Archaeological Reassessment of Byzantine Domestic Architecture. In *Archaeology in Architecture: Studies in Honor of Cecil L. Striker*, edited by Judson J. Emerick and Deborah M. Deliyannis, pp. 119–128. Verlag Philipp von Zabern, Mainz.
  2007   Review of Robert Ousterhout's A Byzantine Settlement in Cappadocia. *Journal of the Society of Architectural Historians* 66(3):395–397. https://doi.org/10.1525/jsah.2007.66.3.395
  2018   Zaraka Surrounded: The Archaeology of Settlements in the Peloponnesian Countryside. In *The Cistercian Monastery of Zaraka, Greece*, edited by Sheila Campbell, pp. 193–213. Monastic Life II. Medieval Institute Publications, Western Michigan University, Kalamazoo.
  2019   Wool and Rubble Walls: Domestic Architecture in the Medieval Peloponnese. *Dumbarton Oaks Papers* 73:165–185.

Kremmidas, V.
  1984   Δημογραφικά της Μάνης [Demography of Mani]. In *Αμητός: Στη μνήμη του Φώτη Αποστολόπουλου [Harvest: In Memory of Photis Apostolopoulos]*, pp. 73–78. Centre for Asia Minor Studies, Athens.

Laiou, Angeliki E.
  2005   The Byzantine Village (5th–14th Century). In *Les villages dans l'empire byzantin (IVe–XVe siècle) [Villages in the Byzantine Empire (4th–15th Centuries)]*, edited by Jacques Lefort, Cécile Morrisson, and Jean-Pierre Sodini, pp. 31–54. Réalités Byzantines 11. Lethielleux, Paris.

Liakopoulos, Georgios C.
  2019   *The Early Ottoman Peloponnese: A Study in the Light of an Annotated* editio princeps *of the TT10-1/14662 Ottoman Taxation Cadastre (ca. 1460–1463)*. Ibrahim Pasha of Egypt Fund Series. Gingko, London.

Longnon, Jean, and Peter Topping
1969 *Documents sur le régime des terres dans la principauté de Morée au XIVe siècle [Documents on the Land Regime in the Principality of Morea in the 14th Century]*. Mouton, Paris.

Lowry, Heath W.
1992 The Ottoman *Tahrîr Defterleri* as a Source for Social and Economic History: Pitfalls and Limitations. In *Studies in Defterology, Ottoman Society in the Fifteenth and Sixteenth Centuries*, pp. 3–8. Analecta Isisiana IV. Isis Press, Istanbul.

Mac Sweeney, Naoíse
2011 *Community Identity and Archaeology: Dynamic Communities at Aphrodisias and Beycesultan*. University of Michigan Press, Ann Arbor.

McDonald, William A., William D. E. Coulson, and John Rosser (editors)
1983 *Excavations at Nichoria in Southwest Greece: III. Dark Age and Byzantine Occupation*. University of Minnesota Press, Minneapolis.

Megaw, H.
1932/1933 Byzantine Architecture in Mani. *The Annual of the British School at Athens* 33:137–162.
https://doi.org/10.1017/S0068245400011862

Menenakou, Sophia
2007 Άγιος Σπυρίδων στους Μπουλαριούς Μάνης (1792). Παρατηρήσεις στις επιγραφές, την αρχιτεκτονική και το εικονογραφικό πρόγραμμα [Ayios Spyridon in Boularioi, Mani (1792): Observations on Inscriptions, Architecture and the Pictorial Program]. *Lakonikai Spoudai* 17:163–178.

Mexia, Angeliki
2008/2009 Άγνωστοι βυζαντινοί ναοί στον Μαντοφόρο του Πύργου Διρού [The Unknown Byzantine Churches in Mantophoros in Pyrgos Dirou]. In *Επιστημονικό συμπόσιο στη μνήμη Νικολάου Β. Δρανδάκη για τη βυζαντινή Μάνη, Καραβοστάσι Οιτύλου 21–22 Ιουνίου 2008, πρακτικά [Proceedings of the Scientific Symposium in Memory of Nikolaos V. Drandakis on Byzantine Mani, Karavostasi Oitylo, 21–22 June 2008]*, edited by Evangelia P. Eleftheriou and Angeliki Mexia, pp. 127–142. Ministry of Culture and Tourism, 5th Ephorate of Byzantine Antiquities, Sparta.

2011 Βυζαντινή ναοδομία στην Πελοπόννησο: η περίπτωση των μεσοβυζαντινών ναών της Μέσα Μάνης [Byzantine Church Architecture in the Peloponnese: The Case of the Middle Byzantine Churches of Inner Mani]. PhD dissertation, Department of History and Archaeology, National and Kapodistrian University of Athens, Athens.

Moatsos, Errikos
1976/1978   Ὁ υπ' αριθ. 1645 (Κατατ. 7753) Κώδιξ VII κλάσ. ιταλ. χειρ. της Μαρκιανής Βιβλιοθήκης [Cod. cl. VII No 1645 (coll. 7753) in the Marciana Library in Italy]. In *Πρακτικά του Α΄ διεθνούς συνεδρίου Πελοποννησιακών Σπουδών (Σπάρτη, 7–14 Σεπτεμβρίου 1975), τόμος Γ΄ Νεώτερος Πολιτισμός [Acts of the First International Congress of Peloponnesian Studies (Sparta, 7–14 September 1975), Vol. III: Modern Civilization]*, pp. 67–72. Peloponnisiaka Parartima 6. Society for Peloponnesian Studies, Athens.

Moschos, Takis, and Leda Moschou
1981   Παλαιομανιάτικα: Οι βυζαντινοί αγροτικοί οικισμοί της Λακωνικής Μάνης [Palaiomaniatika: The Byzantine Rural Settlements of Laconian Mani]. *Athens Annals of Archaeology* 14(1):3–28.
1982   The Palaeomaniatika: The Transition from Ancient Polis to Byzantine Chora. *Ekistics* 49:261–270.

Moschou, Leda
1982   Μια αγροτική περιοχή της Ανατολικής Λακωνικής Μάνης στον Κώδικα Ambrosianus Trotti 373 [A Rural Area of Eastern Laconian Mani in the Codex Ambrosianus Trotti 373]. In *Akten des XVI. Internationalen Byzantinistenkongresses, Wien 4.-9. Oktober. II. Teil: Buch und Gesellschaft in Byzanz. Theologie und Philosophie in der Palaiologenzeit. Byzantinische Architektur [Acts of the 16th International Byzantine Congress, Vienna 4–9 October. Part II: Book and Society in Byzantium, Theology and Philosophy in the Palaeologan Period, Byzantine Architecture]*, pp. 639–656. Jahrbuch der Österreichischen Byzantinistik 32.4. Verlag der Österreichischen Akademie der Wissenschaften, Vienna.

2004 Ruined Byzantine Rural Settlements in Lakonian Mani. In *Settlements of Mani*, edited by Pari Kalamara and Nikos Roumeliotis, pp. 30–36. Hellenic Ministry of Culture, Network of Mani Museums 1. Kapon, Athens.

Moutsopoulos, N. K., and G. Dimitrokallis
1976/1978 Τα μεγαλιθικά μνημεία της Μάνης [The Megalithic Monuments of Mani]. In *Πρακτικά του Α διεθνούς συνεδρίου Πελοποννησιακών Σπουδών (Σπάρτη, 7–14 Σεπτεμβρίου 1975), τόμος Β Αρχαιότης και Βυζάντιον* [*Acts of the First International Congress of Peloponnesian Studies (Sparta, 7–14 September 1975), Vol. II: Antiquity and Byzantium*], pp. 135–169. Peloponnisiaka Parartima 6. Society for Peloponnesian Studies, Athens.
1980 Νεώτερες έρευνες στα μεγαλιθικά μνημεία της Μάνης [New Research on the Megalithic Monuments of Mani]. In *Πρακτικά του Α συνεδρίου Λακωνικών Σπουδών (Σπάρτ-Γύθειον, 7–11 Οκτωβρίου 1977), τεύχος Β'* [*Proceedings of the 1st Conference of Laconian Studies (Sparta–Gytheio, 7–11 October 1977), issue II*], pp. 385–390. Lakonikai Spoudai 5. Society for Laconian Studies, Athens.

Nash, Donna J.
2009 Household Archaeology in the Andes. *Journal of Archaeological Research* 17(3):205–261.
https://doi.org/10.1007/s10814-009-9029-7

Netting, Robert McC., Richard R. Wilk, and Eric J. Arnould (editors)
1984 *Households: Comparative and Historical Studies of the Domestic Group.* University of California Press, Berkeley.

Nevett, Lisa C., E. Bettina Tsigarida, Zosia H. Archibald, David L. Stone, Timothy J. Horsley, Bradley A. Ault, Anna Panti, Kathleen M. Lynch, Hannah Pethen, Susan M. Stallibrass, Elina Salminen, Christopher Gaffney, Thomas J. Sparrow, Sean Taylor, John Manousakis, and Dimitrios Zekkos
2017 Towards a Multi-Scalar, Multidisciplinary Approach to the Classical Greek City: The Olynthos Project. *The Annual of the British School at Athens* 112:155–206.
https://doi.org/10.1017/S0068245417000090

Ousterhout, Robert G.
  2005   *A Byzantine Settlement in Cappadocia.* Dumbarton Oaks, Washington, D.C.
  2017   *Visualizing Community: Art, Material Culture, and Settlement in Byzantine Cappadocia.* Dumbarton Oaks, Washington, D.C.

Panagiotopoulos, Vasilis
  1987   Πληθυσμός και οικισμοί της Πελοποννήσου: 13ος–18ος αιώνας *[Population and Settlements of the Peloponnese: 13th–18th Centuries].* Historical Archive, Commercial Bank of Greece, Athens.

Pawlowski, Mark James
  2020   Intensive Architectural Survey of Byzantine Rural Settlements: A Case Study from the Mani. *Journal of Greek Archaeology* 5:495–513.

Pluckhahn, Thomas J.
  2010   Household Archaeology in the Southeastern United States: History, Trends, and Challenges. *Journal of Archaeological Research* 18(4):331–385. https://doi.org/10.1007/s10814-010-9040-z

Pullen, Daniel J., Michael L. Galaty, William A. Parkinson, Wayne E. Lee, and Rebecca M. Seifried
  2018   The Diros Project, 2011–2013: Surface Survey and Site Collection in Diros Bay. In *Neolithic Alepotrypa Cave in the Mani, Greece,* edited by Anastasia Papathanasiou, William A. Parkinson, Daniel J. Pullen, Michael L. Galaty, and Panagiotis Karkanas, pp. 407–425. Oxbow Books, Oxford.

Rapoport, Amos
  1969   *House Form and Culture.* Prentice-Hall, Englewood Cliffs, New Jersey.
  1982   *The Meaning of the Built Environment.* Sage Publications, Beverly Hills, California.

Reimer, Paula J, Edouard Bard, Alex Bayliss, J Warren Beck, Paul G Blackwell, Christopher Bronk Ramsey, Caitlin E Buck, Hai Cheng, R Lawrence Edwards, Michael Friedrich, Pieter M Grootes, Thomas P Guilderson, Haflidi Haflidason, Irka Hajdas, Christine Hatté, Timothy J Heaton, Dirk L Hoffmann, Alan G Hogg, Konrad A Hughen, K Felix Kaiser, Bernd Kromer, Sturt W Manning, Mu Niu, Ron W Reimer, David A Richards, E Marian Scott, John R Southon, Richard A Staff, Christian S M Turney, and Johannes van der Plicht
- 2013   IntCal13 and Marine13 Radiocarbon Age Calibration Curves 0–50,000 Years cal BP. *Radiocarbon* 55(4):1869–1887. https://doi.org/10.2458/azu_js_rc.55.16947

Saïtas, Yanis
- 1983a Ορθόλιθοι στη Μέσα Μάνη [Menhirs in Inner Mani]. In *Πρακτικά του Α΄ τοπικού συνεδρίου Λακωνικών Μελετών, Μολάοι 5–7 Ιουνίου 1982 [Proceedings of the 1st Local Conference of Laconian Studies, Molaoi, 5–7 June 1982]*, pp. 151–168. Peloponnisiaka Parartima 9. Society for Peloponnesian Studies, Athens.
- 1983b Μάνη: οικιστική και αρχιτεκτονική εξέλιξη στους μέσους και νεότερους χρόνους [Mani: Residential and Architectural Development in Medieval and Modern Times]. *Deltio tes Etaireias Spoudon Neoellenikou Politismou kai Genikes Paideias* 6A:79–100.
- 1990   *Greek Traditional Architecture: Mani*. Translated by Philip Ramp. Melissa Publishing House, Athens.
- 2004   Chores and Villages, Houses, Towers and Fortified Complexes. In *Settlements of Mani*, edited by Pari Kalamara and Nikos Roumeliotis, pp. 54–65. Hellenic Ministry of Culture, Network of Mani Museums 1. Kapon Editions, Athens.
- 2009a Social and Spatial Organization in the Peninsula of the Mani (Southern Peloponnese): Medieval, Post-Medieval and Modern Times. In *Medieval and Post-Medieval Greece: The Corfu Papers*, edited by John Bintliff and Hanna Stöger, pp. 133–152. BAR International Series 2023. Archaeopress, Oxford.
- 2009b The Cemeteries of Mani in Mediaeval and Later Periods: A First Contribution. *British School at Athens Studies* 16:371–385.

> 2011 Cemeteries and Settlements of Mani in Medieval and Later Periods: A Second Contribution. In *Honouring the Dead in the Peloponnese: Proceedings of the Conference Held at Sparta 23–25 April 2009*, edited by Helen Cavanagh, William Cavanagh, and James Roy, pp. 657–718. CSPS Online Publication 2. University of Nottingham, Nottingham.

Sanders, Guy D. R.
> 2014 Landlords and Tenants: Sharecroppers and Subsistence Farming in Corinthian Historical Context. In *Corinth in Contrast: Studies in Inequality*, edited by Steven J. Friesen, Sarah A. James, and Daniel N. Schowalter, pp. 103–125. Brill, Leiden.

Santley, Robert S., and Kenneth G. Hirth (editors)
> 1992 *Prehispanic Domestic Units in Western Mesoamerica: Studies of the Household, Compound, and Residence*. CRC Press, Boca Raton, Florida.

Scott, James C.
> 2009 *The Art of Not Being Governed: An Anarchist History of Upland Southeast Asia*. Yale Agrarian Studies Series. Yale University Press, New Haven, Connecticut.

Seifried, Rebecca M.
> 2015 The Shifting Tides of Empires: Using GIS to Contextualize Population Change Within the Landscape of Seventeenth to Nineteenth-Century Mani, Greece. *International Journal of Historical Archaeology* 19(1):46–75. https://doi.org/10.1007/s10761-014-0281-2
> 2016 Community Organization and Imperial Expansion in a Rural Landscape: The Mani Peninsula (AD 1000-1821). PhD dissertation, Department of Anthropology, University of Illinois at Chicago, Chicago.
> 2020a Seascapes and Fresh Water Management in Rural Greece: The Case of the Mani Peninsula, 1261–1821 CE. *Levant*. 51(2):131-150. https://doi.org/10.1080/00758914.2020.1789316
> 2020b Measurements of 406 Medieval and Post-Medieval Houses in the Southern Mani Peninsula, Greece. Zenodo. https://doi.org/10.5281/zenodo.4307903

2021 The Legacy of Byzantine Christianity in the Southern Mani Peninsula, Greece, after Imperial Collapse. In *Rituals, Collapse, and Radical Transformation in Archaic States*, edited by Joanne M.A. Murphy, pp. 56–76. Routledge, New York.

Seifried, Rebecca M., and Tuna Kalaycı
2019 An Exploratory Spatial Analysis of the Churches in the Southern Mani Peninsula, Greece. *Open Archaeology* 5(1):519–539. https://doi.org/10.1515/opar-2019-0032

Sigalos, Lefteris
2004a *Housing in Medieval and Post-Medieval Greece*. BAR International Series 1291. Archaeopress, Oxford.
2004b Middle and Late Byzantine Houses in Greece (Tenth to Fifteenth Centuries). In *Secular Buildings and the Archaeology of Everyday Life in the Byzantine Empire*, edited by Ken Dark, pp. 53–81. Oxbow Books, Oxford.

Souvatzi, Stella
2008 *A Social Archaeology of Households in Neolithic Greece: An Anthropological Approach*. Cambridge University Press, Cambridge.
2012 Space, Place, and Architecture: A Major Meeting Point between Social Archaeology and Anthropology? In *Archaeology and Anthropology: Past, Present and Future*, edited by David Shankland, pp. 173–196. Berg, London.
2014 The Social Dynamics of Everyday Life. *Reviews in Anthropology* 43(4):238–259. https://doi.org/10.1080/00938157.2014.964067

Stedman, Nancy
1996 Land Use and Settlement in Post-Medieval Central Greece: An Interim Discussion. In *The Archaeology of Medieval Greece*, edited by Peter Lock and Guy D. R. Sanders, pp. 179–192. Oxbow Monograph 59. Oxbow Books, Oxford.

Topping, Peter
   1976/1978   The Population of the Morea (1684–1715). In Πρακτικά του Α διεθνούς συνεδρίου Πελοποννησιακών Σπουδών (Σπάρτη, 7-14 Σεπτεμβρίου 1975), τόμος Α Ολομέλεια [Acts of the First International Congress of Peloponnesian Studies (Sparta, 7–14 September 1975), Vol. I: Plenary], pp. 119–128. Peloponnisiaka Parartima 6. Society for Peloponnesian Studies, Athens.

Traquair, Ramsay
   1908/1909   The Churches of Western Mani. *The Annual of the British School at Athens* 15:177–213.
       https://www.jstor.org/stable/30096410

Tzortzopoulou-Gregory, Lita
   2010   Remembering and Forgetting: The Relationship Between Memory and the Abandonment of Graves in Nineteenth- and Twentieth-Century Greek Cemeteries. *International Journal of Historical Archaeology* 14(2):285–301.
       https://doi.org/10.1007/s10761-010-0109-7

Tzortzopoulou-Gregory, Lita, and Timothy E. Gregory
   2017   The Karavas Water Project: An Archaeological and Environmental Study of Interaction and Community in Northern Kythera. *Journal of Greek Archaeology* 2:343–376.

Vionis, Athanasios K.
   2009   Material Culture Studies: The Case of the Medieval and Post-Medieval Cyclades, Greece (c. AD 1200–1800). In *Medieval and Post-Medieval Greece: The Corfu Papers*, edited by John Bintliff and Hanna Stöger, pp. 177–197. BAR International Series 2023. Archaeopress, Oxford.
   2016   A Boom-Bust Cycle in Ottoman Greece and the Ceramic Legacy of Two Boeotian Villages. *Journal of Greek Archaeology* 1:353–384.
   2020   Landscape Approaches to the Evolution of the Byzantine/Medieval Village-Community in Greece. *Journal of Greek Archaeology* 5:468–494.

Wagstaff, J. Malcolm
   1977   Settlements in the South-Central Peloponnisos, c. 1618. In *An Historical Geography of the Balkans*, edited by Francis W. Carter, pp. 197–238. Academic Press, New York.
   2000   Change in the Agriculture of the Mani 1960/62–1992/93. *Lakonikai Spoudai* 15:127–174.

Wilk, Richard R., and Wendy Ashmore (editors)
   1988   *Household and Community in the Mesoamerican Past*. University of New Mexico Press, Albuquerque.

Wilk, Richard R., and William L. Rathje
   1982   Household Archaeology. *American Behavioral Scientist* 25(6):617–639. https://doi.org/10.1177/000276482025006003

Yaeger, Jason
   2000   The Social Construction of Communities in the Classical Maya Countryside: Strategies of Affiliation in Western Belize. In *The Archaeology of Communities: A New World Perspective*, edited by Marcello A. Canuto and Jason Yaeger, pp. 123–142. Routledge, New York.

Zarinebaf, Fariba, John Bennet, and Jack L. Davis (editors)
   2005   *A Historical and Economic Geography of Ottoman Greece: The Southwestern Morea in the 18th Century*. Hesperia Supplement 34. The American School of Classical Studies at Athens, Athens.

PART II

Abandonment in the Recent Past

Chapter Five
Landscapes of Home and Thereafter: The Condition, Educational Potential, and Natural Environment of Penteskouphi Hamlet

Isabel Sanders, Miyon Yoo, and Guy D. R. Sanders

This paper offers no hypothesis that is intended to advance our understanding of desertification (Friesem et al. 2011). However, we do have an agenda. We wish to show that Penteskouphi is an exemplary educational tool for archaeologists to learn that open-minded observation, multidisciplinary communication, and an ability to relate personally to what one sees can provide a logical, in-depth understanding of archaeological sites and their formation processes. We will demonstrate this by describing the geology, geomorphology, flora, and archaeology of Penteskouphi, as well as by outlining its creation, occupation, and desertion as observed through the deterioration of its built structures back into the natural environment from which their materials were extracted. By doing so, we will highlight the types of characteristics integral to comprehending sites and their formation. Another vital element to our thesis is the relationship between people and their physical environment. People and the landscapes they inhabit are mutually defining. Referring both to an urbanized and pastoral environment, the term *landscape* itself has been defined as a manifestation of the interaction between people and their physical context. The physical formation and metaphysical conceptualization of the landscape are, therefore, coeval to that of human social existence (Schama 1995). It is a place that is neither natural nor artificial. Indeed, it is not so much a place as a symbiosis between humans and their environment (Rackham and Moody 1997). Neither contributing organism would or could be what it is without the other. Though it may seem plainly obvious, we believe that it is important to highlight this connection inherent in the term *landscape* as it is often taken for granted. When the focus, as it too regularly has been, is on civilizations as viewed through the more grandiose material culture they produce, an asymmetrical vision of the past materializes that gives little insight into what people populating these civilizations were actually like. Learning to view people as products as well as manufacturers of their environments (and vice versa) is vital for archaeologists to understand what they are seeing while studying or excavating a site.

The houses at Penteskouphi are made of materials gathered or processed locally: limestone, marl clay, *kalamia*,[1] timber, ceramic, and lime. The immediate environment also sustained those who created the settlement. There is also another, perhaps less tangible, dimension to the place. The settlers selected the location, made productive and even decorative homes and gardens, and built churches, thereby ascribing their landscape with an extended cultural purpose. They made their settlement a real place, a *topos*. It is important to describe both the life of the settlement as well as its demise, as the importance of one defines the other. The panoramic views, physical beauty, varied geology, and flora it supports, as well as the history of human exploitation, play vital roles in the formation of the symbiosis that is the subject of this paper. They also make it a place of particular interest for touristic and wide-ranging educational purposes. Since plants and the landscape in which they grow provide invaluable clues for understanding how land has been used and managed over time, we will provide an as-thorough-as-possible characterization of the area in order to assist the reader in understanding its physical and metaphysical context (Figure 1).

As we have said, the deserted hamlet at Penteskouphi, located a short drive from the base of the American School of Classical Studies at Ancient Corinth, is an ideal place for introducing students of archaeology to site formation processes at first hand. The site is an ephemeral one; the remains of one building, in particular, which we will discuss at length below, show that one day it will require a trained eye to understand that the place was ever inhabited. As the buildings fall into ruin, accumulations of tiles and clay, like the ones sometimes seen when excavating, are an unforgettable lesson in distinguishing between in situ archaeological deposits and those which are not. Roof and wall collapses are primary deposits, whereas earth spread after digging a foundation trench, pipeline, or garbage pit is not. Features encountered while digging that are difficult to discern and understand include animal scuffs, erosion channels, puddles, patches of water-sorted gravel and clay, piles of earth, and evenly trampled surfaces with embedded bones and sherds. Additionally, inside some of the now-abandoned houses, one can still see the material culture

---

[1] *Kalamia* (καλάμια) can refer to any number of reed-like plants that grow beside water or in wet areas. In most cases, however, it is used to describe the plant *Arundo donax*, commonly known as Spanish cane or giant reed.

Figure 1. *Campanula andrewsii* subsp. *andrewsii* is a chasmophytic plant endemic to the northeastern Peloponnese. Here it is seen growing out of the conglomerate cap of the as-yet-unrecorded Penteskouphi marine terrace (see "Geology" section and **Figure 5**, **Figure 6**, and **Figure 7**), with Penteskouphi and Acrocorinth in the background. This image brings together some of the facets that make Penteskouphi a *topos*, with points of interest for amateurs, professionals, and scholars alike. Image courtesy of Isabel Sanders.

left behind by seasonal as well as once-permanent residents. It is a relic of a rural settlement before the plastics- and concrete-dominated Anthropocene era impacted the Peloponnesian countryside. By becoming sensitized to observing and recording the mundane occurrences responsible for the degradation of mud-brick buildings—site formation process in action—both students and, for that matter, established archaeologists can better understand what they are seeing during excavations and what those things may signify.

Two of the authors have visited deserted houses in and around Ancient Corinth for over 20 years, but the ruins only became the subject of study about 15 years ago. The original intent of the study was to develop a personal understanding of how stone houses dilapidate and mud-brick houses dissolve. Since it was never intended for publication but instead only for experiential learning purposes, there was no systematic recording of the buildings, their contents, or processes beyond photographic images. Although the photographs do record and transmit what we have observed and learned about formation processes to others, in retrospect, it is regrettable that we did not carry out any sustained systematic recording. Suitable subjects for study are already and will become increasingly difficult to find. Even at Penteskouphi, some of the initial subjects of our study have since been bulldozed. Happily, this incomplete record of Penteskouphi is amply mitigated by a recent study of Chelmis, a hamlet in the western Argolid (Erny and Caraher 2020), Lakka Skoutara in the eastern Corinthia (Pettegrew and Caraher, this volume), and Wheelock in North Dakota (Rothaus et al., this volume).

Having been given the opportunity to write this paper, we have undertaken more rigorous analyses of the site. The conclusions we draw are based on multidisciplinary personal observation. Each participant—through education, experience, and intuition—identified different characteristics in the landscape, which pointed to different aspects of the inception, creation, and demise of Penteskouphi. It is with pleasure that, via this publication, we can share our conjoined observations and understanding of a site that bears such experiential learning potential.

Environmental Context

Location and Topography

Penteskouphi, 4.5 km southwest of Ancient Corinth as the crow flies, is situated beside a modest streambed at the lower point of a small valley that slopes gently upwards to the south and southeast (Figure 2 and Figure 3). Within the settlement, houses and their auxiliary structures are grouped around yards, but fields are interspersed between these residential complexes, forming an irregular patchwork. To the south of the village, the fields continue and fan out in long, narrow strips, a typical method of dividing land in this area. The settlement is flanked to the east by the hill of Kastraki, which rises away from the streambed; there, claggy-soiled olive groves merge with the tougher, stonier lands on which grows a dense and diverse patchwork of phrygana and maquis plants. To the northwest, the ground rises to the oxblood-colored Ayios Tryphonas plateau, upon which fields are laid out in a random tessellated pattern; the plateau culminates to the south in an odd narrowing strip capped with a large slab of conglomerate, which was exposed by erosion after a wildfire in the summer of 2012. Beyond this, the land falls abruptly away into a network of ravines and badlands. To the north, the cultivated land tumbles gradually away into the wrinkles and furrows of the deep gorges of the Litsa stream that runs past the Neolithic to Late Bronze Age (4000–1100 BC) site of Aetopetra (Blegen 1920; Chatzipouliou-Kalliri 1984).

The fields that surround the settlement and spread atop the plateau are remarkably level, a characteristic that can be attributed to the nature of the soil and underlying rock as much as to human interference. Some are regularly plowed and irrigated, while others have been left to their own devices; all are of clay. Otherwise, the environment is highly variable and includes sheer rocky cliffs, shady watery pockets, thin impoverished soils, and patches of coniferous forest. The complex topography and geology make it possible for a remarkable variety of plants to flourish in a relatively condensed area, which, in turn, made it such a lucrative and desirable place for the settlers of Penteskouphi to build an extension of their agricultural community. Some believe Penteskouphi is situated on the road from Corinth to Kleones (Marchand 2009), but early maps of the region show that this road actually followed the Longopotamos valley (Figure 4; Blegen 1920; Morosini 2018 [1687]; Pelet 1832; Steffen 1884). As we will see, the village occupies a pivotal spot within a very specific landscape and was always an intentional destination, not merely a point along the way to somewhere else.

Penteskouphi literally means "five hoods" (imagine the hood of a medieval cape) but the etymology is uncertain. Some historians and archaeologists have speculated that it is a modern Greek corruption of Mont Escovée, one of the names given to a Frankish stronghold built as part of the siege works to remove Leon Sgouros from Acrocorinth in the early thirteenth century (Finley 1932:485; Miller 1908:36). This speculation relies on the hypothesis that Mont Escovée is the small fortified hill (locally known as Kastraki) that rises immediately to the east of our

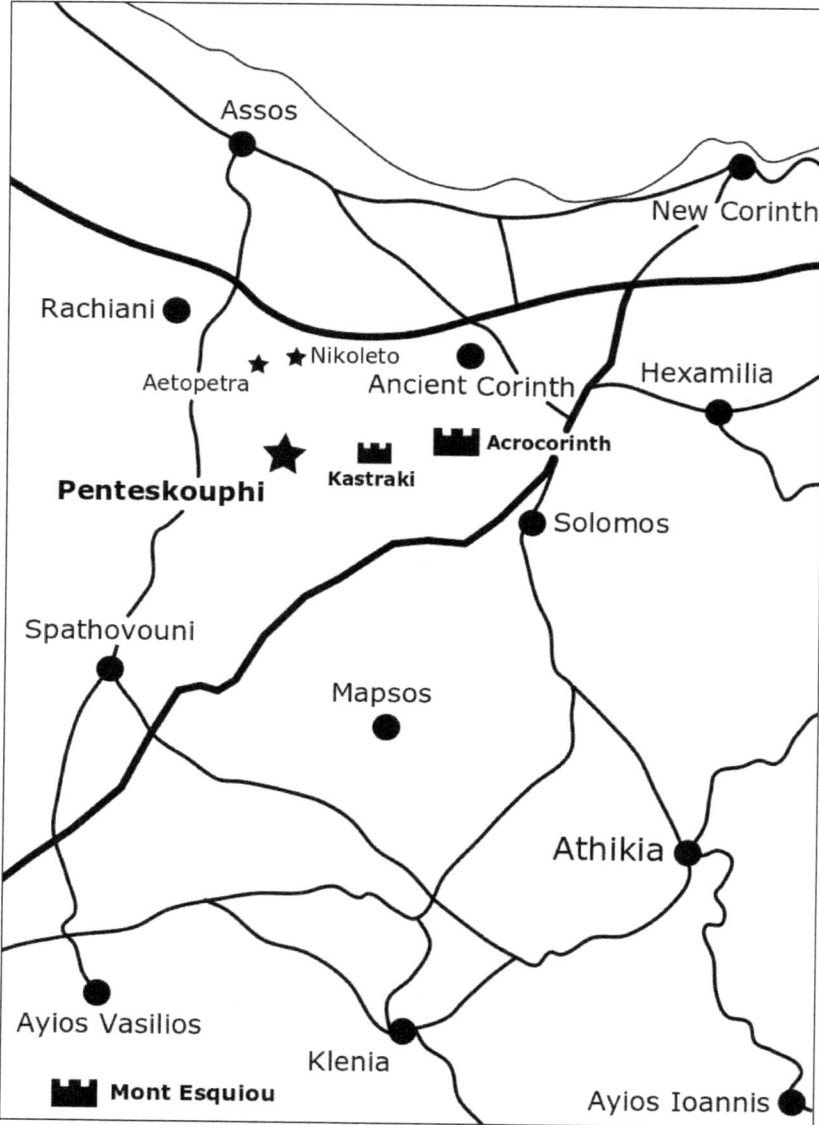

Figure 2. Map showing location of Penteskouphi in relation to Ayios Vasilios, Athikia, and Ancient Corinth. Image courtesy of Guy Sanders.

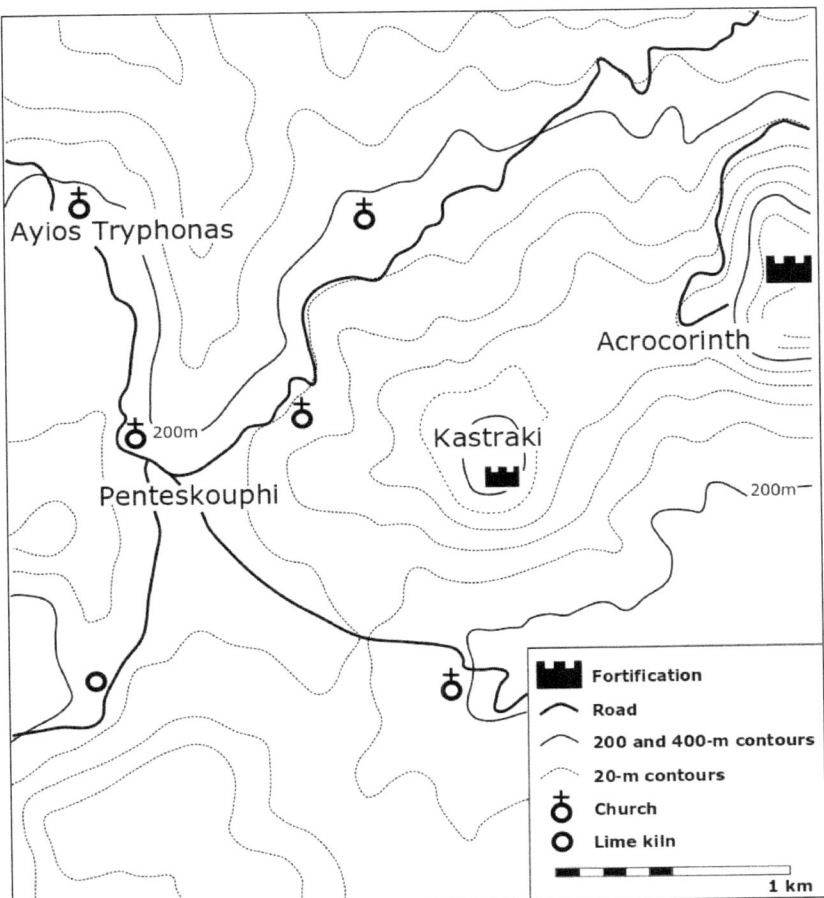

Figure 3. Penteskouphi and its environs. Image courtesy of Guy Sanders.

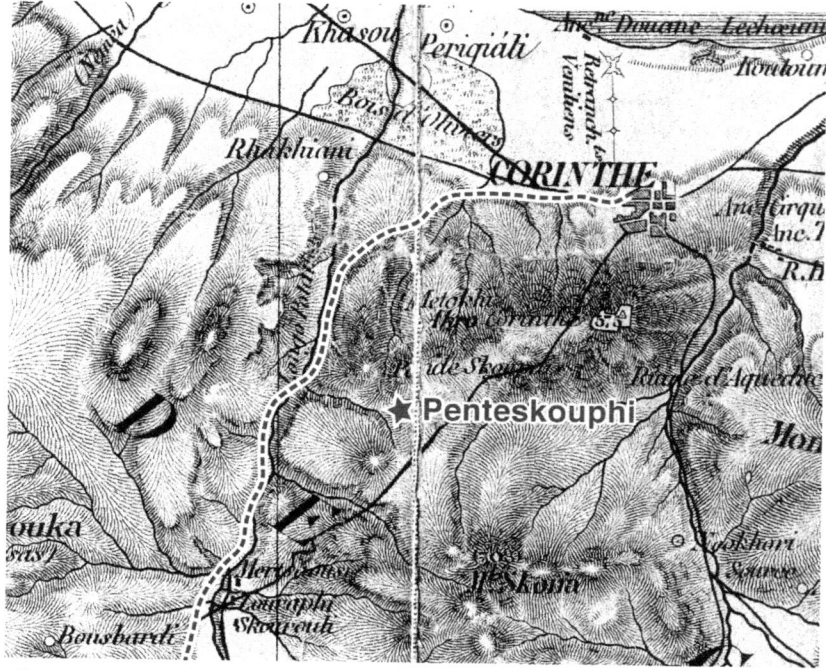

Figure 4. General Pelet's *Carte de la Morée* showing the Corinth–Kleones road (here accentuated in dashed line) heading west out of Corinth before entering the Longopotamos valley. Image courtesy of Guy Sanders.

village, between it and Acrocorinth (Figure 5; Bon 1969). Although the tower on Kastraki can be said to be Frankish, the actual cannon platform is later, probably dating to the Venetian period (Athanasoulis 2009:103). According to Teresa Shawcross (2009:85), the fourteenth-century *Chronicle of the Morea* places Mont Escovée (or Esquiou) on Mount Niphitsa, which rises above the Ayios Vasilios plain over 10 km to the south-southwest of Kastraki (see Figure 2). In fact, the *Chronicle of the Morea* vaguely says that Mont Escovée was built on a plateau dominating a ravine to the south of Corinth (Buchon 1840:69, 763), and while Kastraki is neither south of Acrocorinth nor on a plateau, it could be said to be flanking a ravine. Possible support for Shawcross's assertion is that the nearby village of Kontostavlos (ancient Kleones) may have been so named because its lands were held by the Constable of the Frankish army ("Kontostavlos" in the *Chronicles of the Morea*; Buchon 1840:181, 756). There is evidence of prior occupation dating to the Middle Byzantine period at Penteskouphi. This can be deduced from the findings of surface pottery at Penteskouphi as well as a scatter of tiles and medieval pottery near the church of Ayios Tryphonas 700 m to the north-northwest of the modern village. There

Figure 5. Miyon Yoo standing upon the Penteskouphi terrace southwest of Penteskouphi with Kastraki and Acrocorinth in the background. Image courtesy of Isabel Sanders.

are also remains of a small medieval church 750 m to the northeast. So, although the Penteskouphi settlement is coeval to Frankish Mont Escovée, based on our evidence, it is unlikely that the name Penteskouphi is derived from it. Modern Greek name derivation and word formation is such that the settlement's name could have any number of random etymologies. For example, the first published citation of Penteskouphi was in 1827 when it was said to contain five houses (Pouquville 1827:182), but as it does not appear on the *Carte de la Morée* (Pelet 1832) there is little supplementary evidence to support this citation as a name derivation.

Figure 6. Conglomerate capping on the marl clay bed of the Penteskouphi terrace. Image courtesy of Isabel Sanders.

Geology

The immediate area preserves a remarkable diversity of soil types. There is the acidic *kokkinochoma* (red earth, or *terra rossa*) clay, which is a chemical disintegration of the limestone on the Ayios Tryphonas plateau. This is largely a limestone conglomerate that caps the otherwise ubiquitous pelagic deposits of white marl clay, which is alkaline (Figure 6). In places, the soils are sharply drained, and in others they are apt to become waterlogged. These conditions support a broad diversity of flora and fauna, including humans, that are particular to them.[2]

The oldest geological feature of the area is Kastraki hill to the east. This is a steeply dipping (ca. 70° northwest) Middle Jurassic, pale grey limestone with a fine grain, overlain by a series of conglomerates, siliceous cherts (green and dark red mudstone), and white porcelanite. There are five marine terraces attested in the eastern Corinthia (Figure 7). Respectively, these are the Nikoleto terrace at an elevation of 222 m above sea level (masl), dated to ca. 580 ± 5 thousand years (kyr), the Temple terrace (100 masl, 310 ± 5 kyr), the Ancient Corinth terrace (80 masl, 240 ± 5 kyr) below it, the Sataika terrace at Kato Hexamilia (43 masl, 195 ± 5 kyr), and the New Corinth terrace on the coast (14 masl, 123 ± 7 kyr; Armijo et al. 1996; Karymbalis et al. 2016). In addition to these five, there is the remnant of an undated sixth terrace, which we call Penteskouphi terrace, now mostly eroded and not yet investigated by geologists. This survives on a small, low hill south of the village and on a larger hill to the south-southeast at an elevation of between 285 and 320 masl (Figure 8). This terrace is contextually important because it is the backbone of the formation of the raw materials that were so key to the settlers of the area.

An example is the marl capped by this oldest terrace. This provides a potting clay that is almost unparalleled in the region and that is frequently found with mudstone, an ingredient used by potters in antiquity. A kiln site exploiting both this clay and a local red clay exists on the low hillock south of the path leading from Acrocorinth to Kastraki. Historically, the mudstone was used as temper (e.g. in tiles, *pitharia*, etc.) in order to make the clay stronger and allow for a better transfer of heat during firing. What is more, as we shall see, this mudstone has been found to have good agricultural qualities as well.

---

[2] Indeed, the hills of Acrocorinth and Kastraki have been deemed "Sites of Community Importance and Special Areas of Conservation" by the Natura 2000 initiative. The area is protected due to the unique combination of archaeological interest, natural beauty, and the presence of rare or highly endemic species of plants and animals (European Commission 2017).

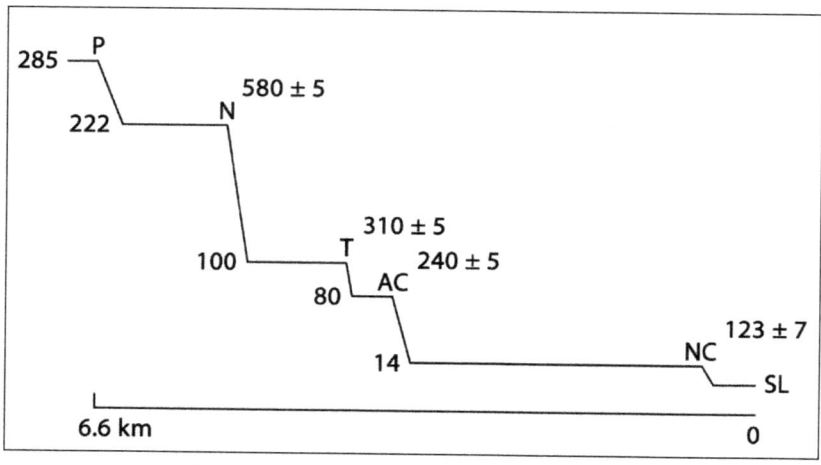

Figure 7. Section from the terrace above Penteskouphi to the sea with elevation in meters above sea level (masl) and age in thousands of years (kyr). P = Penteskouphi terrace, N = Nikoleto terrace, T = Temple terrace, AC = Ancient Corinth terrace, NC = New Corinth terrace, SL = sea level. Vertical scale exaggerated 400%. Note that the Sataika terrace is omitted because it does not appear in the transect from the Penteskouphi terrace to the sea. Image courtesy of Guy Sanders.

Agricultural Production

The fields of the Penteskouphi valley mainly belong to farmers from the village of Athikia, a brisk 12-km—or approximately two-hour walk—to the southeast. The Athikiotes also had property in the upland plain of Ayios Ioannis in the hills that backed the village. Where the land is not covered with pine woods, it is stony with thin, poor soils only suitable for keeping flocks and cultivating barley. For this reason, they acquired the land at Penteskouphi for cultivating what they could not grow closer to home: mainly vines for making wine or currants and more palatable, nutritionally rich cereals. These both require periods of prolonged and intense seasonal activity.

The grapes were harvested and processed in early autumn, and the fields were plowed twice later in the season: once to break up the soil and promote water penetration, and a second time to plow in the weeds that sprang up. With this done, the fields were then sown with wheat. In January or February, the settlers performed the time-consuming and laborious but vital tasks of pruning, tilling, and welling the vines (Leake 1830:144).[3] A third long stint of agricultural work took place in summer,

---

[3] There are two churches at Penteskouphi. The saints to whom they are dedicated both have their feast days at this momentous time of year and represent the

Figure 8. From the hill southwest of Penteskouphi looking across the plain toward Mount Skoria and Mapsos. The elevated plateau covered with pine saplings is a remnant of the Penteskouphi terrace south of the village. Image courtesy of Isabel Sanders.

all-important tasks taking place in the vineyards during this time. One is dedicated to Ayios Antonios (January 17), who is the patron saint of basketry, among other things. The baskets used for collecting grapes were often woven from the vine prunings themselves. The other church is dedicated to Ayios Tryphonas (February 1), the patron saint of gardeners and viticulturists.

when the crops were harvested and the wheat was likely threshed, although we have not found evidence of an *aloni* (threshing floor) at Penteskouphi. Between these long periods of work at Penteskouphi, the farmers could return to their upland pastures for lambing, cheesemaking, resin collecting, and other necessary chores. When donkeys were the main form of transport, the distance between Penteskouphi and the primary home in Athikia meant that a wine press, a storeroom, a stable, and accommodation were essential for several months every year when they were working. Hence, it was worth the time to build permanent structures.

As for the cereal crops, despite some pessimistic assessments by historians of Greek and Roman Corinthia, who assume wheat yields of only 3:1 (Engels 1990:27; Salmon 1984:130), crop yields in the region appear to have been relatively high. A consortium of nineteenth-century cash croppers who rented land from the government along the coastal plains and terraces of Corinthia declared yields of 5:1 (Andreades 1996:198–199; Sanders 2014:106). According to Carl Blegen (1920:13), in 1918 the village of Ancient Corinth produced about 300 tons of wheat, 300 tons of barley, and 700 tons of barley cut green for fodder. It was a productive year, although the harvest would have been better had not a shortage of grain from the previous year's poor harvest forced the farmers to sow lightly. In the same year, the village also produced 300 tons of currants, 50,000 gallons of wine, and 20,000 gallons of oil. Neighboring Hexamilia's *kokkinochoma* soil was considered to be much superior to the marl soils. In the 1940s and 1950s, the Arberores family expected wheat yields on the lower terrace at Ancient Corinth of about 4:1 or 5:1. They had one memorably bad year when their yields were slightly less than 2:1 and one memorably good year when their fields produced a yield of over 6:1 (Aristomenes Arberores, personal communication 2003; Sanders 2014:106). On the other hand, in the early nineteenth century the Vocha, the coastal plain to the north cut through with a high density of seasonal streams, gave yields of 10:1 for a wheat variety called Asprositi and 12:1 for the Mavrogani variety (Walpole 1817:292). Based on these collected sources, it can be realistically assumed that the people cultivating the land at Penteskouphi in the twentieth century could have expected similar yields on the marl, slightly more from fields on the *kokkinochoma* of the Ayios Tryphonas plateau, and probably even more from the fields situated alongside the small seasonal streambed.

Plowing was a slow and all-encompassing business. In the first plowing, the family members would plow the field together, breaking up the clods by hand in the wake of the plow; only 3.5 stremmata (3,500 m^2) could be completed this way in a single day (Sanders 2014:106). The second plowing, intended to curb newly sprouted weeds, took place about one month later. In the mid twentieth century, wheat was sown at a rate of 220 kg per half hectare so that, in an average year at the aforementioned rates, five stremmata sown would provide wheat for the entire family, and the surplus would provide an income (Sanders 2014:106). Although formerly an important staple, barley was sown only in small quantities, mixed together with wheat for use as fodder. Thus, due to its crucially varied collection of soil characteristics, Penteskouphi could provide high yields of wheat and fodder barley, making it worthwhile for the Athikiotes to build and maintain a permanent settlement there.

The majority of the vineyards were planted with stock that produced the renowned small, sweet, black Corinthian grape (**Figure 9**). After harvest, these were sun-dried to produce currants, a name derived from "Reysyns de Corauntz" or "pasa di Corinto." The two or three remaining wine presses attest that grapes for winemaking were also cultivated. Grapes for drying into currants and grapes for eating and turning into wine require very different conditions. Currants do very well in the marl and mudstone-rich soils of the coastal plains, which are moisture retentive but also have good drainage. The vines that produce grapes for eating and making into wine, on the other hand, do much better on hilly limestone slopes. Penteskouphi provides all these geological, geomorphological, and climactic characteristics (clay, aggregate, rocky slopes, and proximity to the sea) in a compact area, thereby forming small biotopes that lend themselves to the productive and easy cultivation of grapes for different uses.

Other Plant Resources

In their publication on the flora of Acrocorinth and its surrounding area, Gregoris Iatrou and colleagues (2007) present over 400 plants (nearly half for the first time) and identify a variety of chorological spectra. Although Penteskouphi falls just outside the study area of that paper, we can attest to the likeness between the geology, plant zones, and floral typologies and diversity of the two areas. This collection of biotopes, in conjunction with the patches of groundwater close to the surface and seasonal running water, also supported a variety of edible, herbal, and otherwise useful plants. Furthermore, these conditions made it easy to grow other useful plants with a minimum of effort. In the wet months, local wild salad vegetables were gathered and either cooked or eaten raw, a common practice even today. Although the most abundant of these—mustard (*Sinapis alba*), chicory (*Cichorium intybus*), and rocket (*Eruca vesicaria*)—may have

Figure 9. Black Corinth cultivar grapevine (*Vitis vinifera*) for making currants, photographed in a deserted vineyard at Penteskouphi. Image courtesy of Miyon Yoo.

been considered too strongly flavored by the locals, we have recorded many other types of edible greens during numerous visits throughout the seasons. Wild carrot (*Daucus carota*), dandelion (*Taraxacum* spp.), nettle (*Urtica* spp.), poppy (*Papaver rhoeas*), amaranth (*Amaranthus* spp.), and sorrel (*Rumex* spp.) are some examples of perfectly edible and nutritious greens that would have been collected and enjoyed by the people of the village (Athanasiou 2014; Papoulias 2006). These appear on disturbed soils, especially where there is a glut of nitrogen-rich manure. Thus, the very activities of everyday life passively enriched the seasonal wild food crops available to the villagers.

Several planted fruit trees, including quince (*Cydonia oblonga*; Figure 10), loquat (*Eriobotrya japonica*), and fig (*Ficus carica*) further testify to the advantages of creating a part-time settlement at Penteskouphi. Other planted trees include mulberries (*Morus* spp.), almonds (*Prunus dulcis*), thickets of walnuts (*Juglans regia*), and domestic pears grafted onto naturally occurring wild pear (*Pyrus amygdaliformis*) rootstocks (Figure 11). Not serendipitously, the fruits of these trees ripen when the Penteskouphians were spending the most time at the settlement. Also present in the gardens of the dwellings are artichokes (*Cynara cardunculus* subsp.

scolymus), a vegetable that has been highly prized in the Mediterranean for thousands of years because all its parts can be eaten in a variety of humble and luxurious ways (Papoulias 2006:26-27).

Even decorative plants such as bearded Iris (*Iris x germanica*) were brought and planted to enrich the lives of the settlers. During our most recent visit, while observing the changes that have affected a specific building, we discovered that rue (*Ruta graveolens*) must have been another plant either present at the site or brought by the settlers. It is customary, even today, to gift a rue plant to owners of new shops or houses. The plant is to be placed by the door to ward off the evil eye. At this building, we found a handful of dried rue sprigs tied together with a cloth and wedged between the wall and the doorframe; at one time it had been covered in mortar and lime wash (Figure 12). These obvious plantings and more subtle behaviors show that the visitors were thinking toward their future at Penteskouphi, making sure they had food and good luck for the years to come (Figure 13).

Many of the indigenous plants occurring along the field margins and beyond the cultivated fields in the surrounding maquis and phrygana (*garrigue*) would also have provided food and useful material. Caper (*Capparis spinosa*) and wild asparagus (*Asparagus acutifolius*) are delicious, nutritious, and still much sought after, and they exist in some abundance at Penteskouphi. Spiny burnet (*Sarcopoterium spinosum*), covered by a woolen rug, was commonly used as a mattress and, attached to a wooden pole, as a chimney brush. It was also used as a packing material when transporting fragile items in baskets and saddlebags (Figure 14). In the wetter area along the seasonal streambed grows an abundance of *kalamia* (see note 1), a plant with similar properties to bamboo that may well have been introduced by the settlers for use as roofing in their abodes, as supports in their vegetable gardens, and along with vine prunings in their basketry. This exemplary selection of plants shows that the presence of wild food and useful plant matter, as well as a water source and the opportunities for cultivation provided by varied biotopes, were integral factors in the Athikiotes' decision to settle at Penteskouphi.

Architecture in the Settlement

The old houses at Penteskouphi are built of locally sourced materials. The foundations and lower walls are of roughly coursed limestone boulders set with a marl mortar. The upper walls are mud brick made from the marl mixed with straw from the wheat fields. One can tell that these were

Figure 10. Quince (*Cydonia oblonga*) grafted onto wild pear (*Pyrus amygdaliformis*) in Penteskouphi. Image courtesy of Isabel Sanders.

Figure 11. Domesticated pear grafted onto wild pear (*Pyrus amygdaliformis*) in Penteskouphi. Image courtesy of Isabel Sanders.

228

Figure 12. A sprig of rue (*Ruta graveolens*) wrapped in cloth and inserted into the doorframe of House B in Penteskouphi. Image courtesy of Isabel Sanders.

229

Figure 13. A horseshoe above the door of House B in Penteskouphi. Image courtesy of Isabel Sanders.

Figure 14. Spiny burnet (*Sarcopoterium spinosum*), here seen in a field margin at Penteskouphi, was often used to make mattresses and chimney brushes. Image courtesy of Isabel Sanders.

made in situ with the local marly earth because the bricks contain a moderate quantity of pebbles and even broken bits of tile, both of which are present on and within the soil at the site (Figure 15).

The 1947 film *Triumph Over Time*, directed by Oscar Broneer and produced by Margaret Thompson (Vogeikoff-Brogan 2007), features sequences of mud-brick and tile production at nearby Solomos (southwest of Penteskouphi) or, as the voice-over calls it, "Sow-low-mow." As seen in this production, to make mud brick, one dug a hole in a place with

Figure 15. Penteskouphi Houses A to I on Google Earth satellite imagery. North at top.

a high marl content, added water and straw while digging in the soil from the edges, and used the feet and legs to mix it all thoroughly. The resulting mixture was slopped into wooden forms to dry before being turned out. The Penteskouphi mud bricks were mortared in place with an altogether cleaner marl, perhaps brought from the marl beds to the west of the village, while the earth for the bricks probably came from the fields (Figure 16).

The presence and density of young cypress trees (*Cupressus sempervirens*) that have sprouted since the abandonment of some of the land at Penteskouphi make it plain that there used to be more adult trees scattered in the area (**Figure 17**). Furthermore, the absence of these parent trees suggests that their trunks were used to produce the main load-bearing beams for the roofs, floors, and doorways of the houses, as cypress trunks tend to be quite straight and also strong, dense, and slow to rot (**Figure 18**). Timber from the softer, more workable, and more prolific local pine woods provided the lesser (and shorter) beams, floor planks, and other necessary timber structures. The roof beams were covered either with *kalamia* or with pine planks and then slathered with a thick layer of marl clay mixed with straw to bind it. This acted both as a sealant and as a bedding for the roof tiles. Small boulders were used to weigh down any tiles that became loose.

Figure 16. From abandonment to ruin (see also **Figure 27**). The top image is House B in 2009, whereas below is the same house in 2017. Images courtesy of Guy Sanders.

Figure 17. Young cypress (*Cupressus sempervirens*) seedling in an abandoned field at Penteskouphi. Image courtesy of Isabel Sanders.

Figure 18. Cypress door lintel of House B. Image courtesy of Isabel Sanders.

The tiles were made of fired marl and probably came from either the tile factory at Bekianika near Solomos or the factory near Nikoleto in the Litsa valley. This was a low-temperature ceramic production, as local marl clays fire best at about 800° +/- 50°C. Calcium carbonate acts as a flux, accounting for the low firing temperature required to sinter the silicate content. Over time, calcium silicate forms, clogging the pores and thereby making the tiles less porous and more waterproof.

The ground floors were made of marl mixed with a cow-dung stiffener. Our local sources tell us that they were resurfaced with this mixture twice per year, once in the spring and again in the autumn. The interior walls received a marl base coat and were then painted with lime; the same procedure was applied to exterior walls to protect them from rain. The protective lime coating had to be reapplied annually, and so a regular supply of lime was needed. For the process to be sustainable, the residents of Penteskouphi needed ready access to sufficient quantities of raw materials for making lime, as well as the means by which to process them. Both were readily available, another characteristic that made the area so advantageous as a settlement site.

There is a small lime kiln, almost certainly coeval to the settlement, about 1 km south of the village (**Figure 19**). Its location was likely determined by the proximity of the pine woods as abundant fuel is required

Figure 19. Lime kiln south of the village. Image courtesy of Guy Sanders.

to reduce calcium carbonate to calcium oxide at a temperature of about 900°C. The presence of pine woods closer to the settlement can also be ascertained from the numerous pine saplings growing in and around the fields, which are likely the progeny of the trees used to fuel the lime kiln. The local grey limestone is hard to break up for making lime, so we can be fairly sure that the local residents were processing the ubiquitous marl instead. The local marls, depending on the beds, have a calcium carbonate content of between 25% and 40%. The practice of using marl for making calcium oxide is extremely old and may date back to the Neolithic period. To make lime, one slakes the calcium oxide with water, which was, as we know, also available within the settlement.

Many of the houses, whether built on a slope or on flat ground, have a stable-cum-storeroom below with a stair and veranda to access one or two living rooms above. If there is no cellar, additional rooms tacked onto the living rooms serve for storage and stabling. At least two of the surviving houses have a wine press, and at least three have an outdoor wood-burning bread oven for baking. These resources could be shared with neighbors, as they are today, but every house observed had its own stable, discernible from the feeding troughs and the characteristic layer of hardened dung.

Aftermath of Abandonment

From the 1950s to early 1970s agriculture in Greece changed radically. Migration of farmers to other countries, the coastal plains, and cities (especially Athens) led to a shortage of rural labor. Lacking sufficient hands, fields were left fallow for long periods, terraces collapsed, and patches of land reverted to phrygana (Wagstaff 1968). An agricultural revolution in the 1960s saw the introduction of fertilizers, pesticides, hybridized seed, and mechanization (Petmezas 2016:235–237). With the subsequent increase in efficiency and yield, farmers turned away from staple crops such as wheat. In the Argos plain, for instance, the years between 1964 and 1972 saw a 33% decline in cereal production and a 116% increase in the number of tractors (Green and Lemon 1996:191).

Penteskouphi was not immune to these changes. About fifty years ago, a switch from cereal cultivation to olive groves began to take place. The cultivation of olive trees is generally more profitable than cultivating either grain or currants; moreover, it became less labor-intensive after the influx of more affordable specialist machinery, and it provided added benefits such as the provision of firewood. The interest of the settlers thus moved away from their laborious vines and cereals, and the seasonal workload changed. Plowing in the autumn decreased and almost ceased altogether, and there was no harvest in summer. On the other hand, the olives were now picked later in the autumn or early winter. With precedence given to the trees over the vines, the vineyards were gradually abandoned.

At about the same time, tractors replaced animal traction for plowing between the olive trees, and pickup trucks replaced donkeys for transport; thus, the stables were no longer necessary. With a truck, the two-hour commute by foot was reduced to a 15-minute drive, so accommodation and, to a certain extent, a storeroom at Penteskouphi became redundant. As a result, much less effort was expended in maintaining the buildings. Modernization was the beginning of the end for the vernacular culture of the village. While some of the structures were still marginally usable one decade ago, today only four spaces out of at least 16 original properties are maintained as storage facilities. These are all either stone or cement-embellished structures. The remainder are in various stages of collapse and are beyond repair.

Structural Dilapidation

When their owners no longer maintained them rigorously, these houses began to dilapidate—at first slowly and then at an accelerating pace. In time, the lime flaked off the walls, exposing the mud brick to winter rain (Figure 20 and Figure 21). Even a small spot of exposed mud brick allowed the water to seep and then run behind the lime wash, hollowing out the walls and forcing the lime crust to fall off in ever larger pieces. The rain dissolved the mud brick, eroding it to form a talus of clay at the base of the wall (Figure 22). Drying winds also played their part in eroding the exposed bricks. A tile turned by the wind, a beech martin, or a cat allowed the rain to soak into the roofing, and the *kalamia* or planks and beams began to rot at the point of exposure (Figure 23). An infestation of termites exacerbated the process. When a tile was turned near the wall head, rivulets from a steady rain cut channels in the mud brick on the inside (Figure 24). Tiles flipped off the roof and broke on the ground outside, where they were trodden into the ground's surface and enveloped by the marl washing from the walls (Figure 25). The remaining contents of the house tended to be thrown around by intruders, and breakables were broken and scattered over quite a large area inside and even outside (Figure 26).

Eventually one of the beams became so rotten that it could no longer support the weight of the roof. It began to slump, admitting more rain and directing it to an area of the roof and floor, thereby accelerating the rotting process. Some tiles began to slide through the rotting roof and onto the floor. Over the course of a few years, more beams rotted and broke. Eventually there was a major but incomplete collapse, so that the fallen tiles were unevenly distributed over the floor. In some places the piles were relatively high; in other places there may have been only a few (Figure 27). If there was a second floor, the wooden planks of the floor under the tile fall also began to rot. Where the roof had already collapsed, these sections of floor broke and collapsed first, dumping their load onto the ground floor (Figure 28).

Roofless and exposed to the elements, the mud-brick walls dissolved, covering all the debris of the collapsed roofing (Figure 29). When equilibrium was finally achieved, the dissolved clay deposits protected the lowest courses of walling from further erosion. Drystone walls gradually shed their uppermost stones. Mortared walls became swollen by the rain, their mortar becoming slightly liquid and unable to maintain the weight of the stones set into it. Throughout these destructive processes, there are continued sporadic human, plant, and animal agencies, all of which create

Figure 20. Though taken at the village of Koutsomodi close to Ancient Nemea, this photograph shows the erosion of mud brick when it is no longer protected by lime plaster. Image courtesy of Isabel Sanders.

Figure 21. Patches of plaster still protecting a rapidly eroding mud-brick wall belonging to the same house in Koutsomodi. Image courtesy of Guy Sanders.

Figure 22. Damage caused by wind and rain once the protection of the roof and lime plaster was lost (House F, 2009). Image courtesy of Guy Sanders.

discernable disturbances. For instance, humans and animals walking inside and outside the spaces create compressed surfaces that resemble floors. Animals like chickens and dogs create pit-like scuffs in these surfaces. Plants and even trees root in the ground floor and walls of the structures while the process is playing out. While dilapidation is generally a gradual process, catastrophic events with major collapses do occur. Either way, when the stone or clay pile is level with the surviving stone-wall head,

Figure 23. A rotting and collapsing roof beam (House H, 2009). Image courtesy of Guy Sanders.

there is a point of near equilibrium where the erosion slows so dramatically as to seem unchanging. Formerly part of the suburban landscape, the house is reunited with the materials from which it was built and becomes a part of the natural landscape, essentially invisible (**Figure** 30).

Ecological Change

One aspect of the village that must be considered alongside the built remains and their contents is what happened in the fields once they were abandoned. Abundant are all the plant species characteristic of soil disturbance and abandoned cultivation: the proverbial weeds. More important, though, is the presence of plants that are defined by slow growth and long-term stability. These will not grow in soil that is deeply plowed regularly, nor in places where chemical fertilizers or herbicides are used (Tan and Iatrou 2001:33). Key examples observed in the fields of Penteskouphi include geophytic plants such as orchids (*Ophrys* spp., *Orchis* spp., *Himantoglossum robertianum*), gladioli (*Gladiolus italicus*; **Figure** 31), phrygana plants, and small, woody, aromatic shrubs and trees. These are all good signifiers of the timescale of abandonment.

Figure 24. Flaked-off plaster and rivulets of clay eroded by water penetrating the roofing (House B, 2009). Image courtesy of Guy Sanders.

We have deduced that this process was gradual and erratic because the recolonizing vegetation in various areas of the inner-settlement fields is of different ages. In one of the currant-drying platforms, for example, grows a stand of young cypresses that are about fifteen years old (**Figure 32**). Up the road, a vineyard of currant vines, turned now to a thicket of wild vines sprouting from the uncontrolled rootstocks, has been infiltrated by

Figure 25. Fallen tiles at the base of an exterior wall (House B, 2009). Image courtesy of Guy Sanders.

243

Figure 26. Living room and kitchen area with scattered belongings (House B, 2009). Image courtesy of Guy Sanders.

Figure 27. Three stages of the collapse of the roofing of House B, also illustrated in Figure 16: (A) slumped roof in 2009; (B) the same corner after the collapse; (C) the same room after total roof collapse. Images courtesy of Guy Sanders.

244

Figure 28. Cellar of House B: (A) in 2010, before the ceiling collapse; (B) in 2017, after the collapse. Images courtesy of Guy Sanders.

Figure 29. Degradation of a house once its roof has fallen through (House F, 2010). Image courtesy of Guy Sanders.

Figure 30. Former House I, south of House J, colonized by lentisc (*Pistacia lentiscus*) and pine. Image courtesy of Guy Sanders.

seedlings of olive (*Olea europaea*), almond, and lentisc (*Pistacia lentiscus*) that are only about five years old (**Figure 33**). In other abandoned fields and vineyards, one can find figs, junipers (*Juniperus turbinata*), wild pears, cypresses, and mulberries of varying ages. These are all very obvious signs of abandonment as the cultivated and built components are still visible within the recolonizing vegetation. But what of identifying the buildings and fields that are no longer visible? At Penteskouphi, signs of these abandoned structures are there if one can learn to see them.

Uniform colonization—dense clusters of trees and shrubs of the same age, size, and type—almost always signify that an event such as fire or field abandonment has dramatically altered the site, but it also indicates what may have existed there before that event took place (Rackham 1983:307). At Penteskouphi there is a small area that is entirely populated by olive trees, spaced cheek to jowl, that are of the same age and height. Clearly, a singular event changed this spot entirely. Such irregularity in the landscape inspires further exploration. Other areas with uniform colonization include a large and age-stunted clump of artichokes on the edge of an unassuming piece of flat land, and the presence of mint (*Mentha longifolia*), salad burnet (*Sanguisorba minor*), and moss—all moisture-loving plants—growing only on an elevated flatness. The latter instance is one of the more complex and interesting sites. Upon closer scrutiny of its

Figure 31. Wild gladiolus (*Gladiolus italicus*), a bee orchid (*Ophrys mammosa*) and a giant orchid (*Himantoglossum robertianum*) found growing in fields, in field margins, and around houses at Penteskouphi. Image courtesy of Isabel Sanders.

characteristics, we realized that it was the site of an already completely deteriorated mud-brick house, as were the other flattened areas with irregularities in the vegetation. The settlement grew to proportions we had not originally expected. This new reading of the landscape would not have been possible without the cooperation between disciplines, which we so strongly advocate.

Archaeology of the Poor

Penteskouphi is also an excellent example of the archaeology of the poor. Obviously, none of the students now coming to dig in Greece witnessed Greek rural life in the early 1970s, when the abandonment of the village began. In truth, it was not far removed from the romanticized portrait presented in *Triumph Over Time*. Older observers can remember being invited into homes where they were given water from the only glass in the house, or coffee from the only cup. Nor was the material culture of the 1970s so different from that of the eighteenth or nineteenth centuries, when cooking pots were made of tinned copper, goods were stored in large wicker baskets coated with clay, and people ate from wooden bowls because ceramics were uneconomical (Sanders 2016:9–16). Eugène Peytier's 1830 description of a house in Corinth, recorded in an unpublished letter,[4] evokes the houses at Penteskouphi:

---

[4] A photocopy of the letter was provided to the authors by Elizabeth French many years ago; however, additional details about the provenance of the original are currently unavailable. A curious reader may have luck exploring archival materials from the Expédition Scientifique de Morée (the scientific team that brought

Figure 32. Young cypresses in a currant-drying platform, estimated to be about fifteen years old. When the platforms were in use, this tree would have been immediately removed. Image courtesy of Isabel Sanders.

> ... in the custom of the country the roof consists of trimmed branches as thick as an arm, spaced from 5 to 6 inches apart which serve as rafters and the tiles are held in place thereon. The houses in general lack chimneys and the smoke from the fires goes out through the cracks between the tiles. Inside the single domestic space of the house is a

Peytier to the Peloponnese) that are housed in the Service Historique de la Défense in Paris.

Figure 33. Lentisc (*Pistacia lentiscus*) seedling (approximately five years old) entangled with an aged currant vine in an abandoned vineyard at Penteskouphi. Image courtesy of Isabel Sanders.

small oven in which they bake maize bread made like a pancake. As often as not they make it at the time of eating and bake it on the ashes of an ordinary fire. Next to the oven and the hearth are coffers made of wood and of (unbaked) clay resembling terracotta pots leaning against the wall, which are used to store grain. The front door is only 4 feet high and in the room one or two small windows. They do not know the usage of iron work for the closing of doors and windows. The bed of the family and the stranger alike is on either side of the fire. The more comfortably off cover it with a woolen blanket and the poorer with a straw mat [translation by Guy Sanders; quoted in Sanders 2016:9].

Although not systematically recorded, frequent visits impressed upon the authors that the original material culture of Penteskouphi was nearly all biodegradable, made mainly of wood, leather, and iron. Ceramics and glass, even window glass, are exceptional but not entirely absent. In one house (House C), there is one room with a table, a chair, and two beds, their mattresses exploding from the damp. On one bed was a ceramic plate (Figure 34). Sometime during 2017 the roof of this room finally collapsed, crushing the bed, but the plate remains in situ at a steep angle from the horizontal. By far the greatest proportion of ceramic material is roofing, but even this does not necessarily remain in situ; tiles are expensive and reusable. Outside another house (House G), there is a stack of tiles removed from a neighboring building that have been safely stored to serve a new roof elsewhere.

Conclusions

Our visits to Penteskouphi have made us aware of the importance of observation for collecting new, field-based data that may bestow new potentials for understanding (and possibly reevaluating) the archaeological record. For instance, after rereading the field notebooks for the excavation of the Frankish Area at Corinth, we were able to reinterpret some of the recorded findings. The complex was thought to date to the second half of the thirteenth century and to have been destroyed ca. 1310. In each building, excavators uncovered a layer of marl overlying the trodden marl of the ground floor. On top of this, in some rooms, was a layer of fallen floor tiles from a second story. These were followed by a layer of broken Laconian roof tiles, and the deposits were all capped with collapsed walling. This was interpreted as a destruction event resulting from an earthquake or the sack of the city in the early fourteenth century (Sanders 2016:4–5).

Since the sequence accurately reflects the observed pattern of degradation and collapse at Penteskouphi, a more fitting explanation may be that the complex at Corinth was abandoned rather than destroyed. The marl overlying the floors had washed out of the roofing and walls; the roofs had rotted and collapsed onto upper floors with floor tiles (where present) and then finally onto the ground floors and the washed-out marl that accumulated on them. Finally, the walls collapsed, spilling over the tile debris both inside and outside the rooms. It now emerges that most

Figure 34. Chairs and plate (House C, 2009). Image courtesy of Guy Sanders.

of the Frankish Area was not constructed until several generations after the events that had been thought to have destroyed it, and that it may have been abandoned over a century later, perhaps due to mounting pressures from Ottoman troops raiding south over the Isthmus in the early fifteenth century. Based on this misreading, one wonders how Penteskouphi would be interpreted during an archaeological survey if it had been abandoned a thousand years ago.

We recently visited Rachiani, which was still inhabited in the early nineteenth century, on the plateau above the Longopotamos River west of Corinth (see **Figure 2**). Today there is hardly even a tile scatter at the site. Rachiani was built on the limestone capping of the Ancient Corinth terrace (see **Figure 7**), and the only surviving remains are a tile scatter on the exposed bedrock. We suggest that, in 50–100 years, Penteskouphi village will comprise a series of large hummocks with a very limited scatter of tile fragments. The walls and tile falls will have been completely buried under a tumulus of marl, like that covering House I (see **Figure 30**). Indeed, based on the profile of House I, we were able to discern traces of older abandoned houses north of the fork in the road between Houses A and B.

As we said in the introduction, this was never meant to be a scientific paper but rather a narrative of the processes of the birth, demise, and rebirth of Penteskouphi settlement. To some it may seem overly sentimental. Our argument is that deduction through observation and personable narrative reminds the scholar that when dealing with archaeology one is dealing with real people in a real environment. These people and the relationship they had with their surroundings were the conductors of the collective conscience, unconscious, and norms of today. As we have shown in this article, the observation, description, and recognition of the realities of the present gives one an understanding of the very past that made the present what it is. This educated reading of the landscape can also aid in finding archaeological sites in the first place. Penteskouphi, therefore, has not become redundant or insignificant because of its abandonment. Instead, its significance has been transformed and it can now be considered a strong teaching and learning tool for introducing students, amateurs, professionals, and tourists alike to this method of study, as long as they are prepared to view things holistically and with sensitivity toward the human element within the natural and heritage landscapes. Most importantly, though, is the fact that these deductions about Penteskouphi were drawn by a group of curious and wonder-prone people who pointedly used a multidisciplinary and symmetrical approach to the subject. To see the potential of places like Penteskouphi, it only took us walking along a track together, overgrown with wild grapevines and towering fennel, looking at the world around us, and seeing different things but nevertheless reaching the same conclusion.

References Cited

Andreades, Matthaios
 1996 Η Κορινθία την Οθωνική περίοδο (1833-1862) [The Corinthia During the Othonic Period (1833–1862)]. Stapepas, Athens.

Armijo, Rolando, Bertrand Meyer, Geoffrey Charles Plume King, Alexis Rigo, and Dimitris Papanastasiou
 1996 Quaternary Evolution of the Corinth Rift and its Implications for the Late Cenozoic Evolution of the Aegean. *Geophysical Journal International* 126(1):11–53. https://doi.org/10.1111/j.1365-246X.1996.tb05264.x

Athanasiou, Zacharias
 2014 *Άγρια βότανα και χόρτα οδηγός αναγνώρισης: 125 είδη* [Wild Herbs and Grasses Identification Guide: 125 Types]. Psychalos, Athens.

Athanasoulis, Demetrios
 2009 *Το Κάστρο Ακροκορίνθου και η ανάδειξή του: 2006-2009* [The Castle of Acrocorinth and its Enhancement Project (2006–2009)]. Hellenic Ministry of Culture and Tourism, Ancient Corinth.

Blegen, Carl William
 1920 Corinth in Prehistoric Times. *American Journal of Archaeology* 24:1–20, 274. https://doi.org/10.2307/497547

Bon, Antoine
 1969 La Morée Franque. Recherches historiques, topographiques et archéologiques sur la principauté d'Achaïe (1205-1430) [The Frankish Morea. Historic, Topographical, and Archaeological Research of the Principality of Achaia (1205–1430)]. *Bulletin Monumental* 127(3):254–256.

Buchon, Jean Alexandre C.
 1840 *Chroniques étrangères relatives aux expéditions françaises pendant le XIIIe siècle* [Foreign Chronicles Relating to French Expeditions During the 13th Century]. Auguste Desrez, Paris.

Chatzipouliou-Kalliri, Elisabet
  1984   Λείψανα πρωτοελλαδικού και μεσοελλαδικού οικισμού στο λόφο Αετόπετρα. Πρώτα αποτελέσματα δοκιμαστικής ανασκαφικής έρευνας [Remains of the Early and Middle Helladic Settlement on the Hill of Aetopetra. The First Results of a Pilot Excavation]. Meletai A. *Archaiologikon Deltion* 33(1978):325–336.

Engels, Donald
  1990   *Roman Corinth: An Alternative Model for the Classical City*. University Chicago Press, Chicago.

Erny, Grace, and William Caraher
  2020   The Kingdom of Chelmis: Architecture, Material Culture, and the Modern Landscape of the Western Argolid. *Journal of Field Archaeology* 45(3):209–221. https://doi.org/10.1080/00934690.2019.1704990

European Commission
  2017   Site GR2530003, Akrokorinthos. Natura 2000 – Standard Data Form, Database Release 25/05/2018. Electronic document, https://natura2000.eea.europa.eu/Natura2000/SDF.aspx?site=GR2530003, accessed November 1, 2020.

Finley, John H., Jr.
  1932   Corinth in the Middle Ages. *Speculum* 7(4):477–499. https://doi.org/10.2307/2850425

Friesem, David, Elisabetta Boaretto, Adi Eliyahu-Behar, and Ruth Shahack-Gross
  2011   Degradation of Mud Brick Houses in an Arid Environment: A Geoarchaeological Model. *Journal of Archaeological Science* 38(5):1135–1147. https://doi.org/10.1016/j.jas.2010.12.011

Green, Sarah, and Mark Lemon
  1996   Perceptual Landscapes in Agrarian Systems: Degradation Processes in North-Western Epirus and the Argolid Valley, Greece. *Ecumene* 3(2):181–199. https://doi.org/10.1177/147447409600300204

Iatrou, Gregoris, Panayiotis Trigas, and Nicolaos Pettas
 2007   The Vascular Flora of Akrokorinthos Castle and its Surrounding Area (NE Peloponnese, Greece). *Phytologia Balcanica* 13(1):83–93.

Karymbalis, Efthimios, Dimitrios Papanastassiou, Kalliopi Gaki-Papanastassiou, Maria Ferentinou, and Christos Chalkias
 2016   Late Quaternary Rates of Stream Incision in Northeast Peloponnese, Greece. *Frontiers of Earth Science* 10:455–478. https://doi.org/10.1007/s11707-016-0577-0

Leake, William Martin
 1830   *Travels in the Morea: With a Map and Plans,* Vol II. John Murray, London.

Marchand, Jeannette C.
 2009   Kleonai, the Corinth–Argos Road, and the "Axis of History." *Hesperia* 78(1):107–163. https://www.jstor.org/stable/40205745

Miller, William
 1908   *The Latins in the Levant: A History of Frankish Greece (1204–1566).* John Murray, London.

Morosini, Francesco
 2018 [1687]   Pianta Topografica dell'Istmo del Regno di Morea e della piazza e borgi di Corinto [Topographic Plan of the Isthmus of the Kingdom of Morea and of the Town of Corinth]. In *Βενετικοί χάρτες της Πελοποννήσου, τέλη 17ου–αρχές 18ου αιώνα από τη Συλλογή του Πολεμικού Αρχείου της Αυστρίας [Venetian Maps of the Peloponnese, Late 17th–Early 18th Centuries from the Collection of the War Archives of Austria],* edited by Olga Katsiardi-Hering, pp. 228, 249–254. MIET, Athens.

Papoulias, Thanasis
 2006   *Τα άγρια φαγώσιμα χόρτα του βουνού και του κάμπου [Wild Edible Plants of the Mountains and Plains].* Pyschalos, Athens.

Pelet, Jean-Jacques Germain
   1832   *Carte de la Morée [Map of the Morea]*. Expédition Scientifique de Morée. Ministre de la Guerre, Paris.

Petmezas, Socrates
   2016   The Long Term Development of Greek Agricultural Productivity in a Euro-Mediterranean Perspective (1860–1980). *Neoellinika Istorika* 4:215–244.

Pouqueville, Françoise Charles Hugues Laurent
   1827   *Voyage de la Grèce [Travels in Greece]*, Vol. V. 2nd ed. Firmin Didot, Paris.

Rackham, Oliver
   1983   Observations on the Historical Ecology of Boeotia. *Annual of the British School at Athens* 78:291–351. https://doi.org/10.1017/S0068245400019742

Rackham, Oliver, and Jennifer Moody
   1997   *The Making of the Cretan Landscape*. Manchester University Press, Manchester.

Salmon, John B.
   1984   *Wealthy Corinth: A History of the City to 338 BC*. Oxford University Press, Oxford.

Sanders, Guy D. R.
   2014   Landlords and Tenants: Sharecroppers and Subsistence Farming in Corinthian Historical Context. In *Corinth in Contrast: Studies in Inequality*, edited by Steven J. Friesen, Sarah A. James, and Daniel N. Schowalter, pp. 103–125. Brill, Leiden.
   2016   Recent Finds from Ancient Corinth: How Little Things Make Big Differences. Paper presented at the Tenth BABESCH Byvanck Lecture, Leiden.

Schama, Simon
   1995   *Landscape and Memory*. Harper Collins, New York.

Shawcross, Teresa
   2009   *The Chronicle of Morea: Historiography in Crusader Greece*. Oxford University Press, Oxford.

Steffen, Bernhard
   1884   *Karten Von Mykenai [Map of Mycenae]*. Reimer, Berlin.

Tan, Kit, and Gregoris Iatrou
   2001   *Endemic Plants of Greece: The Peloponnese*. Gads, Copenhagen.

Vogeikoff-Brogan, Natalia
   2007   *Triumph Over Time: The American School of Classical Studies at Athens in Post-War Greece*. Film by the American School of Classical Studies at Athens.

Wagstaff, J. M.
   1968   Rural Migration in Greece. *Geography* 53(2):175–179. https://www.jstor.org/stable/40566911

Walpole, Robert
   1817   *Memoirs Relating to European and Asiatic Turkey*. Longman, Hurst, Rees, Orme and Brown, London.

Appendix: Plants Identified at Penteskouphi (2016–2017)

E: edible, aromatic, or medicinal properties
O: often planted for ornamental purposes
U: other uses (e.g. building, beekeeping, etc.)

	Botanical name	English common name	Greek common name	Family	Distribution and habitat in Greece
	Acanthus spinosus	Spiny bear's breech	Άκανθος	Acanthaceae	Dry and rocky grasslands, scrub, woodlands, agricultural habitats
E	*Adiantum capillus-veneris*	Maidenhair fern	Κόμη της Αφροδίτης, Πηγαδόχορτο	Pteridaceae	Damp and shady rocks, ravines, walls at low altitudes
U	*Alkanna tinctoria*	Dyer's alkanet	Βαφόριζα	Boraginaceae	Phrygana, dry and stony grasslands, coastal habitats
	Allium hirtovaginatum	Wild onion		Amaryllidaceae	Dry and grassy places, phrygana
U	*Anchusa azurea*	Italian bugloss	Αγόγλωσσο, Βοϊδόγλωσσα	Boraginaceae	Dry and grassy places, agricultural and ruderal habitats
	Anemone coronaria	Crown anemone	Ανεμώνη	Ranunculaceae	Widespread in dry and grassy places, agricultural habitats, woodland clearings, and phrygana
	Anemone pavonina (syn. *Anemone hortensis* subsp. *pavonina*)	Broad-leaved anemone	Ανεμώνη	Ranunculaceae	Widespread in dry and grassy places, woodlands, and phrygana

Appendix: Plants Identified at Penteskouphi (2016–2017). Continued.

	Botanical name	English common name	Greek common name	Family	Distribution and habitat in Greece
U	*Anthyllis hermanniae*		Αλογοθύμαρο, Σμυρνιά	Fabaceae	Phrygana; dry, rocky, and grassy places
E U	*Arbutus unedo*	Strawberry tree	Κουμαριά	Ericaceae	Woodlands, scrub, rocky hillsides
U	*Arundo donax*	Giant cane	Καλαμιά	Poaceae	Coastal waste places, streambeds, riverbeds
E	*Asparagus acutifolius*	Wild asparagus	Άγριο Σπαράγγι	Asparagaceae	Phrygana, grasslands, agricultural and ruderal habitats
E	*Asphodelus ramosus*	Asphodel	Ασφόδελος	Asphodelaceae	Widespread in phrygana, woodland clearings, and dry grasslands
E U	*Atriplex halimus*	Sea orach, saltbush	Αλιμιά, Χαλιμιά	Chenopodiaceae	Coastal habitats
U	*Ballota acetabulosa*	Garden horehound	Λυχνaράκι	Lamiaceae	Dry grasslands, phrygana, agricultural margins, ruderal habitats
E U	*Bituminaria bituminosa*	Pitch trefoil	Πισόχορτο, Ασφάλτιο	Fabaceae	Common in grassy and ruderal habitats
E	*Calendula arvensis*	Marigold	Καλέντουλα, Νεκρολούλουδο, Αδράχτι	Asteraceae	Common in phrygana and grassy, agricultural, and ruderal habitats
U	*Calicotome villosa*	Thorny broom	Ασπάλαθος	Fabaceae	Maquis, phrygana, and ruderal habitats, especially after fire or clearance

Appendix: Plants Identified at Penteskouphi (2016–2017). Continued.

	Botanical name	English common name	Greek common name	Family	Distribution and habitat in Greece
	Campanula andrewsii	Bellflower	Καμπανούλα	Campanulaceae	Endemic to the Peloponnese on limestone rocks and cliffs
E	*Centaurea raphanina*		Αλιβάρβαρο, Κενταύριο	Asteraceae	Grasslands, woodlands, rocky places
E	*Capparis spinosa*	Caper	Κάππαρη	Capparaceae	Dry and rocky places; grasslands; coastal, agricultural, and ruderal habitats
E	*Capsella bursa-pastoris*	Shepherd's purse	Αγριοκαρδαμούρα	Brassicaceae	Widespread in grasslands, clearings, and agricultural and ruderal habitats
E U O	*Ceratonia siliqua*	Carob	Χαρουπιά	Fabaceae	Grasslands and scrub as a stand-alone tree or as part of maquis; also cultivated
O	*Cercis siliquastrum*	Judas tree	Κουτσουπιά	Fabaceae	Scrub, rocky slopes, maquis; also planted as an ornamental
	Cerinthe major	Honeywort		Boraginaceae	Grassy, agricultural, and ruderal habitats
	Cerinthe retorta	Honeywort		Boraginaceae	Grassy, agricultural, and ruderal habitats
E	*Cichorium intybus*	Chicory	Πικρορόδικο, Κιχώριο, Πικραλίδα	Asteraceae	Grasslands, agricultural and ruderal habitats
E	*Cistus creticus*	Cretan rockrose	Λαδανιά	Cistaceae	Widespread in phrygana, woodland margins, and grasslands up to 1,400 m

Appendix: Plants Identifed at Penteskouphi (2016–2017). Continued.

	Botanical name	English common name	Greek common name	Family	Distribution and habitat in Greece
	Cistus salviifolius	Sage-leaved rockrose	Ασπροκουνουκλιά	Cistaceae	Phrygana, grasslands, and open woodlands up to 900 m
E	*Convolvulus arvensis*	Field bindweed	Περικοκλάδα	Convolvulaceae	Grassy, agricultural, and ruderal habitats up to 1,900 m
	Convolvulus elegantissimus (syn. *Convolvulus althaeoides* subsp. *elegantissimus*)	Mallow-leaved bindweed	Περικοκλάδα	Convolvulaceae	Phrygana, grasslands, and agricultural and ruderal habitats up to 1,300 m
E	*Crataegus monogyna*	Hawthorne	Κράταιγος, Μουρτζιά	Rosaceae	Maquis, woodlands, grasslands, ruderal habitats
U	*Cupressus sempervirens*	Italian cypress	Κυπαρίσσι	Cupressaceae	Woodlands and scrub; often planted
	Cyclamen graecum	Greek cyclamen	Κυκλάμινο	Primulaceae	Phrygana, open woodlands, grasslands, rocky slopes, and a variety of other habitats
E	*Cydonia oblonga*	Quince	Κυδωνιά	Rosaceae	Widely cultivated; hedges and woodland margins
E	*Cynara cardunculus* subsp. *scolymus*	Globe artichoke	Αγκινάρα	Asteraceae	Cultivated
	Cynoglossum creticum	Blue hound's-tongue	Κυνόγλωσσο	Boraginaceae	Phrygana, grasslands, agricultural and ruderal habitats

Appendix: Plants Identified at Penteskouphi (2016–2017). Continued.

	Botanical name	English common name	Greek common name	Family	Distribution and habitat in Greece
E	*Daucus carota*	Wild carrot	Άγριο Καρότο	Apiaceae	Phrygana, grasslands, and coastal, agricultural, and ruderal habitats up to 1,500 m
	Delphinium peregrinum		Λαγός, Καρφόχορτο	Ranunculaceae	Phrygana, grasslands, and agricultural and ruderal habitats up to 1,000 m
U	*Dittrichia viscosa*	Sticky fleabane	Ακονιζιά	Asteraceae	Common in agricultural, ruderal, and dry and stony habitats up to 800 m
	Dorycnium hirsutum	Canary clover	Μελιγκάρι	Fabaceae	Grasslands and phrygana up to 1,500 m
E U	*Drimia numidica*	Sea squill	Σκυλοκρέμμυδο	Asparagaceae	Phrygana, dry and stony places, coastal habitats
E	*Ecballium elaterium*	Squirting cucumber	Πικραγγουριά, Πεταχτούλα	Cucurbitaceae	Common in agricultural and ruderal habitats at low levels
E U	*Eriobotrya japonica*	Japanese loquat	Μουσμουλιά	Rosaceae	Cultivated as an ornamental and for its fruits
E	*Eruca vesicaria*	Garden rocket	Ρόκα	Brassicaceae	Agricultural and ruderal habitats; also cultivated
E U	*Eryngium creticum*	Small blue eryngo	Μοσχάγκαθο	Apiaceae	Phrygana, grasslands, and agricultural and ruderal habitats up to 1,100 m

Appendix: Plants Identified at Penteskouphi (2016–2017). Continued.

	Botanical name	English common name	Greek common name	Family	Distribution and habitat in Greece
	Euphorbia apios			Euphorbiaceae	Woodlands, scrub, phrygana, dry grasslands
E	*Ficus carica*	Fig	Συκιά	Moraceae	Scrub, grasslands, ravines, walls, streambeds, and also cultivated up to 1,500 m
E	*Foeniculum vulgare*	Fennel	Μάραθος	Apiaceae	Widespread in agricultural and ruderal habitats
	Fumana arabica	Needle sunrose		Cistaceae	Phrygana and dry grasslands up to 1,250 m
E U	*Fumana thymifolia*	Thyme-leaved sunrose		Cistaceae	Phrygana and dry grasslands up to 1,000 m
E U	*Fumaria officinalis*	Common fumitory	Καπνόχορτο	Fumariaceae	Agricultural and ruderal habitats; also often on walls
	Gagea graeca		Γαγέα	Liliaceae	Phrygana, grasslands, and rocky slopes up to 1,400 m
E	*Galium aparine*	Goosegrass, cleavers	Κολλητσίδα	Rubiaceae	Agricultural and ruderal habitats, woodland margins
	Genista acanthoclada	Spiny broom	Αχινοπόδι	Fabaceae	Phrygana and dry and stony grasslands up to 1,300 m
	Gladiolus italicus	Field gladiolus	Τσαλαπετεινός	Iridaceae	Grasslands, agricultural and ruderals habitats
E	*Glebionis coronaria*	Crown daisy	Μαντηλίδα	Asteraceae	Widespread in grassy places and cultivations
E U	*Globularia alypum*	Shrubby globularia	Στουρέκι, Τσουκλάδι	Globulariaceae	Phrygana and dry and stony grasslands up to 800 m

Appendix: Plants Identified at Penteskouphi (2016–2017). Continued.

	Botanical name	English common name	Greek common name	Family	Distribution and habitat in Greece
	Helianthemum syriacum	Syrian rockrose		Cistaceae	Phrygana, dry grasslands
E	*Helichrysum stoechas*	Everlasting	Αμάραντο	Asteraceae	Phrygana and dry grasslands up to 700 m
	Himantoglossum robertianum	Giant orchid	Γιγαντορχιδέα	Orchidaceae	Phrygana, grasslands, fields, woodland clearings
	Hypericum empetrifolium	Saint John's wort	Αγουδουρας	Hypericaceae	Phrygana, woodlands, rocky slopes, walls
	Hypericum triquetrifolium			Hypericaceae	Agricultural and ruderal habitats, dry and stony places
E U O	*Iris x germanica*	Tall bearded iris	Ίριδα	Iridaceae	Dry, stony, and rocky habitats; widely cultivated as an ornamental
E U	*Juglans regia*	Walnut	Καρυδιά	Juglandaceae	Naturalized in hillside forests; widely cultivated
E U	*Juniperus turbinata*	Juniper	Άρκευθος, Θαμνοκυπάρισσο	Cupressaceae	Phrygana, woodlands, grasslands, coastal habitats
E	*Knautia integrifolia*		Κουφολάχανο	Dipsacaceae	Phrygana, grasslands, and agricultural and ruderal habitats up to 700 m
	Lamium moschatum	Deadnettle	Λαβρόχορτο	Lamiaceae	Agricultural and ruderal habitats
E	*Malva sylvestris*	Common mallow	Μολόχα	Malvaceae	Agricultural and ruderal habitats up to 1,000 m
E	*Matricaria recutita*	Chamomile	Χαμομήλι	Asteraceae	Agricultural and ruderal habitats

Appendix: Plants Identified at Penteskouphi (2016–2017). Continued.

	Botanical name	English common name	Greek common name	Family	Distribution and habitat in Greece
	Matthiola fruticulosa	Perennial stock	Ματθιόλα	Brassicaceae	Phrygana, grasslands, rocky slopes
E	*Mentha longifolia*	Horsemint	Αγριοβάλσαμο	Lamiaceae	Damp meadows and stream margins up to 1,900 m
E U	*Micromeria juliana*		Πολύκομπο, Τραγορίγανη	Lamiaceae	Phrygana and grasslands up to 2,200 m
	Minuartia attica	Sandwort		Caryophyllaceae	Phrygana, grasslands, woodland clearings, high-altitude slopes and grasslands
	Misopates orontium			Plantaginaceae	Phrygana, grasslands, agricultural and ruderal habitats
	Moraea sisyrinchium	Barbary nut	Γυναvδρίρις	Iridaceae	Phrygana, dry grasslands, scrub, woodland clearings
E O U	*Morus* spp.	Mulberry	Μουριά	Moraceae	Agricultural and ruderal habitats; cultivated and often planted as a shade tree
	Muscari commutatum	Grape hyacinth	Σταφυλοϋάκινθος	Asparagaceae	Common in phrygana and dry and grassy habitats
E	*Leopoldia comosa* (syn. *Muscari comosum*)	Tassel hyacinth	Βολβός	Asparagaceae	Grasslands up to 1,450 m; agricultural and ruderal habitats
	Odontites linkii			Orobanchaceae	Greek endemic; phrygana, grasslands, ruderal habitats
E U	*Olea europaea*	Olive	Ελιά	Oleaceae	Cultivated

Appendix: Plants Identified at Penteskouphi (2016–2017). Continued.

	Botanical name	English common name	Greek common name	Family	Distribution and habitat in Greece
	Ophrys lutea	Yellow bee orchid		Orchidaceae	Phrygana, stony grasslands
	Ophrys speculum	Mirror orchid		Orchidaceae	Phrygana, stony grasslands, woodlands, scrub
	Ophrys sphegodes	Spider orchid		Orchidaceae	Phrygana, stony grasslands
	Orchis italica	Naked man orchid		Orchidaceae	Phrygana, stony grasslands
	Ornithogalum umbellatum	Star of Bethlehem	Ορνιθόγαλο	Asparagaceae	Grasslands, agricultural and ruderal habitats
	Osyris alba	Osyris	Σκουπόχορτο	Santalaceae	Phrygana, grasslands, scrub, woodlands
E	*Oxalis pes-caprae*	Bermuda buttercup	Ξινήθρα	Oxalidaceae	Common and invasive weed of agricultural and ruderal habitats
E	*Parietaria judaica*	Pellitory-of-the-wall	Περδικάκι	Urticaceae	Cliffs, ravines, walls, agricultural and ruderal habitats
	Phagnalon rupestre		Αστροθύμαρο	Asteraceae	Phrygana, grasslands, scrub, woodlands
	Phlomis fruticosa	Jerusalem sage	Ασφάκα	Lamiaceae	Phrygana; often dominant in grazed hillsides
	Pinus halepensis	Aleppo pine	Πεύκο	Pinaceae	Common woodland-forming tree below 800 m
E	*Pistacia lentiscus*	Lentisc	Σχίνος	Anacardiaceae	Phrygana, woodlands, grasslands, scrub, coastal habitats
	Plantago albicans	Plantain	Πεντάνευρο	Plantaginaceae	Phrygana; grasslands; agricultural, ruderal, and coastal habitats

Appendix: Plants Identified at Penteskouphi (2016–2017). Continued.

	Botanical name	English common name	Greek common name	Family	Distribution and habitat in Greece
E	*Populus nigra*	Black poplar	Μαύρη λεύκα	Salicaceae	Woodlands, scrub, and freshwater habitats below 800 m
E	*Prasium majus*	White hedge nettle	Λαγουδόχορτο	Lamiaceae	Phrygana, grasslands, woodlands, scrub
E	*Prunus armeniaca*	Apricot	Βερικοκιά	Rosaceae	Cultivated; not native
E	*Prunus dulcis*	Almond	Αμυγδαλιά	Rosaceae	Rocky places, field margins; cultivated
E	*Prunus webbii*	Wild almond	Πικραμυγδαλιά	Rosaceae	Phrygana, grasslands, scrub, rocky slopes, field margins
E U	*Pyrus amygdaliformis* (syn. *Pyrus spinosa*)	Almond-leaved pear	Γκορτσιά	Rosaceae	Phrygana, grasslands, scrub, rocky slopes, and field margins up to 1,600 m
E U	*Quercus coccifera*	Kermes oak	Πουρνάρι	Fagaceae	Phrygana, maquis, scrub, and woodlands up to 1,500 m
	Ranunculus sp.	Buttercup		Ranunculaceae	Moist ground
E	*Reseda alba*	White mignonette	Λευκή ώχρα	Resedaceae	Phrygana, grasslands, and agricultural and ruderal habitats up to 500 m
E U	*Reseda lutea*	Yellow mignonette	Κίτρινη ώχρα	Resedaceae	Phrygana, grasslands, agricultural and ruderal habitats
	Rubia peregrina	Wild madder	Ριζάρι	Rubiaceae	Scrub, hedges, woodlands
E U	*Rubus canescens*	Bramble	Βάτο, Βατομουριά	Rosaceae	Woodland clearings and scrub up to 1,800 m
E U	*Rumex* sp.	Sorrel	Λάπαθο	Polygonaceae	Agricultural and ruderal habitats

Appendix: Plants Identified at Penteskouphi (2016–2017). Continued.

	Botanical name	English common name	Greek common name	Family	Distribution and habitat in Greece
E U	*Sambucus nigra*	Elder	Σαμπούκος, Κουφόξυλο	Adoxaceae	Woodlands, hedges, and agricultural and ruderal habitats up to 1,400 m
E	*Sanguisorba minor*	Salad burnet	Μαυρόφυλλο	Rosaceae	Common in damp meadows up to 2,100 m
U	*Sarcopoterium spinosum*	Thorny burnet	Αστοιβίδα, Αφάνα	Rosaceae	Common in phrygana and grasslands up to 2,000 m
E	*Satureja thymbra*	Savory	Θρούμπι	Lamiaceae	Phrygana, grasslands; often cultivated
	Sedum sediforme	Stonecrop		Crassulaceae	Phrygana, grasslands, rocky slopes
E	*Silybum marianum*	Holy/Milk thistle	Γαϊδουράγκαθο	Asteraceae	Agricultural and ruderal habitats up to 1,000 m
E	*Sinapis alba*	White mustard	Σινάπι	Brassicaceae	Agricultural and ruderal habitats up to 800 m
E	*Smilax aspera*	Common smilax	Αρκουδόβατος	Smilacaceae	Woodlands, scrub
	Solanum americanum	Black nightshade	Στύφνος	Solanaceae	Common but non-native in agricultural and ruderal habitats up to 1,000 m
E	*Spartium junceum*	Spanish broom	Σπάρτο	Fabaceae	Woodlands, scrub, and agricultural and ruderal habitats up to 1,300 m
	Stachys cretica	Downy woundwort		Lamiaceae	Phrygana, grasslands, woodlands, agricultural and ruderal habitats
E	*Teucrium capitatum*	Felty germander	Αγαποβότανο	Lamiaceae	Phrygana and dry and stony or rocky grasslands up tp 2,000 m

Appendix: Plants Identified at Penteskouphi (2016–2017). Continued.

	Botanical name	English common name	Greek common name	Family	Distribution and habitat in Greece
	Teucrium chamaedrys	Wall germander		Lamiaceae	Phrygana, grasslands, woodlands, rocky outcrops
	Teucrium divaricatum	Hedge germander		Lamiaceae	Phrygana, grasslands, rocky slopes
E	*Thymbra capitata*	Thyme	Θυμάρι	Lamiaceae	Widespread in phrygana and dry grasslands up to 1,100 m
U	*Thymelaea tartonraira*		Φυνοκολιά	Thymelaeaceae	Phrygana and grasslands up to 1,000 m
EU	*Ulmus minor*	Smooth-leaved elm	Φτέλια	Ulmaceae	Woodlands, scrub
E	*Urtica pilulifera*	Roman nettle	Τσουκνίδα	Urticaceae	Widespread in agricultural and ruderal habitats
E	*Urtica urens*	Small nettle	Τσουκνίδα	Urticaceae	Widespread in agricultural and ruderal habitats
	Verbascum undulatum	Wavy-leaved mullein	Φλόμος	Scrophulariaceae	Grasslands, agricultural and ruderal habitats
	Vicia cracca	Tufted vetch	Βίκος	Fabaceae	Scattered in grasslands, scrub, and woodland margins
E	*Vicia peregrina*	Vetch	Βίκος	Fabaceae	Dry and open scrub, grasslands, and agricultural and ruderal habitats at low levels

Chapter Six
Life in Abandonment:
The Village of Lakka Skoutara, Corinthia

David K. Pettegrew and William R. Caraher

The prospect of documenting an abandoned modern settlement first attracted teams of the Eastern Korinthia Archaeological Survey to the valley of Lakka Skoutara (i.e. the Skoutara basin) in the southeastern Corinthia in 2001. A rural church, surrounded by over a dozen houses of various types and in different states of use, reuse, and abandonment, seemed to offer a perfect laboratory for studying the processes by which the settlements of the region entered the archaeological record. The signs of life in the upland valley (*lakka*) and the evident complexities of occupation made it an interesting case study for understanding the modern period in its own right.

Over the course of 17 years, a small team of researchers including Lita Tzortzopoulou-Gregory, Timothy Gregory, and the present authors returned intermittently to the valley to interview its inhabitants, document the settlement, and rephotograph the houses.[1] Our initial visit to the houses led to a hypothesis that assumed a rather linear understanding of how villages developed. We regarded the settlement at Lakka Skoutara as a village that was abandoned in the process of nucleation around a church and as an active crossroad in the countryside. However, revisiting the valley over time revealed a wide range of ongoing formation processes

---

[1] We discovered and originally studied the village in 2001, more systematically documented it in 2002, and restudied and photographed it in 2004, 2006, 2009, and 2018. Earlier studies of our work in the area appear in Caraher and Diacopoulos 2004; Caraher et al. 2009; Diacopoulos 2004; Pettegrew and Caraher 2012, 2016; Tartaron et al. 2006:460. This paper is based on text originally written in 2009, which we revised first for the session at the Annual Meeting of the Archaeological Institute of America in 2016 and again in 2018 after a final visit to the valley. We thank our collaborators, Lita Tzortzopoulou-Gregory and Timothy Gregory, for their significant contributions, including interviews with local informants, analysis of ceramic remains, and productive conversations about the Greek countryside. We also thank Professor Albert Sarvis of Harrisburg University of Science and Technology for working with us to conduct drone photography in summer 2018; that imagery forms the background of Figure 20 and Figure 30. All photos, tables, and maps were generated by the authors.

that manifested the broader historical contingencies shaping the landscape over time. We recorded the dynamism of the valley evident in a variety of activities—seasonal settlement, building refurbishment, olive cultivation, shepherding, investment in road infrastructure, among others—which complicated our simple notion of abandonment (for comparative studies, cf. Cameron and Tonka 1993; Erny and Caraher 2020; Gould 1988).

The longevity of this work potentially contributes to a rich array of scholarship, including the study of vernacular Greek architecture (Foster 2002; Sigalos 2004) and the modern Greek countryside. Indeed, a number of scholars in recent years have sought to situate the archaeology of nineteenth- and twentieth-century Greece within the developing field of historical archaeology (Diacopoulos 2004; Erny and Caraher 2020; Gallant 2018; Kardulias 1994; Vionis 2012; cf. Brenningmeyer et al., this volume, for a broad overview of the archaeology of the recent past). Charles Orser (1996:57–88) has famously proposed that the "haunts" of historical archaeology include "colonialism, Euro-centrism, capitalism, and modernity." The history of the settlement of Lakka Skoutara clearly conforms to the history of modernization in the Greek countryside, the situation of small places in the tumultuous events of the mid twentieth century, and the role of regional and global economic connectivity in agricultural practices. While we will touch on few of these issues directly, the narrative of abandonment and rural change presented here will offer material for the kind of microhistorical case study recently called for by Gallant and others in a roundtable on the social history of modern Greece (Avdela et al. 2018). In particular, our work, along with other contributions to this volume, will add to the growing body of literature concerned with changes to rural life, the economy, and labor practices in the postwar decades (for a survey of this literature, see Yannitsiotis 2007:110–115).

Our focus in this article will center especially on site formation processes that were documented over multiple visits, expanding upon similar efforts in Greece pioneered by P. Nick Kardulias, Priscilla Murray, and Claudia Chang in the southern Argolid (Murray and Chang 1981; Murray and Kardulias 1986, 2000) and considered by others in this edited collection (see, for example, Sanders et al., this volume). Kardulias, Murray, and Chang collected ethnoarchaeological data from contemporary herder sites to understand the structure of discard practices in the countryside through careful study of assemblages. This work, however, served to contextualize the various discard, recycling, and curation practices present in the ancient countryside. Pettegrew (2001) drew upon this research to argue that, in many cases, the dynamic formation processes that are associated with Classical farmsteads could result in relatively faint artifact signatures in the landscape, especially after roof tiles were removed, broken pottery discarded, and complete vessels carried off with the departing residents. More recently, Constantinos Papadopoulos (2013) drew upon work from elsewhere in the Mediterranean basin in his effort to document dynamic abandonment and postabandonment processes in a Cretan village through both careful observation and accounts from ethnographic informants. Indeed, as the other essays in this volume illustrate (e.g. Brenningmeyer et al.; Caraher et al.; Rothaus et al.; Tzortzopoulou-Gregory and Gregory, this volume) abandonment was a dynamic and often unfinished process of fluid settlement and its contingent connections to economy, labor demand, markets, regional and global networks, and so on (Sutton 2000).

Our contribution highlights the value of the long-term study of site formation processes, an approach also recommended in the study of the hamlet of Penteskouphi near ancient Corinth (Sanders et al., this volume). Through photographs and detailed descriptions of the houses and their assemblages at Lakka Skoutara over time, we considered evidence for both the abandonment and repurposing of the houses and their assemblages over the last generation. Most importantly, our repeated visits to the valley revealed evidence of the numerous and constant short-term processes of habitation, abandonment, and reuse in the Corinthia that continuously shape this rural landscape. Documenting the ongoing transformation of the site made it clear that Lakka Skoutara was far more than simply a settlement frozen at the stage of abandonment, but rather a living place in the Greek countryside.

The Settlement of Lakka Skoutara

Lakka Skoutara is one of a series of fertile upland basins whose fortunes and functions shifted through time in response to a broader changing world (Figure 1). Work by the Saronic Harbors Archaeological Research Project (Tartaron et al. 2011) and various earlier extensive surveys of the region (Dixon 2000) have demonstrated the valley's historical connections to both the Saronic Gulf and the wider northeastern Peloponnese. Michael Dixon (2000:77) has argued that the area around Korphos and Sophiko marked the Classical-period boundary between the Corinthia and the Epidauria and saw action during the Peloponnesian War (Thuc. 8:10.2–8.11.2). The villages of Korphos and Sophiko preserve Late Roman remains and several Byzantine and post-Byzantine-period monuments in

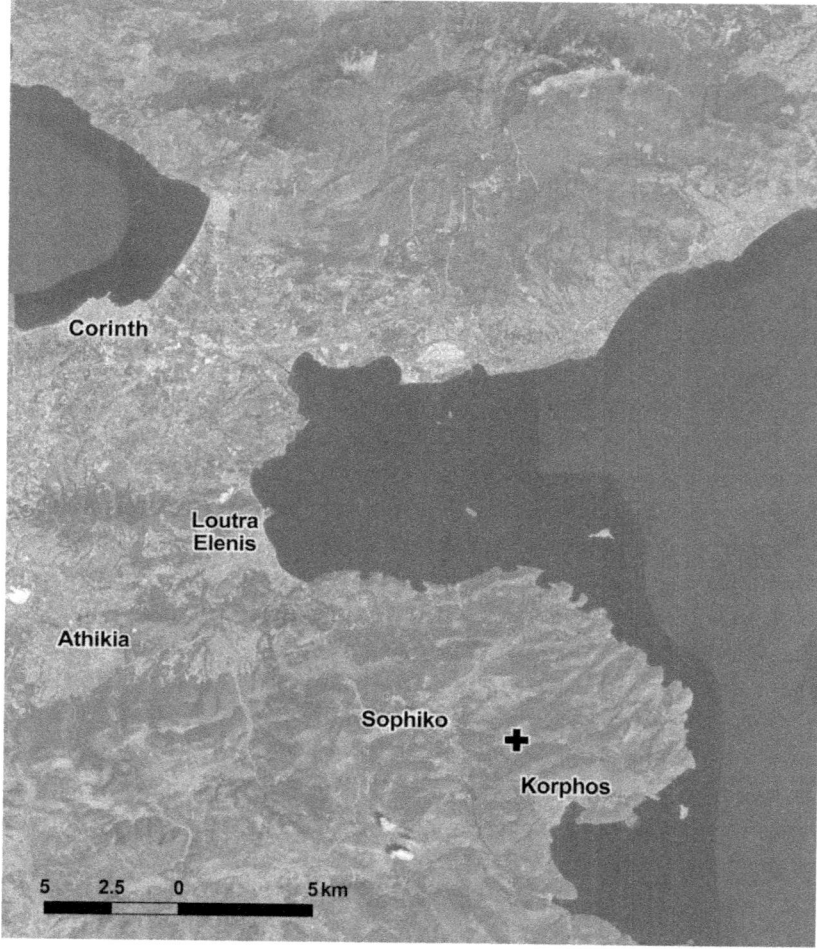

Figure 1. Map showing the location of Lakka Skoutara (+) in the southeast Corinthia. Background imagery courtesy of Esri.

the region, including the Early–Middle Byzantine monastic church at Steiri (Orlandos 1935) and a large, possibly Frankish-period fortification atop Mount Tsalika overlooking Sophiko (Gregory 1996).

The settlement today stretches over approximately 100 ha and is a loose collection of structures that date broadly to the early modern and modern eras. These include a church, six standing buildings, a dozen abandoned and ruined houses, and a variety of rural installations like cisterns, wells, threshing floors, resin-processing basins, and baking ovens (Figure 2). The presence of threshing floors throughout the site and the existence of

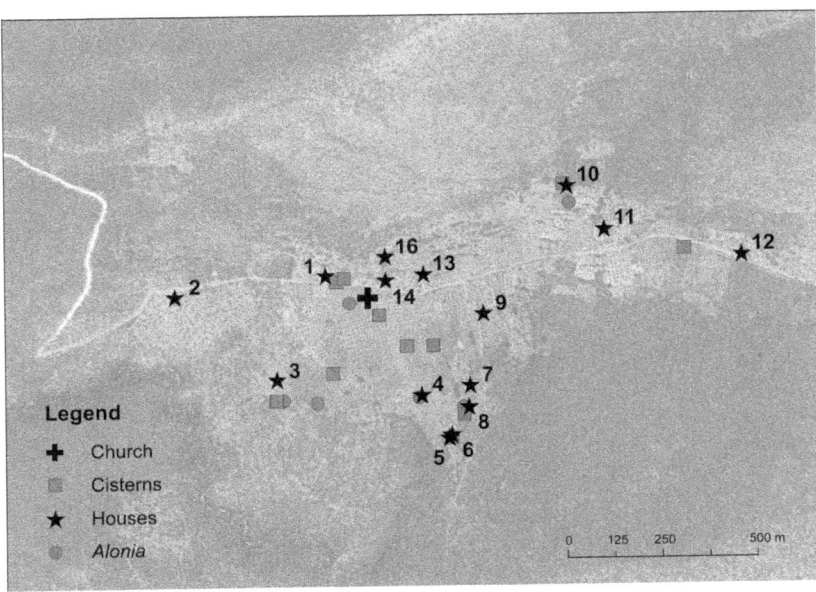

Figure 2. Aerial image of Lakka Skoutara with the locations of buildings and features. Background imagery courtesy of Esri.

terracing on the slopes indicate past use of the basin for cereal cultivation. Indeed, massive piles of stones cleared from the fields stand as reminders of the long-term and systematic effort required to prepare fields in the rocky uplands of the Corinthia for cultivation. At the same time, enormous olive trees and a premodern crusher base of an olive press demonstrate that the basin was bi-cropped in the medieval to modern eras (Figure 3), and the presence of younger groves reveals that the area has remained important for olive cultivation. The basin is punctuated with a dozen constructed cisterns for collecting rainwater (Figure 4), along with one well (Figure 5). Several houses feature large basins that informants told us were used for collecting resin from the pine trees that line the slopes of the valley (Figure 6). A large, ramshackle sheepfold (*mandri*) has gradually taken over the southern edge of the upland basin, and shepherding activities seem to have expanded in this area during the years we have documented the valley. Many houses have corbeled bread ovens. The basin features a relatively recent church dedicated to Ayia Ekaterina which, according to local informants, replaced an earlier church (Figure 7).

In the early modern period, mountain paths crisscrossed the rugged Corinthian landscape, connecting the basin to other valleys, settlements, monasteries, and trade routes. The eastern edge of the village of Sophiko

Figure 3. Premodern crusher base of an olive press.

Figure 4. A typical cistern at Lakka Skoutara.

Figure 5. Well at Lakka Skoutara.

Figure 6. Resin-collector basin.

Figure 7. Church dedicated to Ayia Ekaterina.

is just over 3.5 km away, or less than an hour's walk. From Lakka Skoutara to the coastal village of Korphos, the walk is more difficult and slightly longer (ca. 5 km). The route departs the basin from its southeast corner and follows a series of ridges and ravines and enters the village of Korphos near the church of Ayia Anna. There are sections of a built path along this route as it follows the edge of a steep ravine on the bank opposite the more substantial Ottoman-period built cobblestone road (*kalderimi*) that leads from around Ayia Anna to the fields near the fortification of Are Bartze (Dixon 2000). To the west of Lakka Skoutara are a series of similar, if smaller, basins with contemporary clusters of buildings. The intersection of the east–west route linking Sophiko to the upland basins east of Lakka Skoutara with the route that descends from Lakka Skoutara to Korphos likely accounted for the cluster of buildings in this basin. The hills around the *lakka* are dotted with installations that are associated with the movement of flocks through this area, including small apsidal shepherd's huts and sheepfolds.

Today, a bulldozed road links Lakka Skoutara to Sophiko and the coastal town of Korphos. Recent development of vacation homes in the various small embayments on the Saronic coast has led to the widening of the still-unpaved road through the *lakka*, making this upland basin even more connected to modern movement in the Corinthian countryside. Landowners continue to visit the church on occasion and take care of the olive trees in the basin, and a few farmers move into the standing houses during the fall harvest. The only consistent visitors to the valley, however, are a family of shepherds who use a well in the basin to water their herd of goats, and G.Z. who, for decades now, has driven out daily from Sophiko to maintain his country house, take care of his aging donkey, and escape the bustle of village life (Figure 8). Despite the absence of regular visitors today and the widespread remains of an earlier, more bustling time, the settlement at Lakka Skoutara continues to undergo changes and interventions owing to its place along a modern road through the region. As colleagues on the Western Argolid Regional Project note elsewhere in this publication, the occupation and abandonment "of routes and settlements goes hand-in-hand" (Caraher et al., this volume).

Figure 8. Mr. G.Z. standing in front of his house in 2009. Note the tile pile as provisional discard.

Overview of Method

In the summer of 2001, a small team from the Eastern Korinthia Archaeological Survey visited Lakka Skoutara to record the numerous abandoned houses, their architecture and associated features, and archaeological assemblages. Our aim was to document the houses and their environment in a way that would permit inferences about the cultural formation processes affecting the landscape, such as construction phases, habitation and discard, abandonment, and postabandonment uses. Aware of broader scholarly discussions about the interpretation of rural sites (Alcock et al. 1994; Bintliff and Snodgrass 1988; Osborne 1992), ethnoarchaeological and modern survey approaches in Greece (Murray and Chang 1981; Murray and Kardulias 1986, 2000; Whitelaw 1991), and the dynamic nature of the Greek village (Sutton 1994, 2000), we intended our study to contribute to an understanding of the character of settlement, the nature of abandonment, and archaeological signatures and meanings of habitation in diachronic landscapes.

We documented several houses in a preliminary way in 2001, which allowed us to refine the methods the following year. Our methodology, as it developed, consisted of three distinct components:

1. recording the houses and their assemblages through detailed description and photographs,
2. collecting information on artifact densities around the modern structures through surface survey, and
3. conducting oral interviews with the house owners and inhabitants in nearby Sophiko.

In this paper, we will not delve into the complexities of artifact densities on the surface but rather focus on the changes that are visible in the houses and their assemblages between 2001 and 2018. We will also draw on a series of interviews conducted between 2002 and 2005 in as much as they relate to the interpretation of the houses.

Our recording procedures included basic descriptive fields (e.g. "Artifactual Material") as well as interpretive assessments (e.g. "Function and Land Use"). To facilitate the process of description, we assigned numbers to the houses that we later associated with individual homeowners through interviews (see **Figure 2**). We noted the location of each house, its size and dimensions, orientation, and associated features; the artifacts present inside and outside (within 15 m) of the house in terms of their types, quantities, and conditions; the different phases of habitation, construction styles, and building functions; and the current condition of buildings and area, including ground cover and visibility. In addition to descriptions, we photographed the interior and exterior of the houses to capture the physical changes through time.

Following our initial systematic study of the houses in 2002, we returned to the area in subsequent seasons (2004, 2006, 2009, and 2018) to record the cultural processes and patterns of land use altering the houses, their functions, and their assemblages (**Table 1**). As the houses vary in their current function, condition, and position in the valley, we were unable to record every house during every season. Several houses or house foundations (#s 1, 7, 8, 9, and 15) were physically inaccessible to us, either occupied during our visits or bounded by fencing; these were documented only from a distance. One house (#12) seems to have disappeared sometime after our initial study in 2002, perhaps in connection with the widening of the unpaved road running through the valley. Several other houses (#s 11, 16, and 17), which lie high on the northern slopes of the basin, survive only in their wall foundations and are overgrown with weeds; we recorded these only during our 2002 and 2009 visits. Nonetheless, we still collected information on a dozen houses, including a number with still-standing architecture.

Table 1. General Overview of the Domestic Buildings in the Valley of Lakka Skoutara.

House No.	Description of Building	Dimensions (N–S x E–W)	Area (m²)	Orientation (degrees)
1	House	—	—	—
2	Longhouse	9.80 x 6.00	58.80	338
3	Longhouse	11.30 x 5.80	65.54	150
4	Longhouse	6.9 x 11.0	75.9	82
5	Longhouse	7.55 x 4.50	33.98	330
6	Longhouse	9.35 x 5.50	51.43	—
7	Longhouse	—	—	148
8	Longhouse	5.80 x 10.10	58.58	88
9	Storehouse	4.20 x 5.90	24.78	84
10	Longhouse	12.50 x 6.20	77.50	355
11	Longhouse	11.40 x 5.50	62.70	2
12	Longhouse	—	—	—
13	Storehouse / House	3.28 x 6.41[a]	21.03	80
14	Longhouse	10.30 x 6.00	61.80	4
15	Longhouse	—	—	—
16	Longhouse	6.50 x 4.20	27.30	350
17	Longhouse	12.00 x 5.00	60.00	—

[a] The dimension and area for House #13 is based on 2009 measurements and does not reflect the updates to the building made by 2018.

Table 1. Continued.

House No.	Current Condition	Owner	Years of Study
1	Maintained	C.S.	—
2	Collapsing	Y.K.	2002, 2004, 2006, 2009, 2018
3	Collapsing	S. Family	2002, 2004, 2006, 2009, 2018
4	Wall foundations	N.G., D.G.	2002, 2004, 2006, 2009, 2018
5	Collapsing	M.P.	2002, 2004, 2006, 2009, 2018
6	Wall foundations	M.P.	2002, 2004, 2006, 2009, 2018
7	Maintained	G.Z.	—
8	Wall foundations	I.M.	—
9	Maintained	G.M.	—
10	Maintained	A.K.	2002, 2009, 2018
11	Wall foundations	G.K.	2002, 2009
12	Demolished	G.S.	2002
13	Maintained	I.K.	2002, 2009, 2018
14	Collapsing	N.K.	2002, 2004, 2006, 2009, 2018
15	Maintained	K.S.	—
16	Wall foundations	—	2002, 2009
17	Wall foundations	—	2009

Figure 9. A typical fieldstone longhouse.

The Architecture and Building Phases of the Houses

Most of the houses at Lakka Skoutara are single-story "longhouse" types common to the Peloponnese and southern central Greece in the early modern era (see Brenningmeyer et al., this volume). Sigalos draws attention to the longhouse type with a broad façade, which is predominant in the Greek mainland and especially the Peloponnese during the Ottoman and early modern periods (Sigalos 2004:57, 61–63, 169–176). At Lakka Skoutara, these buildings were typically 9–12 m long and 4–6 m wide with total area between 50 and 70 m² (mean: 52.01 m; median: 59.40 m), and they were constructed with fieldstone walls, mud mortar, and tiled roofs (Figure 9). The houses are oriented roughly north–south, with windows and doors on the long east–west walls; the doors are almost always on the east façade. Courtyards defined by low walls appear at some houses immediately outside the main doorway, and they are often associated with external installations like cisterns, gardens, chicken coops, and bake ovens (Table 2; for the courtyard as an integral component of the house, see Sigalos 2004:61–62).

Only four buildings (#s 5, 9, 13, and 16) have noticeably smaller dimensions, which made them more difficult to categorize. House #9 was small enough (24.78 m²) that it appeared obvious it was used as a storehouse. In our original estimation, House #13, constructed of cinder block (Figure 10), was built for purposes of storage rather than residence (cf. Murray

Table 2. Features and Installations Associated with the Houses.

House No.	Threshing Floor	Oven	Resin Basin	Cistern	Enclosure	Older House Foundation	Field Walls	Other
2		X			X	X		
3		X	X	X	X			Circular stone structure
4	X	X			X	X		
5				X		X	X	
6				X	X			
10		X		X				Chain-link fence
11					X			
13						X		Large earth pile
14			X	X				Cemented porch
16								Retaining walls
17								

Note: As discussed above, some houses were inaccessible to us, and we were unable to document internal or external features. This explains why six houses (#s 1, 7, 8, 9, 12, and 15) are not listed here or in Tables 3–5.

Figure 10. House #13 before renovation.

Figure 11. House #13 after renovation.

and Kardulias 1986:31). In our most recent visit to the valley in 2018, however, this small cinder-block construction had gained an impressive façade, an extension to the east, a covered front porch, a bake oven, and installations for a future electrical hookup, all set within a yard defined by gravel patches and terraces constructed of cinder block and fieldstone (Figure 11). The changes in building architecture over time demonstrate the challenges of our interpretive categories and the possibilities for rapid change—a shabby storehouse today may become the proudest house tomorrow (cf. Brenningmeyer et al., this volume, for a parallel observation in the village of Aigition). That the original cinder-block construction of House #13 was also built over the remains of an earlier longhouse further complicates archaeological interpretation.

The sizes of all the structures in the valley (including the smaller buildings) are comparable to houses documented elsewhere in central Greece and the Peloponnese. Murray and Kardulias (1986:Table 1, 28–29) provide figures of 9–20 m^2 for storehouses and 50–93 m^2 for houses. Cooper (2002:37), suggests typical dimensions of 10–12 x 6–8 m for nineteenth- and early twentieth-century houses in the regions of Achaia and Eleia, which is the same length but greater width than these Corinthian houses. Sigalos (2004:88–109) notes dimensions for late Ottoman and early modern longhouses in towns and villages in Boeotia generally in the range of 11–14 x 5–8 m, although houses are occasionally much longer. Clarke (2000:112–113) indicates 10 x 6 m houses are common for late nineteenth- to early twentieth-century houses in the villages of nearby Methana.

The floor plans of the house reflect an agricultural mainland style with interior space arranged linearly into one or two rooms (Table 3; Sigalos 2004:59). Several of the houses (#s 4, 6, 11, 16, and 17) collapsed long ago and survive only in low foundation walls (Figure 12). Overgrowth of vegetation makes it difficult to reconstruct floor plans but nonetheless suggests division into one or two rooms. The houses that remain standing and were accessible to us point to comparable plans, with the long north–south dimension of the house divided into southern and northern rooms by a low ledge of plastered stone or cement that steps up from an earth floor and/or a partition wall constructed of vertical branches covered with mud and whitewashed plaster (Figure 13).[2] The elevated room (usually the northern one) is smaller and contains a fireplace, windows, and niches on the east or west walls and furniture such as beds, benches, and tables

---

[2] House #14 is the only house we documented with a cement floor at the same level throughout.

Figure 12. Rubble foundation walls of an older house.

Figure 13. Partition wall creating an internal division in a house.

287

Figure 14. Room with a fireplace, window, niche, table, and bedframe.

Figure 15. Larger room with an earthen floor.

Table 3. Floor Plans and Construction Materials Used in the Houses.

House No.	Floor Plan
2	Floor space divided into northern room and southern room: northern room has elevated stone and cement floor and fireplace on north wall; southern room has earth floor. Door on east wall, and windows and wooden niches on east and west walls.
3	Floor space divided by mud-and-mortar partition wall into northern and southern rooms: northern room has elevated, plastered stone floor (now covered by thin layer of manure), fireplace and low bench on north wall, windows on east and west walls, and niche on west wall; southern room has earth floor (now covered by manure), door on east wall, wooden niches in south and east walls.
4	House survives only in wall foundations and overgrown with weeds. Divided into a larger east room and narrower west room. Door on east wall.
5	Floor space divided into elevated southern and northern rooms: southern room has elevated cement floor and fireplace; northern room has earth floor. Wooden niches in south wall, windows in east wall, door on east wall.
6	House survives only in wall foundations and now overgrown with weeds—floor plan unclear.
10	Floor space divided by mud mortar partition wall into northern and southern rooms: northern room has raised cement floor, fireplace and niche on north wall, window and niche in east wall, window in west wall, and stone bench; southern room has stone and earth floor, concrete basin (1.73 x 2.47 m, 1.70 m deep) for processing resin, and door on west wall.
11	House survives only in wall foundations and now overgrown with weeds—floor plan unclear.
13	Small cinder-block house built over older longhouse; concrete floor throughout; door on south wall, fireplace on east wall, windows in south and north walls.
14	Floor space divided by mud mortar partition wall into northern and southern rooms with concrete floor at one level throughout house: northern room has fireplace and niche on north wall, window and niche on west wall, window on east wall; southern room has doorway and window on east wall and two concrete basins (2.00 x 2.50 m, 1.50 m deep) for processing resin.
16	House survives only in wall foundations and now overgrown with weeds—floor plan unclear. Door on east wall; possible windows on north, east, and west walls.
17	House survives only in wall foundations and now overgrown with weeds—floor plan unclear. Windows on north and east walls.

Table 3. Continued.

House No.	Construction Materials	Roof
2	Fieldstone walls (0.57 m), mud mortar, plaster on interior, whitewash; repaired with cinder blocks and concrete capping.	Pitched roof, wooden beams and tresses, tiles; vertical concrete roof support.
3	Fieldstone walls (0.53 m), mud mortar, plaster on interior; repaired with brick, concrete cinder blocks, and concrete and plaster capping.	Pitched roof, wooden beams and tresses, tiles.
4	Fieldstone walls (0.70 m), mud mortar, chinking with pottery and tile.	Tile fragments indicate tile roof.
5	Fieldstone walls (0.60 m), mud mortar, chinking with tile, plaster on interior, whitewash; repaired with cinder blocks and concrete.	Pitched roof, wooden beams and tresses, tiles.
6	Fieldstone walls (0.75 m), mud mortar.	Tile fragments indicate tile roof.
10	Fieldstone walls (0.60 m), mud mortar, plaster, whitewash; repaired with concrete.	Tile, pitched (hip).
11	Fieldstone walls (0.60 m), mud mortar, plaster, whitewash.	Tile fragments indicate tile roof.
13	Cinder blocks, concrete, bricks, metal supports.	Pitched, wooden beams, modern tiles
14	Fieldstone walls (0.60 m), mud mortar, chinking with tile, plaster.	Pitched roof, wooden beams and tresses, tiles.
16	Fieldstone walls (0.68 m), mud mortar, chinking with tile, plaster, whitewash.	Tile fragments indicate tile roof.
17	Fieldstone walls (0.70 m), mud mortar.	Tile fragments indicate tile roof.

Figure 16. The timber frame of a longhouse roof after tiles were stripped.

Figure 17. Tiled longhouse #10.

(Figure 14); it comprised the main living and sleeping space for the residents. The larger room typically features a simple earth floor, the house door, and an additional window, and among other things it was used for an interior work space, storage, and sometimes the housing of animals (Figure 15; Sigalos 2004:103); this much is evident in the agricultural implements (e.g. ladder), straw on the floor, and resin-processing basins visible in some of the houses. However, it is important to note that we had access to few functioning longhouses, and the one we did visit changed in notable ways over a 17-year period in respect to furniture, partition walls, and interior objects (#10, see below).

The houses have low pitched roofs constructed of long beams, a lattice of intertwined branches, and tiles (Figure 16 and Figure 17). The most common type of tile covering the typical house in the valley is the buff and (red) brown Laconian tile, although other types of machine-produced tile such as the glossy red "Marseilles" type are also occasionally found. Most of the houses have now lost their full set of tiles, but where they remain suggests that 2,000 tiles are common (e.g. #7); the longest house (#10) makes use of about 2,700 tiles (Figure 17). Although the houses tend to be roofed with the same type of tile, our survey and study demonstrated different tile types at several of the houses that point to successive roofing episodes.

The architecture itself shows building phases that can be dated by construction styles and evident refurbishment (Foster 2002:130). On the one hand, it is relatively easy to differentiate early modern (pre-1950) from modern construction episodes in the houses since the former make use of a traditional vernacular style of construction common to longhouses—coursed fieldstone walls about 0.50–0.75 m thick, chinked with small stones and tiles, filled with mud mortar, plastered, and whitewashed—while the latter make use of construction materials like cinder blocks and concrete reinforcements that have been in use in the region only since the 1960s. Cinder blocks, which were added to reinforce pediments (#s 2 and 5) and walls (#s 3 and 5) or were used to rebuild the structure altogether (#s 9 and 13), indicate distinct modification episodes in recent decades (Figure 18); the same is true of brick-and-concrete capping used in conjunction with older building materials. On the other hand, the mixture of different kinds of materials sometimes speaks to complex patterns of remembrance and the intention of evoking the past by refurbishing with traditional materials (fieldstone). One informant (M.P.) noted, for example, that the incorporation of fieldstones into a cinder-block house represented an intentional effort to create continuity with the original house of the 1920s.

Figure 18. Cement cinder block incorporated into fieldstone house construction.

Figure 19. Foundation rubble remains of former house phase (right) below its now collapsing successor (left).

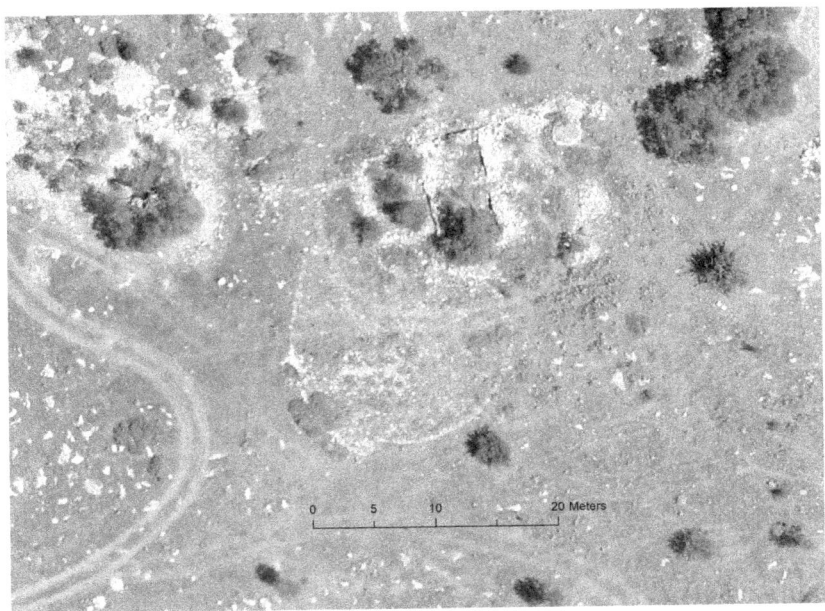

Figure 20. Aerial (drone) image of House #4 showing threshing floor and building phases. Image courtesy of Albert Sarvis.

The same complexities are evident in examining the relationship between adjacent house remains that could suggest building migration, additions, or phases in accordance with changing household needs and the necessity of occasional reconstruction. We have already commented on the complicated lifecycle of House #13, a cinder-block storehouse constructed in recent decades, which underwent a major upgrade and refurbishment between 2009 and 2018 and sits atop the remains of a longhouse whose fieldstone walls are still visible today. Other buildings demonstrate similar complexities of construction and rebuilding. House #2 reuses the eastern wall of a former house lying immediately to the west, which survives only in low foundation walls and a sunken depression in the earth (1–2 m deep) that must have been caused by the collapse of the bedrock beneath the former house (**Figure 19**); the current house clearly is a newer version of its neighbor and recycles the fieldstones into the new building. In other cases, however, the exact relationship of associated structures or the multiplicity of enclosed spaces is less clear. At House #4, for instance, low foundation walls of two rooms to the west of the house could represent, variously, earlier phases of the structure, later extensions to accommodate new members, associated buildings and enclosures, or, as M.P. explained, the divided living space of two brothers who did not get along (Figure 20; cf. the discussion of house clusters documented at Aigition: Brenningmeyer et al., this volume).

Oral interviews add interesting details about the human experiences of the changing household that take us back as far as the later nineteenth century. According to one informant, House #3 dates to the 1920s, but it was maintained and refurbished in the same place for nearly a century—even if there is nothing obvious in the architecture that distinguishes the earlier from the later phases of habitation. Coulton and Foster's (2002) enormous catalogue of village houses for the *nomoi* of Achaia and Eleia give numerous examples of houses dated by oral testimony or datestones to the nineteenth century, a pattern that is not uncommon elsewhere (Whitelaw 1991:417). The longevity of houses in the same location is understandable in terms of property boundaries, the expenditure of energy in an initial investment, and intergenerational family ownership. Forbes (2007:229–230) has even observed for Methana that inhabitants often thought of a rebuilt house as the *same* house as the one it replaced.

In other cases, neighboring structures reflect the complex dimensions of intergenerational housing needs that are only clear from oral testimonies. G.Z.'s house (#7) is situated within 20 m of the foundations of the house (#8) of his grandfather, I.M., who died in 1947 at 103 years old. His own house marks a more recent construction of the family that has outlived that of his grandfather's home. On the other hand, M.P.'s house (#5), which is also a more recent refurbishment (early 1980s) in cinder block, lies immediately over his father's house built in the 1920s and intentionally incorporates the former structure's foundations and fieldstone walls to foster continuity of place. Interestingly, though, the low foundations of nearby House #6 represent not a house preceding his father's (#5) but one that his father built during the German occupation in the early 1940s to accommodate the new needs of the inhabitants who were then living in the valley year-round. The seemingly old foundations of House #6 are much more recent in time than the foundations that are now incorporated into a structure that uses cinder blocks.

These kinds of intricacies in building life cycles appear to be common to all the houses in the valley, even if we have neither the archaeological clues nor the stories to decode them. Although the construction of adjacent houses often occurs to accommodate new members (such as daughters-in-law and grandchildren) of the extended families, building function can be quite complex. Clarke (2000:119, 123) offers an example of a large family in Methana purchasing a house in the 1920s immediately adjacent to their own and using it, successively, for storage, a temporary village school, and the residence of the families of their son, daughter-in-law, and eventually, grandparents. Sigalos (2004:62) documents the use of adjacent houses as residences for married children and as stables for animals. Property owners at Lakka Skoutara referred to older houses in several places that are totally invisible today, the ephemeral building material presumably incorporated into later structures and features (cf. Sanders et al., this volume, for the melting of abandoned houses into the landscape over time). G.Z., for example, pointed out a place near his grandfather's house (#8) where he remembered his great-grandfather's hut (*kalyvi*) with its dirt roof. Elsewhere, M.P. noted that House #10, belonging to A.K., was the ancestor to a house just to the north (now gone) that was owned by his grandfather. The remains of now-vanished houses are often incorporated into later constructions (Clarke 2000:116–117). The oldest inhabitants of the basin remember seeing as children some of these houses built of mud-brick walls and with mud roofs (see Given 2018 for an example of this type of construction on Cyprus). Mud-brick construction is common to vernacular architecture of the Peloponnese generally (Foster 2002:139) but is nearly absent at Lakka Skoutara, and the informants' memory in this respect adds a vital clue to the longevity of this village.

The different construction styles that can be observed at the houses, then, manifest the multiple phases of building, repair, and refurbishment that are always present, albeit not always obvious at houses that survive only in foundation or at those that have vanished altogether. In fact, as the following section will explore, the houses are constantly being transformed even within the dynamic landscape of a valley that can often seem abandoned.

Settlement Lifecycles

If the agricultural installations and houses themselves reflect episodes of habitation over time, the equipment and artifacts at the houses represent the varied processes of habitation, functional shift, reuse, and abandonment in a landscape tied to the broader global forces transforming the northeastern Peloponnese in the twentieth and twenty-first centuries. Hence, while habitation was typically seasonal in the valley, with land owners residing permanently in Sophiko and visiting their land during peak agricultural months, we have also learned of times when people inhabited the valley semi-permanently, as, for example, during the turbulent

Table 4. Archaeological Assemblages Found within the Houses.

House No.	2001/2002	2004/2006
2	Glass fragments, plastic, manure bags.	Now large quantities of tile, wood, cinder block.
3	Plastic medicine bottle, three burlap sacks filled with wool, a few tile fragments, manure, metal can for gas, cloth, empty burlap bags, cigarette lighter.	South end of roof collapsed; tiles and beams have obscured southern part of house.
4	Tiles (vegetation obscures ground); piles of pruned olive branches.	No piles of branches.
5	Dense scatter: bed spring, kitchen ware (metal cooking pot lid, plastic cups, silverware), cloth (pants, jacket, other), plastic container, glass bottle, metal can, cord, hundreds of tiles.	Unchanged.
6	Overgrown with weeds.	Unchanged.
10	Northern room: wooden bed; large key in wall niche; scissors, metal, and leather in wall niche; overturned table. Southern room: hay throughout; metal plow, wooden ladder, small metal basin, metal can, broom, plastic cup, wood pile, a few tiles.	—
13	Ladder, plastic chair, bricks, cinder blocks, stacked tiles, wood, metal containers, burlap bag.	—
14	Northern room: bedspring, wooden dresser, door on floor; containers and glass bottles on shelves; burnt wood. Southern room: metal, wooden, and plastic containers, barrels, and cases; cups, metal, wood, numerous tiles.	Unchanged.

Table 4. Continued.

House No.	2009	2018
2	Now goat bones, plastic water bottle.	Roofless and crumbled; cinder block and tiles still visible.
3	Roof totally collapsed, inside now covered over with wood beams, tiles, stones, and cinder blocks.	Collapse now covers over interior objects; inside, noted brick, cinder block, some plastic, rubble, tiles.
4	Piles of pruned olive branches.	Unchanged, but tiles still visible in and around structure.
5	Roof totally collapsed, inside now covered over with large quantity of wood beams, tiles, and cinder blocks.	Roof collapse with tiles and rafters covering artifacts; noted plastic plates, resin collectors, and two glass bottles.
6	Unchanged.	Unchanged, but significant vegetation growth within; noticed Corinthian tile on wall.
10	Northern room: wooden bed, large key in wall niche, table (not overturned). Southern room: long saw, plastic container, agricultural chemical barrel, broom, plastic cup, pile of 219 tiles.	No clear division of rooms any longer (internal partition wall gone); interior clean: three wooden blocks, neatly stacked pile of tiles, saw blade in resin basin.
13	Unable to access.	Provisional discard / storage of construction material in northeast extension: wood, hoses, brick, fieldstone.
14	Tile roof now fully collapsed, tiles cover ground, overgrown with weeds (2006, unchanged in 2009)..	Total collapse, with walls standing only 1–2 m above ground; overgrown with thistles and weeds; only tile fall still visible and pink plastic container.

1940s when World War II and the subsequent Civil War made life in Sophiko difficult. The abandoned landscape that seems to characterize the valley today is itself a product of changes to small-scale agriculture across Greece since the 1960s. The introduction of mechanized agriculture (and small trucks), the decline in cereal cultivation in the northeast Peloponnese, and the widespread ownership of vehicles undermined agriculture and more permanent forms of settlement in the valley. The last family residing permanently in the valley had moved out by the early 1980s, and since then most of the standing houses have been occupied only for short duration during the fall olive harvest by villagers who otherwise reside in the larger settlement of Sophiko. On the other hand, G.Z. has continued to drive out to his country house nearly every day from his permanent residence in neighboring Sophiko, while the owners of the other standing buildings continue to maintain, refurbish, and even expand their residences. Such contingent forms of settlement and land use have left material correlates in the landscape that defy facile definitions of "habitation" and "abandonment."

The associated artifact assemblages offer glimpses into the functions of the buildings (Table 4; see Murray and Chang 1981; Murray and Kardulias 1986). We would expect that these "farmsteads" should produce a range of artifacts that point to domestic function, including at least the basic furnishings common to early modern seasonal houses, which typically included utilitarian equipment like a bed, chairs, tables, wine barrels, olive oil containers, and utensils for cooking, eating, and drinking (Clarke 2000:110–113, 117, 124). Obviously, such domestic assemblages are exceptional, however, and most of the houses in the basin are missing these furnishings. This was partly a result of our sample as we were unable to access and document several of the functioning houses that are still in use. One seasonally occupied house that we were able to consistently study over the years—a house high on the slopes above the eastern end of the valley (#10)—revealed many small changes of internal objects and features over the 17-year period (see Table 3). Our original documentation recorded a space divided by an internal partition wall into a northern and southern room. A wooden bed frame, overturned table, and some tools (scissors, leather) were found in the one room, and farming equipment (ladder), tools (plow, broom), metal and plastic containers, and some construction material (a few tiles, wood) in the other; the hay across the southern room indicated animal keeping. In 2009, the same furniture was found in the northern room in a different arrangement, but the tools were gone, while different tools (a long saw) and some new objects (a large metal barrel, plastic cup) and a greater quantity of tiles were found in the southern room. By 2018, the internal partition wall was gone, and the interior was completely clean, without furniture or objects except for three wooden blocks, a saw blade in the resin basin, and neatly stacked tiles. Our visits evidently captured glimpses of the normal movement and circulation of agricultural goods that must be common to all functioning homes in the valley. Interestingly, very few characteristic domestic items, such as plates, utensils, or food or drinking vessels, were visible.

Collapsing or abandoned houses rarely showed substantial domestic debris. The houses that survive only in their foundations (#s 4, 6, 11, 16, and 17) preserve only light tile scatters and occasional artifacts inside and outside the structure, while most of the assemblages at other houses indicate non-domestic functions. Only two collapsing houses (#s 5 and 14) showed a variety of habitation material including furniture, containers, clothing, tiles, and various assorted metal and plastic artifacts. At M.P.'s house (#5), the material was scattered in the collapse all about the floor of the house, but in House #14 containers and glass bottles were still present on wooden shelves. Both houses fell into disuse but had not been depleted of the household goods, perhaps because the homeowners were unable to visit in their older age or because the children inheriting the properties saw no point in continuing their parents' investment. M.P. himself was 80 years old in 2001 when he first showed us around the valley and, although he had not visited his house in some 10 years, he became upset when he saw it in ruins (on the emotional power of abandoned lands, see **Forbes 2007:326–327**).

Most of the houses produce the sorts of assemblages that we would expect from abandonments in which the objects and equipment were recycled elsewhere. Half of the houses recorded (#s 4, 6, 8, 11, 16, and 17) survive only in their foundations, and very few tiles and sherds were visible. Since these were abandoned long ago during the period when the basin was used regularly, it is probable that the materials were carried off and reused elsewhere before or during abandonment. Domestic objects and equipment were essentially stripped from Houses #2 and #3 before their conversion into animal pens, while some houses (e.g. #10) that are still standing and in use today no longer have the most basic household equipment, such as storage vessels, plates, and utensils. It is also possible, however, that vegetation and earth cover some scattered debris on the floors of these buildings; we ourselves observed the burial of postabandonment debris from collapsing roofs and the growth of new vegetation over a 17-year period (see **Table 4**).

Figure 21. The largely inaccessible interior of House #2 with collapsed roof.

Figure 22. Goats roaming in the collapse of House #3.

Assemblages at several of the houses reflect specific shifts in building function following occupation. The domestic assemblages of Houses #2 and #3 were so depleted during and after abandonment that there is nothing visible inside the houses that specifically suggests habitation (Figure 21). The burlap bags, wool, medicine bottles, glass and plastic containers, and manure, among others, reflect first the conversion of these buildings into animal pens and, now that the roofs have collapsed, an area open to grazing animals. In 2009 and 2018, we observed goats stationed in an animal pen 50 m to the south and moving among the ruins of House #3 (Figure 22). The reuse of houses as animal pens is not uncommon in the Greek countryside (Forbes 2007:231–233). The small cinder-block house (#13), on the other hand, replaced a longhouse years ago and clearly seemed to have been built with storage in mind, at least until its more recent expansion with new porch and space revealed a clear domestic character. In 2018, we recorded provisionally discarded material within one of the new rooms of that structure (construction material such as bricks, cinder blocks, hoses, stacked tiles, and wood); in an earlier year, we had observed equipment useful during the fall olive harvest such as a ladder, plastic chairs, and a burlap bag.

Few of the artifacts found outside the houses contribute to positive assessments about habitation even though the courtyard and surrounding fields would have been principal arenas for domestic activities (Table 5; Sigalos 2004:61–63). Most objects found outside the houses point especially to construction or agricultural activities. The tractor tires, resin collectors, shotgun shells, pallets, and branch piles present around several buildings indicate the relatively recent use of the land for plowing, resin processing, hunting, and olive cultivation. The light scatter of ceramic, metal, plastic, and glass containers found outside some houses (#s 2, 4, 6, and 13) indicates storage or consumption of food and liquids (e.g. sardine cans, a Nescafe frappe shaker) and reflects either seasonal visits to the valley during olive cultivation or behaviors completely unrelated to the use of the houses. For example, the laundry detergent and plastic water bottle around House #2 were observed in 2009 and were discarded from the gravel road above and not from the house. Some of the plastic water bottles have fallen from olive trees where they had been hung as warnings of pesticide spray. Other objects, such as the sole of a shoe, a comb, a sock, and small mirror, are too random to suggest anything other than low-intensity activity in the area, and such finds have clear parallels with discard patterns documented in the southern Argolid (Murray and Chang 1981:Figure 3; Murray and Kardulias 1986:33). The fabric of the houses

Table 5. Archaeological Assemblages Surrounding the Houses.

House No.	2001/2002	2004/2006
2	Light scatter of artifacts: metal cans, wood, glass fragment, plastic bottle, pithos fragment, resin collector, ca. 160 tile fragments	Unchanged, except more tile fragments from roof collapse
3	Cinder blocks, bricks, earth, and tile at southeast and northwest corners	Unchanged
4	Scatter of artifacts: ca 50. tile fragments, 50 potsherds, glass fragments; metal barrel holder, bottles, oil can, sardine can; 12 shotgun shells, sole of a shoe, plastic comb	Unchanged
5	A few tile fragments, piece of metal	Unchanged
6	Metal container	—
10	Scatter of tile fragments	—
13	Stacked tiles behind structure; scattered artifacts: tile and pottery fragments, cement fragments, wood; bottle of plastic cleaning solution, metal cans, sock, small mirror, pruned olive branches	—
14	Scattered artifacts: tractor tires, plastic and metal pieces, bricks, containers	Unchanged
16	A few tile fragments, shotgun shells	—

Table 5. Continued.

House No.	2009	2018
2	New piles of pruned olive branches; plastic water bottle and laundry detergent container near road	Tiles on exterior
3	Collapsed debris (stone, cinder blocks, earth, tile) now on east and west sides	Greater collapse to exterior
4	New piles of pruned olive branches	Some tiles around structure; no olive branches
5	New piles of pruned olive branches	—
6	Unchanged	—
10	Tile fragments gone; overturned water trough outside door	None noted
13	Stacked tiles and barrel behind structure; scattered artifacts: tile and pottery fragments, cement fragments, wood; metal can, olive branches	Water bottles and pallets, otherwise clean yard
14	Unchanged	Cigarette pack, plastic cup, and roadside debris
16	New Nescafe frappe shaker, metal spring, plastic bottle	—

Figure 23. Tile fragments from collapsed House #3 becoming part of surface deposits.

themselves created halos throughout the basin in the form of slumped and collapsed walls and roofs (#s 2 and 3), stacked tiles or wood (# 13), and light scatters of tile and brick (#s 4, 10, 11, 13, 14, and 16). This much is obvious already from the surviving fieldstone walls, but these eventually will dissolve into the landscape, and the construction debris will become more important in defining the former habitation (Figure 23; cf. Sanders et al., this volume).

Overall, the quantity of artifacts noted in and around most of the houses is low. Fewer than half (5 of 11) of the carefully documented houses contained assemblages inside that were substantial; fieldstones and a few tile fragments were the principal signature of the other six buildings. Outside the houses, artifact scatters were typically small, with only occasional clusters of potsherds and trash (#s 4 and 13). As we noted earlier, our area of pedestrian survey incorporated several houses and showed that tile especially was an important signature of these buildings, while light scatters of table wares, kitchen wares, and storage vessels were observed in the fields around the houses. These observations at least allow us to conclude that, while artifact clusters (including especially tile) may sometimes form a signature of habitation, lower-density scatters are often all that is left of former houses in the modern countryside.

Among the most interesting data we collected in our study was a series of observations about the state of the houses. While in many of the houses we noted no discernible changes, the alterations that we did observe were

Figure 24. House #2 with tiles in place in 2001.

Figure 25. House #2 after tiles were stripped.

sometimes significant. As one example, we obtained two quite different snapshots of the objects inside House #10. In 2002, we observed the large southern room covered with hay, and in both rooms an overturned table, plow, small metal basin, ladder, wood pile, and several small objects (scissors, metal, leather, key), suggesting use for storage and animals. In 2009, the northern and southern rooms were cleaner and neater (the hay had disappeared) and still included the table and key, but otherwise they had a quite different assemblage: a wood saw, an empty barrel, a broom, and a stack of 219 tiles. Both years suggest that the house was being used mainly for storage of agricultural and domestic implements, but the artifacts being stored were different; the artifacts parallel the range of agricultural or pastoral implements documented at "storehouses" in the southern Argolid (Murray and Kardulias 1986:31).

Even abandoned houses in the basin show signs of artifact movement. We documented the stripping of hundreds of whole tiles from the roof beams of House #2 between 2001 (Figure 24) and 2002 (Figure 25), an event that resonates with a story told by M.P. about tile stripping. He described two brothers who together owned an old house and had an irresolvable dispute, which resulted ultimately in one brother leaving and stripping his half of the roof tiles. The story highlights the curate behavior common to rural activities at Lakka Skoutara as well as the relational and personal dimensions behind the observed archaeological patterns. Such kinship disputes that involved property ownership remain relatively common in twenty-first-century Greek villages (Forbes 2007:164, 168, 232–234) and clearly shape recycling behaviors that are common at the houses.

Outside the houses, we observed small changes between 2002 and 2018 indicating that the houses remain centers of active land use. At two of the maintained houses (#s 10 and 13), tiles, a small mirror, and socks disappeared between 2002 and 2009 while a barrel and water trough appeared. A Nescafe frappe shaker and plastic water bottle at House #16 were newly discarded probably during the October harvest in 2009, while the laundry detergent container above House #2 suggests random discard from the road. Additionally, abandoned and ruined structures were evidently good places to pile pruned olive branches both inside and around the houses.

Finally, we observed in this brief span of time the rapid deterioration of the walls and roofs of the abandoned houses themselves. We documented the gradual collapse of tile roofs of several abandoned houses (#s 2, 3, 5, and 14), resulting in the wooden beams and hundreds of tiles falling inside and partially outside the structures (Figure 26 and Figure 27). At two

Figure 26. Standing House #3 with a tile roof in 2001.

Figure 27. Same collapsed house in ruins in 2009.

of the structures (#s 3 and 14), the house floors were no longer visible by 2009 and, in fact, were largely inaccessible, with roof beams and debris blocking entry; the household items left in the house were buried beneath the bulk of the building itself. The loss of the roof typically entailed also the rapid deterioration of the walls as exposure to the elements eroded the mud mortar and the fieldstone walls collapsed.

In sum, the life cycles of settlement, rebuilding, and abandonment at Lakka Skoutara were highly contingent. The houses and their physical assemblages today reflect only a small part of the complicated formation processes shaped by human factors such as kinship practices, inheritance, interpersonal conflict, mobility, transportation, land use, and agricultural activities. Human behaviors and formation processes can quickly reshuffle the physical artifacts of settlements within the short order of a decade or even a few years, a fact that complicates our definitions of terms such as *habitation, abandonment,* and even *village*. The archaeologist of the contemporary world and the archaeologist of the future must recognize this inherent dynamism in the landscape.

Conclusion

In the preceding paper, we have highlighted how rural agricultural houses and their associated artifacts, features, and environments in this small world reflect the contingency of habitation and abandonment over periods of time that range from decision-making moments to centuries. Ultimately, these dynamic processes complicate, if not confound, our definitions, categories, and interpretations. Given the tendency for seasonal occupation in the valley, can we say that Lakka Skoutara was ever fully inhabited in the early modern era other than during the war years of the 1940s? On the other hand, has it ever really been abandoned? The seasonal return of the inhabitants of Sophiko for the olive harvest, at least, shows how much life continues even in "abandoned" habitations in the Greek countryside. The maintenance and new investments in standing architecture—even while surrounding buildings fall—show the entanglement of new settlement in the old.

Our experience documenting the site of Lakka Skoutara has itself demonstrated the very real limitations of our methods for recording the dynamic landscape. While our field methods included many of the standard practices of intensive pedestrian survey, we were regularly reminded of how incomplete these methods were for capturing an archaeological landscape that continued to develop even as our fieldwork took place. In a similar way, it has been obvious to us that the several total weeks we have

309

Figure 28. Cinder-block storehouse that is new to the valley.

Figure 29. Mobile concession stand recently brought into Lakka Skoutara.

spent in the valley since 2001 can hardly capture the manifold natural and human processes that reshape it on a day-to-day level. Even our tendency to visit the valley in June or July can produce an incomplete view of a quiet countryside interrupted only by the sounds of bleating goats, buzzing bees, or the shepherd's call. Our visit one year in early November during olive season offered an altered view of the settlement.

Even in early summer 2018, as we were putting the final touches on this article, we had a chance to return to the area and make a final record of the contingent countryside. In some respects, the village appeared like the one we had first visited 17 years earlier. Although a couple of buildings had crumbled to the point of partially preserved wall foundations and one house had disappeared entirely, most of the houses standing in 2001 were still at least partially standing in 2018 and their yards were still maintained. The valley felt familiar as we walked across plow furrows and through prickly vegetation, collecting sharp Corinthian thistles in our socks. The "hover bees," basking sheepdog, singing cicadas, and sound of wind blowing through the valley in late May almost felt timeless.

But the closer view revealed change and aspects of new life in so many subtle ways. Several buildings and their yards were largely maintained. On the western end of the valley, about 170 m north of House #3, a small tiled structure made of cinder block—a storehouse perhaps—had newly appeared since 2009, as had surrounding piles of building material, plastic piping, and blue tarp (Figure 28). Twenty-five m northwest of the storehouse was a small mobile concession stand (4 x 3 m) covered with a tin shed roof of corrugated metal (Figure 29). We noticed three bikes inside but wondered who would be riding them and where, and whether the concession stand served any specific role here for the shepherds. As we walked around, we ran into a hiker on his way to Korphos. I.K.'s former storehouse (#13) had received an attractive new porch and an extension with sockets for electrical hookup. When or how electricity will come to the village is unknown, but new buildings speak to a potential optimism about the region's future connectedness and agricultural character that was less visible two decades ago.

We as archaeologists had also changed over the years, and not just in age and bodily wear. As we walked around the valley over rough cobble, with chirping birds and the clinging bells of sheep to the west, we could also make out a new kind of whirring above like the distant sound of buzzing bees. We had brought a drone this time, in partnership with new collaborators, and we captured nearly a thousand images over the

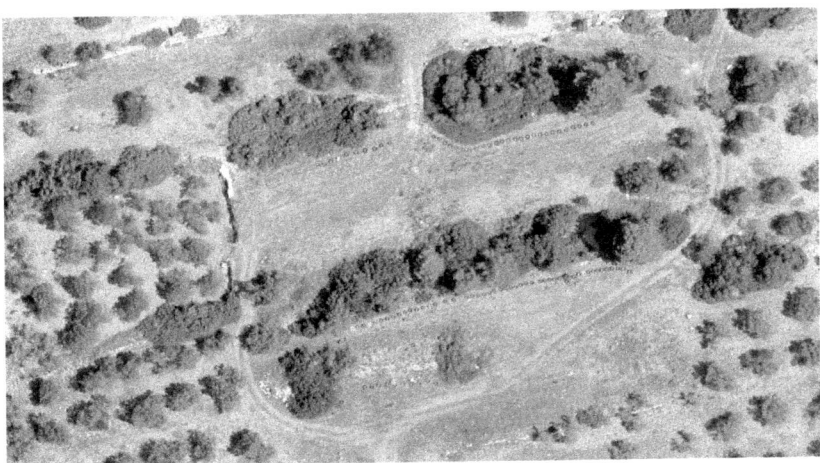

Figure 30. Drone photograph of the valley showing terraces neatly defined by tires. Image courtesy of Albert Sarvis.

course of two hours.[3] We ourselves did not imagine surveying the valley in this way 20 years ago in the days of the Eastern Korinthia Archaeological Survey, but the arrival of the drones, which themselves reflect global contingencies of technology, have allowed us to see the landscape in a whole new way (Figure 20; cf. Brenningmeyer et al., this volume). The threshing floors (*alonia*) and houses appear crystal sharp from 100-m altitude, and the clear photographs reveal patterns we had never noticed before with boots on the ground: the frequency of large ash circles from burning olive branches, terraces neatly defined by tires, pockets of dense cobble alternating with rich brownish-red soils, and the sharp lines of field walls (Figure 30).

The settlement of Lakka Skoutara continues to change with each passing year, and these changes transform any traditional view of abandonment at the site. Seasonal habitation at Lakka Skoutara largely ceased in the 1970s, but the buildings have attracted continued activity in the landscape as farmers harvested olives, tended their sheep, and maintained rural storage and retreat. Our own return visits to the valley have left only the faintest traces, but everywhere we see signs of life in abandonment.

---

[3] The work was carried out in partnership with Professor Albert Sarvis of Harrisburg University of Science and Technology.

References Cited

Alcock, Susan E., John F. Cherry, and Jack L. Davis
   1994   Intensive Survey, Agricultural Practice, and the Classical Landscape of Greece. In *Classical Greece: Ancient Histories and Modern Archaeologies*, edited by Ian Morris, pp. 137–170. Cambridge University Press, Cambridge.

Avdela, Efi, Thomas Gallant, Nikolaos Papadogiannis, Leda Papastefanaki, and Polymeris Voglis
   2018   The Social History of Modern Greece: A Roundtable. *Social History* 43(1):105–125. https://doi.org/10.1080/03071022.2018.1394037

Bintliff, John, and Anthony Snodgrass
   1988   Off-Site Pottery Distributions: A Regional and Interregional Perspective. *Current Anthropology* 29:506–513. https://doi.org/10.1086/203668

Cameron, Catherine M., and Steve A. Tonka (editors)
   1993   *The Abandonment of Settlements and Regions: Ethnoarchaeological and Archaeological Approaches*. Cambridge University Press, Cambridge.

Caraher, William R., and Lita Diacopoulos
   2004   Less than a Village: Patterns of Rural Settlement in the Landscape of the Southeastern Korinthia. Paper presented at the 105th Annual Meeting of the Archaeological Institute of America, San Francisco, California.

Caraher, William R., Timothy E. Gregory, David K. Pettegrew, and Lita Tzortzopoulou-Gregory
   2009   Between Sea and Mountain: The Archaeology of a 20th Century 'Small World' in the Upland Basins of the Southeastern Korinthia. Paper presented at the 21st Biennial Symposium of the Modern Greek Studies Association, Vancouver, British Columbia.

Clarke, Mari H.
   2000   Changing House and Population Size on Methana, 1880–1996: Anomaly or Pattern? In *Contingent Countryside: Settlement, Economy, and Land Use in the Southern Argolid Since 1700*, edited by Susan Sutton, pp. 107–124. Stanford University Press, Stanford.

Cooper, Frederick
   2002   *Houses of the Morea: Vernacular Architecture of the Northwest Peloponnesos (1205–1955)*. Melissa, Athens.

Coulton, Mary B., and Helen B. Foster
   2002   Catalogue of Village Architecture. In *Houses of the Morea: Vernacular Architecture of the Northwest Peloponnesos (1205–1955)*, edited by Frederick Cooper, pp. 146–413. Melissa, Athens.

Diacopoulos, Lita
   2004   The Archaeology of Modern Greece. In *Mediterranean Archaeological Landscapes: Current Issues*, edited by Effie F. Athanassopoulos and LuAnn Wandsnider, pp. 290–324. University of Pennsylvania Museum of Archaeology and Anthropology, Philadelphia.

Dixon, Michael
   2000   Disputed Territories: Interstate Arbitrations in the Northeastern Peloponnese, ca. 250–150 B.C. PhD dissertation, Department of History, Ohio State University, Columbus.

Erny, Grace, and William R. Caraher
   2020   The Kingdom of Chelmis: Architecture, Material Culture, and the Modern Landscape of the Western Argolid. *Journal of Field Archaeology* 45(3):209–221.
            https://doi.org/10.1080/00934690.2019.1704990

Forbes, Hamish
   2007   *Meaning and Identity in a Greek Landscape: An Archaeological Ethnography*. Cambridge University Press, Cambridge.

Foster, Helen B.
   2002   Village Architecture of the Morea. In *Houses of the Morea: Vernacular Architecture of the Northwest Peloponnesos (1205–1955)*, edited by Frederick Cooper, pp. 130–145. Melissa, Athens.

Given, Michael
   2018   Conviviality and the Life of Soil. *Cambridge Archaeological Journal* 28(1):127–143. https://doi.org/10.1017/S0959774317000609

Gallant, Thomas W.
   2018   Social History and Historical Archaeology in Greece. The Kefalonia and Andros Project, 2010–2014. In *An Age of Experiment: Classical Archaeology Transformed (1976–2014)*, edited by Lisa Nevett and James Whitley, pp. 177–193. McDonald Institute for Archaeological Research, Cambridge.

Gould, Richard A.
   1988   Life Among the Ruins: The Ethnoarchaeology of Abandonment in a Finnish Farming Community. In *The Social Implications of Agrarian Change in Northern and Eastern Finland*, edited by Tim Ingold, pp. 99–120. Suomen Antropologinen, Helsinki.

Gregory, Timothy E.
   1996   The Medieval Site on Mt Tsalika near Sophiko. In *The Archaeology of Medieval Greece*, edited by Peter Lock and Guy D. R. Sanders, pp. 61–76. Oxbow Monographs 59. Oxbow Books, Oxford.

Kardulias, P. Nick
   1994   Towards an Anthropological Historical Archaeology in Greece. *Historical Archaeology* 28(3):39–55. https://doi.org/10.1007/BF03374189

Murray, Priscilla, and Claudia Chang
   1981   An Ethnoarchaeological Study of a Contemporary Herder's Site. *Journal of Field Archaeology* 8:372–381. https://doi.org/10.2307/529576

Murray, Priscilla, and P. Nick Kardulias
- 1986   A Modern-Site Survey in the Southern Argolid, Greece. *Journal of Field Archaeology* 13:21–41. https://doi.org/10.1179/009346986791535726
- 2000   The Present as Past: An Ethnoarchaeological Study of Modern Sites in the Pikrodhafni Valley. In *Contingent Countryside: Settlement, Economy, and Land Use in the Southern Argolid Since 1700*, edited by Susan Sutton, pp. 141–168. Stanford University Press, Stanford.

Orlandos, Anastasios K.
- 1935   Βυζαντινοί ναοί της ανατολικής Κορινθίας [Byzantine Churches of the Eastern Corinthia]. *Archeion ton Byzantinon Mnimeion tis Ellados* 1:53–90.

Orser, Charles E., Jr.
- 1996   *A Historical Archaeology of the Modern World*. Springer, New York.

Osborne, Robin
- 1992   'Is it a Farm?' The Definition of Agricultural Sites and Settlements in Ancient Greece. In *Agriculture in Ancient Greece*, edited by Berit Wells, pp. 21–28. Svenska institutet, Stockholm.

Papadopoulos, Constantinos
- 2013   An Evaluation of Human Intervention in Abandonment and Post-abandonment Formation Processes in a Deserted Cretan Village. *Journal of Mediterranean Archaeology* 26(1):26–50. https://doi.org/10.1558/jmea.v26i1.27

Pettegrew, David K.
- 2001   Chasing the Classical Farmstead: Assessing the Formation and Signature of Rural Settlement in Greek Landscape Archaeology. *Journal of Mediterranean Archaeology* 14(2):189–209. https://doi.org/10.1558/jmea.v14i2.189

Pettegrew, David K., and William R. Caraher
- 2012   Producing Peasants in the Corinthian Countryside. Paper presented at the 113th Annual Meeting of the Archaeological Institute of America, Philadelphia, Pennsylvania.

2016 Life in an Abandoned Village: The Case of Lakka Skoutara. Paper presented at the 117th Annual Meeting of the Archaeological Institute of America, San Francisco, California.

Sigalos, Eleftherios
2004 *Housing in Medieval and Post-Medieval Greece.* BAR International Series 1291. Archaeopress, Oxford.

Sutton, Susan B.
1994 Settlement Patterns, Settlement Perceptions: Rethinking the Greek Village. In *Beyond the Site: Regional Studies in the Aegean Area*, edited by P. Nick Kardulias, pp. 313–335. University Press of America, Lanham, Maryland.

Sutton, Susan B. (editor)
2000 *Contingent Countryside: Settlement, Economy, and Land Use in the Southern Argolid Since 1700.* Stanford University Press, Stanford.

Tartaron, Thomas F., Timothy E. Gregory, Daniel J. Pullen, Jay S. Noller, Richard M. Rothaus, Joseph L. Rife, Lita Tzortzopoulou-Gregory, Robert Schon, William R. Caraher, David K. Pettegrew, and Dimitri Nakassis
2006 The Eastern Korinthia Archaeological Survey: Integrated Methods for a Dynamic Landscape. *Hesperia* 75(4):435–505. https://www.jstor.org/stable/25068001

Tartaron, Thomas F., Daniel J. Pullen, Richard K. Dunn, Lita Tzortzopoulou-Gregory, Amy Dill, and Joseph I. Boyce
2011 The Saronic Harbors Archaeological Research Project (SHARP): Investigations at Mycenaean Kalamianos, 2007–2009. *Hesperia* 80(4):559–634. https://doi.org/10.2972/hesperia.80.4.0559

Vionis, Athanasios K.
2012 *A Crusader, Ottoman, and Early Modern Aegean Archaeology: Built Environment and Domestic Material Culture in the Medieval and Post-Medieval Cyclades, Greece (13th–20th Century AD).* Leiden University Press, Leiden.

Whitelaw, Todd M.
  1991   The Ethnoarchaeology of Recent Rural Settlement and Land Use in Northwest Keos. In *Landscape Archaeology as Long-Term History: Northern Keos in the Cycladic Islands*, edited by John F. Cherry, Jack L. Davis, and Eleni Mantzourani, pp. 403–454. Monumenta Archaeologica 16. University of California Press, Los Angeles.

Yannitsiotis, Yannis
  2007   Social History in Greece: New Perspectives. *East Central Europe* 34(1-2):101–130. https://doi.org/10.1163/18763308-0340350102006

Chapter Seven
Roads, Routes, and Abandoned Villages in the Western Argolid

William R. Caraher, Dimitri Nakassis, and Ioanna Antoniadou

Over the last 20 years, scholars have come to view the Greek countryside through the lens of contingency. The work of Susan Buck Sutton (1988, 2000), P. Nick Kardulias (2015), Paul Halstead (2014), Evi Karouzou (2014) and others (Forbes 2007, 2017; Lee 2001) has emphasized that the modern and early modern countryside of Greece is not a stable, stagnant manifestation of some idealized (and classicized) traditional Greek rural life, but a dynamic and contingent space that adapted constantly to local, regional, and global economic and political pressures. These approaches have, for example, pushed back against the notion that the Greek village was an isolated and timeless unity bearing witness to a continuous historical tradition of rural life only recently disturbed by modernity, by embracing the full complexity of the landscape, including sites beyond formally constituted villages (Sutton 2000:21). They also have reconfigured the formal village as historically constituted: Sutton's work demonstrates how a complex variety of factors are at play in the dynamics of Greek villages, which are characterized by significant change over time, including in- and out-migration (Sutton 1988). In this context, the palimpsest of abandoned villages in the contemporary Greek landscape appears not as the ruins of a collapsed tradition but rather as a record of the adaptability and connectivity inherent in Greek rural life.

This recognition of a historically dynamic Greek countryside coincides with a growing interest in archaeological formation processes in intensive pedestrian survey (Bintliff et al. 1999; Pettegrew 2001). The dynamism of the Greek countryside in the early modern and modern periods resisted the simplistic ways that survey archaeologists understood settlement at a regional scale (Papadopoulos 2013; Pettegrew and Caraher, this volume). The processes that formed abandonment—from the recycling of ceramic roof tiles to the rhythms of seasonal use and discard—produced diverse surface assemblages that complicated the analysis of the surface remains of the Greek landscape. Greater attention to specific sites of abandonment, including the kind documented in this volume, has contributed to how we interpret survey data of all kinds. At the same time, the complex relationship between formation processes and surface assemblages has pushed archaeologists of the countryside to understand the modern landscape as more than an ethnoarchaeological case study for ancient farmsteads: the countryside is a complex record of habitation and activity; environmental, social and political interactions; and spatial and historical contingencies (Forbes 2007; Halstead 2014; Murray and Kardulias 1986). Renewed attention to both natural and human features in the countryside provides essential context to understanding the dynamism of abandonment as an archaeological, social, and economic process.

This interest in formation processes through ethnographic methods has periodically informed efforts to understand abandoned rural places in the landscape. Robson Bonnichsen's (1973) famous study of "Millie's Camp," for example, demonstrated the tension between archaeological and ethnoarchaeological readings of an abandoned contemporary camp site. The archaeologist's misreading of the abandoned site revealed the limits of archaeological practices and the value of ethnographic collaborations. Richard Gould's (1988) study of an abandoned Finnish village, likewise, drew upon an ethnoarchaeological approach to propose a typology of abandonment that emphasized the potential for ethnoarchaeological readings to contribute to a behavioral archaeology. Gould's notion of "progressive abandonment" fits most of the early modern and modern sites in Greece which encountered changes in function and population in response to particular historical situations as well as longer-term economic trends. For example, Tzortzopoulou-Gregory's (Diacopoulos 2004) and Pettegrew and Caraher's (this volume) work on the settlement of Lakka Skoutara in the Corinthia showed episodes of full-time habitation during the disruptions of World War II and the Greek Civil War, as well as progressive abandonment that continued at the site into the twenty-first century in response to changing aricultural practices and mechanization. Papadopoulos's (2013) study of an abandoned site in contemporary Greece arrived at similar conclusions, which emphasize how ethnography reveals the complex and episodic character of abandonment assemblages. The influence of methods developed in the context of North American and world archaeology coincides with research questions that are increasingly informed by the larger project of historical archaeology (e.g. Orser 1996), particularly the impact of capitalism, colonialism, and modernity on the Greek landscape, as Thomas Gallant (2018) and Athanasios Vionis (2012) have noted.

These scholarly developments provide the intellectual background to the research of the Western Argolid Regional Project, which documented two abandoned seasonal settlements, Chelmis and Koutsopoulou, in the rolling hills to the south of Inachos River in the Western Argolid (Figure 1). Today, access to these settlements involves traveling along rough dirt roads that disappear into olive groves or hiking through agricultural fields and along overgrown paths. In contrast, the modern villages of the Inachos valley sit astride paved roads that connect them to Argos. The relative invisibility of smaller, unimproved roads and tracks that connect the abandoned settlements to major routes and villages suggests that the major routes do not tell the entire story of movement and settlement in the landscape and hints at the changing relationships between places in the Greek countryside.

Conventional studies of paved or improved roads frame them as a projection of the centralized authority of the state (Alcock et al. 2012:3–4; González-Ruibal 2019:121–122, 142; Harvey and Knox 2015; Pikoulas 2007). Indeed, the modern roads connecting the villages of the Inachos valley to the modern political and market center of Argos represent just this kind of byway. These roads have seen significant investments by the state for their upkeep, and this contributes to both their visibility in the archaeological record and, in some cases, their continued use (Chatzikonstantinou and Sakellaridou 2017). As with the sustained investment required for monumental architecture, formal built roads can produce a notable signature in the landscape that is preserved in field boundaries, terraces, surfaces, bridges, and telltale depressions. In contrast, less formal paths and routes offer less persistent traces in the landscape (Gibson 2007). Despite their more elusive material traces, these byways nevertheless contribute to the formation of social ties, the structure of settlement, and, in some cases, opportunities for various forms of resistance in the landscape. As archaeologists have become more aware of the contingent countryside, routes that never acquired significant investment by the state have taken on new importance in understanding how communities and groups adapted to changing economic and political pressures. The relationship between abandoned routes and abandoned settlements provides an oft-overlooked context for short-term change at the regional level. Koster's (1976) famous "Thousand Year Road," for example, represented a persistent—yet materially unimproved—track from the southern Argolid to the summer pastures at Mount Kyllini above Stymphalos. This route may well trace a part of a significant medieval "inland road" that linked the Corinthia to other parts of the northeast Peloponnese and remained

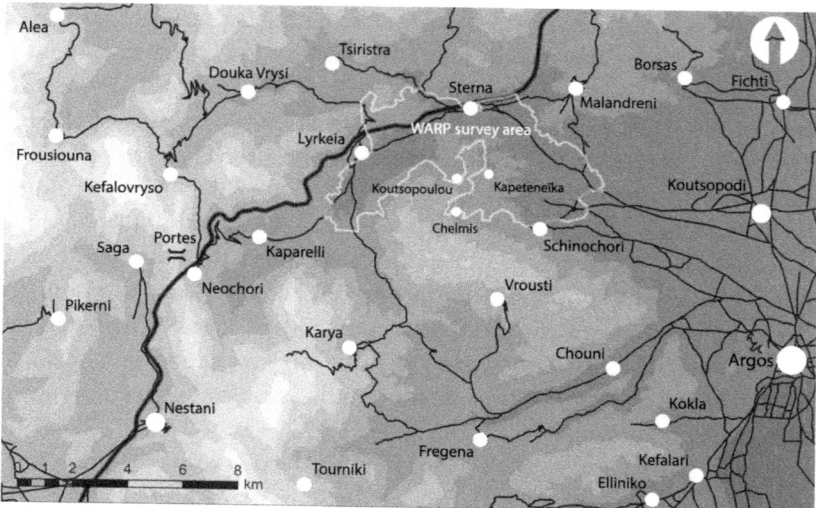

Figure 1. Map of modern settlements and major roads of the western Argolid. Map courtesy of Dimitri Nakassis.

significant until the early modern period (Kourelis 2018). These abandoned, seasonal, and occasional routes existing outside the roads that connect modern long-term political nodes (with their ancient and medieval predecessors) offer another way to subvert the idyllic imagining of a Classical countryside and reinforce arguments for dynamism and contingency that have formed the contemporary Greek landscape.

The Western Argolid Regional Project (WARP)

Our study of the routes and settlements of the Inachos valley is part of the Western Argolid Regional Project (WARP). From the start, WARP set out to study not just the landscape and settlement of the Inachos valley, but also its role in the terrestrial networks of the Argive Plain to the southeast, Arcadia to the west, and the Corinthia to the north (Gallimore et al. 2017). We anticipated varying degrees of connectivity between the premodern and modern settlements of the valley and what has historically been the political center of the region: the city of Argos, situated at the center of the fertile Argive Plain. The modern villages of Kaparelli, Lyrkeia, Sterna, and Schinochori stand more or less along the route of the river, connected by a paved trunk road which continues east on the river's left bank towards Koutsopodi before bending south toward the city of Argos. Modern travelers to Greece are probably most familiar with this region from the vantage of the Moreas Motorway, the modern highway cut into the northern slope of the valley between Sterna and Kaparelli that connects the Argolid to Arcadia via a tunnel through Mount Artemision. From 2014 to 2016, WARP conducted intensive and extensive survey in the vicinity of the villages of Lyrkeia, Schinochori, and Sterna (Figure 1).

Today, most local traffic follows the paved, two-lane road that runs alongside the valley bottom and the river. Smaller, largely unpaved roads extend from the main road and crisscross the region, conducting traffic to agricultural installations and fields. These roads invariably shape our view of the landscape as archaeologists who work in the area both in terms of how we move through and between these microregions and how we understand the historical development of this territory. For example, the modern road that provides access to the site of Orneai climbs from the modern village of Lyrkeia over a saddle (Diaselo) to the villages of Douka Vrysi and Kefalovryso, and makes clear the significance of this pass from the Inachos basin to valley systems to the north, east, and west (Figure 2). Sections of Ottoman-period bridges near this route indicate that parts of this impressive road were built perhaps as early as the eighteenth century, but the route has likely existed for centuries. Elsewhere in the survey area, northeast of the modern village of Schinochori, remains of a Venetian-period fortification at the site of Skala overlook the modern road in the narrow gap between a steep ridge and the Inachos River (Banaka-Dimaki 1992/1998; Pikoulas 1995:188–191, 263–267; Pritchett 1980:12–15). The topography here dictated a limited number of possible routes for a road heading both west and north departing the Argive Plain and keeping to the north of the Inachos (Figure 3). The fortification stands at a particularly narrow point, where ancient, medieval, and modern routes likely coincided, and indeed a modern inn (*chani*) was located nearby (Lehmann 1937). These patterns have sometimes led ancient historians to propose that ancient and modern roads largely tend to follow similar routes through passes and along valley bottoms. Indeed, Pritchett (1994:5) proposed as much for the route through the Inachos River valley.

More recently, however, scholars of the ancient landscape have complicated this apparent coincidence of ancient and modern routes by observing that pedestrian and animal traffic—and even carts—tend to prefer the shortest route between two places and are more tolerant of slope than even the modern bulldozer (Lee 2001:69). Likewise, despite the convenience and pervasive presence of modern roads, intensive pedestrian survey has sought to distance its view of the ancient landscape from the modern through its focus on landscapes at the margins of modern

324

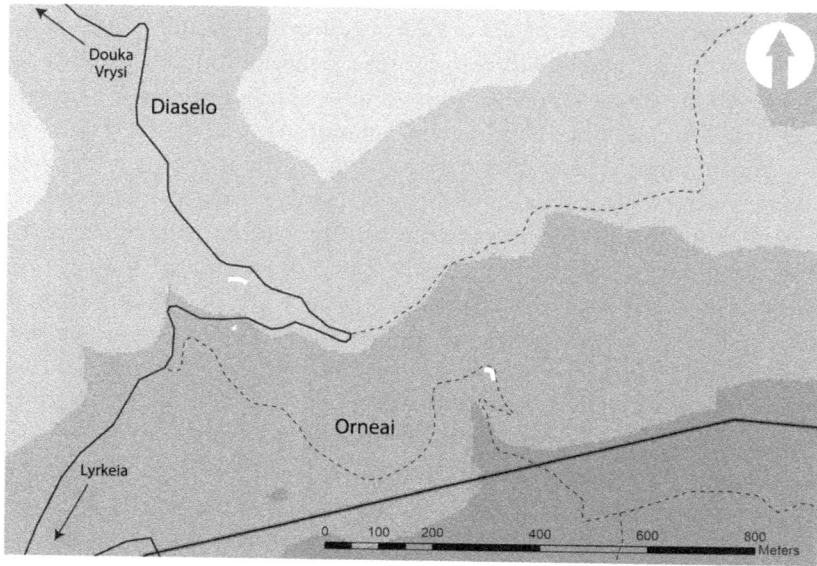

Figure 2. Map of the Diaselo region. Paved roads are indicated by solid black lines, unpaved roads by dashed black lines, and the remains of Ottoman bridges with solid white lines. Map courtesy of Dimitri Nakassis.

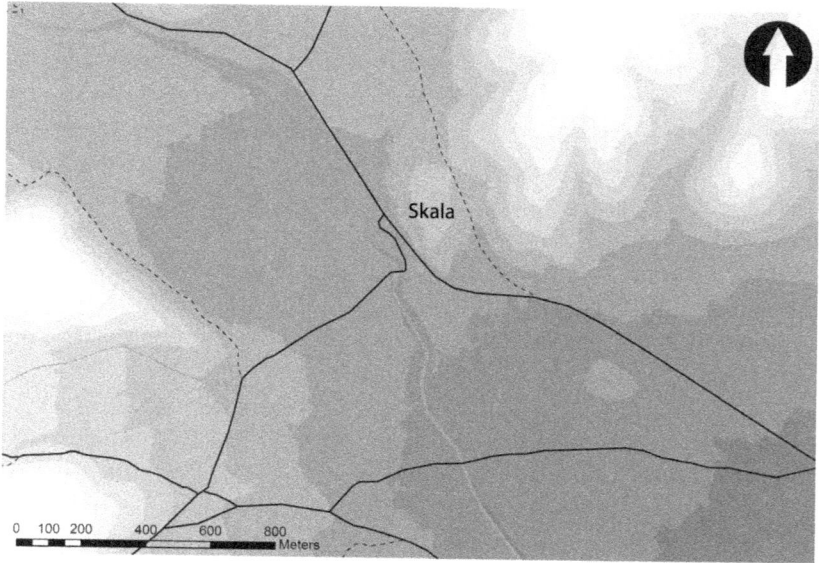

Figure 3. Map of the Skala region. Paved roads are indicated by solid black lines, unpaved roads by dashed black lines, and river and stream beds by solid blue lines. Map courtesy of Dimitri Nakassis.

use and by adopting practices designed to identify "hidden landscapes" that are independent of modern settlement and land use (e.g. **Forbes and Mee 1997**). Our contribution to this volume will focus on a number of relatively short-term sites that appear to fall outside of the main modern routes through the western Argolid, and we will trace how the contingent intersection of these abandoned settlements and abandoned routes shapes the formation processes, archaeological remains, and history of the Inachos valley.

Chelmis

In 2015, WARP spent two weeks documenting the ancient and modern material around a settlement called Chelmis, which is located approximately 3 km west of the modern village of Schinochori at the base of Mount Bachriami, which forms the western boundary of this section of the Inachos valley. W. Kendrick Pritchett (1980:16–17) visited the small church of the Panayia (which he calls the Pantanassa) nearby, which is surrounded by a high-density scatter of Classical and Hellenistic material, numerous graves (Papachristodoulou 1970), and architectural blocks. WARP field teams discovered high densities of ancient material, mostly Archaic to Hellenistic in date, extending over an impressive area (38 hectares). Local inhabitants tell the story that the region was once ruled by a poor king named Chelmis, who somewhat paradoxically hid his treasure in one of the wells adjacent to the small church.

Pritchett rejected the claim of Papachristodoulou (1970) that Chelmis should be identified with the ancient settlement of Lyrkeia (or Lyrkeion). That settlement is known only from a handful of ancient sources, principally Pausanias (2.25.4–5), whose description makes clear that Lyrkeia lies 60 stades from Argos on the northerly route to Mantineia via Orneai. Although Pausanias thought that the town had been abandoned from the time of the Trojan War, a third-century BC Argive inscription (*SEG* 17 [1960] 143.3) makes it clear that Lyrkeia continued to be inhabited in the Hellenistic period. Pritchett (1980:17) argued not only that Chelmis is further than 60 stades from Argos, but also that "… no main road would have continued on up the valley of the Inachos from the settlement [of Chelmis]. The valley or ravine is situated in a recess too far into the mountain. There are wheel-ruts in the rocks, and these could only have marked a road which terminated at the settlement." In other words, the ancient route through the region must have followed the modern road along the Inachos River. Since modern Chelmis apparently represented

Figure 4. A modern oven at Chelmis showing the reuse of tiles; exterior (above) and interior (below). Photographs courtesy of William Caraher.

for Pritchett a "suburb" of the village of Schinochori, to which it was connected by a local road, so too was the ancient site of Panayia a peripheral Argive village (*komi*) at the edge of a classic central-place system focused on Argos. In this reading of the landscape, ancient Chelmis is like modern Schinochori, a village located at the end of a major road whose function is to connect the village to the main artery that runs alongside the Inachos River.

Modern Chelmis is a small and largely abandoned settlement of over a dozen Balkan-style longhouses, stretching along the slopes of a narrow valley cut by a deep drainage that brings mountain runoff to the Inachos

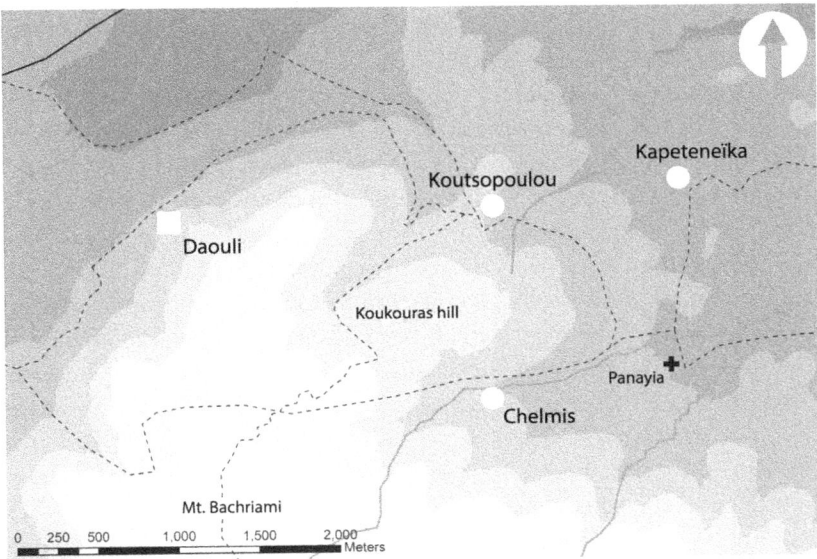

Figure 5. Map of Chelmis and its environs. Paved roads are indicated by solid black lines, unpaved roads by dashed black lines, and river and stream beds by solid blue lines. Map courtesy of Dimitri Nakassis.

River (Erny and Caraher 2020). Houses in the settlement featured animal pens for sheep or goats (*mandria*), corbeled ovens (Figure 4), and, in at least three cases, large threshing floors (*alonia*). The settlement saw activity as recently as the 1970s; in fact, at least one house, associated with a particularly elaborate *mandri* infested with fleas, continues to function as a seasonal residence. It is likely that the settlement was initially founded in the late nineteenth century (or perhaps slightly later), but it does not appear in the official demographic records until 1951 with a population of 119. Archival records from the Metropolis of Argolis indicate that the small church of the Panayia was constructed in the same year. This church is located 1 km to the east of Chelmis, where the east–west road toward Schinochori meets a dirt road that heads north to the settlement of Kapeteneïka (see Figure 5).

The houses of Chelmis demonstrated considerable variation in their states of abandonment, which ranged from the completely collapsed to at least one house that continues to function on a seasonal basis. Ethnographic work conducted by Ioanna Antoniadou connected the settlement at Chelmis with the village of Frousiouna, located some 15 km to the west (as the crow flies, but about twice that on modern roads) on the southern side of the Alea valley (see Figure 1). Agropastoralists from Frousiouna founded the settlement at Chelmis in order to winter their flocks from November to April. The practice was largely abandoned in the 1970s, and today only two residents continue to make the annual trek with their flocks. Villagers from Frousiouna also cultivated grain in this narrow valley and would venture to Chelmis in the early summer; the women would reap for 10 days in mid June, after which the men would descend from Frousiouna to thresh. Any connection between Frousiouna and Chelmis even today remains elusive in material terms. Indeed, it could be argued that the only material connection that remains is the ownership of land and houses in Chelmis, which are still largely in the hands of families from Frousiouna who have now settled in various places on the Argive Plain, although some properties have been broken up by intermarriage and inheritance.[1]

WARP described these houses and related features in significant detail and documented the artifact scatters in the immediate vicinity of each building. While a detailed analysis of the artifact scatters and buildings appears elsewhere (Erny and Caraher 2020), it is worth noting several patterns that are significant for understanding the history and function of the site. The Balkan-style longhouses represent the typical agglomeration of buildings commonly associated with seasonal settlement in Greece (Bintliff 2014; Sigalos 2004). The area now remains active primarily for cultivating olives and apricots, as demonstrated by a few buildings that remain in use for storage. Several houses are in a state of collapse and neglect; two have had their tile roofs removed for use elsewhere. A cluster of completely collapsed houses stands well beyond the reach of the rough field roads that currently provide access to the region and can be reached only by walking through terraced fields and across small stretches of built footpaths. The overgrown and neglected corbeled ovens associated with most houses in Chelmis preserve recycled tiles that likely were transported to the site as roof tiles (see **Figure 4**). Houses with preserved roofs or with significant complements of roof tiles stand closer to the modern dirt road that links Chelmis to Schinochori. This likely reflects the reciprocal relationship between access to the building, the utility of the structure, the desire to maintain the building, and the age of the house. In fact, someone

---

[1] In the absence of official documentation, property ownership is often established through continuous and intergenerational use of the fields. In light of the impending implementation of the land and property register (*ktimatologio*) in the Peloponnese, it would be interesting to observe how the ownership of "abandoned" land will be managed and compromised and the ways in which this will, in turn, give rise to new notions and significations of landscape.

recently used a bulldozer to extend a road across the ravine to give access to a house that has been meticulously restored and locked. In this context, formation processes and byways are clearly related.

Ethnographic interviews reinforce the marginality of Chelmis in terms of both its geographic location and its place in the Greek image of the countryside. Spatially, it sits between the "home" village of Frousiouna in the highlands at the Arcadian border and the established lowland villages that ring the central market town of Argos and in which many former residents of Chelmis now live. Chelmis is also marginal with respect to the ways that rurality is imagined in modern Greece. The "backward" and "traditional" countryside can be reductively opposed to the "sophisticated" and "modern" urban centers. The twenty-first-century economic crisis, however, has led to some Greeks imagining the countryside as the destination for a counter-urban movement back to ancestral homes and properties, often driven by romantic and idealistic images of rural life (Anthopoulou et al. 2017). We have observed these processes operating in the villages of the western Argolid, but they have not affected "in between" settlements such as Chelmis.

Chelmis' connection to the other settlements in the Argolid challenges the most obvious evidence from the material record. For example, Pritchett interpreted modern Chelmis as a hamlet connected to Schinochori and imagined that the ancient road, like its modern counterpart, ended at the head of the valley. Yet, the present link between the settlement at Chelmis and the main road along the valley bottom via Schinochori is largely a function of the modern state rather than any kind of persistent imperative derived from the most plausible route through the region. In modern times, the connection between Chelmis and the nearby village of Schinochori largely appears to have been tied to the formal status of Schinochori as a village with a school for the children of Chelmis and a church for Sunday services over the winter. None of the few former inhabitants of Chelmis who live in Schinochori today (for reasons of marriage) visit their prior homes. Economically, Chelmis looked to the Saturday markets in Argos, where the cheeses produced by the pastoralists were sold; once these families had returned to Frousiouna for the summer, they sold their products at the markets of Tripoli.

Koutsopoulou

The site of Koutsopoulou, which is part of a broader area known locally as Davrou, stands a little over 1 km to the north of Chelmis (Figure 1, Figure 5). It is located in the rugged highlands between Chelmis and the Lyrkeia valley, accessed by ascending the eastern side of a deep ravine that opens onto the southeastern corner of the relatively broad valley, about 3.5 km east of the modern village of Lyrkeia. Today, a steep unpaved road makes its way up to Koutsopoulou; however, before trucks and tractors were common in the Greek countryside, the sides of these ravines had paths that led to the rolling alluvial fans that form the southern edge of the Inachos River valley. Davrou is divided into smaller toponyms that indicate the names of previous—and in some cases the first—owners. Thus, Iliopouleïka indicates the settlement associated with a family from Frousiouna who had purchased the land after 1914 from its previous owners, the Dimopoulos family from Lyrkeia.

Like Chelmis, the site consists of a small agglomeration of abandoned and roughly contemporary houses situated on the south slope of a narrow, steep valley. Its toponym is indicative of its first owner: Koutsopoulos, a shepherd from Lyrkeia. In 2016, we documented the houses and their associated features and material. The houses of Koutsopoulou are Balkan-style longhouses similar to those at Chelmis. The overgrown condition of the houses made it difficult to identify associated features, but two houses are clearly connected to *mandria*; another has an oven and a possible cistern. None of the houses have preserved roofs, and they all have substantial tile falls, indicating that the tiles were not removed after the houses were abandoned. Only one house is easily accessed from the modern dirt road, and this house has attracted a large and varied assemblage of modern trash that ranges from objects associated with agricultural work to an obsolete and broken computer, contemporary pots and pans, shipping pallets, and so on. As at Chelmis, the presence of a modern dirt road shaped the abandonment process at the site, as the most accessible house became a site of discard.

From Koutsopoulou to Chelmis

The relationship between Koutsopoulou and Chelmis is more than typological. The two sites also stand along a premodern route through the low hills that separate Chelmis from the widened Inachos River valley near the village of Lyrkeia. To be clear, Pritchett's intuition—that no main road continued through the hills north of Chelmis—may well be correct, but these hills were far from impassable. Indeed, Pritchett (1980:xi; cf. Pikoulas 1999) himself observed that early modern "mule paths, or short cuts ... often on examination prove to follow the course of ancient routes." A 1944 map from the British War Office clearly shows the existence of routes linking Lyrkeia to Koutsopoulou and Chelmis (**Figure 5**). The route departs the neighborhood of Koutsopoulou to the south, crosses a ravine, and then traverses the lower slopes of a hill that is named Koukouras on the Hellenic Army maps. The settlement of Chelmis stands on the southern slope of Koukouras hill, from which it is possible to cross at a shallow section of a deep ravine and descend to the area of Panayia. Today, this walk takes about half an hour at a leisurely pace. It is telling that both Koutsopoulou and Chelmis stand near points where it is possible to cross the deep ravines that carry the runoff from Mount Bachriami to the Inachos River. While seasonal torrents surely transform these ravines on a regular basis, the ability to cross the ravines and walk along the slopes of this hilly region demonstrates that, despite Pritchett's assessment that the settlement of Chelmis and the Panayia stood at the end of the cart road, it is entirely possible that significant traffic continued on foot through the region.

Daouli

A small fortification called Daouli ("Drum") lies 2 km west of Koutsopoulou, tucked into a craggy cliff on the southern slope of the Inachos River valley (**Figure 5**, **Figure 6**). The earliest post-Roman material from the site dates to the early nineteenth century. This site offers spectacular views of the village of Lyrkeia and its valley, including the rugged acropolis of Orneai and the pass north toward the village of Douka Vrysi and the upland valleys of the Corinthia. Daouli also sits above the route that runs along the valley bottom from the city of Argos to Portes, the western pass to Arcadia that is clearly visible from Daouli. On September 19, 1826, Ibrahim Pasha crossed Portes on his way from Tripolitsa into the Inachos valley and raided several villages in the upper part of the valley before withdrawing (**Chrysanthopoulos** 1899:2:353–355). Such raids were common for Ibrahim Pasha during the summer of 1826, although their impact in the Argolid seems have been minimal compared to the devastation elsewhere in the Peloponnese (**Dakin** 1973:186–187; **Finlay** 1861:2:113–114). While it is impossible to connect the fortification of Daouli with these events, the threat of Ibrahim Pasha's troops certainly reflected the potential for an invading force from Arcadia to attack Greek positions in the

Argolid over the Portes pass. Chrysanthopoulos (1899:1:165–166, 2:353) does refer to multiple fortifications in the area (*ta frouria*), and to a captain named Kladouris who was responsible for guarding the Portes pass that connected the Argolid to Arcadia. Locally, the surname Kapetanos

Figure 6. The fortification at Daouli. Photograph courtesy of William Caraher.

is believed to indicate an ancestral link to captains from the Greek War of Independence, and the area below Daouli is known as Braïmi, after Ibrahim Pasha's incursion.

The site of Daouli extends over three levels and is accessible only by scaling narrow rock ledges. Both the lowest and the highest levels have lined cisterns that are fed through natural fissures in the rock. The fortification itself consists of mortared walls with narrow slits that partly enclose the rock shelter. Graffiti in the mortar of the upper cistern testifies to the site's use in the mid twentieth century. We learned from locals that the site was visited regularly. A local quarry used in the early twentieth century was located nearby, the area below was and is still used to herd goats, and the site itself was used as a refuge during World War II and the Greek Civil War. The complex is clearly earlier in date, but its exact date and function remain uncertain. Villagers from Lyrkeia assert that it was used as a place of refuge for the villagers when the Ottomans were in Argos, which would be consistent with the early nineteenth-century date of the pottery we found. The view from Daouli alone ensured that a person stationed there could monitor traffic approaching Lyrkeia from any direction, as well as any attempt to pass through Koutsopoulou to Chelmis, Schinochori, and Argos. While individuals at Daouli could monitor traffic, the small size of the fortification and its remote location surely meant that they could hardly control it. On the other hand, it would have been an effective (albeit highly visible) refuge and a valuable launching point for raids, acting as a place of local resistance during the Ottoman period. It certainly seems well suited to and well positioned for the harrying tactics that were often employed by Greek forces during the War of Independence.

The fortification at Daouli, in conjunction with the settlements at Chelmis and Koutsopoulou, shed light on movement through the region in the nineteenth and early twentieth centuries. The primary roads through the region largely appear to have followed the course of the Inachos River, as they do today, but north–south passes to mountainous communities like Frousiouna, whence the pastoralists who founded Chelmis originated, were also important routes. The fortification at Daouli, then, stood not as a secluded hideaway but rather as a lookout at an intersection of important east–west and north–south routes.

Modern Settlement in Historical Context

The houses at the sites of Chelmis and Koutsopoulou and the fortification at Daouli are not ancient, and the settlement patterns presented by these sites reflect particular historical contingencies. Chelmis stands in the intermediate zone between the valuable agricultural lands on the Argive Plain and the land surrounding mountain villages (Lehmann 1937:113); the latter, although limited and perhaps marginally productive, required heavy investment over time and hence represented valuable assets to their communities (Karouzou 2014:49). The need to maintain terraces and carefully manage fertility, erosion, and access added value to these fields. Intermediate lands in the Argolid saw increased activity in the mid nineteenth century (Lehmann 1937:97–103). Prior to that time, these lands remained uncultivated and underdeveloped because they did not offer the easy access that characterized the relative flat plains of the river valleys or the Argive Plain, and they lacked ready access to water (which was obtained primarily by digging wells). As a result, these zones had low population densities that supported extensive agropastoral strategies (Karouzou 2014:128) and often served as seasonal grazing grounds for the winter flocks from mountain villages. The public lands in these zones were sold cheaply in the land distribution of 1871. Evi Karouzou (2014:85) has shown that families from the mountainous demes of Alea and Lyrkeia purchased over 40% of the national land available in the vicinity of Malandreni and Schinochori. Since it is generally true that the land distributions of the late nineteenth century gave priority to those families who were already working national lands, it seems likely that the agropastoral exploitation of these fields predates 1871. Most of the land purchased in the 1870s was bought by small farmers or pastoralists rather than wealthy urbanites; the latter had generally abandoned direct investment in agriculture by the later nineteenth century (Karouzou 2014:82). At sites like Chelmis, access to affordable land allowed pastoralists who hailed from mountain villages an opportunity to expand their economic reach through a mix of agropastoral activities suited to these intermediate lands.

The presence of threshing floors (*alonia*) at Chelmis that predate the middle decades of the twentieth century reflects the use of these fields for dry farming of cereals. It was not until the middle of the twentieth century that deep drilling and mechanized pumps made it possible to irrigate these intermediate lands, which now feature both dry and irrigated farming of olive trees as well as irrigated apricot groves. These areas were largely unirrigated in the nineteenth and early twentieth centuries, unlike the fields on the plain which could be more easily irrigated in order to grow cash crops like tobacco and vegetables. Karouzou's (2014) study of agriculture in the Argolid amply illustrates the ways in which the Argive economic system responded to changes in broader market, demographic, and state forces in the late nineteenth and early twentieth centuries. She argues that communities and smallholders in the Argolid shifted agricultural strategies in response to the growing demands of both Athens and industrial markets across Europe. Lower European import duties made local access to external markets through the port at Nafplio—as well as links to Corinth and Patras—all the more significant. At the same time, the growing reach of substantial roads and, by the 1880s, railroads, also provided access to markets and introduced new competition from outside the region as well as new sources of capital. These developments tended to benefit residents of the plain, who exploited these new economic opportunities by intensifying labor. The increase in market gardens is the most obvious manifestation of this response, but so too is the increase in animal husbandry, which is in fact directly tied to the increase in garden production by the supply of manure. Yet, most labor at that time was limited and defined by the family.

Intermediate settlements like Chelmis maintained close ties to the Argive Plain as well as the regional and Mediterranean economy throughout the twentieth century. Market-driven agricultural production on the plain could absorb surplus labor from families who were engaged in mixed agropastoral production in the intermediate zone and in mountain villages. The demand for this labor continued to increase through the first decades of the twentieth century, which saw the use of canning to preserve food for sale outside of the region—especially in Athens—and the greater availability of credit to finance more intensive agriculture on the plain. The poor quality of soils and the absence of water for irrigation at settlements like Chelmis in the intermediate zone limited their capacity for intensive agriculture and marked their productivity as marginal, even in comparison to the fields in the valley bottom associated with nearby villages of Schinochori and Malandreni. At the same time, the opportunities for employment in the expanding market agriculture of the plain provided mountain villages like Frousiouna the resources and incentive to expand their cultivation at intermediate settlements like Chelmis. Karouzou's study shows how families in these marginal zones used a variety of strategies to maximize their economic production. In fact, families in these regions tended to rely on a more diverse set of economic strategies than their counterparts on the plain, who were far more focused on a single economic strategy: the intensification of the production of specific cash crops.

The balance between the low-cost and marginal character of land also encouraged economic activities that shaped the political organization of late nineteenth- and twentieth-century Greece. The economic relationship between Karya and Lyrkeia (then known as Kato Belesi) informed the political relationship between the two villages, which in the nineteenth century served as the respective seats of the summer (March 9–September 9) and winter (September 9–March 9) capitals of the *demos* of Lyrkeia (which was dissolved in the 2011 Kallikratis reform). This organization represented the political formalization of economic relationships between the mountain villages and villages in the intermediate zone (**Nouchakis 1901:451**). Late nineteenth- and early twentieth-century sources indicate that a major cart road existed between Argos and Sterna along the route of the Inachos River (**Great Britain Naval Intelligence Division 1920:427; Miliarakis 1886:14; Nouchakis 1901:451**). The Inachos valley road provided access to the market at Argos for the surplus produce of the *demos*. By the middle of the twentieth century, it was the place of Lyrkeia in the Inachos corridor that ensured its continued importance, while the mountainous Karya shed its population precipitously: of the 1,547 residents in 1940, only 402 remained in 1951. While mountain villages progressively lost their populations, villages in the intermediate zone like Lyrkeia, Schinochori, and Malandreni have been able to retain stable, if modest, populations by shifting their economic strategies towards the cultivation of olives, citrus, and apricots (and in Malandreni, grapes). Only in the postwar period does Chelmis appear as a settlement with population statistics in official government records: from 1940 to 1951, Frousiouna's population declined from 437 to 161 (a loss of 267 people or 61% of the total population of the village), while Chelmis appears for the first time in 1951 with a population of 119. Kostakeïka and Kapeteneïka—seasonal settlements that, like Chelmis, were founded by agropastoralists from Frousiouna and Kefalovryso, respectively—appear in the census for the first time in the same year with populations of 50 and 49.

These population figures can hardly reflect permanent residence; we know from our interviews that the transhumance between Chelmis and Frousiouna continued until it was largely abandoned by the 1970s. It does, however, indicate an increasing economic orientation toward the Argive Plain and its markets, and it explains the de-emphasis on the routes through the countryside that were inscribed by humans and animals on

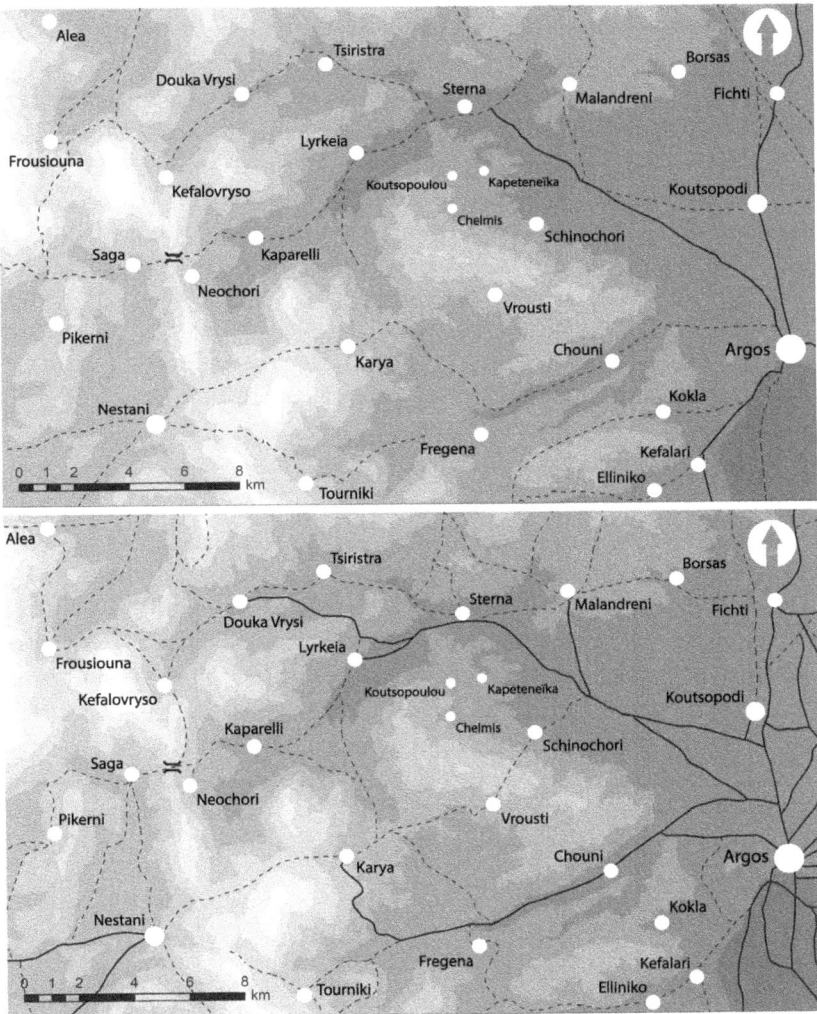

Figure 7. Major routes in the western Argolid, 1900 (above) to 1950 (below). Major roads are indicated by solid black lines, secondary roads by dashed black lines. Map courtesy of Dimitri Nakassis.

foot. The built stone footpaths (*kalderimia*), used in recent memory by transhumant pastoralists, were abandoned, especially as newly paved asphalt roads were constructed in the interwar period (Chatzikonstantinou and Sakellaridou 2017). A comparison between the road networks of 1900 and 1950 shows how markedly different the pattern is (Figure 7).

The abandonment of the network of paths and routes that connected the mountain villages to their counterparts on intermediate lands likewise shaped the abandonment of these settlements. The absence of strong social or economic ties between the villages in the Inachos valley (like Schinochori) and the settlements on nearby marginal lands—as well as the relative distance between settlements like Chelmis and Frousiouna in the mountains—mitigated efforts to maintain settlements in the intermediate zone or to engage in other curation strategies. Moreover, contemporary dirt roads provided only modest access to these settlements from villages in the Inachos valley, reflecting the diminished value of the marginal land in the late twentieth century economy as well as the lack of strong connections between these seasonal settlements and the nearby villages. As a result, the abandonment of routes and settlements goes hand-in-hand, and the presence of modern roads connecting nearby villages to those in intermediate lands tends to encourage a mix of curation and discard practices that are tied more to contemporary access to a structure than to the persistence of its original use. Thus, archaeological formation processes and abandonment intersect with ongoing contingency in the contemporary countryside and are mediated as much by road construction and route abandonment as by social and economic practices that structure the Greek landscape.

Conclusions

Roads both represent and reinforce the political and economic structures of settlement in the modern Greek landscape, but, like the villages and settlements they serve, roads are historically contingent. The cart road that ran along the Inachos valley bottom seems to have always followed the projection of state power into the region, perhaps even in antiquity (cf. Pikoulas 1999). The importance of this road became particularly prominent in the modern period as the state rationalized the political relationships between centers—especially (former) administrative seats—and the capital of the *eparchia*, Argos. Modern road systems, then, encourage us to "see like a state" (*sensu* Scott 1998). "Real" villages get well-built roads that are paved with asphalt by the middle of the twentieth century.

They also receive the administrative apparatuses of the state, including schools, post offices, and government offices, as well as the attendant private amenities that parallel the state's interests, from bank branches to local businesses. On the other hand, seasonal settlements like Chelmis and their regional connections are left out. As Scott (2009) and Harvey and Knox (2015) point out, being bypassed by major roads is not always detrimental to nonstate actors and, in some cases, is a desirable expression of the "art of not being governed." The position of Daouli may well speak to such resistance to state authorities, if indeed it was used as a fort in the Greek War of Independence in the early nineteenth century.

Settlements like Chelmis did not receive improved links to their home villages nor amenities befitting a "real" village. Chelmis did get electricity, however, and a series of electric lights that run parallel to the dirt road, perhaps designed to guide the children of Chelmis—often accompanied by their parents—who in the winter would walk each day to the school in Schinochori. Contingency in the countryside was not just a manifestation of settlement or the changing economic roles for various communities, but also of the state's role in mediating the connections between communities, markets, and political centers. For instance, Karouzou (2014:239–247) has argued persuasively that secondary education—reserved almost entirely for boys, however—was a strategic alternative to crop intensification that families in mountainous villages disproportionately used, as indicated by records of secondary school enrollments by village and anecdotally confirmed by Ioanna Antoniadou's ethnographic interviews. One woman in her 60s from Lyrkeia recalled that, although she was a better student than her brother, she was not allowed to continue in school: "They did not send girls, they did not take them to school then" ("τα κορίτσια δεν τα στέλνανε τότε, δεν τα πηγαίνανε στο σχολείο τότε"). The secondary schools were located in Argos, so that, while mountain villages could (and did) hire teachers to follow transhumant communities from the mountain to the plain, secondary education required a significant investment by the family. Beyond the costs of living in town, the families of students from distant villages were required to pay tuition (35–65 drachmas annually).

Such contingency impacts the visibility of links between settlements as well as the visibility of settlements in the countryside over time. Pritchett's argument for the major road through the Inachos valley running along the valley bottom near the modern route reflects the historical primacy of Argos as the regional political center in antiquity and in modern times, as well as an understanding of the countryside as being essentially static through time. The state invested in both the route and the settlements along the route, ensuring their persistent visibility in the landscape. Settlements and routes that fell outside the scope of direct state influence tended to see less investment and so were correspondingly less visible and, perhaps, more variable in their prosperity and prominence in the countryside. The declining fortunes of the village of Karya, as well as the settlements of Chelmis and Koutsopoulou, demonstrate how abandonment and connectivity work in tandem.

In microcosm, the varied access to the buildings at these sites shaped the character of their abandonment. At Chelmis, one building that is accessible by a modern road has remained in use as a seasonal residence, and two others near the road have seen recent use for storage. At Koutsopoulou, the proximity of the road made one house the site for provisional discard, while collapsed houses that are accessible only by foot never had their tiles removed. At Chelmis, many houses lost their tiles, which were likely reused either at other houses in the settlement or for corbeled ovens. The formation processes that create the visible remains encountered by archaeologists are in no way independent from the contingency that shapes settlement and connectivity at the regional scale. The development of paved roads through the Greek countryside not only follows and reinforces the structure of regional settlement, but also shapes how archaeologists understand the countryside. In contrast, the relative invisibility of early and premodern roads, routes, and byways has tended to obscure the historical reasons for the abandonment of settlements like Chelmis and Koutsopoulou. The collapse of the buildings associated with these settlements and the disappearance of the buildings in the landscape reinforce their relative isolation from contemporary routes and create the impression that modern routes and settlements preserve a persistent, historical structure of the past countryside. Only by understanding the interrelationship between history, archaeology, and formation processes can the history of Greek rural life come to light.

References Cited

Alcock, Susan E., John Bodel, and Richard J.A. Talbert (editors)
   2012   *Highways, Byways, and Road Systems in the Pre-Modern World.* Wiley-Blackwell, Chichester.

Anthopoulou, Thesodosia, Nikolaos Kaberis, and Michael Petrou
   2017   Aspects and Experiences of Crisis in Rural Greece. Narratives of Rural Resilience. *Journal of Rural Studies* 52:1–11. https://doi.org/10.1016/j.jrurstud.2017.03.006

Banaka-Dimaki, Anna
   1992/1998   Το Μαλανδρένι στην αρχαιότητα [Malandreni in Antiquity]. *Horos* 10–12:245–250.

Bintliff, John
   2014   The Archaeology of Ottoman to Early Modern Greece. *Pharos* 20:347–369. https://doi.org/10.2143/PHA.20.1.3064547

Bintliff, John, Phil Howard, and Anthony Snodgrass
   1999   The Hidden Landscapes of Prehistoric Greece. *Journal of Mediterranean Archaeology* 12:139–168. https://doi.org/10.1558/jmea.v12i2.139

Bonnichsen, Robson
   1973   Millie's Camp: An Experiment in Archaeology. *World Archaeology* 4:277–291. https://doi.org/10.1080/00438243.1973.9979539

Chatzikonstantinou, Evangelia, and Areti Sakellaridou
   2017   History of Mobility in Greece: The Building of the National Road Network as a Defining Episode. In *History of Technology in Greece from the Nineteenth to the Twenty-First Century*, edited by Stathis Arapostathis and Aristotle Tympas, pp. 281–297. Bloomsbury, London and New York.

Chrysanthopoulos, Fotios (Fotakos)
   1899   *Απομνημονεύματα περί της Ελληνικής Επαναστάσεως* [Memoirs of the Greek Revolution]. 2 vols. P. D. Sakellarios, Athens.

Dakin, Douglas
  1973   *The Greek Struggle for Independence, 1821–1833*. University of California Press, Berkeley and Los Angeles.

Diacopoulos, Lita
  2004   The Archaeology of Modern Greece. In *Mediterranean Archaeological Landscapes: Current Issues*, edited by Effie Athanassopoulos and LuAnn Wandsnider, pp. 183–198. University of Pennsylvania Museum of Archaeology and Anthropology, Philadelphia.

Erny, Grace, and William Caraher
  2020   The Kingdom of Chelmis: Architecture, Material Culture, and the Modern Landscape of the Western Argolid. *Journal of Field Archaeology* 45:209–221.
        https://doi.org/10.1080/00934690.2019.1704990

Finlay, George
  1861   *History of the Greek Revolution*. 2 vols. William Blackwood and Sons, Edinburgh and London.

Forbes, Hamish
  2007   *Meaning and Identity in a Greek Landscape: An Archaeological Ethnography*. Cambridge University Press, Cambridge.
  2017   Surplus, Storage and Status in a Rural Greek Community. *World Archaeology* 49:8–25.
        https://doi.org/10.1080/00438243.2016.1260356

Forbes, Hamish, and Christopher Mee (editors)
  1997   *A Rough and Rocky Place: The Landscape and Settlement History of the Methana Peninsula, Greece*. Liverpool University Press, Liverpool.

Gallant, Thomas W.
  2018   Social History and Historical Archaeology in Greece. The Kefalonia and Andros Project, 2010–2014. In *An Age of Experiment: Classical Archaeology Transformed (1976–2014)*, edited by Lisa Nevett and James Whitley, pp. 177–193. McDonald Institute for Archaeological Research, Cambridge.

Gallimore, Scott, Sarah A. James, William Caraher, and Dimitri Nakassis
   2017   To Argos: Archaeological Survey in the Western Argolid, 2014–2016. In *From Maple to Olive: Proceedings of a Colloquium to Celebrate the 40th Anniversary of the Canadian Institute in Greece, Athens, 10–11 June 2016,* edited by David W. Rupp and Jonathan E. Tomlinson, pp. 421–438. Canadian Institute in Greece, Athens.

Gibson, Erin
   2007   The Archaeology of Movement in a Mediterranean Landscape. *Journal of Mediterranean Archaeology* 20:61–87. https://doi.org/10.1558//jmea.2007.v20i1.61

González-Ruibal, Alfredo
   2019   *An Archaeology of the Contemporary Era.* Routledge, London.

Gould, R. A.
   1988   Life Among the Ruins: the Ethnoarchaeology of Abandonment in a Finnish Farming Community. In *The Social Implications of Agrarian Change in Northern and Eastern Finland,* edited by Tim Ingold, pp. 99–120. Suomen Antropologinen Seuran Toimituksia 22. Finnish Anthropological Society, Helsinki.

Great Britain Naval Intelligence Division
   1920   *A Handbook of Greece.* H.M. Stationery Office, London.

Halstead, Paul
   2014   *Two Oxen Ahead: Pre-Mechanized Farming in the Mediterranean.* Wiley-Blackwell, Chichester.

Harvey, Penny, and Hannah Knox
   2015   *Roads: An Anthropology of Infrastructure and Expertise.* Cornell University Press, Ithaca, New York.

Kardulias, P. Nick
   2015   Island Pastoralism, Isolation, and Connection: An Ethnoarchaeological Study of Herding on Dokos, Greece. In *The Ecology of Pastoralism,* edited by P. Nick Kardulias, pp. 243–266. University Press of Colorado, Boulder.

Karouzou, Evi
2014   *Les jardins de la Méditerranée: agriculture et société dans la Grèce du sud, 1860–1910 [The Gardens of the Mediterranean: Agriculture and Society in Southern Greece, 1860–1910]*. Académie d'Athènes, Athens.

Koster, Harold
1976   The Thousand Year Road. *Expedition* 19:19–28.

Kourelis, Kostis
2018   Zaraka Surrounded: The Archaeology of Settlements in the Peloponnesian Countryside. In *The Cistercian Monastery of Zaraka, Greece*, edited by Sheila Campbell, pp. 193–213. Medieval Institute Publications, Kalamazoo, Michigan.

Lee, Wayne
2001   The Pylos Regional Archaeological Project, Part IV: Change and Material Culture in a Modern Greek Village in Messenia. *Hesperia* 70:49–98. https://doi.org/10.2307/2668487

Lehmann, Herbert
1937   *Argolis: 1. Landeskunde der Ebene von Argos und ihrer Randgebiete [Argolis 1: Regional Study of the Argive Plain and its Peripheral Areas]*. Deutsches Archäologisches Institut, Athens.

Miliarakis, Antonios
1886   *Γεωγραφία πολιτική νέα και αρχαία του νομού Αργολίδος και Κορινθίας: Μετά γεωγραφικού πίνακος του νομού [A Modern and Ancient Political Geography of the Prefecture of the Argolid and Corinthia: With a Geographical Map of the Prefecture]*. Estia Editions, Athens.

Murray, Priscilla, and P. Nick Kardulias
1986   A Modern-Site Survey in the Southern Argolid, Greece. *Journal of Field Archaeology* 13:21–41. https://doi.org/10.1179/009346986791535726

Nouchakis, Ioannis E.
1901 Ελληνική χωρογραφία: Γεωγραφία, ιστορία, στατιστική πληθυσμού και αποστάσεων [Greek Chorography: Geography, History, Population Statistics, and Distances]. Spyridon Kousoulinos, Athens.

Orser, Charles E., Jr.
1996 A Historical Archaeology of the Modern World. Plenum Press, New York.

Papachristodoulou, Ioannis
1970 Λύρκεια–Λύρκειον [Lyrkeia–Lyrkeion]. Athens Annals of Archaeology 3:117–120.

Papadopoulos, Constantinos
2013 An Evaluation of Human Intervention in Abandonment and Post-abandonment Formation Processes in a Deserted Cretan Village. Journal of Mediterranean Archaeology 26:27–50. https://doi.org/10.1558/jmea.v26i1.27

Pettegrew, David K.
2001 Chasing the Classical Farmstead: Assessing the Formation and Signature of Rural Settlement in Greek Landscape Archaeology. Journal of Mediterranean Archaeology 14:189–209. https://doi.org/10.1558/jmea.v14i2.189

Pikoulas, Giannis A.
1995 Οδικό Δίκτυο και Άμυνα. Από την Κόρινθο στο Άργος και την Αρκαδία [Road Network and Defense: From Corinth to Argos and Arcadia]. Horos, Athens.
1999 Κυθηραϊκά [Kytheraika]. Horos 13:71–80.
2007 Travelling by Land in Ancient Greece. In Travel, Geography and Culture in Ancient Greece, Egypt and the Near East, edited by Colin Adams and Jim Roy, pp. 78–87. Oxbow Books, Oxford.

Pritchett, W. Kendrick
1980 Studies in Ancient Greek Topography: Part III. Roads. University of California Press, Berkeley.
1994 Essays in Greek History. Gieben, Amsterdam.

Scott, James C.
    1998   *Seeing Like a State: How Certain Schemes to Improve the Human Condition Have Failed.* Yale University Press, New Haven.
    2009   *The Art of Not Being Governed: An Anarchist History of Upland Southeast Asia.* Yale University Press, New Haven.

Sigalos, Eleftherios
    2004   *Housing in Medieval and Post-Medieval Greece.* Archaeopress, Oxford.

Sutton, Susan B.
    1988   What is a "Village" in a Nation of Migrants? *Journal of Modern Greek Studies* 6:187–215.
            https://doi.org/10.1353/mgs.2010.0331
    2000   Introduction: Past and Present in Rural Greece. In *Contingent Countryside: Settlement, Economy, and Land Use in the Southern Argolid since 1700*, edited by Susan B. Sutton, pp. 1–24. Stanford University Press, Stanford.

Vionis, Athanasios K.
    2012   *A Crusader, Ottoman, and Early Modern Aegean Archaeology: Built Environment and Domestic Material Culture in the Medieval and Post-Medieval Cyclades, Greece (13th–20th Centuries AD).* Leiden University Press, Leiden.

Chapter Eight
Drones and Stones:
Mapping Deserted Villages in Lidoriki, Greece

Todd Brenningmeyer, Kostis Kourelis, and Miltiadis Katsaros

The village was burned by the Germans on July 23, 1943. About one hundred families lived here before the villages burned. The Germans burned other villages in the area but, I think, Aigition was the last one. Not all the houses were burned, but most of them were. The walls of the houses were left standing. The walls hadn't fallen down, only the roofs and the floors. You could only see the walls, nothing else. The roof and everything inside burned [Demetris Kaphritsas, interview, June 28, 2015].

Demetris Kaphritsas was two years old when his village, Aigition, was burned by the Axis Powers in World War II and its residents were interned in a detention camp in Athens. "After the war," Kaphritsas continues, "we returned to the village on foot from Athens. And once we came back, we found nothing. It's not just that they burned the houses; they burned our clothes, everything. There was nothing left." Kaphritsas' story is not unique to the village of Aigition but characterizes the fate of one-quarter of all of Greece's rural villages destroyed by the Axis Powers in reprisal for partisan resistance.

Abandonment and occupation are topics that the discipline of archaeology is most uniquely qualified to address. Nevertheless, modern villages have not been the central focus of Greek archaeology. When interviewed at the age of 74, Kaphritsas provided the last living testimony of a village destroyed in 1943, reoccupied in 1944, and abandoned by 1980. We were fortunate to record him—just a year before his death—at his house, which was surveyed during the Lidoriki Project in 2015. His interview also revealed an earlier engagement with modernity, the mass immigration of Greeks to America in 1891–1924: "My house belonged to someone else. My father bought it from a man who traveled to America three times to build it. His name is marked on the cornerstone: I. M. Boviatsis, 1915." Transnational migration in the 1900s, war in the 1940s, and urbanization in the 1960s are central to the national Greek narrative, but the

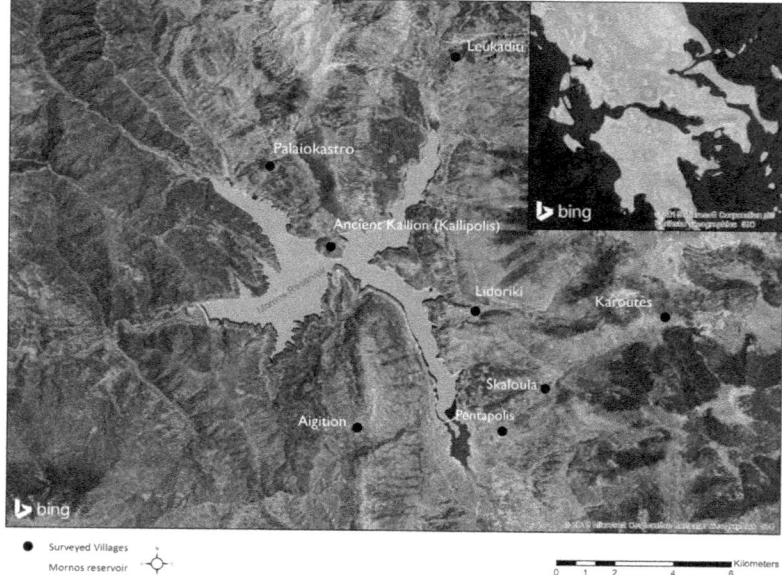

Figure 1. The location of Aigition and surrounding villages.

relationship between these processes and villages has not been explored archaeologically. The Lidoriki Project was conceived as a field school for undergraduate students in three universities carried out between 2010 and 2016. Its general objective was to map the cultural topography of a typical Greek landscape in the region of Lidoriki, named after its largest village. In 1972, the region was devastated by the construction of a reservoir along the Mornos River valley (Figure 1). Robbing the region of its water resources, arable lands, and ecological heritage, the Mornos Reservoir had the single objective of providing drinking water to the national capital of Athens, 200 km away. The second major intervention that radically changed this region's ecology was intensive bauxite mining on the slopes of Mount Giona. The area of Lidoriki thus offered an excellent laboratory to study the intensive changes that characterize the modern Greek rural environment. Included in this area was the abandoned village of Aigition. We chose it as a good case study to survey the processes of occupation, abandonment, and postabandonment.

Archaeological field surveys have proven the precarious nature of the Greek landscape as settlements are abandoned, relocated, or founded anew from century to century. A demographic and agricultural revolution precipitated a rapid increase in settlement during the modern period, particularly during the nineteenth century. In contrast, during the early twentieth century, a progressive decrease in agricultural growth led to the abandonment of villages that culminated in emigration and urbanization. The violent first half of the century caused unprecedented destruction and movement, which was mitigated by a peaceful second half of the century facilitated by an urban economy centered in Athens. The scars of desertion during the turbulent twentieth century are evident in the fallen walls, concrete patches, and ad hoc interventions that make most Greek villages incoherent and difficult to romanticize. Text historians of the Annales School began to study deserted Greek villages in the mid 1960s, at the same time that processual archaeologists developed field methods to model the landscape through surface survey, as evident in this volume (the Australian Paliochora-Kythera Archaeological Survey in Tzortzopoulou-Gregory and Gregory, this volume, the Eastern Korinthia Archaeological Survey in Pettegrew and Caraher, this volume, and the Western Argolid Regional Project in Caraher et al., this volume). Collaborating with pedestrian surveys, ethnoarchaeologists also created a documentary record of village life and abandonment. Although the village was the epicenter of all three perspectives, its physical actuality was not the primary source material. Between textual analysis (historians), surface survey (landscape archaeologists), and oral narratives (ethnoarchaeologists), the Greek village as a complex and stratified material artifact has received less attention. The Greek village has been the direct subject of architectural studies, which has focused on typological and morphological features rather than the nuanced accumulation of change.

Part one of this paper reviews the study of deserted Greek villages and situates our study of Aigition within that historiography. Part two discusses our survey of the village. Part three examines the postabandonment transformation of the village.

The Study of Deserted Villages

Since its foundation as a nation-state, Greece has experienced continuous devastation through wars, civil wars, forced migration, and economic collapse. The long Greek War of Independence produced much destruction and abandonment that early travelers read as the foundation for a national rebirth. Focusing on ancient rather than modern ruins, however, scholars paid little scientific attention to ruined villages. Archaeology was dominated by study of the Classical period that justified the existence of the nation-state. During the Balkan Wars, architect Aristotelis Zachos started to interpret the vernacular architecture of Macedonia in terms of ethnic repositories of folk knowledge that privileged the Greek traditions of the region. Importing notions of *Heimat* or homeland from German Romanticism, Zachos and other intellectuals sought evidence of an essential Greekness in vernacular architecture that justified contested territorial claims during the collapse of the Ottoman Empire. This search for the remnants of a pure premodern Greek identity started in the 1880s with the study of folk songs and customs. The study of folk material culture followed in the 1920s. The first formal surveys of Greek vernacular architecture were conducted in the region of Phocis by Demetrios Loukopoulos (1925), in northern Greece by Zachos (1922/1923), and on the island of Skyros by Angeliki Chatzemichali (1925). British archaeologists under the influence of the Arts and Crafts movement also contributed to this body of research, most notably R. M. Dawkins (1902/1903).

In the 1930s, architect Dimitris Pikionis institutionalized the study of traditional houses in the architectural curriculum of the National Technical University of Athens. The search for Greekness in the rural house involved the documentation of traditional villages in field campaigns of architectural morphology, a formal class that continues to be taught at the architectural schools in Athens and Thessaloniki till today. Architecture faculty like Anastasios Orlandos promoted the careful analysis of vernacular forms and the hope that this morphology would be replicated in modern design (Kourelis 2011/2012). Loukopoulos' study of Aetolia, moreover, highlighted research on typological forms and chronological change more than the aesthetic articulation of unchanging forms (Philippidis 1984:157). The book was illustrated with architectural drawings by Pikionis, who developed what architectural historians have called a school of Critical Regionalism in the modernist movement (Frampton 1985). Loukopoulos' study does not identify individual houses, making it difficult to return to the evidence and reassess their condition, but it analyzes the general character of houses similar to those surveyed by the Lidoriki Project. The early date of Loukopoulos' fieldwork in the 1920s, however, captured a house type that had disappeared by the middle of the twentieth century. This was the unitary single-space house with a central indoor hearth (Loukopoulos 1925:12). No traces of unitary houses are extant today in Phocis with the exception of a room associated with the national hero, Athanasios Diakos. It is a cell in the Monastery of St. John Prodromos in Artotina and dates to 1728. The room's association with a hero of the War of Independence has guaranteed its preservation. Reported by early travelers in the late nineteenth century, these earlier houses are distinguished by a hearth set in the middle of the single room, a lack of fireplaces, and a roofing structure loose enough to allow for the passage of smoke.

Studies of vernacular architecture took a prominent role in national conversations after the 1922 Asia Minor Catastrophe and population exchange with Turkey. Without an expansionist dream toward Constantinople and Turkey to frame national greatness, Greek architects turned their search for the nation's roots inward, within the hinterland of the old state. The pedagogy of village surveys initiated by Zachos, Pikionis, and Chatzemichali fueled a synthetic cultural appraisal across all Greek arts and literature, later characterized as the Generation of the Thirties. The collaboration of international scholars interested in the preservation of folk arts traditions, moreover, led to the foundation of a Greek Arts and Crafts movement, led by Chatzemichali, whose house—designed by Zachos—became a showpiece of a vernacular craft revival. Employing craftsmen and refugees in craft workshops produced a short-lived renaissance of folk arts. The first mass destructions of villages in the Balkan Wars, in World War I, and in the Asia Minor Catastrophe made modernity's mechanized ruthlessness manifest. Now under threat and in the process of desertion, the Greek village galvanized sentiments of preservation and activism as part of the national project. Before the 1920s, Greek vernacular architecture had been dispensable. The medieval and early modern villages that covered the ancient sites of Delphi, Olympia, or Athens were hastily dismantled in order to reveal the foundations of the more valuable ancient temples below them. After the 1920s, Greek villages entered the scholarly horizon that only ancient temples possessed.

The house studies of the 1920s and 1930s were interrupted by World War II and the Greek Civil War, during which an unprecedented number of villages were destroyed and abandoned. Postwar renewal focused on rapid urbanization and the wholesale abandonment of craft traditions for the architecture of reinforced concrete. As more and more villages were deserted in the 1960s and 1970s, students of architecture at the National Technical University of Athens and the Aristotle University of Thessaloniki continued to document vernacular architecture in seasonal excursions outside their urban classrooms. In the process, both universities amassed the greatest archives of vernacular architecture. A small selection of this research was published in the 1980s in individual monographs by Melissa Publishing House, edited by Dimitris Philippidis (1982). The vernacular style of the Aegean islands, in particular, was endorsed by modernist architects like Le Corbusier as an important precedent for the International Style. The architectural focus on Greek houses culminated in the 1964 exhibition at The Museum of Modern Art, "Architecture without Architects" (Rudofsky 1964). The exhibition's curator, Bernard Rudofsky, began his architectural career in 1929, writing his dissertation on the vaulted houses of Santorini (Architekturzentrum Wien 2007:102–111). The centrality of the Greek house in global vernacular discourse was highlighted by Paul Oliver (1975:8), the founder of vernacular architectural studies; he noted, "the shelter of Greece has claimed more attention than that of any other country." Whether motivated by the Greek search for indigenous folk culture or by the modernist search for pure form, the study of Greek villages was extensive, but the methodology of study was aesthetic and typological. Architects and folklorists documented the purest unadulterated examples and sought general design ideals rather than archaeological particulars. It was essentially an ahistorical project.

The study of Greek architecture took a little-known forensic turn during World War II and the Civil War. During the Axis occupation of Greece, the urban planner Constantinos Doxiadis began a clandestine project of mapping the destruction of villages (Theocharopoulou 2012). He deployed architects trained in the practices of village documentation to record war destruction. This approach pushed the discipline toward a more evidentiary methodology whose target was the presentation of evidence in the court of law. Doxiadis presented his collaborative grassroots survey to the Nuremberg trials and to an international conference in San Francisco. Serving as Under-Secretary of the Department of Reconstruction after the war, he published a series of booklets recording war calamities, including a brochure devoted to destroyed towns and villages (Doxiadis 1947). The American press reported extensively on the destruction of villages, especially in the two most horrific examples of the massacre in Kalavryta and Distomo. Destructions at Distomo, located 60 km east of Lidoriki, were featured in the December 1942 issue of *Life Magazine* with photographic documentation of the life conditions of those returning to reinhabit the ruins of their villages. "In roofless house the Greek family Zaphiris sets up housekeeping. Along the road all that remained to the Greeks was the land walls of their stone houses and what they could carry on their backs" (Life Magazine 1944:25). As Greece entered a phase of postwar prosperity, reconstruction, and reconciliation with Germany, both scholarly and popular records turned their attention away from German destruction and reparations. American engagement during the Civil War contributed indirectly to the destruction of villages, such as in the deployment of napalm bombs in September 1948 at Mount Vitsi in Macedonia. Beyond the records of destroyed villages collected and mapped by Doxiadis (1947:45), there is yet unstudied documentary data in archives with rich photographic records. The Contemporary Social History Archives in Athens have digitized thousands of photographs "with a significant concentration of material relating to the Axis Occupation, the National Resistance movement, the Greek Civil War and the postdictatorship period" and made them available online (ASKI 2015). Susan Heuck Allen (2015) has studied the photographs taken by a Greek-American dentistry student serving in the U.S. Army. The experiences of Greek-American GIs stationed in Greece provides a fascinating perspective, and it has been captured in one local history project by Philadelphia's Greek-American Veterans of Foreign Wars (VFW) Post (Eleftheria Post 2013:264, 395). The continuous political conflict between right and left has overshadowed the willingness to study the destruction of villages and associated loss of civilian life. Unlike in Spain or Argentina, where the archaeology of the recent past has been used as a strategy of national reconciliation, Greek archaeology has shunned the study of the recent past because of the unresolved traumas of the Civil War. In their study of the rare excavation of a mass grave in Lesbos, Katerina Stefatos and Iosif Kovras (2015:166) have called the Greek paradox a "reconciliation through silence." In spite of Greece's extraordinary national resources devoted to archaeology, none of them are directed to the archaeology of the recent past.

For most of the twentieth century, the Greek village has been studied through the lens of aesthetics as an object of architectural ingenuity, simplicity, efficiency, formal clarity, beauty, and authenticity. The study of deserted Greek villages as a historical topic began under the auspices of the Annales School. As a student of Fernand Braudel, Eleni Antoniadis-Bibicou (1965) collated all extant historical sources on village desertion. The conversation initiated by Antoniadis-Bibicou was picked up by the Anglo-American school of geography headed by Malcolm Wagstaff and the economic historian Elena Frangakis-Syrret, who questioned some of Antoniadis-Bibicou's explanations of desertion based on war (Frangakis and Wagstaff 1987; Wagstaff 1978). As the French Annales School's discussion of the 1960s migrated into the Anglo-American economic-geographical positivism of the 1970s, increasing attention was placed on archaeological evidence. Geographers like Wagstaff participated in the revolution of processual archaeology that focused on the Greek countryside. In 1961 the Minnesota Messenia Expedition developed the methodologies of regional survey by relying on pottery scatters and spatial modeling. Although the Bronze Age was the early subject of research, processual archaeology's pedestrian surveys in Greece promised a diachronic perspective that included the study of the recent past. Figuring out how the modern Greek countryside worked was a central research agenda for many foundational surveys, including the Minnesota Messenia Expedition (Aschenbrenner 1972), the Argolid Exploration Project (Jameson et al. 1994; van Andel and Runnels 1987), the Pylos Regional Archaeological Project (Davis 1998), the Nemea Valley Archaeological Project (Wright et al. 1990), the Boeotia Survey (Bintliff 2012), and the Eastern Korinthia Archaeological Survey (Gregory 2007). This regional perspective continues today with ongoing research projects in the Peloponnese, as evident in the contributions of this volume.

Independently of archaeology, cultural anthropologists began to study the Greek village as a sociological organism, moving the study of Greece beyond the aesthetic romanticism that characterized earlier studies. Survey archaeologists capitalized on the intellectual developments of Ernestine Friedl's (1962) study of Vasilika and invited anthropologists to help them collect data on contemporary rural life. Thus, during the late 1970s and 1980s this collaboration created a new discipline of the ethnoarchaeology of village life represented by the work of Harold Koster (1977), Susan B. Sutton (2000), and Hamish Forbes (2007). The work of this generation is particularly important for the study of deserted Greek villages because it took place at the peak of abandonment, when the majority of villagers deserted their homes for the economic opportunities of Athens. Sutton (personal communication 2015) remembers interviewing villagers who were packing up to leave while being interviewed, leaving the keys in the door.

The new methods of archaeological regional survey arrived at Lidoriki in the 1980s, when the Netherlands Institute at Athens conducted its Aetolian Studies Project (Bommeljé et al. 1987). The survey carried out in 1985 and 1986 by Peter Doorn was innovative in its collection of oral history through a computerized questionnaire. General interpretations, a site catalogue, and the analysis of the interviews were included in the project's monograph but, as Doorn informed us, there is more unpublished data (Doorn 1987, 1989, 2009). The Aetolian Studies Project covered an extensive area and noted every historical site encountered during fieldwork. In the course of collecting oral histories for our own project, we learned that the Dutch team used the abandoned village of Aigition as its residence. Although we have not yet discerned which exact structures were used for lodging, they must have stayed in one of the houses around the central square.

Until the 1990s, the study of deserted Greek villages focused on scatters of pottery, ethnography, and limited textual sources. Research on the physical buildings was still dominated by the methodologies developed by architectural pedagogy in search of great examples rather than by the development of complete data sets. One innovation was introduced by Eleftherios Pavlides (1995), who studied alteration, fashion, and change in a village in Lesbos. Using a semiotic approach, Pavlides focused on what caused change in the vernacular architecture of Eressos. Houses were seen as more than static repositories of meaning but also constantly changing markers of identity, social stratification, and intergenerational renovation.

Just as Pavlides changed the depth of study in one village, the Morea Project introduced complexity in studying large regions and quantifying large datasets of buildings and villages. The Morea Project was designed by Frederick Cooper, Helen B. Foster, Mary Coulton, and Joseph D. Alchermes as part of the Minnesota Archaeological Researches in the Western Peloponnese. Until this project, one of the greatest difficulties in the study of deserted villages was the impediment of scale. At a middle scale between regional distribution maps of pottery scatters and human individuals, the archaeology of houses had to invest in technical surveying technologies to overcome the complexity of 3D forms. Cooper deployed early technologies of the global positioning system, database management, and remote sensing onto the villages of the Peloponnese in the 1990s and 2000s. All three authors of this paper worked on the Morea Project, which surveyed 150 villages and 3,000 houses between 1990 and 2000 (Brenningmeyer et al. 1998; Cooper et al. 2003; Kourelis 2003). Work on the Lidoriki Project was seen as an opportunity to update the Morea Project's technological innovations into the twenty-first century.

Our survey of Aigition began in 2010. A decade after the completion of the Morea Project, the authors returned to the field with a toolkit of helium balloons, kites, and drones along with streamlined applications on tablets and cell phone devices. Digital photogrammetry allowed us to create a 3D record of villages that was cheap, quick, efficient, and teachable. By placing unique targets on the ground, flying a camera on a kite or balloon, and processing those images photogrammetrically, we produced architectural surveys of much greater detail than we had in the

Morea Project. Our first project, in fact, was to resurvey the village of Taxiarches, which was the first village surveyed by the Morea Project in 1990 (Cooper et al. 2003:187–188).

Acutely aware of the Greek economic crisis, coupled with the drying up of research funds in the U.S., it became important for us to devise a collaborative project structure that would allow the grand ideals of the golden age of archaeological survey to survive in a climate of shortages. The Deserted Greek Village Project was conceived as an informal partnership of collaborations with whom we could share data and resources. The two panels at the 2016 Annual Meeting of the Archaeological Institute of America in San Francisco were the first result of this collaborative ethos. Work by our students was also presented in the conference's poster session (Bierman et al. 2016). As the village mappers, we collaborated with the Mt. Lykaion Excavation and Survey Project (in 2013) to study Ano Karyes, the Corinth Excavations by the American School of Classical Studies at Athens to survey the village of Penteskouphi (in 2015), and the Western Argolid Regional Project to survey Chelmis (also in 2015; see Caraher et al. and Sanders et al., this volume). The Deserted Greek Village Project hopes to continue studying the unpublished house data of the Morea Project and to collaborate with other legacy projects, such as the Nemea Valley Archaeological Project (NVAP). Susan B. Sutton, the ethnographic director of NVAP, has shared with the authors samples of the vast archive collected by the project around the villages of Ancient Nemea (Sutton 1995).

Beyond these collaborative projects, our research and teaching focused on the region of Lidoriki, where the deserted village of Aigition offered the most interesting case study. Miltiadis Katsaros established the institutional connections between the National Technical University of Athens and the Greek Archaeological Service. Working intimately with a community of local preservation activists, moreover, has afforded us access to local knowledge and a new form of public archaeology. The work in this paper comes from four seasons of collaboration between American undergraduates from two liberal arts colleges (Maryville University in Missouri and Franklin & Marshall College in Pennsylvania) and Greek undergraduate students in architecture from the National Technical University of Athens (2010, 2014, 2015, and 2016). Sofia Klossa supervised the collection of ethnographic information. Nikos Lakafosis and Kostas Georgiou helped in the topographical studies. The students who participated in the field school are Shelby Biermann, Sara Loynd, Austin Nash, Nicole Thompson, Lizzy Woods, Cassie Garison, Joel Naiman, Jordan

Dietl, Jessica Lange, Bethany Pohlman, Megan Sparks, Cherie Zeppo, Andrea Herschelman, Brennan Loynd, Stathis Kotridis, Maria Christofi, Paris Demetriou, Marina Naki, Maroula Bacharidou, and Demetris Karakostas.

Aigition Survey

The survey of Aigition and the surrounding area owes much to lessons learned during the Morea Project. Initiated in 2010, the Lidoriki Project, like its predecessor in the Peloponnese, was designed as both a research project and a teaching laboratory with student volunteers. Survey methods embraced both traditional and technological approaches for the collection of architectural and topographic information. Traditional land survey with the total station was supplemented with aerial reconnaissance using balloon aerial photography, kite aerial photography, and pole aerial photography. By 2014, the acquisition of a small DJI Phantom II uncrewed aerial vehicle (UAV) simplified the acquisition of aerial data, allowing a broader and more systematic collection of imagery for the site, including areas where vegetation and wind patterns limited the use of earlier methods (Brenningmeyer et al. 2016). Aerial photographs were captured with 60% minimal overlap, enabling the creation of detailed orthophotographs and digital elevation models using structure from motion software, specifically Agisoft's Photoscan Professional platform. The orthophotographs provide a record of the site and its topography and, in some cases, capture the gradual decline of structures during the brief period of our investigation.

Documentation of individual houses was undertaken using multiple techniques. Crew members noted architectural features specific to individual structures and plotted building clusters using both mobile geographic information systems (GIS) software and project notebooks. Houses and storage buildings were typologically differentiated. Houses were built with quoins and windows and contained fireplaces. Storage structures were smaller buildings (averaging between 2.5 x 2.5 m to 5 x 6 m in size) without a fireplace or quoins and with walls typically constructed of unmortared rubble. In some cases, structures with dimensions slightly larger than those noted above were classified as storage structures. In these instances, the structures were among the smallest in a group or cluster of buildings and in each case did not preserve evidence of quoins or a fireplace. When the Axis powers burned the village on July 23, 1943, they set fire to houses but did not bother with ancillary spaces like sheds or animal pens. After returning from detainment, the villagers used the storage structures as their primary residences. Although the site's history eroded the typological distinction between home and storage, it remained a significant distinction.

Architecture students from the National Technical University of Athens developed hand-drawn plans for a small number of structures. Additional buildings were documented using close-range photogrammetry and videogrammetry (Brenningmeyer et al. 2020). These approaches allowed us to rapidly document the site and develop 3D reconstructions for study and dissemination. Video captured during the final year of the survey provided the foundation for many of the house reconstructions and captured additional contextual information for houses as they existed at the time of the survey. Although not directly connected to the village of Aigition, the project also created a photographic record of 125 objects collected by the Lidoriki Folklore Museum. A dozen of the objects were 3D-modeled. Our data was made available on three online platforms: the Deserted Greek Villages database through Maryville University, a Lidoriki Folklore Museum Omeka site through Franklin & Marshall College (both sites no longer available), and a Sketchfab page hosting the 3D models (https://skfb.ly/67CoB).

Aigition

Like most rural villages, the textual sources for Aigition are scarce. Its original name, Strouza, was hellenized in 1928 to match the attested classical site of Aigition nearby. Strouza is a postrevolutionary village. It did not exist when Françoise Pouqueville compiled a list of villages in the region around 1820 (Pouqueville 1826:45–46). The foundation of the village church, dated by inscription to 1852, marks the consolidation of what would have begun as seasonal shelters into a full-fledged village. With zero inhabitants reported in the 1971 census, Aigition's chronological horizon covers approximately 120 years. The village encompasses an area of roughly 23 ha spread along two high ridges on the southwestern side of Mount Pirina (Figure 2). Both its topographical siting and its buildings illustrate the two main economic activities of the village: agriculture and husbandry. It is located close to fertile valleys below and to pastures above. A series of threshing floors on the west side of the main ridge take maximum advantage of prevailing winds during harvest. Structures are positioned along two broad ridges bisected by a drainage basin, forming a settlement of theatrical shape. Built terraces extend along all sides of the settlement.

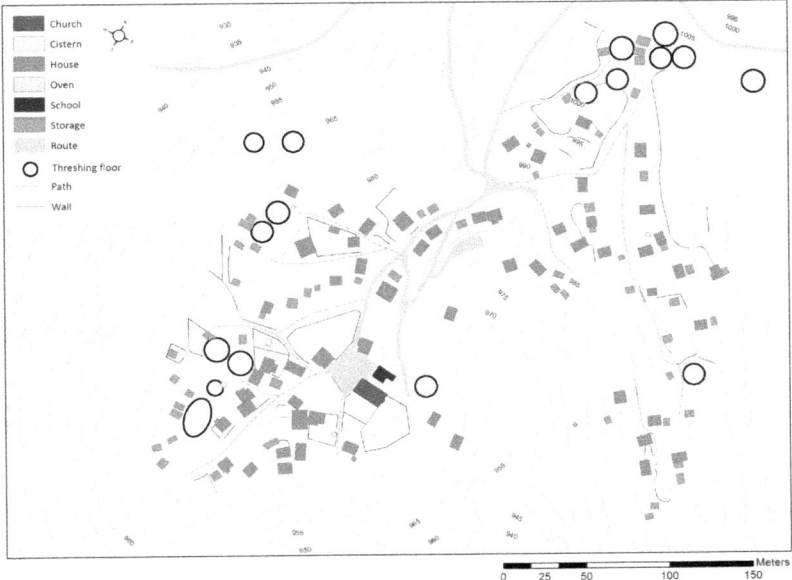

Figure 2. Map illustrating the classification and location of structures throughout the village of Aigition.

The ruined buildings of the village are preserved in a landscape of sparse scrub vegetation interspersed with oak. The Archaeological Survey School of Holland (ASSH) suggested that this landcover is a relatively recent development, likely deriving from substantial erosion that occurred during the nineteenth century as woodlands were deforested and converted into shrubbed pasturelands (ASSH 1989:239). The village today is abandoned with most buildings in some degree of ruination. Of the more than 140 buildings surveyed by the team, only 11 retain a roof, and several of these are in danger of collapse. Aerial photographs taken during the 2014 and 2015 field seasons documented the collapse of one such roof in the northeastern section of the village (AIG086). It is likely that without some intervention many of the remaining roofs will fail within the next decade.

Shared threshing floors and storage structures highlight the communal role that agricultural activities played during harvest (**Figure 2**). In the south and northwest areas of the site, the threshing floors are primarily positioned along the west slope of the ridge (**Figure 3**). In the northeast area, the threshing floors are positioned primarily at a high point along the western edge of the plateau to capitalize on wind patterns. In the summer

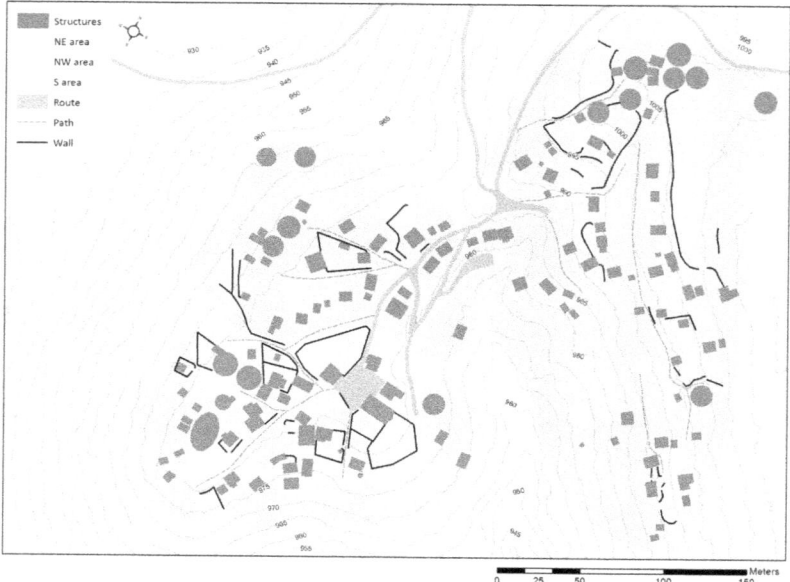

Figure 3. Map illustrating the distribution of features across Aigition in the south, northwest, and northeast areas.

months of harvest, there is little wind in this region. Threshing floors are positioned at the highest slopes to take maximal advantage of wind energy required to separate the wheat from the chaff in a process called winding (*aerisma*). A series of small, irregular rubble constructions is located near the threshing floors. Some of these abut the outer perimeter of the floors, and others are positioned just a few meters away. Although the small buildings are poorly preserved, their size and construction suggest that they functioned as storage buildings for grain associated with threshing activities. Two additional threshing floors (AIG137 and AIG133) were identified along the eastern edge of the site. Like the previously described features, both are situated near the edge of slope to take advantage of northerly winds.

The South Area

Houses are positioned at varying distances from these harvest processing areas and were often built in tightly spaced clusters along the midline of the ridge, extending down to the southern slope of the plateau (**Figure 4**). In some instances, buildings were constructed directly above earlier buildings or abutting existing walls. For example, AIG014 is located in a cluster of five buildings (**Figure 5**). A datestone carved into a quoin on the

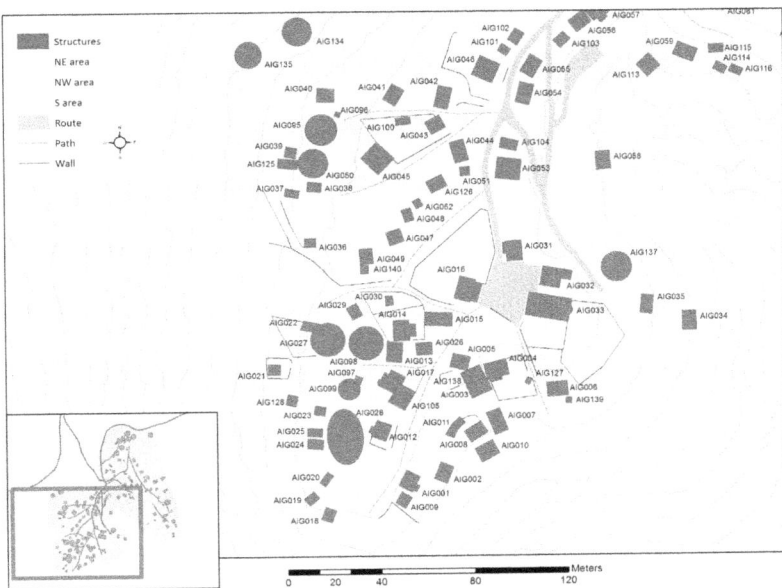

Figure 4. Features and their project IDs in the south and northwest areas.

northeast corner marks 1915 as the year of construction. The building's roof is in a good state of preservation, and it is likely that until recently the house was used as a seasonal residence. Four structures surround this building to the east, south, and north. AIG013 is located immediately to the south. Its surviving courses preserve evidence of robbed quoins, suggesting that the building functioned as a house. AIG015, to the east, may also preserve a house foundation. AIG026 (ca. 7 x 6 m) is preserved by partial segments of three rubble walls with no evidence of quoins or a fireplace. The size and quality of this structure suggest that it may have functioned as a storage building. AIG030, located just to the north, is a cistern. In addition to these structures, AIG014 is surrounded by a modern fence. The space delineated by these walls and fences likely served to contain animals that were kept close to the home, or more recently to keep grazing animals and intruders from entering the property. Heavily built perimeter walls are a feature of the few houses that continued to be inhabited among the ruins. These walls were not original features of the village when occupied but signify the demarcation of private property in the absence of a living community to enforce the customary boundaries. The structures just described are circumscribed by narrow roads to the north, south, and east and a retaining wall to the west, separating this cluster from nearby buildings.

Figure 5. Building cluster in the south area surrounding AIG014.

Figure 6. Dipla house (AIG045).

Clusters of spatially proximal structures, like those surrounding AIG014, should be seen as buildings belonging to the same extended family. The houses were single-family dwellings whose clustering suggests a familial pattern of development similar to that documented for other villages in Greece (Aschenbrenner 1972; Friedl 1962). In a typical Greek family, the eldest son inherited the patrimonial house. When the younger sons married, they needed a separate household, which was built next to the original family house. Daughters would move to the house of their husbands. This process led to the clustering of buildings or the designation of entire neighborhoods of a village occupied primarily by members of the same family. Aschenbrenner (1972:62) documented this process in Karpofora, and Friedl (1962:62) identified a similar situation at Vasilika, noting that houses were typically built near one another as they were constructed on family-owned property. In nineteenth-century Methana, it was not unusual to find two or three brothers living together with their wives in their parents' house (Clarke 2000:179). The length of cohabitation within a household depended on a variety of factors, and the economic advantages of cohabitation could encourage a delayed separation of the families into independent households (Friedl 1962:59). In Vasilika, brothers sometimes continued to live in their father's house (along with their wives and children) after their father's death, and in some instances they chose to share a single house after separation. In these houses, a wall constructed between the upstairs and downstairs rooms created two separate living units for each brother and his family. Friedl (1962:59–60) documented four such houses (called *dipla*) at Vasilika in 1961. Whereas most houses in Aigition were of the single-family type, AIG045 represents a duplex unit like that noted by Friedl, a single house divided in two by a solid wall (Figure 6). According to our interview with Kaphritsas, the house indeed was the residence of two brothers, and it included an iron workshop on the first floor.

364

Figure 7. Aerial photograph of the village square.

Figure 8. Carved limestone block indicating the date (1852) and name of the village church (AIG033).

The Village Square (Plateia) *in the South Area*

The most prominent and best-preserved buildings in Aigition are located around the village square (*plateia*; **Figure 7**). The largest of these is the village church dedicated to the Holy Spirit (Ayio Pnevma). This structure constitutes the only religious building in the village. A carved limestone block set into the apse marks the construction of the church in 1852; this is the earliest preserved inscribed date and likely represents the foundation date for the village (**Figure 8**). The carving includes a cross with the Christogram of "Jesus Christ Conquers" (ΙΣ.ΧΣ.Ν.Κ.) and names the church's dedication (The Church of the Holy Spirit). Most unusual about this church is its double role as parish and funerary chapel. More commonly, villages have two religious buildings: a village church for the services of the living at the center of the village and a funerary chapel for the services of the dead at the cemetery. Aigition is unusual in having its cemetery within the village and adjacent to the square, with only one church serving both functions. The church is a basilica type with a hipped gabled roof typical of churches built in central and northern Greece from the sixteenth to the nineteenth centuries. According to our interviews, a recent fire destroyed the Holy Spirit's wooden interior decoration, which included an ornate wooden templon screen that was purported to have been carved by a Macedonian workshop. Although it does not survive for

Figure 9. Schoolhouse (AIG032).

inspection, interviewers who had seen it before the fire compared it in quality to the templon screen in nearby village of Klima (6 km north of Aigition) at the Church of the Taxiarches. The templon screen at Klima is dated to 1842 by inscription and has been attributed to Macedonian artists, who were the most elite woodcarvers of the Late Byzantine and Ottoman periods.

The four other structures that surround the *plateia* were constructed at the beginning of the twentieth century. AIG032 was built as a schoolhouse in 1909 (**Figure 9**). The datestone located on the southeast quoin names five individual donors, but only two names—G. K. Boviatsis and I. P. Boviatsis—are legible. The Boviatsis family, specifically Ioannis Boviatsis, also built a house (AIG016) across from the school in 1915. Mr. Kaphritsas, the last resident of AIG016, narrated the story that his father had passed on to him. Accordingly, Boviatsis travelled to the United States on three separate occasions, sending remittances to the village for the construction of this house. Ship manifests at the Statue of Liberty–Ellis Island Foundation confirm that Ioannis Boviatsis entered the U.S. in 1910 and 1914. His declared destination was Milwaukee, Wisconsin, and specifically, 682 E. Water Street, a wooden house a few blocks away from the Greek Orthodox Church constructed in 1914. Neither the house nor the church is still standing. Milwaukee's tanneries offered good employment opportunities for Greeks, along with the more typical florist, confectionary, and shoe-shining professions (Saloutos 1970). With vast experience in the dairy and livestock industries, the émigrés from Aigition would have easily transitioned their skills to the tanneries and stockyards of Milwaukee. We know from other interviews that Milwaukee's Greek-American community today has members that maintain contact with their original villages in the Lidoriki area. Similarly, the Lidorikiotes of Chicago lived in their own neighborhood (Hegewisch) and established their own church, the Assumption, in 1924 (Sellers 2001). The list of inscribed donors in the schoolhouse likely commemorates the individual who sent remittances directly from Milwaukee and Chicago. Building a schoolhouse, renovating a church, and building a clock tower are the most typical public forms of immigrant benefaction (in addition to building private homes for their families). The 1909 datestone of the school is important because it notes private investment in schooling by migrants three years before Prime Minister Venizelos made primary education obligatory by law. The 1911 school reform necessitated the construction of state-operated elementary schools such as the old school in Lidoriki, which currently serves as the local archaeological museum. The Lidoriki school stands out as a large state building with distinct polygonal masonry and steel beams over the lintels. The Aigition school, on the other hand, is indistinguishable from a house and represents the investment from a private patron. The Aigition school remained in use through the 1960s. Kaphritsas noted that, when he was a student here in the 1950s, there were 80 students. A small generator located next to the school was purchased during the 1970s and was the only source of electricity prior to the arrival of power lines in the 2010s.

A datestone on the southwest corner of AIG016 commemorates the absentee immigrant owner, Ioannis Boviatsis, through his initials carved between a cross and two trees (typical decorative motifs in dedicatory house inscriptions; Figure 10). The building was later purchased by Kaphritsas' father. Like many of the buildings in Aigition, this structure was burned by the Axis powers during World War II. Evidence of charred wood is still visible on the lintel of the main door. After the war, the Kaphritsas family returned to the village and lived in a two-room storage shed located near the house. Over the course of many years, they procured lumber from the forest and rebuilt the wooden interiors of the destroyed house. The house has been continuously maintained by the family, which means that it is heavily modified by later additions, such as a concrete porch and balcony. The two-room storage shed that the family inhabited after the war is visible today as piles of rock.

Figure 10. Datestone from the house west of the church (AIG016).

Figure 11. House north of the church (AIG031) showing polygonal masonry and semi-circular stone arches.

The fourth structure, located on the north side of the village square, is a house with an intact roof (AIG031). Architecturally, the building shares similarities with AIG016 and AIG014 located southwest of the *plateia*. All three structures are constructed of polygonal masonry set in mortar with large dressed quoins and stone tympanum arches above wooden lintels at the windows and doorways (Figure 11), suggesting that AIG031 was constructed at approximately the same time as AIG016 and AIG014 (i.e. 1915).

The Northwest Area

The area northwest of the *plateia* (see Figure 4) is organized in a manner similar to that in the south. Houses and storage structures extend along the center and eastern sides of the ridge with agricultural processing areas positioned along the steep slope to the west. Most of the structures are oriented along the main road and several small paths that extend from this main artery. Building groups or clusters in this area are more difficult to define than in the south. Few shared walls and fences are preserved that delineate spatial relationships. Many of the buildings are preserved only by foundation walls and small piles of rubble, making the interpretation of their function and relationship difficult.

AIG046, located just west of the main road, is among the more interesting structures in this area of the site. The building preserves a large cistern on its western side. The eastern half of the structure consists only of a large pile of rubble situated within and around the building's foundation walls. The structure is one of only two buildings with attached cisterns that were documented in the village. A damaged floor of steel-reinforced concrete caps part of the cistern, suggesting that the cistern and perhaps the house date to the twentieth century.

A building cluster can be identified west of the main road just north of AIG044 (Figure 12). This group includes buildings AIG045, AIG100, and AIG043. A low wall connects each of these structures, enclosing a large area that opens to the east. AIG100 is a small structure located just south of this perimeter wall on the north side of the group. AIG043, positioned at the east end of the group, is composed of coursed rubble masonry with a chimney on its east wall. Based on its material remains, it is the house occupied most recently and is contemporary to the enclosing wall (Figure 13). Dressed ashlars in the doorjamb appear to have been reused from another building. The size of the building and the presence of windows and a chimney suggest that this structure functioned as a house. It is currently in a poor state of preservation with a partially collapsed roof, which

Figure 12. Aerial view of building cluster in the northwest area.

Figure 13. Building (AIG043).

Figure 14. Renovated building (AIG058).

was haphazardly rebuilt when the structure was used for storage and seasonal or temporary housing. The building is directly associated with the walled area and storage building to its west, with the entrance to this area positioned next to the building itself. The enclosed area to the west of AIG043, like similar spaces found in the southern area of the village, was likely used to contain animals that were kept near the home. What is unclear is how AIG045, located at the west end of the cluster, relates to this enclosed space. The structure's rear wall forms part of the perimeter wall, but the house does not open onto this area. As discussed above, our informants noted that the building was the home of two brothers who divided the structure in half; one brother lived in the southeast side with his family, and the other brother's family lived in the northwest side. A central wall divides the house into two distinct units that were homes to the two families. The property wall abuts AIG045 and must postdate the construction of this house. As with the houses to the south, it is unclear if the spatial relationship seen in this cluster is associated with rooms related for a single family or if it accrued over multiple generations.

A notable example of restoration can be identified in AIG058 (Figure 14), located east of the main road and down the slope from AIG053. The structure is composed of large stones set in mortar with preserved, dressed limestone quoins. Wooden tie beams that were used to stabilize and level the stone courses are visible along the exterior walls. The building was damaged at some point in its history and has been heavily renovated. The structure is now separated into two parts. The west section of the building is now a storage structure that reuses the west wall and a small section of the south corner of the original house in its construction. This building is covered by a corrugated roof and is open at the east. The east side of the house has been converted into a separate seasonal shelter. A new wall was constructed against the west side of this half of the original house, and a door and window were installed in the south wall. A corrugated roof covers this structure, and another corrugated roof supported by metal posts extends from the south wall to cover a small patio. The walls have been reinforced with mortar. The plan and elevation of the original building is obscured by the later renovations. AIG053, like AIG043 described above, illustrates the process of structural renovation through the modification of previously abandoned structures and recycling of building material from other houses. The restored houses seem to be occupied seasonally by owners who return to the village for herding or hunting.

The Northeast Area

The northeast area of the site extends along the southwestern edge and upper slopes of the broad southeastern plateau of Mount Pirina (Figure 15). A narrow draw separates this section of the settlement from the buildings described above. A particularly large concentration of threshing floors was found along the top of the slope in the northwest section of this area (AIG075, AIG074, AIG073, AIG108, AIG109, AIG110, and AIG136). The threshing floors average 13–15 m in diameter and have associated buildings for storage. A cluster of structures was positioned just south of these threshing floors (Figure 16). Of particular interest are house AIG071 and storage structures AIG106 and AIG072. These buildings are surrounded by walls that delineate a plot of land that runs upslope to threshing floors AIG075 and AIG074. Three openings in these walls provide access to houses AIG121 and AIG119 and their storage structures (AIG131, AIG130, AIG120, and AIG122). House AIG069 is also positioned near the access to house AIG0171 and its nearby threshing floors. The proximity of house AIG071 to the threshing floors and the definition of this space through the construction of the perimeter walls may indicate some control over access to the floors.

373

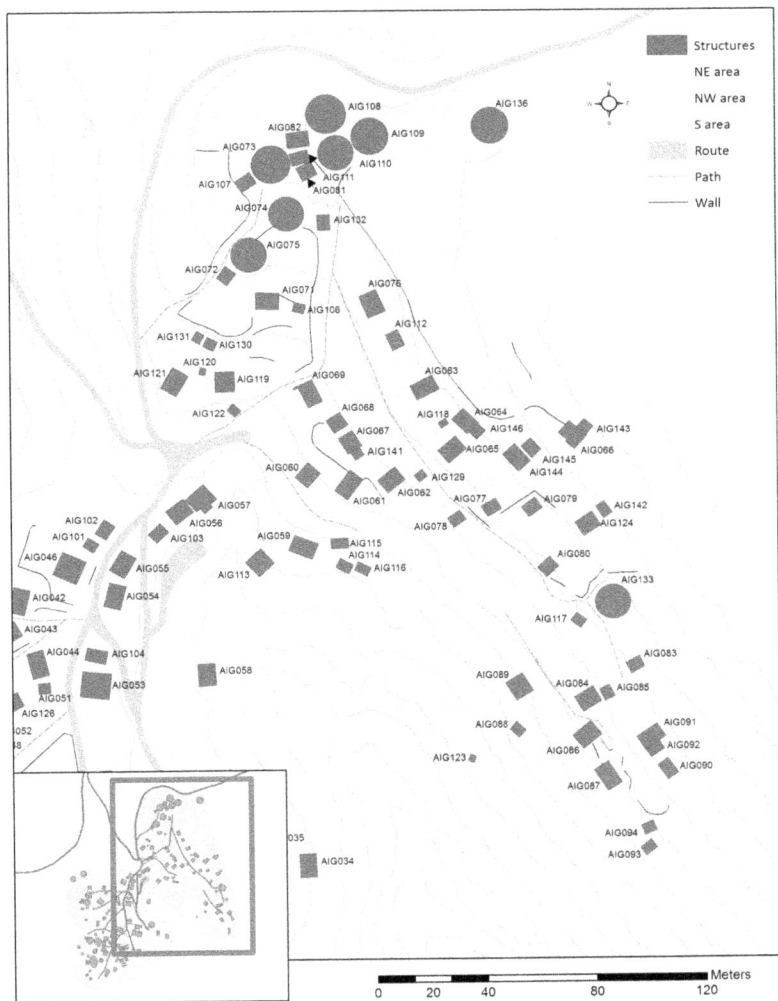

Figure 15. Features and their project IDs in the northeast area.

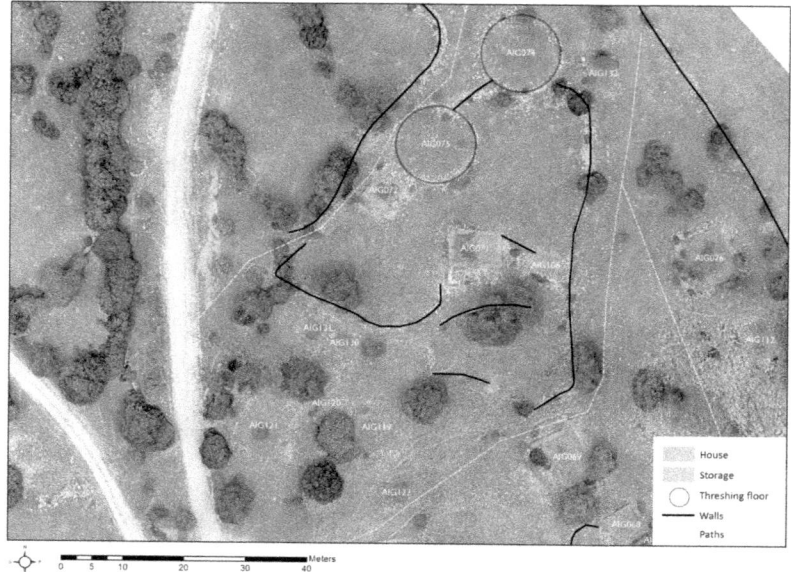

Figure 16. Building cluster at the west edge of the northeast area.

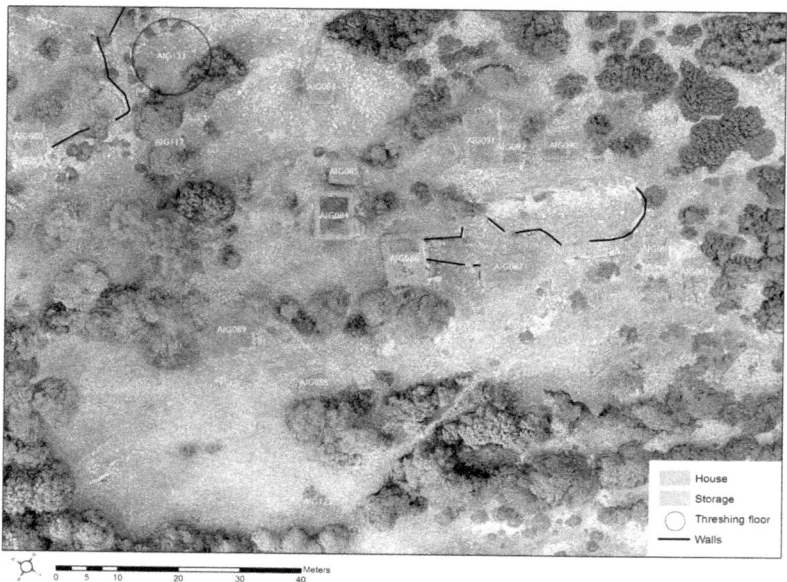

Figure 17. Building cluster at the east side of the northeast area.

Buildings erected to the east of the threshing floors are spread along the plateau and slope and in many cases are oriented to a series of paths that extend from threshing floors and the main road to the west. Overall, two concentrations containing smaller clusters of structures can be identified in this dense area of habitation, each with a number of houses, related storage structures, and access to threshing floors. The first concentration of structures is positioned just east of the threshing floors described above. This grouping includes buildings AIG076, AIG112, AIG063, AIG064, AIG118, AIG146, AIG065, AIG077, AIG144, AIG145, AIG066, and AIG143. These structures are all situated just north of the main east–west path that cuts across this area of the site. AIG068, AIG067, AIG141, AIG060, AIG061, AIG062, AIG129, and AIG078 are located just south of this route. At the eastern end of this area is a second concentration of buildings that is set apart spatially from the other structures in this area. These structures include AIG079, AIG142, AIG124, AIG080, AIG117, AIG083, AIG084, AIG085, AIG086, AIG087, AIG088, AIG089, AIG123, AIG090, AIG091, AIG092, AIG093, and AIG094. A threshing floor (AIG133) located nearby is associated with these buildings, providing a separate agricultural processing area for the houses.

Some clusters can be identified among buildings within these two concentrations, but in general the spatial relationships were not clear in the field or in aerial photos. AIG059 is a house with three smaller storage structures (AIG115, AIG114, and AIG116) positioned nearby. AIG062 and AIG067 likewise represent houses with nearby storage structures (AIG129 and AIG068, respectively). AIG084, AIG085, AIG086, and AIG087 are positioned at roughly similar elevations (Figure 17). AIG086 and AIG087 are further connected by rubble walls that define a shared space between the two structures. AIG084 and AIG086 are the best preserved of the group and are impressive structures with commanding views of the village to the south. The quoins of AIG086 were robbed, but AIG084 retains its rusticated, pillowed quoining. AIG085, AIG094, and AIG093 are positioned nearby at similar elevations to the houses just described and likely represent small storage buildings. AIG083 may be another storage structure related to this group. AIG091, AIG092, and AIG090 appear to form a second cluster. The buildings are situated at a similar elevation but slightly higher on the slope than the buildings just described. AIG092 was constructed against the outer wall of house AIG091 and served as a storage structure for the building. AIG090 may have served a similar capacity. The other buildings at this end of the ridge are separated somewhat from the two groups just described and do not have a clear relationship to these buildings.

In general, the storage areas in the northeast area were positioned along the paths that connected domestic architecture to the threshing floors. The orientation of these structures makes sense if they were used to store grains after threshing and winnowing activities. Transportation of grain from the threshing floor would have moved along the paths just described. Positioning storage structures along these routes would have simplified the transport and storage of grains that were carried downhill from the threshing floors.

The organization of space in this area is also interesting in terms of the placement of property and retaining walls. The long east–west path that connects the threshing floors to the east end of the ridge was quite broad at the west end of the ridge, offering easy access to and from the threshing floors located at the higher elevations. Threshing floors AIG073, AIG108, AIG109, AIG110, and AIG136 were easily accessed using this broad path. It seems likely that these floors were used by many of the families in the northeast area. Threshing floors AIG074 and AIG075 are positioned near house AIG071 and are located partially within the property and retaining walls that seem to outline the boundaries associated with this house. As noted above, these walls open onto the houses (AIG121 and AIG119) and related structures to the south, providing access to these threshing floors from that location. It is possible that threshing floors AIG074 and AIG075 were primarily used by the houses nearby and that the threshing floors to the north were shared by the community more broadly. The lone threshing floor at the eastern edge of the site (AIG133) presents a similar situation and was likely used by the cluster of houses located near this structure. While the proximity of the threshing floors to nearby building clusters does suggest a relationship, it should be noted that this division of ownership and use is speculative, as the informants did not note any specific behaviors related to these features.

The Village as History

The remains of Aigition outlined above represent a typical Greek village centered around a *plateia* with a church. The location of the cemetery in the main square is more unusual. The houses are clustered along the natural topography and form residential units. The architecture of the houses is consistent: they are two stories in height, with space for animals and storage on the ground floor and human residence on the upper floor. There is no communication between the stories. Small, one-story buildings are attached or clustered around the primary residential unit. Evidence of exterior bake ovens was identified either attached to or near the main house. Two of the houses, moreover, have water cisterns. Otherwise, water was carried from a public well outside the village. Three concrete water storage units were built along the ridge of the village at the threshing floors and date to after the 1940s.

The village developed gradually from the 1850s until the 1940s. We do not have sufficient chronological evidence to reconstruct the sequence of development. There are subtle differences in the treatment of openings, the articulation of lintels, and how the masonry walls adhere to the wooden casements of doors and windows. There is also a variety of iron pins and bronze hardware used in the joining between carpentry and masonry elements. It is not clear whether these morphological differences in construction are indicators of chronology or rather of mason preferences. One morphological difference, for example, can be found in the treatment of the corner quoins of two houses in the northeast sector (AIG084). Each block has a rusticated pillowing extrusion, which has also been found in two houses in Lidoriki. This is a self-conscious neoclassical detail that derives from the cosmopolitan architecture of Paris, London, and Vienna and migrated to Athens in the 1880s. Its employment here in two houses exhibits the ambitions of the itinerant stone masons to dress the peasant installations with the aesthetic fashions of European urbanism. One potential mode of transmission might be the national road network constructed during the last two decades of the nineteenth century. It includes bridges with similarly stylized features, a few of which have been identified in the area. A second potential mode of transmission might be through the rusticated train stations and railroad infrastructure built by French engineers.

One of the central themes from our survey is the differentiation of three key phases of abandonment: following immigration to the U.S. in 1900, the burning of the village by the Axis powers in 1943, and migration in the 1960s to other towns, Athens, or Germany. The archaeological profile of immigration to the U.S. was identified positively not by house desertion but by house and school construction with remittances. The archaeological evidence for the destruction of the village in 1943 is twofold. In AIG016, which was reconstructed after the war, we identified the charred remains of wood over the reinforced lintel of the front door. More prominent, however, is the coexistence of ruins and renovations. Returning from internment in the concentration camp of Athens, the residents of Aigition lived in the animal pens, which were single-story structures that had not been burned. The Nazi soldiers burned the interior of the houses by breaking doors and windows and throwing into the space ignited cloth doused in petrol. The house contents and furniture caught fire, and then the wooden structure (i.e. the beams supporting the upper floor and the roof) burned. The vertical masonry walls survived. The task of the returned residents, therefore, was to scavenge for wood so that they could rebuild floors and roofs. Only some of the houses were rebuilt, while the others remained as piles of stone. Stone was not in shortage. Many of the burned houses were left to collapse upon themselves and disintegrate though entropy.

A more pervasive form of reuse can be seen in fittings that secured the house openings at its doors and windows. Many of the original wooden door and window fixtures were surely burned during the fires that destroyed the interior beams and ceilings. The ones that survived were appropriated. The recycling of casements, sashes, windowpanes, and shutters from different houses is prevalent. In some cases, the original direction of opening between interior glass windows and exterior wooden shutters was reversed. Some shutters, for example, were placed inside the house, while the windows are on the outside. Some reused windows swing outwards, while others open inwards. There is a clear differentiation of carpentry between doors used for the animal/storage floor below and doors (and windows) used for the human floor above. Doors for the storage spaces are made locally of unmilled cedar. Doors for the residential half, in contrast, are milled in an urban style of panels and decoration, typically painted in blue or green. These doors would have been manufactured in a central mill at the larger town of Lidoriki. Following the reinhabitation of the village by its displaced citizens, the hierarchy between openings is eroded.

Between 1944 and the 1960s, Aigition existed in a precarious state as its residents lived among the ruins but made piecemeal improvements in some select houses. During the 1960s, there was a mass exodus to Athens. Recognizing the devastation of villages during the Axis occupation and the Civil War, the Greek government attempted to consolidate the population of five villages (Aigition, Vraila, Karoutes, Lidoriki, and Skaloula) into a new village aptly named the "City of Five," or Pentapoli, in 1951. The village accommodated a small part of the population (394 people in 1961) but failed to become a new urban center. Lidoriki remained the regional center (1,302 people in 1961). After the war, Aigition's returning population was 84% of its prewar size, but by 1961 it diminished to 31% and by 1971 it was fully depopulated. The populations recorded by the national census were 114 in 1928, 384 in 1940, 324 in 1951, 120 in 1961, 0 in 1971, 0 in 1981, and 8 in 1991 (Stamatelatos and Stamatelatos 2006:

52, 437, 612). Even through the village lacked any permanent residents, it was seasonally used by a handful of people. A few owners kept their houses locked but visited them in the spring and summer. Kaphritsas, who lived permanently in the Peloponnese, visited his house once per month and stayed longer with friends during the winter hunting season. When we first visited the village in 2010, it was clear that a large population of sheep, goats, and cows herded through the village. We met one elderly woman who was the single year-round resident. The installation of a paved access road, a water system, and electricity in the 1970s made the village attractive for seasonal visitors and itinerant shepherds. As an electrified, watered, and paved ruin twice over, the village continued to be renovated, particularly in the central *plateia* of the church and cemetery. A concrete picnic area was built next to the church, along with a monument for war heroes. The picnic area signified a transition of the village's main usage from an inhabited community to an outdoor destination for seasonal visits associated with church festivals and memorials. The lack of permanent inhabitants, moreover, turned the village into an unmonitored open landscape for animal grazing. Absentee owners who lived nearby and could occasionally visit the village built high fences to keep animals from entering their property. These new fences created a demarcation of private property that never existed during the life of the village. It is in this late phase (between the 1980s and the present) that owners began to hoard building material for future projects and to build large concrete porches where modest wooden balconies might have once been. We observed piles of building material stacked along walls in fenced areas. We also noted the fresh robbing of the nicer ashlar blocks located at the corners of half-ruined houses (AIG086). The most aggressive renovations and transformations of a small number of houses (AIG058, AIG043, AIG016, AIG017) date, interestingly enough, to the last phase of occupation in the 2000s. They represent a desperate attempt to turn what was once communally maintained (even in ruin) into a site with a handful of seasonal private installations that had to survive in the wilderness.

Conclusion

When Loukopoulos and Pikionis surveyed the domestic architecture of Aetolia and Phocis in the 1920s, they inadvertently gave birth to the discipline of vernacular architectural studies. The perspective adopted by Greek architects of the Generation of the Thirties and revived in the 1960s privileged morphologically pure architectural features that could illustrate in formal terms the essence of a Greek experience during multiple centuries of agricultural life rooted in the Greek landscape. When processual archaeology developed new scientific tools to study that landscape in the 1960s, the Greek village was contextualized within a framework of ecological and social forces. A rigorous approach to the study of material culture was coupled with ethnography to produce a variated historical landscape. The field of architecture prefers to study well-preserved standing monuments that can reveal the synthetic life world of buildings. Archaeologists, on the other hand, prefer to study the evidence of change and alteration.

The Greek countryside contains many Greek villages that were deserted after World War II and the Greek Civil War. The vast majority of archaeological resources, both Greek and non-Greek, are devoted to the study of ancient monuments. Although deserted Greek villages have entered archaeological discourses, they are rarely investigated with the same rigor. With the deaths of its original inhabitants, the availability of oral histories is dramatically waning and the window of opportunity for an anthropology of Greek villages is closing. The material evidence of deserted Greek villages is becoming increasingly central in the writing of Greek social history. With the passage of time, the villages are being overcome by forest as they return to a state of nature. They offer excellent case studies of postabandonment site-formation processes, as illustrated at Penteskouphi (Sanders et al., this volume).

The study of Aigition illustrates the marriage of architectural and archaeological perspectives. The Lidoriki Project, more broadly, served as a training ground and pedagogical experiment to bring different types of students to one region and develop a systematic methodology for recording the physical remains of a medium-sized village in a short period of time. Miltiadis Katsaros and his Greek students from the National Technical University of Athens brought to the site the long architectural tradition of studying Greek houses evolved from Loukopoulos and Pikionis. Todd Brenningmeyer, Kostis Kourelis, and their U.S. students brought the Anglo-American tradition of landscape archaeology. The photogrammetric survey of Aigition is possibly the first 3D digital survey of a deserted village in Greece. It provides a dataset (freely available online) that will hopefully generate the cultivation of better methodologies and other village surveys.

The combination of oral histories, architectural survey, landscape survey, and object analysis brings light into a typical Greek village over the course of a tumultuous century, from its foundation in the 1850s to its abandonment in the 1970s. The study of the physical remains offers points of entry into multiple historical moments that are traditionally studied through textual and oral sources. The survey illustrates the progressive construction and disintegration of an agricultural shepherd community in ways that textual and oral sources do not capture. Individual family houses developed into clusters of family complexes. The village grew along two ridges, but its public life centered around the church of 1852 and the schoolhouse of 1909. The houses fit a typology of two-story dwellings but differ enough in their construction methods and furnishings to illustrate variations in time and stylistic norms. We were also able to illustrate how some of the houses testify to the architectural agency of global migration, built by remittances from migrant workers in the U.S. The most vivid episode of the village's history is its destruction by the Axis powers. "The Germans burned the village" is a common narrative encountered in Greece, but the material clarification of such an event has not been documented archaeologically. The burning of Aigition translates into the destruction of the wooden elements in its houses, namely its floors and ceilings. The masonry walls survived. Some were rebuilt when the villagers returned from their internment, but others were left as masonry piles. Over the course of two decades, the village was maintained by partial recycling of archaeological ruins. Finally, the survey of Aigition illustrates the process of natural deterioration resulting from the departure of its inhabitants. Even while uninhabited, the site continued to be used by the local population in similar ways as Lakka Skoutara (Pettegrew and Caraher, this volume). Water and electricity were brought to the village, while various inhabitants have preserved the houses from natural deterioration.

The village of Aigition contains in its material history complex processes of site formation that are both cultural and natural in nature. Its ordinariness has made it invisible to most scholars. We have brought our drones in conversation with its stones and, in the process, have rendered a marriage of tools and subjects.

References Cited

Allen, Susan Heuck
    2015   Like Pulling Teeth with ELAS. Paper presented at the 24th Biennial International Modern Greek Studies Association Symposium, Atlanta, Georgia.

Antoniadis-Bibicou, Eleni
    1965   Villages désertés en Grèce: Un bilan provisoire [Deserted Villages in Greece: A Provisional Assessment]. In *Villages désertés et histoire économique, XIe–XVIIIe siècle [Deserted Villages and Economic History, 11th–18th Centuries]*, École Pratique des Hautes-Études – VIe Section, Centre de Recherches Historiques, pp. 343–417. S.E.V.P.E.N., Paris.

Archaeological Survey School of Holland
    1989   Strouza (Aigition): A Historical-Topographical Fieldwork. Chronika B1. *Archaiologikon Deltion* 36(1981):236–248.

Architekturzentrum Wien
    2007   *Lessons from Bernard Rudofsky: Life as a Voyage*. Birkhäuser, Basel.

Aschenbrenner, Stanley
    1972   A Contemporary Community. In *The Minnesota Messenia Expedition: Reconstructing a Bronze Age Regional Environment*, edited by William A. McDonald and George R. Rapp, Jr., pp. 47–63. The University of Minnesota Press, Minneapolis.

ASKI
    2015   Αρχείο σύγχρονης κοινωνικής ιστορίας [Contemporary Social History Archive]. Electronic document, http://askiweb.eu/index.php/en/248-our-collections, accessed July 1, 2020.

Biermann, Shelby, Sara Loynd, Austin Nash, Nicole Thompson, and Lizzy Woods
    2016   Artists at Aigition: Documentation, Design, and the Investigation of Rural Greek Villages. Poster presented at the 117th Annual Meeting of the Archaeological Institute of America, San Francisco, California.

Bintliff, John
   2012   *The Complete Archaeology of Greece: From Hunter-Gatherers to the 20th Century A.D.* Wiley-Blackwell, New York.

Bommeljé, Sebastiaan, Peter K. Doorn, Michiel Deylius, Joanita Vroom, Yvette Bommeljé, Roland Fagel, and Henk van Wijngaarden
   1987   *Aetolia and the Aetolians: Towards the Interdisciplinary Study of a Greek Region.* Parnassus Press, Utrecht.

Brenningmeyer, Todd, Frederick A. Cooper, and Caitlyn Downey
   1998   Satellites, Silicon, and Stone: Spatial Information and Greek Archaeology. *Geo Info Systems* 8(1):20–28.

Brenningmeyer, Todd, Kostis Kourelis, and Miltiadis Katsaros
   2016   The Lidoriki Project – Low Altitude Aerial Photography, GIS, and Traditional Survey in Rural Greece. In *CAA 2015: Keep the Revolution Going. Proceedings of the 43rd Annual Conference on Computer Applications and Quantitative Methods in Archaeology*, Vol. 2, edited by Stefano Campana, Roberto Scopigno, Gabriella Carpentiero, and Marianna Cirillo, pp. 979–988. Archaeopress, Oxford.
   2020   Unsettled Settlements: Documenting Site Abandonment and Transformation in Modern Greece. In *CAA 2017: Digital Archaeologies, Material Worlds (Past and Present). Proceedings of the 45th Conference on Computer Applications and Quantitative Methods in Archaeology*, edited by Jeffrey B. Glover, Jessica Moss, and Dominique Rissolo, pp. 322–335. Tübingen University Press, Tübingen.

Chatzemichali, Angeliki
   1925   Ελληνική λαϊκή τέχνη. Σκύρος *[Greek Folk Art: Skyros]*. Makris, Athens.

Clarke, Mari H.
   2000   The Changing Household Economy on Methana, 1880–1996. In *Contingent Countryside: Settlement, Economy, and Land Use in the Southern Argolid Since 1700*, edited by Susan B. Sutton, pp. 169–199. Stanford University Press, Stanford.

Cooper, Frederick A., Kostis Kourelis, Helen B. Foster, Mary Coulton, and Joseph D. Alchermes
   2003   *Houses of the Morea: Vernacular Architecture of the Northwest Peloponnesos (1205–1955)*. Melissa, Athens.

Davis, Jack L. (editor)
   1998   *Sandy Pylos: An Archaeological History from Nestor to Navarino*. University of Texas Press, Austin.

Dawkins, R. M.
   1902/1903   Notes from Karpathos. *Annual of the British School in Athens* 9:176–210. https://doi.org/10.1017/S006824540000767X

Doorn, Peter K.
   1987   The Village Interviews. In *Aetolia and the Aetolians: Towards the Interdisciplinary Study of a Greek Region*, edited by Sebastiaan Bommeljé, Peter Doorn, Michiel Deylius, Joanita Vroom, Yvette Bommeljé, Roland Fagel, and Henk van Wijngaarden, pp. 114–123. Parnassus Press, Utrecht.
   1989   Population and Settlements in Central Greece: Computer Analysis of Ottoman Registers of the Fifteenth and Sixteenth Centuries. In *History and Computing*, Vol. 2, edited by Peter Denley, Stefan Fogelvik, and Charles Harvey, pp. 193–208. Manchester University Press, Manchester.
   2009   Population and Settlement in Post-Medieval Doris, Central Greece. In *Medieval and Post-Medieval Greece: The Corfu Papers*, edited by John Bintliff and Hanna Stöger, pp. 199–213. BAR International Series 2023. Archaeopress, Oxford.

Doxiadis, Constantine A.
   1947   *Destruction of Towns and Villages in Greece*. Publications from the Undersecretary's Office for Reconstruction 11. Undersecretary's Office for Reconstruction, Athens.

Eleftheria Post
   2013   *Eleftheria Post 6333 Veterans of Foreign Wars of the United States. Honors and Remembrance: A Lifetime of Service to our Country and Community*. Eleftheria VFW Post 6633, Philadelphia.

Forbes, Hamish
   2007   *Meaning and Identity in a Greek Landscape: An Archaeological Ethnography*. Cambridge University Press, Cambridge.

Frampton, Kenneth
   1985   Critical Regionalism: Modern Architecture and Cultural Identity. In *Modern Architecture: A Critical History*, pp. 313–327. 2nd ed. Thames and Hudson, New York.

Frangakis, Elena, and J. Malcolm Wagstaff
   1987   Settlement Pattern Change in the Morea (Peloponnisos) c. A.D. 1700–1830. *Byzantine and Modern Greek Studies* 11:163–192. https://doi.org/10.1179/030701387790203028

Friedl, Ernestine
   1962   *Vasilika, a Village in Modern Greece*. Hold, Rinehart and Winston, New York.

Gregory, Timothy E.
   2007   Contrasting Impressions of Land Use in Early Modern Greece: The Eastern Corinthia and Kythera. In *Between Venice and Istanbul: Colonial Landscapes in Early Modern Greece*, edited by Syriol Davies and Jack Davis, pp. 173–198. American School of Classical Studies at Athens, Princeton, New Jersey.

Jameson, Michael H., Curtis N. Runnels, and Tjeerd H. van Andel
   1994   *A Greek Countryside: The Southern Argolid from Prehistory to the Present Day*. Stanford University Press, Stanford.

Koster, Harold A.
   1977   The Ecology of Pastoralism in Relation to Changing Patterns of Land Use in the Northeast Peloponnese. PhD dissertation, Department of Anthropology, University of Pennsylvania, Philadelphia.

Kourelis, Kostis
   2003   Monuments of Rural Archaeology: Medieval Settlements in the Northwestern Peloponnese. PhD dissertation, Department of Art and Archaeology of the Mediterranean World, University of Pennsylvania, Philadelphia.

2011/2012   Byzantine Houses and Modern Fictions: Domesticating Mystras in 1930s Greece. *Dumbarton Oaks Papers* 65/66:297–331. https://www.jstor.org/stable/41933713

Life Magazine
1944   "What the Germans Did to Greece." 27 November: 21–27. New York.

Loukopoulos, Demetrios
1925   Αιτωλικαί οικήσεις σκεύη και τροφαί *[Aetolian Houses, Utensils, and Food]*. P. D. Sakellariou, Athens.

Oliver, Paul
1975   Introduction. In *Shelter, Sign and Symbol*, edited by Paul Oliver, pp. 6–37. Barrie and Jenkins, London.

Pavlides, Eleutherios.
1995   The Expression of Institutional Meaning in Greek Domestic Architecture. In *Constructed Meaning: Form and Process in Greek Architecture*, edited by Eleftherios Pavlides and Susan Buck Sutton, pp. 345–386. Modern Greek Studies Yearbook, Minneapolis.

Philippidis, Dimitris
1984   Νεοελληνική αρχιτεκονική. Αρχιτεκτονική θεωρία και πράξη (1830–1980) *[Modern Greek Architecture: Architectural Theory and Practice (1830–1980)]*. Melissa, Athens.

Philippidis, Dimitris (editor)
1982   Ελληνική παραδοσιακή αρχιτεκτονική *[Greek Traditional Architecture]*. 2 vols. Melissa, Athens.

Pouqueville, Françoise Charles Hugues Laurent
1826   *Voyage de la Grèce [Travels in Greece]*, Vol. IV. 2nd ed. Firmin Didot, Paris.

Rudofsky, Bernard
1964   *Architecture Without Architects: A Short Introduction to Non-Pedigreed Architecture*. Doubleday, Garden City, New York.

Saloutos, Theodore
   1970   The Greeks of Milwaukee. *Wisconsin Magazine of History* 53(3):175–193. https://www.jstor.org/stable/4634531

Sellers, Rod
   2001   *Chicago Southeast Side Revisited*. Arcadia, Charleston, South Carolina.

Stamatelatos, Michael, and Photeini Vamva-Stamatelatos
   2006   Επίτομο γεωγραφικό λεξικό της Ελλάδος *[Concise Gazetteer of Greece]*. 2nd ed. Ermis, Athens.

Stefatos, Katerina, and Iosif Kovras
   2015   Buried Silences of the Greek Civil War. In *Necropolitics: Mass Graves and Exhumations in the Age of Human Rights*, edited by Francisco Ferrándiz and Antonius C. G. M. Robben, pp. 161–184. University of Pennsylvania Press, Philadelphia.

Sutton, Susan B.
   1995   Crumbling Walls and Bare Foundations: The Process of Housing in Greece. In *Constructed Meaning: Form and Process in Greek Architecture*, edited by Eleftherios Pavlides and Susan Buck Sutton, pp. 319–344. Modern Greek Studies Yearbook, Minneapolis.

Sutton, Susan B. (editor)
   2000   *Contingent Countryside: Settlement, Economy, and Land Use in the Southern Argolid since 1700*. Stanford University Press, Stanford.

Theocharopoulou, Ioanna
   2012   Constantinos A. Doxiadis: The War and the Archive. Paper presented at the conference Front to Rear: Architecture during World War II, Institute of Fine Arts, New York University, New York. Vimeo, https://vimeo.com/5789572, accessed July 1, 2020.

van Andel, Tjeerd H., and Curtis Runnels
   1987   *Beyond the Acropolis: A Rural Greek Past*. Stanford University Press, Stanford.

Wagstaff, J. Malcolm
   1978   War and Settlement Desertion in the Morea, 1685–1830. *Transactions of the Institute of British Geographers* 3(3):295–308. https://doi.org/10.2307/622158

Wright, James C., John F. Cherry, Jack L. Davis, Eleni Mantzourani, Susan B. Sutton, and Robert F. Sutton, Jr.
   1990   The Nemea Valley Archaeological Project: A Preliminary Report. *Hesperia* 59:579–659. https://doi.org/10.2307/148078

Zachos, Aristotelis
   1922/1923   Ältere Wohnbauten auf griechischen Boden [Older Residential Buildings on Greek Soil]. *Wasmuths Monatshefte für Baukunst* 7–8:247–250.

Chapter Nine
Wheelock, North Dakota: "Ghost-Towns," Man Camps, and Hyperabundance in an Oil Boom

Richard Rothaus, William Caraher, Bret Weber, and Kostis Kourelis

The hyperabundance of manufactured material culture, especially in areas subject to extractive industry boom-and-bust cycles, makes nuanced interpretation seemingly impossible. These difficulties are amplified when studying domestic architecture and assemblages, as these themselves are a mix of display and function. The University of North Dakota (UND) Man Camp Project, led by William Caraher and Bret Weber, has been investigating workforce housing and the archaeology of the contemporary world in North Dakota's Bakken oil fields since 2011 (Caraher 2016; Caraher et al. 2017; Caraher and Weber 2017; Caraher et al. 2016). Faced with ubiquitous accumulation of manufactured goods during an oil boom, we have adopted novel research techniques. While our work remains rooted in archaeology's traditional concerns with buildings, objects, and space, we have been faced with the challenge of documenting that which is far too numerous to record and largely uninteresting in its manufactured repetitiveness. Part of that challenge was contextualizing resurgent occupation in the nearly abandoned town of Wheelock, North Dakota. Wheelock, founded in 1904, was one of the earliest towns in western North Dakota, and including it in our study provided some historical context to the fast-paced Bakken boom that started in 2006, peaked in 2012, and continues today—albeit much diminished since a global price decline in 2015. In contrast, Wheelock's history was much slower paced. Founded as a railroad town, it followed a normal North American plains trajectory with waves of new settlers who fared less well than they hoped. By the dustbowl years of the 1930s, Wheelock's fate was sealed, and through attrition it arrived in the 1970s to its local reputation as a ghost town. Initially, Wheelock was to us an annoying aberration in our typology, but it became a precious window into the impact of the boom on human lives.

Man Camp Typology

In cataloguing the man camps, we categorized camps into three broad types. Type 1 camps are the most formal, usually run by international workforce housing groups, interesting mostly in their strictly regimented efficiency and uniformity. Type 2 camps are semiformal, similar to American recreational vehicle (RV) parks, filled with mobile homes, trailers, trucks, and ad hoc structures. Type 2 camps occupied most of our attention, with their wide variety of manufactured housing solutions and pockets of personality where these homes were individualized. Type 3 camps—the most ephemeral—are unregulated gatherings of trailers and tents placed in locations where the authorities would overlook them, until they did not. These variations in housing have long been part of North American oil booms. In Kilgore, Texas, in the 1930s, salaried men lived in the "company camp" free of charge, while hourly workers lived in the "poor-boy camp" for a nominal rent. Those not employed by the company lived rough in "Happy Hollow," enduring a cycle of police clearings and reinhabitations (Weaver 2010). Like all typologies, ours works well in summary paragraphs but falters on the ground.

Wheelock was one of the locations that just did not fit our typology very well. While we were aware of Wheelock from the beginning of the project, we initially spent very little time there. This was largely because we did not know what to do with it, partly because it was rather seedy and unnerving. It was only as we completed our boom-period fieldwork and began publications that the importance of Wheelock became more evident. Wheelock was casually considered a ghost town, so far on the margins that it was hard to shoehorn into our typology of man camps. Wheelock is a village that never took hold, blinking in and out of occupation while situated in a location that had no lasting reason. As such, it is a precious window that pierces the veil of hyperabundance, commodified culture, and performance materiality (Bourdieu 1987). The theatricality of twenty-first-century oil boomtowns should not be underestimated, as everyone is quite aware that they are being closely watched. Just as in contemporary American suburbs, what people own, how they live, and what they leave outside their homes are displays indicative of position and roles, real and desired. How they live is thus a theater of performance (Bourdieu 1970, 1977). Wheelock is a recent example of a marginality that blinks in and out of the wider world's attention in cycle with waves of economic booms—real or anticipated—of the region (Figure 1).

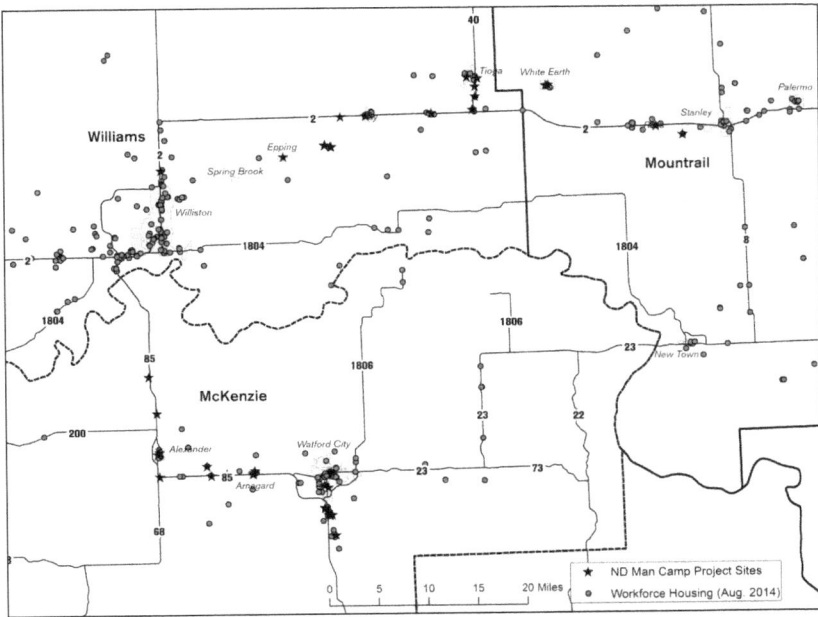

Figure 1. Study area of the North Dakota Man Camp Project. Map courtesy of William Caraher.

Man Camps, Ghost Towns, and Oil Boom Theaters of Performance

The treasure of Wheelock to archaeology is that it happened to blink on right when we were passing through. Rather than an anomaly from long ago that reappeared in an archaeological record complete with tendentious interpretations, we encountered a "ghost town" while the people were still there. Seeing the locale reinhabited by hopeful newcomers during an oil boom, we were given an opportunity to see past the region's tens of thousands of manufactured residences into the deep material culture of time and industry. Wheelock emphasizes to us that oil boom economies in remote locations do not require that housing be livable, just that it exist. In this reality, without the financial backing or public image concerns of the major companies to assist or protect them, the ancillary workers, truckers, store clerks, and bartenders are very much on their own, as they were in earlier booms (Weaver 2010). Removed from visibility, Wheelock shows a raw reality hidden elsewhere.

The monumental scale of industrial shale oil as an extractive industry, matched by the overwhelming number of industrialized housing solutions, can be rather impenetrable. And, as with all such situations, the façades of the solutions are designed with a purpose: to project an image to both outsiders and insiders. This is not a criticism, of course, but a reality. We all do this: the American front yard is cultivated, more or less, to present an image of orderly prosperity; its entryway is designed to transition a family from outside culture to inside culture. This reality, however, combined with the uniformity of a twenty-first-century oil boom and residences all stocked from the same Walmart, makes it difficult to see anything but the façade. Allan Sekula (2002), the photographer-philosopher, struggled with this while studying the global shipping industry, and he emphasized the importance of looking at the places in-between. One can learn only so much about shipping by looking at the mechanized shipping yards and uniform shipping containers at ports of entry and exit, and almost nothing of the material lives of the workers. The solution is to look at the places where the action is not; for Sekula, that meant the vessels traversing the ocean openness and the backside of the shipping yards. Sekula's central idea, as applied to his photographic work, was that simple realism captures the projected image. Critical realism finds a way around the projected image to capture realities that may not be obvious even to participants. Our "critical realism" in the UND Man Camp Project functioned by looking at the personalization of housing, at people's backyards and mudrooms, and at Wheelock (Roberts 2012; Sekula 2002).

While the media lazily tosses about "Wild West" analogies for oil-boom regions, and while individuals may indeed feel elements of chaos as they go about their lives, there is more overt order and monotony than not. The Type 1 camps are run by professionals who know how to maximize uniformity, efficiency, and logistics to maximize profits. Set up in secured areas, with uniformity not only of buildings, but also down to toilets and light fixtures, the Type 1 camps usually sparked the same reaction among visitors: they are like prisons. In our interviews with staff and inhabitants, however, the attitude was usually different. The Type 1 camps, derived from their long association with extractive industries and military deployments, attempt a benign utilitarianism that focuses on their primary function: provide a place for people living a relentless grind of long shifts to bathe, eat, and sleep. The Type 1 camps are not personalized because no one considers them home, and most residents, after working 21 days straight, are both required and glad to leave for their 10 days off. The material culture of Type 1 camps is, however, a masterpiece of extractive industry theater. To the outsider, with their barbed-wire fences, neatly arranged buildings, and security gates, they act as a counterbalance to the never-ending talk of man camps as hazards (Reed 2016). To the insiders, the message is clear and not unwelcome: work, eat, sleep, move on; your home is elsewhere. While not, perhaps, something most of us would aspire to, the Type 1 camps are a simultaneous triumph of efficiency and control propaganda. At the top of the spectrum of uniformity, their message of industrialized progress is clear—no grandiose statues or motivating slogans needed.

In our typology, the Type 2 camps rested firmly in the middle of our tripartite order. While seemingly more chaotic than the Type 1 camps, each Type 2 camp had its own internal order, all more similar than not. Whether known to local authorities and subject to rules or not, one finds rows of trailers and standardized spacing. The theater of the Type 2 camps was internal; the longtime local residents never went into them and saw them only as chaos. We, however, saw in the Type 2 camps what many of the residents also saw: a chance to personalize and make an individualized statement. As a result, we spent a great deal of time documenting the strategies used by inhabitants to personalize their spaces, to adapt structures not designed for winters so they could withstand the North Dakota deep freeze, to maximize their ability to enjoy what little downtime they had, and to transmit their knowledge to their neighbors. Some of the inhabitants of the Type 2 camps told us they had access to Type 1 camps but greatly preferred doing things their own way. The theater in the Type 2 camps was a resistance theater, an act of individual opposition to efforts of the industry to commodify both labor and persons.[1]

Even the rough and fleeting Type 3 camps had a performative nature. Type 3 camps were common only at the start of the boom, and the camps tended to disappear as soon as the authorities grew tired of them. Thus, we were able to visit only a few of them. Our best documented Type 3 camp disappeared suddenly, leaving behind only abandoned supplies and tracks in the snow from the tractor used to remove trailers. Our limited time in Type 3 camps was, however, full of what we came to term "Bakktimism," an abundant belief that everything was going to work out for the better. This relentless optimism is not unique to oil booms; in *Nomadland*, Jessica Bruder (2017) encountered much of the same in the individuals she met who wandered from job to job as part of the precariat class—even those who knew that permanence and retirement was

---

[1] Type 2 camps are not dissimilar to the stacks of the dystopian novel *Ready Player One*, where vast portions of the population live in chaotic trailers stacked upon each other in a precarious grid work (Cline 2011). The shared interest in manufactured material culture led both the UND Man Camp Project team and the novel's author, Ernest Cline, to the Atari graveyard dig of 2014 in Alamogordo, New Mexico (Caraher et al. 2014; Reinhard 2018).

never to be theirs. Similar sentiments appear among the displaced automobile manufacturing workers of Janesville, Wisconsin (Goldstein 2011; Standing 2013). Type 3 camps were focused on short-term existence, as hopeful workers tried to gain initial employment in the oilfield economy. These camps had their own theatrical aspect; the message, shouted perhaps a bit too loud, was that sleeping in a tent while looking for a job was just a normal step on the way to the American dream.

Wheelock was just obscure enough, just far enough off the highway, that we found it escaped the performance art of the Type 1, 2, and 3 camps. The new arrivals in Wheelock were focused on very basic activities: make money, preserve family units, and find food, shelter, and water. With no one watching and with so few people living in town, there was no call for the external-facing theater of the Type 1 camps or the internal-facing theater of the Type 2 camps. Wheelockians were not marginalized labor but critical low-status labor, poised to jump on what Walter Benjamin (2014) called the "carousel of jobs," grabbing whatever they could lest they be forced out of the "production process" and not find their way back in again (see Sekula 2010). Most were there because they were the workers in the unpleasantly real underbelly of an industry that markets order, cleanliness, and workers living the American dream. Wheelock was a non-place, an anonymous, generic crossroads of human existence that gave us a window through which we could see what actually makes a boom function (Augé 1995). While aesthetically unpleasing and socially unpleasant, Wheelock punched through the manufactured façade of boomtown dreams and provided a valid—and indeed preferred—subject of study. Although easy for some to dismiss as delusional in their acceptance of the conditions, Wheelockians embodied a pragmatism reminiscent of Gandalf's now meme-ified advice to Frodo:

"I wish it need not have happened in my time," said Frodo.
"So do I," said Gandalf, "and so do all who live to see such times. But that is not for them to decide. All we have to decide is what to do with the time that is given us." [Tolkien 1965:82]

Wheelock's Early Days

Wheelock, of course, has a history, and we can see that this is not the first time Wheelock has been in this position. The town was incorporated in January 1904 by William Maloney and 19 other individuals. It was named after Ralph Wheelock, a reporter at the *Minneapolis Tribune*, who was an earlier promoter of the town site and the area's perceived potential for wheat farming. Maloney had filed on the land three years earlier, subsequent to the establishment of a Great Northern Railroad depot. By 1903 a general store, hardware store, lumber yard, blacksmith, and livery had opened. Wheelock's main competitors were Epping, about 10 miles to the west along the railroad line, and Ray, about 10 miles to the east. Wheelock's brief history as a railroad town was typical. It was placed in largely roadless country at a location that was convenient for a railroad depot, not settlers. Other than being on a rise, Wheelock's location was unremarkable. There was no nearby lake, no nearby stream, and even the closest spring was several miles away. Unlike other towns in North Dakota that were linked, however tangentially, to the past like Bismarck or Fargo or Minot, Wheelock sprung from nothing, and its ephemeral origin helps explain in part its ephemeral existence. Wheelock as a town does not appear at all in the 1910 or 1920 U.S. census, an indicator of just how tiny it was in the early years. But growth was evident; the census shows Wheelock township (not the town) increasing from a population of 0 in 1910 to a population of 440 by 1920, making it one of the more populated townships in Williams County. It was larger than the nearby jointly listed towns of Epping/Springbrook (321), slightly larger than Tioga (433), slightly smaller than Ray (563), and dwarfed by Williston (4,448). Wheelock's founders had high hopes for it, but in the end those hopes never amounted to much of a reality.

Wheelock's growth peaked in the 1920s before its population dropped to 115 in 1930, mirroring similar towns that were promoted to immigrants as prime wheat-growing territory through the wonders of dry farming (Gilles and Brannan 2006; Kozol 1988; Roet 1985). By the 1920s more business had moved in, and the town celebrated the installation of the region's first cement sidewalks in 1928. Lutheran, Methodist, and Catholic churches were built. In 1927, a brick schoolhouse with a full basement was built. Proponents of dry farming insisted that if the prairie were broken and crops planted, the environment would shift, the rains would come, and all would flourish. This was markedly untrue, and Wheelock—like many communities—was pummeled by the Great Depression and the drought and windstorms of the 1930s. We are fortunate to have a fine series of photos by the famed photojournalist Russell Lee, who visited Wheelock in 1937 while working for the Farm Security Administration (FSA). Lee's charge as an FSA photographer was to capture the plight of farmers in the Dust Bowl. The FSA was in the midst of a movement to relocate sharecroppers, tenant farmers, and poor landowners from marginal land to collective farms, and the agency had broad political

Figure 2. "Ole Thompson, farmer near Wheelock, North Dakota." Photograph by Russell Lee (1937), retrieved from the Library of Congress, https://www.loc.gov/item/2017780824.

opposition (Hurt 1986). The FSA program was not a jobs project, but rather a propaganda program. Already skilled and accomplished photographers, including Russell Lee, Dorothea Lang, and Walker Evans, were dispatched across the United States to create portraits of rural America that have since become iconic in their depiction of depression theater, showing strong people enduring in impossibly hard situations.

Lee's journeys brought him to North Dakota from August through November 1937, with much of his work focusing, not unexpectedly, on the arid western half of the state (Wexler et al. 2018). In September 1937, Lee visited Wheelock and photographed a number of area families and farms. While we have only the photographic evidence to work from—and propaganda photos, at that—there is still much to be gleaned. The photos uniformly record utilitarian, somewhat ad hoc structures. In one image, farmer Ole Tronson poses in front of his home, decorated only with what seems to be mud mortar and a hanging thermometer. In another, Ole Thompson sits at his kitchen table in the unfinished interior of a vertical slat-board structure, with the wooden framing of the structure serving as narrow shelves (Figure 2). Ole is surrounded by items and

Figure 3. "House occupied by farm laborer. Wheelock, North Dakota." Photograph by Russell Lee (1937), retrieved from the Library of Congress, https://www.loc.gov/item/2017780777.

Figure 4. "Farmhouse near Wheelock, North Dakota." Photograph by Russell Lee (1937), retrieved from the Library of Congress, https://www.loc.gov/item/2017780456.

Figure 5. "Home of Herman Gerling. Wheelock, North Dakota." Photograph by Russell Lee (1937), retrieved from the Library of Congress, https://www.loc.gov/item/2017780479.

clutter: some functional, like kitchen condiments and books; others, piles of papers destined for reuse. Lee recorded other utilitarian houses. One is a simple house with a low, sloped roof and siding made of pieces of sheet metal, a shed and car unceremoniously placed in the front yard (Figure 3). Another house is made of two roofed shed buildings of different heights joined together, the exposed end loosely covered in tar paper (Figure 4).

Most memorable, perhaps, is the series of photos focusing on the home and farm of Herman Gerling (Figure 5). The photos indicate that the Gerling family did not live in town; they do not appear as landowners in the 1937 atlas of Williams County, North Dakota, indicating that they were likely tenant farmers (Williams County Board of County Commissioners 1937). Herman Gerling was born in Minnesota but was a resident of Williams County all of his adult life. Herman was in his first marriage to Katie when, in 1912, their mortgage was foreclosed (Williston Graphic [WG], 4 July 1912:7). He was drafted for World War I in 1914 and was back home by August 1916, when he collected an $8.00 bounty on four coyote skins (WG, 10 August 1916:4). By 1920 Herman was living in nearby Springbrook, and Katie had died (U.S. Census Bureau, Schedule for Enumeration of Population for Springbrook Township, Williams

County, North Dakota, 2 January 1920, facsimile, USGenWeb Archives, http://www.usgwarchives.net/nd/williams/census/1920/245-04a.gif). By 1930 Herman, now 49 years old, had relocated to Truax township (about 15 miles south of Wheelock) with his second wife Tirazah (age 29). Three children were living in the house: Doris Hickle (age 4), Gertrude (age 4), and James (age 9; U.S. Census Bureau, Schedule for Enumeration of Population for Truax Township, Williams County, North Dakota, 2 April 1930, facsimile, USGenWeb Archives, http://www.usgwarchives.net/nd/williams/census/1930/55-01a.gif). A decade later, it seems that Doris Hickle and James had left the household, but Herman, Tirazah, Gertrude (now age 14), and son John (age 3) were still in Truax. Herman was buried in nearby Epping in 1966. Gertrude never married—or at least never took another name—and lived in Williston in the late 1990s. She died in 2001 and is also buried in Epping (Williston Herald [WH], 6 February 2001).

The Gerling family seems to have interested Lee (or maybe it was just amenable to his presence) as he recorded multiple scenes with them. The most memorable image is the family in front of their handmade door, Tirazah holding baby John, Herman hand-on-hip (Figure 6). Eleven-year-old Gertrude, wearing clothes so clean and oversized they must be Herman's best outfit, is turned slightly to the side, perhaps self-conscious of the right arm she lost four years earlier (in an accident, according to the photographer's notes). The house, as revealed in other photos, is in rough shape. The attic window is missing completely, with one board over it showing that it has been opened up for ventilation during the hot days of late summer. The front window is missing, the frame boarded up except for a top slat opened for light and air; a second photo shows this window fully "closed," with glimpses of the cloth used to stuff cracks and stop seeping dust. The windows on the sides of the house are in their frames, but all but two panes of glass have been boarded over. The house, however, does have wooden siding and a good roof (Figure 7). A pile of rocks along the side of the house seems aspirational rather than an actual stone socle; the rocks are held in place by a retaining fence, and this style is matched at other houses photographed by Lee. Boards form a ladder up the roof to the stove pipe, suggesting regular maintenance. A crosscut wood saw hangs from the eaves. The Gerling house has an interesting additional feature: a large sheet of wood mounted to serve as a second door that closes over the front door and secures the house. This is an odd feature; perhaps it serves to close out the dust when the storms come, or to better secure the house when the family is away.

Figure 6. "The Herman Gerling family near Wheelock, North Dakota. The daughter lost her arm four years ago." Photograph by Russell Lee (1937), retrieved from the Library of Congress, https://www.loc.gov/item/2017780476.

Figure 7. "Home of Herman Gerling near Wheelock, North Dakota." Photograph by Russell Lee (1937), retrieved from the Library of Congress, https://www.loc.gov/item/2017780477.

Figure 8. "Herman Gerling, farmer near Wheelock, North Dakota." Photograph by Russell Lee (1937), retrieved from the Library of Congress, https://www.loc.gov/item/2017780472.

The interior of the Gerling home is similarly utilitarian. The framing is exposed and used as shelving in the kitchen, where three guns are hung over the boarded-up window. Lee recorded Herman sitting in a chair reading the newspaper, and a hung photo near him is canted to create a storage space for stacks of paper waiting to be reused (Figure 8). The wall finishes are curious; they are sheets of a material perhaps 4 x 3 ft in dimension, with flaps or subdivided panels at one side. They are not placed piecemeal, however, and the Gerlings have aligned them where possible. The yard of the Gerling house is filled with items: barrels for water that Herman fetched from the spring, a discarded tire, a washing machine. To the left of the front door is a metal barrel laid on its side with a metal pan sitting next to it, perhaps to serve as storage or a doghouse. Lee also photographed the Gerling's threshing machine, which, according to Lee's caption, had not been used since the harvest of 1929 eight years earlier. The machine is surrounded by metal debris and forms the core of what is a typical farm junk pile—a not-so-subtle indication that Herman never expects to thresh again, but he will keep the machine just in case.

Wheelock was a railroad town that did not make it. The railroad line survived and even revived during the Bakken boom, as Wheelock now houses a small frac sand depot. But the promises of verdant wheat fields through dry farming proved less than accurate, and families quickly left. The abandoned towns of the west have a strong mythology, and North Dakota history has its own firm interpretation of "too-much, too-fast," which accepts the noble idea of civilizing the state but blames the failures on a lack of proportion (Robinson 1966). This is more moralizing trope than analysis, as it makes the ambitions of citizens the mistake. The realities are more complex. The late railroad towns like Wheelock were instruments of the railroad. They served the purpose of the railroad, were places built alongside the railroads with no regard for long-term survival, and indeed faded when the technology advanced and close-placed service centers were no longer needed. While Wheelock was enjoyed by residents, remembered fondly by descendants, and storied as a ghost town, the reality is that Wheelock was artificial from the beginning and no more likely to become an organic thriving town than the now-dwindling man camps of the recent oil boom (Hudson 1982).

The Great Depression and the Dust Bowl seem to have spelled the end of Wheelock's ambitions, but Wheelock was not suddenly abandoned. Rather, it just stopped growing, and the population drifted away (see Pettegrew and Caraher, this volume). The population stayed roughly level into 1940 (94) and 1950 (101). One of the longest-lived businesses, the hotel (itself a merger of two earlier competing hotels), made it until 1948. The general store, following suit, closed in the mid 1950s. Wheelock's pride, the brick schoolhouse, closed in 1961 when the remaining children were bussed to nearby Ray. The death of the store and the closure of the school were the end for Wheelock, and by 1970 the population had dropped to 21 as the last families abandoned it, presumably for larger towns and cities.

At night, the lights from the drilling rig at North Dakota's first producing well would have been visible from Wheelock. The oil well Clarence Iverson #1 started production in April 1951, a mere eight miles east of Wheelock. Renowned North Dakota journalist and historian Bill Shemorry reported:

> When I reached the hill just west of Wheelock, I could see the glow of a fire in the sky directly to the east. I wondered if the well was on fire. I passed through Ray and headed east. The light of the fire was getting brighter. There was no problem finding the well site in the dark. I came to the turnoff south of Tioga. A gravel road led to the well. It looked like the fire was just over the next hill, but I found it was four miles down the road. There was no room to stop. The glare in the sky had drawn several hundred interested spectators. The drilling rig and surrounding area were lighted by a huge gas flare. It was almost as if it were daylight. [Shemorry 2001]

But the technical difficulties of drilling the Bakken shale limited the growth of the industry. There was a small boom in the late 1970s and early 1980s, but documentation of the impact of that boom is exceedingly slim. The relative paucity of the record of quotidian life during the 1980s boom inspired the UND Man Camp Project in our mania for documentation. Wheelock saw a brief uptick in population, with the 1980 census showing an increase of 13 people since 1970 (for a total population of 34), but by 1990 the population had dropped back down to 23. People still own property, a few residents linger, and others occasionally come and go. The old railroad depot has been used as a clubhouse by the Ramblers Motorcycle Club for several decades. While locals certainly could tell a more nuanced tale, from our perspective, the 1980s boom passed Wheelock by.

Wheelock Resurgent

The most recent oil boom, however, hit Wheelock hard. In the first half of the 2010s a few entrepreneurs quickly brought Wheelock back to life. At the height of the Bakken shale play around 2011 to 2015, all available housing in northwest North Dakota was quickly used up. Hotels went for premium prices—if they could be found—and in response, the man camps sprung up. Wheelock was placed firmly on the informal and diverse end of our camp typology, to the point that it seemed a chaotic wonderland, albeit a bit hazardous and off-putting.

We saw situations in Wheelock that were unparalleled in other Bakken boom residencies. We were so taken aback by the unsanitary and hazardous conditions that one investigator remarked, "I haven't seen anything quite like this except in Tegucigalpa [Honduras]." As noted, Wheelock is a non-place, far enough on the margins that no one is paying much attention, and a place that is not participating in the performances of the extractive economy. What makes Wheelock so invaluable in our study is that people in Wheelock largely just did what they wanted as if no one was watching. Our camp typology, while developed for our use, also reflected some very deliberate intentions on the part of camp owners and residents to message their identity. Type 1 camps say, "we accept this and will excel." Type 2 camps say, "we are proud individuals, more than just our jobs." Type 3 camps say, "the American dream is for us, too." But Wheelock, chaotic and forgotten, sparsely inhabited and fragmented even among those few inhabitants, stands outside the theater of extractive culture as something else, something far more raw.

In our initial observations, Wheelock seemed utterly and hopelessly random. Massive piles and debris fields of reused and potentially reusable materials abounded, reminiscent of the stockpiling evidenced in the Lee photographs. Trailers and RVs were ubiquitous but arranged so randomly that it was nearly impossible to tell what was storage, what was habitation, and what was abandonment. Several old structures in Wheelock were being lived in, most well past any state of decay that would have been tolerated in a managed town or city. Residents were not usually hostile during our visits, but they also were not forcefully enthusiastic in their welcoming as we frequently encountered elsewhere. Some evidenced quite clearly in their furtive motions and disappearances that they were in Wheelock to avoid being found, and this sentiment held overall. Wheelock was a place you could go if you just wanted to be left alone. This sense was captured quite well in the documentary film *The Overnighters*, which chronicles the work of a pastor in Williston during the boom. He visits Wheelock with some trepidation, asks the wrong questions, and is promptly chased away with a shotgun (Mosse 2014).

Over the course of several visits and multiple interviews with residents, we were able to make some sense out of Wheelock. All of our interviews in Wheelock were conducted with approval from the Institutional Review Board at the University of North Dakota, and for this article we have changed names to protect the identity of individuals. The defining characteristic of Wheelock is that it was a place beyond normal rules and expectations. But there were rules and order in the town. Activity was focused in three areas: the orderly area dubbed by a few residents as "Paul's Property" on the northeast corner of town, the chaotic "Wrangle's Heights" in central Wheelock, and the entrepreneurial southwest corner run by self-proclaimed mayor, Theodore Magnus. Each of these areas had its own identifying characteristics, driven by the property owners; but it was also recognizable that there were individuals around just "doing their own thing" regardless of who owned the property. Certainly, the waggishly named Wrangle's Heights dominated the experience of visiting Wheelock, not only because of its centrality and its somewhat frightening character, but also because of the massive sprawl of haphazardly located materials. This imposing declaration of non-order caused many visitors to Wheelock to simply turn around and go the other way, and it solidified the negative reputation of the town.

The center of Wrangle's Heights was Douglas Wrangle, who grew up in nearby Grassy Butte, another almost-ghost-town about 30 miles away that was regionally known—at least among history fans—for its sod-constructed post office. Wrangle purchased a vacant house in Wheelock in 2010 at the beginning of the boom, and property records show that he owned one house located on two lots. His property, however, was the epicenter of activity in Wrangle's Heights; when we interviewed him in 2012, he reported that he was renting space to 12 trailers (Figure 9 and Figure 10). Wrangle divided his trailer park into two sections. One section was dry, meaning that there were only electrical hookups for residents. The other section, which he told us rented for $650 per month (a low price in 2012), had water and sewage hookups. The water and sewage hookups were rather tenuous, however. Wrangle hauled his own water and filled a long holding tank to which the trailers were connected. Near the holding tank was also a septic pit, so there was a tangle of water

Figure 9. Wrangle's property in 2012. Photograph courtesy of Richard Rothaus.

and sewage hoses running side by side. The system obviously did not work well, and we saw raw sewage cutting a rivulet through the property (Figure 11).

In 2012, Wrangle had residents from Nebraska, Nevada, Minnesota, Texas, Vermont, and California. For a time, there was a registered sex offender from Arkansas living there. Tenants found Wrangle via word of mouth, and, unlike in some of the camps we surveyed, the individuals there did not share a single employer. Wrangle feigned ignorance of a county moratorium on trailer parks and emphasized the critical element of growth in Wheelock, the town's distance and thus invisibility from U.S. Highway 2: "They kind of leave you alone if you're out here in the middle of nowhere." Wrangle himself lived in a large house in marked disrepair, along with his brother, his sister-in-law, and their children. Wrangle's Heights had no single female residents, but there were a few couples. Wrangle insisted there were no drugs at all and no crime, echoing sentiments we heard at nearly every camp: "No crime and drugs here; that's only at other camps." Wrangle's positive affirmations of a well-run trailer park did not match our visual inspection of the property. Wrangle's family members also were aware of community issues. In our first encounter with them, upon hearing that some of us were historians, they spoke enthusiastically about the history of Wheelock and even shared with us some maps and documents they had found in their house.

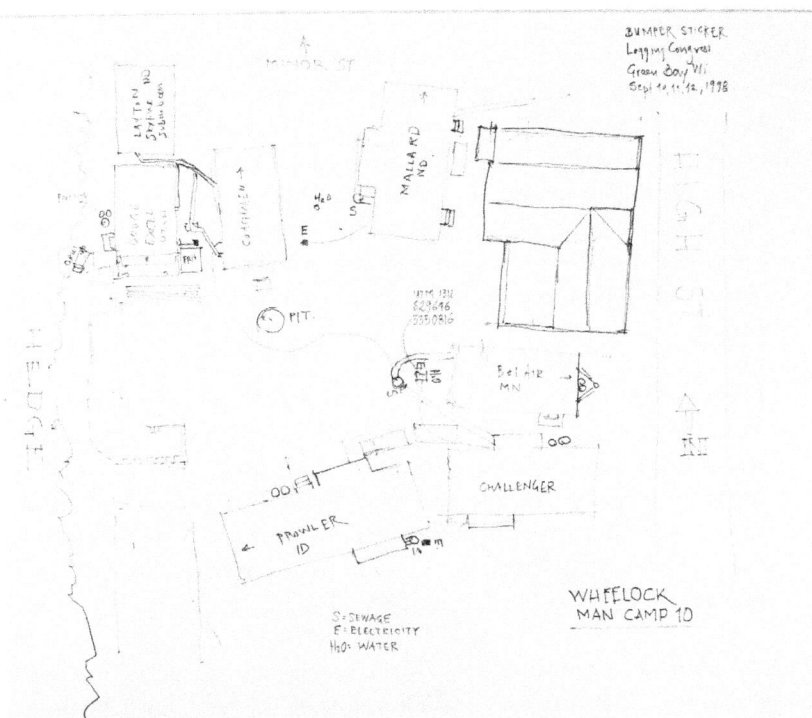

Figure 10. Wrangle's property in 2012. Plan courtesy of Kostis Kourelis.

Figure 11. Wrangle's water system in 2012. Photography courtesy of William Caraher.

In 2015 we were able to interview Walter Winston, who lived in Wrangle's Heights for three years before moving to Paul's Property. Winston reported that the septic system was constantly problematic. According to him, water was a problem in the winter because Wrangle had to borrow and rearrange hoses endlessly to fill his holding tank, which led to frozen pipes. Winston reported that the police were constantly visiting the property for a variety of reasons, including people shooting off guns. He confirmed that there was a methamphetamine problem in Wheelock, which was obvious from our visits, but described the problems more generically:

> Just a million different personalities and people living with their kids and family, and a lot of drinking and fighting, just, I've seen pretty much everything you can possibly think of out here, just random stuff. You come home and everybody's just got chairs set up around your camper having a fire outside your camper, and you can't get any sleep, and blowing flames out of their mouth with alcohol in front of the little kids. [UND Interview FT9_1bw July 11 2015]

This situation was confirmed by Barbara Ardent, who in a 2012 interview noted that the older residents drink and just go to sleep, but "the young ones … start fights and stuff" (UND Interview FT1_9bw Aug 10 2012). Winston reported that the Williams County Planning Division came out and shut Wrangle down for having too many campers on the property but implied that it was the chaos and police calls that were the impetus. Winston remained the only trailer resident on Wrangle's property in 2014, and in 2015 he made the move.

Paul's Property, at the northeast corner of Wheelock, was much more orderly than Wrangle's Heights. We were not able to determine the property ownership and relationships, as a key landowner would not interview with us. This area of Wheelock was less intensely inhabited, occupied by 10 units at peak, but usually far fewer. Paul's Property, across from the Ramblers Motorcycle Club, was just far enough removed from Wrangle's Heights to have a different atmosphere. We conducted interviews here in 2015, when we found an extended Hispanic family living in two trailer units (UND Interview FT2_1bw Feb 9 2013). A young couple with two small children shared that they were happy with the electric, water, and sewage hookups and pleased to be with their family. But Louis and Anna did not speak highly of Wheelock, telling us "It's lonely … It's trouble here … You can't trust a lot of people." While they tried to be discreet, our interviewees noted that they stayed separate from the inhabitants of Wrangle's Heights, because "people over there get into other people's business" and "when people aren't home, they get into houses and stuff." Louis stated that the only reason they were in North Dakota was for the money and that they had moved to Wheelock because he found a space where he could bring his family from Salt Lake City to be with him. Prior to finding the spots in Wheelock, Louis had lived in a Type 1 man camp, which he described as "being in a [place like where] ... minors go when they get in trouble." Between the winter snow and the spring mud, they only found summer pleasant, but they expressed some discontentment; they came for the money, but prices were so high that they were not any better off.

Winston, who formerly had lived in Wrangle's Heights, was entering his fourth year as a resident of Wheelock when we last interviewed him in 2015 at Paul's Property. While Wheelock was full of interesting characters, Winston certainly stood out. A young man from northern Minnesota, Winston was working at the oil-to-rail transfer facility in nearby Epping. Winston was perhaps the most conventionally realistic of the residents of Wheelock. Standing in the chaos and clutter of the town, he did not want us to see the inside of his trailer, as he was in the middle of a renovation. The outside showed the neatly installed insulation on the doors and windows, providing steady temperatures but also never-ending night inside. Winston worked seven days on, seven days off, and chose Wheelock simply because of its proximity to Epping. He said that Paul's Property had full hookups for 12 trailers and an actual permit, unlike Wrangle's Heights, and that the water was clean and electric was reliable, all for $600 per month, plus electricity (UND Interview FT9_1bw July 11 2015). Winston never really articulated why he chose to live this way, but our takeaway sense was that he was a loner. He wanted to work and be left alone, and in Wheelock he found a place to do that. Winston had been interviewed by reporters in 2012 when he was highlighted as one of the "sardines" of Wheelock: three Minnesota boys packed side-by-side in a 17-foot camper looking for work, a process that took several months (Melby 2012). Winston was clearly popular in Wheelock, as he was mentioned in many of our interviews. He thought Paul's Property might thrive because of his investment in good lots, but he joked that perhaps Wrangle would lose his house and that Theodore Magnus (the self-proclaimed mayor) might buy up the property, like so much of the rest of Wheelock. As of 2018, two years after a drop in oil prices, Paul's Property is three years delinquent on taxes, Wrangle hangs on, and Magnus indeed owns 21 parcels in Wheelock.

While Magnus owns property throughout Wheelock, he lives in the southwest corner of the town. We interviewed Magnus and his sister in 2012. Magnus had lived in Wheelock for several years before the boom. He is an entrepreneur who rents tools and equipment and does repairs and other mechanical jobs. Magnus told us he came to Wheelock for space; he had purchased a houseboat, did not have a space to store it, and found inexpensive land in Wheelock. "I was in Savage, Montana, and I thought, 'man, I ain't got no place to park it' … I came back here because I grew up here." Since his arrival in 2008, Magnus has acquired property as he has been able, including a place for his boat. When we interviewed him, he was planning on building small cabins to rent to people for $650 per month, but this plan never came to fruition. Magnus's sister expressed misgivings about Wrangle's Heights, saying "it's going to be scary," and Bill referenced the raw sewage that we had noted. Magnus had called the Health Department on numerous occasions, but they had not visited—probably, as Magnus posited, because they were overwhelmed by the growth. Magnus related that prices for property had skyrocketed; he once bought lots for $50–100, but now people were asking $15,000.

Magnus expressed a great deal of nostalgia for Wheelock as a commercial hub and shared (accurately) much of the town's history (UND Interview FT1_13ab Aug 10 2012). He had childhood memories of the town having nearly "1,000–1,200 people" around on weekends when they came in to shop and get machines repaired. Magnus shared that a few old-timers were hanging on, like Raymond Lynch, who at 71 still kept the old city well thawed with a wood-burning stove that he tended in the early morning hours all winter long, and "Dooby's grandpa" who still walked out to get the mail at 91 years old. Their children, we were told, want to sell as soon as the old-timers pass on, and with the boom they expect huge prices. Magnus described this as a negative consequence of the boom—"North Dakotans don't usually act like this"—but, of course, in Wheelock, no one had had a chance to act like this since the beginning of the twentieth century, and the boasts of innate financial fair play in the recent past are as untested as claims of racial equality in all-white towns. Even after oil prices dropped and the boom faded, Magnus continues as an ever-hopeful entrepreneur. In June 2016 he had several lots of property zoned to commercial for a planned paintball facility (Williams County 2016). Magnus's most ambitious plan yet was unveiled in 2017, when

North Dakota legalized medical marijuana. Magnus and two partners want to open an 18,000 square foot outdoor grow space that will produce 250 pounds of medical-grade cannabis. Included in the plan is their hope to rename the town "Weedlock" (KFYR TV 2017).

One structure above all emphasized Wheelock as a place outside the theater of oil-boom settlement. Located on the east side of the town near the early concrete sidewalk, a structure had undergone so many iterations of additions that it had become nearly incomprehensible, and we assumed it was the construct of someone with a substance abuse struggle (Figure 12). But closer examination brought the realization that the structure does have its own sense. At the heart is a natural stone chimney that must belong to one of the first houses in Wheelock. It seems that half of the original roofline is still in place, and the other half, removed either intentionally or out of convenience, probably allowed a trailer home to be placed adjacent to or conjoined with the structure. That trailer is no longer in place but has been replaced by a flat-roofed shed structure. Both the upper and lower sections of the structure have relatively new windows and incomplete siding, a sharp juxtaposition with the unfinished nature of the rest of the building. At both the east and west ends of the structure are multiple unique shed-like additions that provide a perhaps pure example of agglutinative architecture. The domicile recalls Lee's photo of a building that was just two sheds pushed together, but this one has been amplified by the greater abundance of material in the twenty-first century. Roofing and walls are haphazard at best, with mismatched insulation and siding. All of the additions have separate entrances, and on the north side of the "house" there are two doors next to each other: one for what is clearly the residence, the other for the shed. Useful debris is scattered in the yard, and, as everywhere in Wheelock, there are exposed water and sewer lines and extension cords. When we visited in the winter 2014, we saw in one of the sheds a body-sized object wrapped in blankets. We thought we had made a horrible discovery only to find that, instead, great care had been taken to keep a water tank from freezing with a heating blanket. We were never able to interview the residents of this structure.

Wheelock as Home of the Precariat

Wheelock can easily be dismissed as a marginal town full of marginal individuals, but that is an analysis that adopts the mythos of a benign and regularized extractive industry. By emphasizing the orderly but rough housing, researchers merely mirror the façade that industry and the individuals employed by industry want us to see. In our interviews

Figure 12. The agglutinative structure in 2012. Photograph courtesy of Richard Rothaus.

Figure 13. Trailer in Wrangle's Heights in 2012. Photography courtesy of William Caraher.

in workforce housing across the Bakken, Wheelock's inhabitants do not stand out as particularly different from the inhabitants of other camps. If the inhabitants are the same but the inhabitation is markedly different, we posit that the difference is the absence of controlling forces that want to represent a specific story in material culture. In our other man camp sites, that story, while not always being told successfully, is overwhelmingly one of American gumption, hard work, and success. Wheelock—absent from the industrial, governmental, and societal enforcers of the norm—is our window into a raw reflection of the material reality of an oil boom. This is not dissimilar to the towns in the western Argolid, Greece, that have embraced life off of major roads for the "art of not being governed" (Caraher et al., this volume; Scott 2009). Within that reality we see a grittier form of the precarious life of workers. Certainly, this in part has long been visible in the mobile home styles adopted by oilfield workers nearly a century ago (Weaver 2010). But Wheelock is more visceral. The chaos is uncontrolled because no one feels they need to control it, and we see the manifestations of fractured families, the hoarding of materials that may be needed in a crisis, and the long existence which fills the time waiting for a future that seems most unlikely to exist. The "front yard" of one trailer in Wrangle's Heights provides us with a glimpse of semi-permanence and seasonality. Bales of hay used for winter insulation are tossed aside to make room for a camping chair, fishing poles, a refrigerator, and a child's toy dump truck. The trailer window has a sign, "Caution: Drama Queen Inside," and the door is adorned with a talismanic Jesus fish (Figure 13; Edmondson 2010). Always there are water and electrical lines in sight, representing a never-ending struggle for independence with utilities. Wheelock in the 2010s is very similar to Wheelock of the 1930s, even in the residents' habit of stockpiling material goods. Even the reaction of beneficent outsiders is similar. In the first few years of our fieldwork, the team spoke often of the need for safe housing; the FSA photographers crafted images to facilitate the relocation of the Dust Bowl farmers to the safety of a new agricultural promised land.

For archaeologists, Wheelock provides a glimpse into the material culture of the precarious workers for whom there are no permanent jobs and, increasingly, no permanent abodes. Wheelock evidences certain material cultural habits from both the 1930s and the early twenty-first century that can be associated quite directly with boom-and-bust cycles, including variation from anticipated housing plans, styles, and materials, and accumulation for reuse that probably will never happen. Currently in North Dakota, for example, the two most visible and easily identifiable historical archaeological assemblages are the Dust-Bowl-era homestead and the twenty-first-century man camp, because of the sheer abundance and chaos of objects. Traditional archaeological approaches fail in the face of such assemblages. Analyzing random objects that are long since separated from their use and collected only for some vague hypothetical possible reuse is a methodological conundrum, at best; in Wheelock we did not encounter use middens so much as hopes-and-dreams middens. Just as importantly, perhaps, Wheelock may indicate that, at least in the realm of historical archaeology, we may have been studying the wrong places. If we want to see the material culture underpinnings of an industrial boom, we should look where we are not expected to look. The similarities of railroad-boom Wheelock and oil-boom Wheelock are striking, and they highlight the lives of workers over a century in a region that has always seen extractive industries (including agriculture) as the main source of income. Wheelock, always just outside the performance of permanence and prosperity, displays the much more functional realities of families that struggle to gather the material needs to survive, as well as the mental bolsters to continue.

Acknowledgments. The UND Man Camp Project has been led by William Caraher and Bret Weber, with assistance from Richard Rothaus and Kostis Kourelis. At various times we have been assisted in the field by Aaron Barth, Kyle Cassidy, and John Holmgren. As is often the case in longitudinal studies, while we do not always agree, our data collection and interpretation have mixed and melded so frequently that we all can claim joint custody. Interviews referenced and quoted in this document were conducted by Bret Weber and Aaron Barth and are currently in preparation for publication by Bret Weber.

References Cited

Augé, Marc
    1995   *Non-Places: Introduction to an Anthropology of Supermodernity.* Translated by John Howe. Verso Books, New York.

Benjamin, Walter
    2014   Carousel of Jobs. In *Radio Benjamin*, edited by Lecia Rosenthal, translated by Jonathan Lutes, pp. 283–291. Verso Books, New York.

Bourdieu, Pierre
    1970   The Berber House or the World Reversed. *Social Science Information* 9:151–170. https://doi.org/10.1177/053901847000900213
    1977   *Outline of a Theory of Practice.* Cambridge University Press, Cambridge.
    1987   *Distinction: A Social Critique of the Judgement of Taste.* Translated by Richard Nice. Harvard University Press, Cambridge.

Bruder, Jessica
    2017   *Nomadland: Surviving America in the Twenty-First Century.* W.W. Norton, New York.

Caraher, William
    2016   The Archaeology of Man Camps: Contingency, Periphery, and Late Capitalism. In *The Bakken Goes Boom: Oil and the Changing Geographies of Western North Dakota*, edited by William R. Caraher and Kyle Conway, pp. 181–196. Digital Press at the University of North Dakota, Grand Forks.

Caraher, William, Raiford Guins, Andrew Reinhard, Richard Rothaus, and Bret Weber
    2014   Why We Dug Atari. *The Atlantic*, August 7, 2014. https://www.theatlantic.com/technology/archive/2014/08/why-we-dug-atari/375702/, accessed October 4, 2020.

Caraher, William, Kostis Kourelis, Richard Rothaus, and Bret Weber
    2017   The North Dakota Man Camp Project: The Archaeology of Home in the Bakken Oil Fields. *Historical Archaeology* 51(2):267–287. https://doi.org/10.1007/s41636-017-0020-8

Caraher, William, and Bret Weber
  2017 *The Bakken: An Archaeology of an Industrial Landscape*. North Dakota State University Press, Fargo.

Caraher, William, Bret Weber, and Richard Rothaus
  2016 Lessons from the Bakken Oil Patch. *Journal of Contemporary Archaeology* 3(2):121–294. https://doi.org/10.1558/jca.31771

Cline, Ernest
  2011 *Ready Player One.* Century, London.

Edmondson, Todd
  2010 The Jesus Fish: Evolution of a Cultural Icon. *Studies in Popular Culture* 32(2):57–66.

Gilles, Mora, and Beverly Brannan
  2006 *FSA: The American Vision.* Harry N. Abrams, New York.

Goldstein, Amy
  2017 *Janesville: An American Story*. Simon and Schuster, New York.

Hudson, John C.
  1982 Towns of the Western Railroads. *Great Plains Quarterly* 2(1):41–54.

Hurt, R. Douglas
  1986 Federal Land Reclamation in the Dust Bowl. *Great Plains Quarterly* 6(2):94–106.

KFYR TV
  2017 Entrepreneurs Looking to Capitalize on Medical Marijuana in Wheelock. 26 October. http://www.kfyrtv.com/content/news/Entrepreneurs-looking-to-capital-on-marijuana-453321243.html, accessed October 4, 2020.

Kozol, Wendy
  1988 Madonnas of the Fields: Photography, Gender, and the 1930s Farm Relief. *Genders* 2:2–13.

Melby, Todd
    2012   They Call Us "The Sardines." *Black Gold Boom: How Oil Changed North Dakota*. Prairie Public Radio, Fargo, North Dakota. http://blackgoldboom.com/the-sardines/, accessed October 4, 2020.

Mosse, Jesse
    2014   *The Overnighters*. Drafthouse Films, Austin, Texas.

Reed, Ann
    2016   Unpackaging Boomtown Tropes: Insider/Outsider Dynamics in North Dakota's Oil Patch. In *The Bakken Goes Boom: Oil and the Changing Geographies of Western North Dakota*, edited by William R. Caraher and Kyle Conway, pp. 51–68. Digital Press at the University of North Dakota, Grand Forks.

Reinhard, Andrew
    2018   *Archaeogaming: An Introduction to Archaeology in and of Video Games*. Berghahn Books, New York.

Roberts, Bill
    2012   Production in View: Allan Sekula's *Fish Story* and the Thawing of Postmodernism. *Tate Papers* 18. http://www.tate.org.uk/research/publications/tate-papers/18/production-in-view-allan-sekulas-fish-story-and-the-thawing-of-postmodernism, accessed October 4, 2020.

Robinson, Elwyn B.
    1966   *History of North Dakota*. University of Nebraska Press, Lincoln.

Roet, Jeffery B.
    1985   Land Quality and Land Alienation on the Dry Farming Frontier. *The Professional Geographer* 37(2):173–183. https://doi.org/10.1111/j.0033-0124.1985.00173.x

Scott, James C.
    2009   *The Art of Not Being Governed: An Anarchist History of Upland Southeast Asia*. Yale University Press, New Haven.

Shemorry, Bill
   2001   Shemorry on Hand for Initial Oil Discovery. *Williston Herald* 1 April. Williston, North Dakota.

Sekula, Allan
   2002   *Fish Story*. Richter Verlag, Düsseldorf.

Standing, Guy
   2011   *The Precariat: The New Dangerous Class*. Bloomsbury Academic, New York.

Tolkien, J. R. R.
   1965   *The Fellowship of the Ring: Being the First Part of the Lord of the Rings*. Ballentine Fantasy, New York.

Weaver, Bobby D.
   2010   *Oil Field Trash: Life and Labor in the Oil Patch*. Texas A&M University Press, College Station.

Wexler, Laura, Lauren Tilton, and Taylor Arnold
   2018   Photogrammar. http://photogrammar.yale.edu/, accessed 23 January 2018.

Williams County
   2016   Meeting Minutes of the Williams County Planning and Zoning Commission. June 26, 2016. Electronic document, https://www.williamsnd.com/usrfiles/meeting/6-23-2016_Minutes.pdf, accessed October 4, 2020.

Williams County Board of County Commissioners
   1937   *Atlas of Williams County, North Dakota*. Board of County Commissioners, Williams County, North Dakota.

Williston Graphic (WG)
   1912   "Notice of Foreclosure Sale." 4 July:7. Williston, North Dakota.
   1916   "County Revenue Fund." 10 August:4. Williston, North Dakota.

Williston Herald (WH)
    2001   "Obituaries." 6 February. Williston, North Dakota. Electronic document, https://www.willistonherald.com/obituaries/gertrude-gerling/article_0c739f12-adf9-5727-9485-221db31f1c99.html, accessed 2 December 2020.

The Authors

Rebecca M. Seifried (ORCID: 0000-0002-4372-2164) is the Geospatial Information Librarian at the University of Massachusetts Amherst. Her PhD (University of Illinois at Chicago) investigated the material effects of imperial expansion in the Mani peninsula over the past millennium, building on her interests in GIS, historical and landscape archaeology, and the experience of living in imperial frontiers and peripheries. Her current research is exploring the routes that historical travelers took through Mani, with a special interest in the built environment they did (or did not) document along the way. Email: rseifried@umass.edu.

Deborah E. Brown Stewart (ORCID: 0000-0002-0511-8601) is the Head of the Penn Museum Library at the University of Pennsylvania, a role in which she serves both as the subject specialist for anthropology and archaeology within Penn Libraries and the curator for the Daniel Garrison Brinton Collection. Previously, she served as the Librarian for Byzantine Studies at Dumbarton Oaks Research Library and Collection. Her PhD (Bryn Mawr College) scrutinized the evidence for sacerdotal housing in ancient Greece. Email: browndeb@upenn.edu.

Ioanna Antoniadou (ORCID: 0000-0003-0596-9083) is an archaeologist and ethnographer based in Thessaloniki, Greece. Her PhD (University of Southampton) explores the intersection of professional archaeology and the public conceptions of the past in Kozani, Greece—research that directly informed her ethnographic work as part of the Western Argolid Research Project. She is currently the co-director of the *Oral History Group of Eptapyrgio* in Thessaloniki, documenting oral testimonies and material manifestations regarding the "difficult past" throughout the twentieth century. Email: antoniadou@gmail.com.

Todd Brenningmeyer (ORCID: 0000-0001-9012-7440) is Professor and Director of the Art History Program in Art and Design at Maryville University. He has applied digital reconstruction, GIS, and remote sensing techniques to artifacts, structures, and sites while working on archaeological projects in the United States, Egypt, and Greece. Email: tbrenningmeyer@maryville.edu.

William R. Caraher (ORCID: 0000-0002-4618-5333) is Associate Professor of History at the University of North Dakota as well as Director and Publisher of the Digital Press of the University of North Dakota. In addition to working on archaeological survey projects in Greece, he is the co-director of the Pyla-*Koutsopetria* Archaeological Project in Cyprus. Email: william.caraher@und.edu.

Marica Cassis (ORCID: 0000-0002-9651-5273) is Associate Professor and Department Head in Classics and Religion at the University of Calgary. She serves as the Assistant Director and Byzantine Project Director for the excavations at Çadır Höyük in Turkey. Her research focuses on the archaeology and history of medieval Anatolia. Email: marica.cassis@ucalgary.ca.

Timothy E. Gregory (ORCID: 0000-0003-0038-3382) is Professor Emeritus in the Department of History at The Ohio State University. Throughout his career, he has trained a number of archaeologists, including advising on the doctoral dissertations for several authors in this volume. He served as director of The Ohio State University Excavations at Isthmia for more than three decades, is co-director of the Eastern Korinthia Archaeological Survey, co-director of the Karavas Water Project, and co-director of the Australian Paliochora-Kythera Archaeological Survey Project. Email: gregory.4@osu.edu.

Miltiadis Katsaros (ORCID: 0000-0001-7270-6908) is Associate Professor in the School of Architecture at the National Technical University of Athens. As a practicing architect and consulting engineer, he has designed and supervised several urban renewal, historic preservation, and new building projects in Greece and abroad. His research and teaching involve technology, innovation and sustainability in architectural design, and the exploration of advanced digital tools for surveying, mapping, documenting and simulating built-environments. Email: m.katsaros@m2k.gr.

Kostis Kourelis (ORCID: 0000-0002-1428-568X) is Associate Professor of Art History at Franklin & Marshall College. He is an architectural historian focusing on the archaeology of Greece from Byzantium to the present. Broadly defined as the archaeology of contemporary migration and labor, his recent fieldwork focuses on refugee camps, remittance villages, fracking, and punk. Email: kkoureli@fandm.edu.

Anthony Lauricella (ORCID: 0000-0002-2461-4205) is the Acting Director of the Center for Ancient Middle Eastern Landscapes at the Oriental Institute of the University of Chicago. He has conducted fieldwork in Sicily, Turkey, Palestine, and Azerbaijan. His doctoral dissertation explored the reuse of early Islamic built environments. Email: ajlauricella@uchicago.edu.

Dimitri Nakassis (ORCID: 0000-0002-0783-2702) is Professor and Chair of the Department of Classics at the University of Colorado Boulder. He is co-director of the Western Argolid Regional Project (WARP) and co-director of the Pylos Tablets Digital Project, through which he pursues his research interest in the material and textual production of early Greek communities. He was named a MacArthur Fellow in 2015. Email: dimitri.nakassis@colorado.edu.

David K. Pettegrew (ORCID: 0000-0003-0073-6045) is Professor of History and Archaeology in the Department of History at Messiah University. He is among the co-directors of the Pyla-*Koutsopetria* Archaeological Project in Cyprus and has worked on a number of other archaeological projects in Greece and central Pennsylvania. His research and teaching center on integrating archaeological and textual evidence to narrate local history, especially Mediterranean cities and landscapes at the end of antiquity, with particular interest in the Corinthia. Email: dpettegrew@messiah.edu.

Richard Rothaus (ORCID: 0000-0002-3370-654X) is Dean of the College of Liberal Arts and Social Sciences at Central Michigan University, but he is also a historian and archaeologist who has worked in North America, Europe, and the Middle East, including on the Eastern Korinthia Archaeological Survey Project. For many years, he owned a cultural resource management firm that worked primarily in the Northern Plains and Midwest. His current research interests include the history and archaeology of Japanese-American internment camps. Email: rotha1r@cmich.edu.

Guy D.R. Sanders (ORCID: 0000-0002-1238-0544) is Director Emeritus of the American School of Classical Studies Corinth Excavations at Archaia Korinthos. His career includes several excavations and archaeological surveys in mainland Greece, Melos, Macedonia, Cyprus, and Portugal. Currently, he is involved with the Lechaion Harbour Project and the Western Argolid Regional Project. Email: sanders.gdr@gmail.com.

Isabel Sanders (ORCID: 0000-0001-8335-5015) holds an MA in Art History at the University of Glasgow and a certificate in Horticulture with Plantsmanship at the Royal Botanic Gardens Edinburgh, and she was trained at the flagship garden of the Mediterranean Garden Society in Attica. In addition to working as a gardener, designer, and plant consultant in Greece, she is pursuing a MSc in Sustainable Heritage at University College London with a focus on Mediterranean heritage and the region's natural landscapes and flora. Email: isabel.platani@gmail.com.

Lita Tzortzopoulou-Gregory (ORCID: 0000-0003-0411-5318) is Executive Officer of the Australian Archaeological Institute at Athens. She is also co-director of the Australian Paliochora-Kythera Archaeological Survey and project manager of the Ohio State University Excavations at Isthmia, Greece. Her research interests include landscape archaeology, commemoration and identity, public archaeology, and cultural heritage practices. Email: lita.gregory@sydney.edu.au.

Olga Vassi (ORCID 0000-0003-2239-0348) is Director of the Ephorate of Antiquities of Chios, Ministry of Culture, Greece. She has authored several articles and books about the Byzantine and Ottoman buildings on the island, where she oversees thorough study, conservation, and careful restoration of monuments. Email: ovassi@culture.gr.

Bret Weber (ORCID 0000-0003-4372-3623) is an Associate Professor in the Department of Social Work at the University of North Dakota. His research involves the ways in which built environments and housing policies impact impoverished communities in cities, towns, and reservations. Email: bret.weber@und.edu.

Miyon Yoo (ORCID: 0000-0002-3512-6557) is an ecologist, botanist, and gardener with a double MSc in Biodiversity Management and Spatial Planning and Development. She has worked as a field botanist at various conservation institutions in France and has hands-on experience working in unconventional, water-wise, Mediterranean gardens in Portugal and Greece. Over ten years, she has developed extensive interest in Mediterranean landscapes and flora. Email: miyoneza@gmail.com.

www.ingramcontent.com/pod-product-compliance
Lightning Source LLC
Chambersburg PA
CBHW051031160426
43193CB00010B/905